The *Sams Teach Yourself in 24 Hours* Series

Sams Teach Yourself in 24 Hours books provide quick and easy answers in a proven step-by-step approach that works for you. In just 24 sessions of one hour or less, you will tackle every task you need to get the results you want. Let our experienced authors present the most accurate information to get you reliable answers—fast!

VBA DATA TYPES

DATA TYPE	STORAGE SIZE	RANGE
Byte	1 byte	0 to 255
Boolean	2 bytes	True or False
Integer	2 bytes	−32,768 to 32,767
Long (long integer)	4 bytes	−2,147,483,648 to 2,147,483,647
Single	4 bytes	−3.402823E38 to −1.401298E−45 for negative values; 1.401298E−45 to 3.402823E38 for positive values
Double	8 bytes	−1.79769313486232E308 to −4.94065645841247E−324 for negative values; 4.94065645841247E−324 to 1.79769313486232E308 for positive values
Currency	8 bytes	−922,337,203,685,477.5808 to 922,337,203,685,477.5807
Decimal	14 bytes	Numbers with 28 decimal places of accuracy
Date	8 bytes	January 1, 100 to December 31, 9999
Object	4 bytes	Any Object reference
String (variable length)	10 bytes + string	0 to approximately 2 billion
String (fixed-length)	Length of string	1 to approximately 65,400
Variant (with numbers)	16 bytes	Any numeric value up to the range of a Double
Variant (the characters)	22 bytes + string length	Same range as for variable-length String

COMMON ERROR MESSAGES

ERROR NUMBER	DESCRIPTION
13	This message indicates a Type Mismatch. This is likely to happen when getting user input from an inputBox, field, or control on a user form.
91	This message indicates that an object variable or With structure object isn't assigned.
438	This message indicates an invalid object reference.
4605	This message indicates an object isn't selected. It can crop up if your Selection object needs to contain text, or if you don't have the correct settings in Word—for example, an incorrect View.
5152	This message is generated when a file is missing.
5174	This message is generated when a file is missing, or you are inserting a document as a subdocument based on another template.

continues

Sams Teach Yourself Microsoft® Word 2000 Automation in 24 Hours

ERROR NUMBER	DESCRIPTION
5273	This message is generated when the path or file name used is invalid.
5941	This message is generated when an object (such as a table) is missing for an operation when you want to use Autoformatting.
1004	This message is the missing file message that is generated by Excel.

Steps for Accessing Other Microsoft Applications

1. In the Visual Basic Editor, select Tools, References.
2. Select the appropriate library listed below and click OK.
3. Declare an object variable and assign it to the correct Application object in your code using either CreateObject to get a new instance or GetObject to use an existing instance. Sample code is provided in the following section to assist you with constructing your own procedures. In the case of the ActiveX Data objects, the code is longer.

   With the ADO library, you have to set up a connection to the database and then set up the object you want to reference. This example shows the connection and the creation of a RecordSet object that is used to work with data.
4. Use its objects, methods, and properties to accomplish your task.

THE MICROSOFT APPLICATION OBJECT LIBRARIES AND DECLARATIONS

APPLICATION	LIBRARY AND OBJECT DECLARATION

Excel	Microsoft Excel 9.0 Object Library
	`Dim objExcel as Excel.Application`
	`Set objExcel =`
	`CreateObject("Excel.Application")`

Access	Microsoft Access 9.0 Object Library
	`Dim objAccess As Access.Application`
	`Set objAccess = New Access.Application`

Outlook	Microsoft Outlook 9.0 Object Library
	`Dim objOutlook As Outlook.Application, _`
	`    objNameSpace As NameSpace`
	`Set objOutlook =`
	`CreateObject("Outlook.Application")`
	`Set objNameSpace =`
	`objOutlook.GetNamespace("MAPI")`

Word	Microsoft Word Object 9.0 Library
	`Dim objWord as Word.Application`
	`Set objWord = CreateObject("Word.Application")`

ActiveX Data	Microsoft ActiveX Data Object Library 2.1\
	`Dim cnnEmployees As ADODB.Connection,`
	`rsEmployees As Recordset`
	`Set cnnEmployees = New ADODB.Connection`
	`cnnEmployees.ConnectionString = _`
	`"Provider=Microsoft.Jet.OLEDB.4.0;Data`
	`Source=C:\My Documents\You Name It Toys.mdb"`
	`cnnEmployees.Open`
	`Set rsEmployees = New ADODB.Recordset`
	`rsEmployees.Open "Employees", cnnEmployees,`
	`adOpenStatic, adLockReadOnly`

Pamela Palmer

SAMS Teach Yourself

Microsoft® Word 2000 Automation in 24 Hours

SAMS

A Division of Macmillan Computer Publishing
201 West 103rd St., Indianapolis, Indiana, 46290 USA

Sams Teach Yourself Microsoft® Word 2000 Automation in 24 Hours

Copyright © 2000 by Sams Publishing

International Standard Book Number: 0-672-31652-8

Library of Congress Catalog Card Number: 99-60556

Printed in the United States of America

First Printing: September 1999

02   01   00   99   4   3   2   1

Trademarks

Warning and Disclaimer

Z52.5
.M52
P275
1999x

ASSOCIATE PUBLISHER
Bradley L. Jones

ACQUISITIONS EDITOR
Sharon Cox

DEVELOPMENT EDITOR
Thomas Cirtin

MANAGING EDITOR
Lisa Wilson

PROJECT EDITOR
Heather Talbot

COPY EDITOR
Mary Lagu

INDEXER
Bill Meyers

PROOFREADER
Jill Mazurczyk

TECHNICAL EDITORS
Lowell Mauer
Sundar Rajan

TEAM COORDINATOR
Meggo Barthlow

MEDIA DEVELOPER
Craig Atkins

INTERIOR DESIGNER
Gary Adair

COVER DESIGNER
Aren Howell

COPY WRITER
Eric Borgert

LAYOUT TECHNICIANS
Brian Borders
Susan Geiselman
Mark Walchle

Overview

Contents

PART II   LEARNING THE VBA FUNDAMENTALS

HOUR 5   EXPLORING VBA   79

HOUR 6   UNDERSTANDING DECISION PROCESSING   101

HOUR 7   UNDERSTANDING REPETITIVE PROCESSING WITH LOOPS   119

PART V   WORKING WITH COMPLEX DOCUMENTS AND OTHER APPLICATIONS

HOUR 18   WORKING WITH MAILINGS   333

About the Author

Pamela Palmer is an independent consultant specializing in the development of applications using Visual Basic, Access, and Visual Basic for Applications. Pamela has more than 15 years experience in the computer industry. She divides her time among developing applications, writing books, developing training material, and training users and developers.

After receiving her bachelor's degree in business administration from Wichita State University, Pamela has worked in several industries. She has worked with financial institutions and universities, as well as providing training and software development to technology companies. As a consultant, she has worked with small companies and Fortune 500 companies.

Pamela received the certificate of completion from the Sandia National Laboratories Software Quality Engineering and IEEE Software Engineering Standards program. She is also a Microsoft Certified Instructor.

This book is her tenth. She has co-authored *Sams Teach Yourself Access 2000 in 21 Days*, contributed to Que's *Using Visual Basic for Applications 5*, *Using Word 97*, *Using Excel 97*, *Using Project 98*, *Using Outlook 97*, and *Using Visual Basic 3*, as well as acting as co-author for two other books on Visual Basic 5 and 6.

Dedication

This book is dedicated to my husband, David, and my children, Christopher, Katie, and Deanna.
For without their support and patience, this book wouldn't have happened.

Acknowledgments

As with any book, there are many people who help make it possible. For starters, I couldn't have completed this book without the support of my family. Although my husband laughed at my frustration over the number of pages written each day, and my son (at five) thinks writing books doesn't look that hard, they had great patience through the long hours, makeshift meals, and distractions. I also want to thank my mother for offering her support and confidence.

I would like to thank Sharon Cox for this project. I have worked with many clients to speed up their work with many of Microsoft Word's tools including VBA. I was delighted to turn it into a book. I would also like to thank Tom Cirtin. His input was invaluable. He helped refine the contents and make sure the material met the objectives.

In addition to Tom's contribution, I also had a great editing team. Heather Talbot and Mary Lagu provided wonderful assistance. They kept the text consistent and tightened up the language to make sure that each hour could be completed in an hour.

Lowell Mauer and Sundar Rajan gave each chapter a thorough check to make sure that each step produced the desired results. They also offered great suggestions for improving the content. I would like to thank all of them for their assistance and support.

Last, but not least, I would like to thank Sarah Browning. She was my acquisitions editor for my first book seven years ago. When she called to ask me to contribute to *Using Visual Basic 3*, I disagreed with her assessment that writing was something for me. Thanks for insisting. It couldn't have worked out better.

Tell Us What You Think!

As the reader of this book, *you* are our most important critic and commentator. We value your opinion and want to know what we're doing right, what we could do better, what areas you'd like to see us publish in, and any other words of wisdom you're willing to pass our way.

As an associate publisher for Sams Publishing, I welcome your comments. You can fax, email, or write me directly to let me know what you did or didn't like about this book—as well as what we can do to make our books stronger.

Please note that I cannot help you with technical problems related to the topic of this book, and that due to the high volume of mail I receive, I might not be able to reply to every message.

When you write, please be sure to include this book's title and author as well as your name and phone or fax number. I will carefully review your comments and share them with the author and editors who worked on the book.

Fax: 317-581-4770

Email: adv_prog@mcp.com

Mail: Brad Jones
          Associate Publisher
          Sams Publishing
          201 West 103rd Street
          Indianapolis, IN 46290 USA

Introduction

The *Sams Teach Yourself in 24 Hours* books are designed to give you a fast start with a particular topic, and this book follows that pattern. Please take a few minutes to review the following material to help you understand the format of this book.

Who Should Read This Book

This book is designed for the user who is familiar with most of the advanced features of Microsoft Word, but who is not necessarily a programmer. As you began using the advanced features of Word, you soon identify certain features that you use frequently. You will then begin looking for ways to make these features function faster and more efficiently. This book helps you do that.

This book is not designed to serve as a reference manual, but as a step-by-step tutorial for the "power user." It is designed to meet three objectives:

- *Getting you started*: It is designed to get you started automating your work by introducing automation concepts as well as the macro recorder.

- *Mastering the fundamentals of VBA*: This book is aimed to help you master the fundamentals of programming with VBA. In most cases, the reader isn't a programmer. You might have recorded several macros, and are looking at this book because you want to enhance your recorded macros. For better and for worse, you must learn the language before you can get the most out of VBA.

- *Demonstrating automation*: You will see many solid examples of automation in this book. As you work with Word, you may be very frustrated because you have to repeat tasks frequently. These tasks may not be completed in exactly the same way every time (which would warrant a default setting), but you are performing them often enough to require automating them in some way.

Hours 1–8 are designed to meet the first two objectives. The remainder of the book is task oriented. For example, if you spend time formatting your tables, but the formatting you use isn't one of the types defined in the Table Wizard, you might be interested in Hour 12. It covers automating tasks with tables.

Hours 9–24 are written to explore specific features in Word. By focusing on one aspect of Word, you will get a better understanding of what it takes to automate your own tasks in each area.

What This Book Will Do For You

Hour 1 is designed to provide a blueprint for automating your work. It introduces the process for automation as well as reviews some of the fundamental advanced features. Although you may feel that you already have a grasp of these, don't skip this section. Its purpose is to refresh your memory about features that might save you some time in automation.

The remainder of Part I provides an overview of how you will automate your work. You will experiment with recording a macro and then take a look at the Visual Basic for Applications (VBA) code that was generated.

Part II covers the fundamentals of programming with VBA. When you begin automating your work, you may be satisfied with merely recording macros. As you create more macros to automate specific aspects of document creation, you will find that you will want to incorporate some of the decisions you make into the macro itself. At that point, you must begin working with the language. It allows you to automate more sophisticated actions.

Beginning with Hour 9, the book takes a different tack. Hours 9 through 24 examine how to take advantage of specific features with VBA. Although it isn't a requirement to know the specific feature presented in an hour before you complete it, you will be able to complete the hour more easily if you have used the specific feature before you begin.

For example, automating the creation of a table will be easier if you have created one from scratch first. The features will be covered briefly, except for the process automating them. If you need more information about the features themselves, don't forget that you have online help.

Can This Book Really Teach Word Automation in 24 Hours?

Yes. Each hour is designed to be completed in an hour or less. Every effort is made to keep the duration of each hour consistent, as well as to keep each hour independent from the others. There are some exceptions.

Hours 1 through 8 are the introductory chapters. They focus on the analysis of your automation needs and the fundamentals of the language. Some of these hours may take slightly longer or less time depending on what knowledge you start with. If you have programmed in another language, the hours focusing on the core language will go much faster because in many cases the information will be review.

Hours 1 through 8 are more closely connected to each other than the rest of the book. In these hours, you will often complete a task in one hour and then review the results in a later hour, or improve on the results with additional code.

This interdependence means it is best to complete these hours in sequence. A benefit of doing this is that you can achieve an objective simply by expanding the work done in a previous chapter. This means less typing on your part.

In most cases, the rest of the hours are independent. If you are in a hurry to automate a task, you can jump directly to that hour, because each hour will focus on the language components for only that task.

This doesn't mean that at the end of this book, you will know all there is to know about VBA and Word. This book is designed to give you the fundamentals of automation, as well as an introduction to automating most of the commonly used features. In many cases, if more advanced automation is possible, a reference to online help topics will be included.

What You Need

This book assumes that you have a Windows 95–compatible computer with Windows 95/98 or NT loaded. In addition, you must have Microsoft Office loaded.

Although this book is written for Office 2000, many of the techniques will work just as well with Office 97. Regardless of which version of Office you are using, make sure that the VBA and VBA help items are selected during the installation.

For the completion of Hour 20, you will also need to have the VBA and VBA help items selected for the other products. If you are going to complete the tasks addressing Internet access, you will want Internet Explorer 5, along with the necessary hardware.

Files Included on the Companion Web Site

Most of the lessons include tasks for creating macros. If you prefer to view the completed macros, you can download sample templates with the macros from this book's companion Web site. To access the Web site on the Internet, simply type `http://www.mcp.com/product_support`. Then in the Book Information and Downloads text box, enter the ISBN, which is 0-672-31652-8, and click the Search button.

In Hour 1, you will be introduced to the different locations to store your macros. One of these locations is your Normal template. Given that you will have customized your

Normal template as you worked with Word, you should not overwrite your template with the samples.

To avoid this possibility, any macro that was supposed to be in the Normal template will be stored in a special template. For instructions for using all these templates, please refer to Appendix B.

Conventions Used in This Book

Each lesson highlights new terms as they appear, and a question-and-answer section is provided at the end of each lesson to reinforce what you have learned. In addition, the lessons reinforce your learning further with quiz questions and exercises.

This 24-hour course also uses several common conventions to help teach the programming topics. Here is a summary of the typographical conventions:

- Commands, computer output, and words you type appear in a special `monospaced` computer font.

```
It will look like this to mimic the way text looks on your screen.
```

- If a task requires you to choose from a menu, the book separates menu commands with a comma. Therefore, this book uses File, Save As to indicate that you should open the File menu and choose the Save As command.
- When learning a programming language, you often must learn the syntax or format of a command. Lines similar to the following will be displayed to help you learn a new Visual Basic language command:

```
For CounterVar = StartVal To EndVal [Step IncrementVal]
    Block of one or more Visual Basic statements
Next CounterVar
```

The monospaced text designates code (programming language information) that you'll enter into a program. The regular monospaced text, such as `For` and `Next`, represent keywords you must type exactly. You don't have to worry about capitalization as you type them because VBA isn't case sensitive. Depending on your Visual Basic Editor options, the editor may adjust the capitalization as you enter text. *Italicized monospace* characters indicate placeholders that you must replace with your own program's values.

In many cases, there are some options that can be used with a command. In those cases, the optional keywords or placeholders will be presented in brackets. If there are multiple options with different keywords, the keywords will be separated by vertical bars referred to as pipes. If you don't specify one of the options, the default settings for the command will be used.

In addition to typographical conventions, the following special elements are used to set off various pieces of information and to make them easily recognizable:

NEW TERM The first time a *new term* appears, you'll find a New Term icon and definition to help reinforce that term.

This arrow (➡) at the beginning of a line of code means that a single line of code is too long to fit on the printed page. Continue typing all characters after the ➡ as though they were part of the preceding line.

This is different from the line continuation character in VBA, which is at the end of the code line. It is inserted by typing a space and the underscore. In most cases, the line breaks were inserted into the code as it was created to make it easier to read in the book and in the Visual Basic Editor when you examine the files from the companion Web site. In those cases, you type the lines as they appear in the text.

A Note presents interesting pieces of information related to the discussion at hand.

A Tip offers advice or teaches an easier way to do something.

A Caution advises you about potential problems and helps you steer clear of disaster.

HOUR 1

Introducing Automation Fundamentals

Welcome to the first hour of learning to streamline your word-processing tasks using Word 2000 Automation. After learning the fundamentals of Word 2000, you probably realize that there are many tasks in Word that you perform over and over. Word enables you to eliminate many of these repetitive procedures with the great automation tools described in this book.

The highlights of this hour include

- Developing a strategy for automation
- Evaluating your automation needs
- Learning template fundamentals
- Learning text automation fundamentals

Developing a Strategy for Automation

Choosing this book shows that you recognize the need for automation. You have noticed similarities among documents you create. You may have also noticed that you perform the same series of steps frequently.

Recognizing that you can cut the time required to create documents is half the battle. The second half is knowing what Word tools to use. The choices can be quite overwhelming. To implement automation in your work, you are going to take these steps:

- Evaluate your needs
- Determine what tools are needed
- Determine how you are going to implement the automation

As you complete this hour, you will get a good start on evaluating your needs and selecting the tools to automate tasks. You will make a list of your recurring word-processing chores, and develop a plan to automate the items on your list.

After you plan what needs to be automated, you are going to have to adopt a strategy that works with your schedule. One approach is to set aside time to automate tasks, or small groups of related tasks, one at a time. This approach is good if you are often rushing to get a document out the door. If you are under a tight deadline, focusing on the document is paramount.

Another approach is to take a little extra time when you are creating a type of document you use often. For example, you budget four hours to prepare a proposal. Proposals are completed several times a month. By scheduling an extra hour as you complete your proposal, you can automate the process for the next one. A disadvantage to this approach is that your focus is split between the document and the automation.

You can also combine the approaches. You might find that setting aside some time to automate as much of the document as possible is the best approach. As you work, you can add elements that you missed in your first attempt. Regardless of what plan you adopt, begin by evaluating your needs.

Evaluating Your Automation Needs

By the time you have decided to reduce the time you spend creating documents, you will have already created many of them. Evaluating your needs is frequently a matter of reviewing some of these documents to identify the procedures that need to be automated.

Brainstorming is one technique you might find valuable as you evaluate your needs. Think back over the last day, week, and month. Review some of your existing documents. You can begin to isolate the elements your documents share. As you brainstorm for ideas, create a table to assist with this process. Make three columns:

- *Document/Task*: List frequently used tasks and documents.
- *How Often It Is Used*: Note the frequency of each task and document.
- *Tools That Are Needed*: Fill this in later as you complete the material covered in this hour.

Looking at your directory of files will help generate the list of ideas. To assist you with brainstorming, you may want to consider these areas:

- *Standard documents*: Consider what documents are standard for your office. Letters, faxes, and memos are the first types of documents that spring to mind, but they aren't the only ones.

  If you spend a lot of time in meetings, you might be creating agendas, minutes, and meeting notices. If you work in sales, there are marketing packages, sales flyers, proposals, or postcards. Each occupation will have specific document needs.

- *Paper-based forms*: Review your operation to see whether you are still using a paper-based form for information retrieval. It might be a vacation request, materials request, personnel information update, and so on.

- *Document elements*: Examine the contents of your documents for standard elements, such as a logo, special formatting for tables, special bullets, and so on.

- *Printing*: Are there special settings for printing some of your documents? For example, you might print five copies of a meeting agenda for regular attendees.

- *Merging*: Review the types of merging you perform frequently. Do you mail to the same list of names every time? Do you mail the same document to different lists frequently? Do you use the same settings for sorting or filtering regularly?

- *Accessing outside applications*: Review your integration of information from other sources. Are you frequently adding an Excel spreadsheet to your document? Do you exchange information with PowerPoint regularly?

After you have listed all the documents and tasks to automate, indicate how often you use them to help you prioritize the tasks. If the document or task is something you are using on a daily basis, automating it will have an immediate impact on your work.

Learning Template Fundamentals

Now that you have identified tasks, you are going to determine what tools are required for each document or task. To get a better idea of what is possible, the next step is to review how tasks are automated in Word.

NEW TERM To automate your actions in Word, you use a template. A *template* is a special document that stores specific settings for document creation. It provides a model for a new document. It can store page settings, styles, AutoText entries, custom menus, custom keystrokes, custom toolbars, fixed text, and (last but not least) macros.

NEW TERM A *macro* is a series of actions that have been saved so you can execute them as a unit.

You may not have noticed it, but you use a template every time you create a file. The default template is called the Normal template; its filename is Normal.dot. It creates a very basic document. It has a portrait orientation, with 1-inch top and bottom margins. It has 1.25-inch left and right margins with area specified for a header and footer beginning at .50 inches.

NEW TERM A template also has a set of styles to speed up document formatting. A *style* is a list of attributes that controls the appearance of your paragraphs and characters. The style definition can include settings for font, character spacing, text effects, indents, spacing, line and page breaks, tabs, borders, shading, spelling and grammar checks, frames, bullets, numbers, outline numbers, as well as shortcut keys and what style for the following paragraph.

There are two types of styles: A paragraph style affects the entire paragraph, and the character style affects only the text that is selected. By default, you are creating text using the default Normal paragraph style with the Default Paragraph Font character style.

NEW TERM The Normal template also contains some default AutoText entries to assist with creating letters. An *AutoText entry* is a saved block of text or graphics that can be inserted into any document. It is a great way to store document items you use frequently. It can contain the company logo, directions to your office, contact information, and so forth.

The Normal template doesn't contain any special menus, toolbar keystrokes, or fixed text. It also doesn't include any Visual Basic for Applications (VBA) macros. It can serve as a model for any document.

Word also provides some more elaborate templates for specific types of documents. If you use the New Blank Document button on the standard toolbar, you create a document using the Normal template. If you use New from the File menu, you have more choices in the New dialog as shown in Figure 1.1.

FIGURE 1.1

The New dialog lists all the templates currently available.

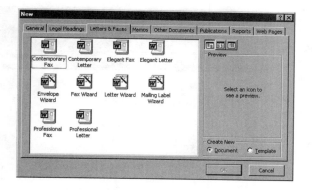

Comparing Templates and Wizards

The New dialog is a tabbed dialog. The templates are divided into categories. To create a letter, select the Letters & Faxes category. In this category, you see two choices: templates and wizards. You are going to create a letter with a template and with the wizard in order to see the difference between the two methods.

NEW TERM   A *wizard* is a different kind of template that automates document creation with VBA. When a wizard is chosen to create a new file, it does more than open a new document based on a specific template. It has a series of dialog boxes asking questions to help complete the document. It will choose a template and fill in information.

Using a Template

To create a letter with a template, perform the following steps:

1. Select File, New, and the Letters & Faxes tab.

2. Select Professional Letter and click OK.

3. Notice that it provides a general framework for the letter. It has the date already inserted, as well as text and macro button fields to assist with completing the letter (see Figure 1.2).

4. Close this letter without saving it.

Using a Wizard

To create a letter with a wizard, perform the following steps:

1   Select File, New, and the Letters & Faxes tab.

2. Double-click the Letter Wizard. Notice it creates a generic letter, and the Office Assistant asks whether you want to send one letter or multiple letters to a mailing list.

FIGURE 1.2

The letter template includes some text and fields to speed up letter creation.

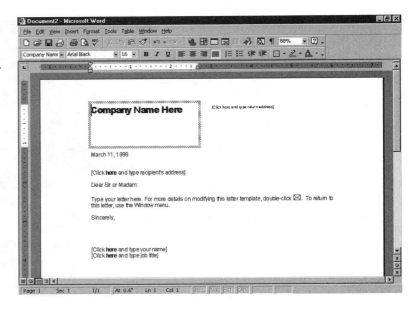

3. Select Send One Letter, and the Letter Wizard dialog will be displayed.

4. Select Professional Letter from the Choose a Page Design drop-down list and click Next.

5. Type `Christopher Palmer` as the Recipient's Name.

6. Type the following as a Delivery Address:

   `123 Oak Terrace`

   `MyTown, IL 55555`

7. Select Informal as the Salutation and select Next.

8. Select Next to skip the Other Elements.

9. Notice your name is included as the Sender's name and the Closing is already selected. Select Finish.

If your name isn't already entered as the Sender, you have not completed the User Info tab in the Options dialog. Select Tool, Options to set this information.

10. Notice the Assistant is offering to assist with some of the other tasks associated with creating a letter. Click Cancel.

    If the Office Assistant isn't displayed and you want assistance, you can turn it on. Select Help, Show Office Assistant to display the Assistant. When the Assistant is displayed, you can right-click and select Options. Select the Use Office Assistant and Help with Wizards checkboxes and click OK.

11. Notice more of the letter is completed for you. All you have to do is complete the body of the letter, as shown in Figure 1.3.

FIGURE 1.3

The wizard completes more of the letter for you than the template did.

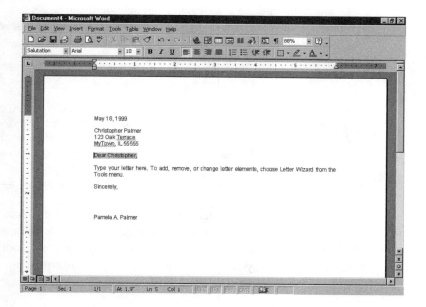

The Letter Wizard is a special template. It asks you a series of questions using a dialog and then builds the letter using your responses. This is accomplished with VBA macros. Concentrate on developing your own custom templates to cut the time it takes you to create documents.

Determining Access

The first step in automating your work is to determine when you want access to a particular automation feature. Do you need a feature with a specific type of document or with all documents? Create separate templates with the particular features needed for specific documents.

If you are adding styles you use in every document or VBA macros that are needed in more than one type of document, you can make these available to all documents. This means placing styles and macros in a global location. You can place these items in the Normal template.

Styles, menus, keystrokes, toolbars, and VBA macros can be accessed from all documents, but this has a disadvantage. Everyone has his or her own Normal template. If you want to share items, you have to give other users your Normal template, which eliminates their customized features.

If you are going to share some of your automation features, consider creating a global template. A global template can be added to Word. As long as it is added, users have access to any styles, AutoText entries, menus, keystrokes, toolbars, and macros without losing their customized Normal templates.

> There are some additional concerns when you are creating a template to be used as a global template. You might need to adjust the implementation of specific features, so they can be accessed from other documents. Creating global templates is covered in Hour 23, "Creating a Global Template or Add-In."

After you have determined what type of access you need for your automation, you are ready to begin automating your work. An important factor in automation success is selecting the right tool for the job. In addition to VBA macros, modifying menus, toolbars, and keystrokes, you also have page setup, styles, AutoText entries, and boilerplate text. To refresh your memory about using these tools, a brief overview of each is included below.

Creating a Template

If you are going to automate a particular document, you will want to create a custom template. There are two different approaches for creating templates. You can create a template from scratch, or you can use an existing document to create a template. Creating a template from scratch is the method you will use if you don't have an existing document to use as a model:

1. Select File, New.
2. Select an existing template, such as the Blank Document template, to use as a model.

3. Select Template from Create New Choices and click OK.

4. Notice that the title bar has Template 1 as a title.

At this point, you can make any changes that are necessary. When you save the template, you will notice that you are not looking at your default directory. There is a special directory for your templates. This directory is controlled by one of the File Location options and can be changed by selecting Tools, Options.

The other method is to use an existing document as a model. In the section "Evaluating Your Automation Needs" earlier in this hour, you generated a list of tasks and documents that you wanted to automate. In most cases, your approach will be to anticipate what needs to be automated and create your templates for each of the tasks in advance. When you find yourself in a rush to get documents out, you will not have time to set up automation procedures.

You had an opportunity to see the Letter Wizard in action (see "Comparing Templates and Wizards" earlier in this hour). It automates many of the tasks for creating a letter, but you still have to complete four steps to finish the letter. These steps pose questions, which may have the same answer in every instance.

The Letter Wizard wasn't quite right for me. One reason was the limited choice of letter styles. One setting for the Letter Wizard is pre-printed letterhead. I don't use pre-printed letterhead, but I do use one of the specialty papers offered through a mail-order firm. It has some great color graphics, but I still need to print my mailing information. This is a situation when starting with an existing document and creating a template from it is a better choice.

To create a template from an existing document, perform the following steps:

1. Open the document that will be used as a model, as shown in Figure 1.4.

2. Select File, Save As.

3. Select Document Template from the Save as type list (see Figure 1.5). It will automatically switch to your template directory.

4. Enter a filename and click Save.

After the file is saved as a template, you can make the changes needed without disturbing the original file. You can modify the page settings or add custom styles, AutoText entries, custom menus, keystrokes, toolbars, macros, or boilerplate text such as fixed text and fields.

FIGURE 1.4

A sample letter to be used to turn into a template.

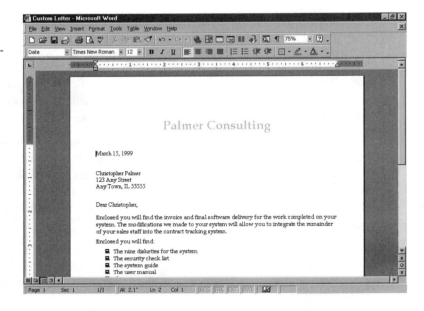

FIGURE 1.5

The Save As dialog will switch directories to your User Templates directory.

Adjusting Page Setup

The first feature to add to your template is a custom page setup. This enables you to set up special margins, paper settings, and layout options. If you are working with an existing document, this process can be very quick because you completed most of these tasks when you created the original document. In the case of my letter template, the margins had to be adjusted to accommodate the graphics at the top and bottom of the page. To adjust the page setup for the template, perform the following steps:

1. Select File, Page Setup, and the Margins tab.
2. Notice in Figure 1.6 that the top and bottom margins are larger than those in the

Normal template, and the left and right margins are reduced. The header is larger and the footer is smaller to accommodate the special paper. Your settings will be different to fit your paper.

FIGURE 1.6

The margins have been adjusted to accommodate the special paper.

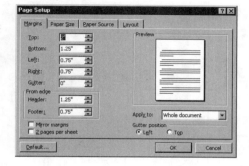

3. Select the Paper Size tab (see Figure 1.7).

FIGURE 1.7

The Paper Size tab enables you to change the size and orientation.

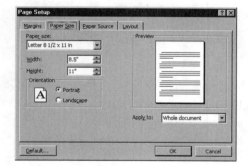

4. Notice that this is a standard paper size with a portrait orientation.

5. Select the Paper Source tab (see Figure 1.8).

6. Notice that you can specify different sources for the first and remaining pages. This tab is very useful if you have special printers.

    If you have a network printer with multiple paper trays, one of them might be dedicated to letterhead paper. On older or smaller printers with one paper tray, you might want to set the first page to manual feed so that you are prompted to insert a page of letterhead paper.

7. Select the Layout tab (see Figure 1.9).

FIGURE 1.8
The Paper Source tab gives you more control over your printer.

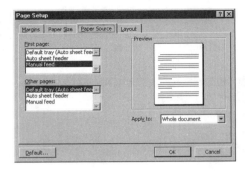

FIGURE 1.9
The Layout tab controls the text on the page, as well as headers and footers.

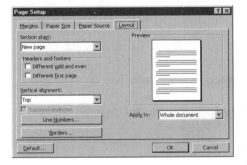

8. Notice that the Layout tab controls sections, headers and footers, vertical alignment, as well as line numbers and borders.

9. Select Different First Page and click OK.

After you have made your choices, you implement them when you click OK. When working with existing documents, you might have some unexpected visual effects.

For example, after you set the Different First Page setting, a header that contains your letterhead information may look as if the information has been deleted (see Figure 1.10). This will be remedied shortly.

Do	**Don't**
Do adjust the Page Setup first when creating a template from scratch. It will eliminate the need to edit your headers and footers.	Don't panic if your headers disappear as you change the Page Setup. If you choose Different First Page for Headers and Footers, Word assumes you want to create a new header and footer for the first page. It is easy to fix using the Clipboard.

FIGURE 1.10

The header is no longer visible.

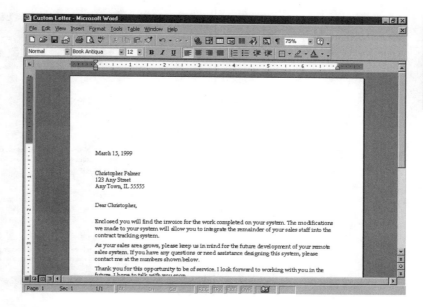

Creating Styles

The next step is to isolate any special formatting you will need on a regular basis. Styles automate formatting when you need to apply more than one attribute to your text. There are two methods for creating styles. You can create styles by example or by definition.

When you are using a document to create your template, you may find that creating styles by example is easier. It is simply a matter of selecting the text with the desired formatting and naming the style. For example, the letter shown in Figure 1.11 has some special bullets in the text.

To create a style by example, perform the following steps:

1. Place the insertion point in the paragraph that has the desired formatting.
2. Click in the Style drop-down list.
3. Type the new name for the style (like `Computer Bullet`).

The other method for creating a style is to define it. This method is great when you do not have an example that has already been formatted. Another style need is illustrated in Figure 1.12. Here is a list that needs some dressing up. Maybe another style of bullets is in order.

FIGURE **1.11**
*The bulleted text has
computer bullets.*

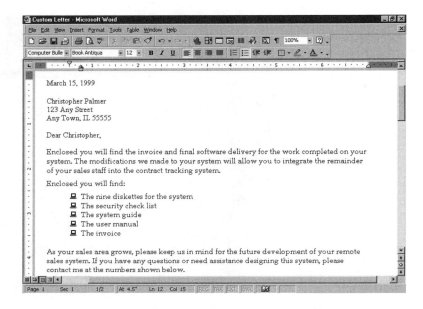

FIGURE **1.12**
*These list items don't
have any special for-
matting.*

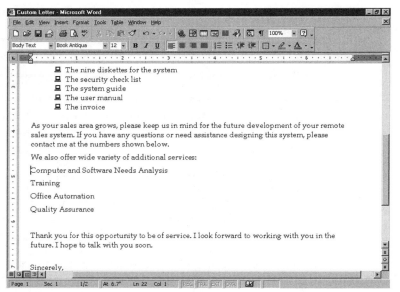

To create a style by definition, perform the following steps:

1. Select the list to be formatted.

2. Select Format, Style to open the Style dialog (see Figure 1.13).

FIGURE 1.13

The Style dialog is used to create and maintain styles.

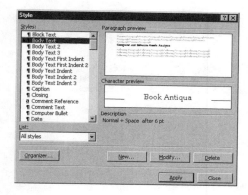

3. Select the New button to open the New Style dialog (see Figure 1.14).

FIGURE 1.14

The New Style dialog is used to define new styles.

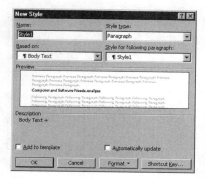

4. Enter a name for the new style, such as Keyboard Bullet.

5. Notice the Style type is Paragraph.

6. Select a style to base the new style on (such as the Computer Bullet style).

7. Notice that selecting the predefined style creates its indention spacing and bullet settings.

8. Click on Format and view the customization choices. See Figure 1.15.

9. Select Numbering to get to the Bullets and Numbering dialog.

FIGURE **1.15**

*The style can contain
any of these settings.*

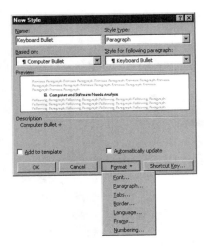

10. Select Customize to change the bullet.

11. Select Bullet to display the Symbol dialog as shown in Figure 1.16.

FIGURE **1.16**

*The Symbol dialog
enables you to select a
new symbol to serve as
the bullet.*

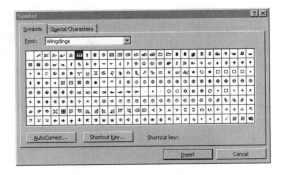

12. Select the symbol three to the left of the currently selected symbol and click OK.

13. Click OK to complete the selection and click OK to save the style.

14. Click Apply to turn the plain list into a bulleted list.

15. Notice it shows Keyboard Bullet in the style drop-down list.

You can also modify styles using the Style dialog or the Style drop-down list. Try to isolate as many regular formatting activities as possible.

> If you have custom formatting for headings, modify the existing Headings 1–9. There are many functions that use these styles automatically, such as Outlining and Table of Contents.

Learning Text Automation Fundamentals

In other word processing programs, one of the primary uses for a macro is to insert standardized text. In Word, you can use a macro for this purpose, but you have several other options for inserting standardized text.

NEW TERM If you have text or graphics that you need some of the time, but not every time, you can use an *AutoText* entry. An AutoText entry is a document that has been saved as part of the template that can be inserted as needed. For text that is a part of the document every time it's created, you can create *boilerplate text*: any fixed text or graphics. Boilerplate text won't be changed as you create new documents. It can also include *built-in fields*, which are placeholders in your document that will fill in specific information at print time, such as a date, the writer's name, and the name of the document.

In Hour 2, "Getting Started with VBA," you will learn how to create a macro to insert text. To see if that is necessary, you must understand what AutoText entries and boilerplate text can do for you. These features are discussed in this section to assist with your decision making.

Adding AutoText Entries

The next step in implementing automation is to consider any text that is standard. For example, the last paragraph in the sample letter shown in Figure 1.10 is a closing paragraph. It thanks the client and solicits future business. It is text that isn't used every time, but is probably used frequently. (If it were used every time, it would qualify as boilerplate text, which is described in the next section.)

Because it isn't used for every letter, this paragraph is better formatted as an AutoText entry. If you are using a sample document to create the template, this process is easy:

1. Select the text such as the last paragraph of your letter. Make sure you select the paragraph mark if you want the entire paragraph.
2. Select Tools, AutoCorrect, and the AutoText tab as shown in Figure 1.17.

FIGURE 1.17

*This AutoText tab
enables you to create
and manage your
AutoText entries.*

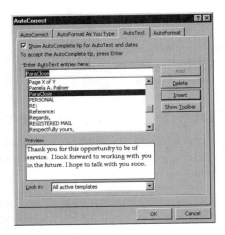

3. Type `ParaClose` (as a name) and click Add.

4. Delete the text and type `ParaClose`.

5. Notice the ToolTip with part of the text and press Enter to add the text to the document to test it.

You can also add an AutoText entry for the close of the letter. The "Sincerely," and your name are already added by default automatically, but you could also add the spacing in between as one entry if desired.

Adding Boilerplate Text

Boilerplate is text, such as your company name and address, that is used every time you create a certain document. In this example, this information is contained in the header and footer, which are currently not visible because they are slated to start on the second page. This can be corrected with the help of the Clipboard:

1. Move to the end of the document and press Ctrl+Enter to add a second page.

2. Select View, Header and Footer.

3. Press Ctrl+A to select the entire header contents and press Ctrl+X to move it to the Clipboard.

4. Select the Default Paragraph font from the Style drop-down list and press Ctrl+E to center the text.

5. Type `Palmer Consulting`.

6. Select the Show Previous button from the Header and Footer toolbar to move to the first page header and press Ctrl+V to paste the contents of the Clipboard.

7. Use the Clipboard to move the footer material to the first page footer.

8. Close the Header and Footer toolbar and delete the second page.

After the header and footers are created in the template, eliminate all the text under the letter opening. Then, you can add some fields to assist with entering the text of the letter such as the date and recipient information.

Introducing Fields

As defined earlier in "Learning Text Automation Fundamentals," a field is a placeholder that retrieves specific information when a document is updated or printed. To assist with automation, Word provides 73 fields that can prompt the user for information or even fill in the information for them.

To assist you with locating the field you can use in your automation, Word divides the fields into categories. For example, there is a category for Date and Time. It has six fields for displaying different dates associated with the document. One of these fields inserts the date into a document:

1. Select the date in the letter.

2. Select Insert, Date and Time to display the Date and Time dialog (see Figure 1.18).

FIGURE 1.18

The Date and Time dialog enables you to insert a field for the date.

3. Select one of the available formats, then select Update Automatically and click OK.

After the date is in place, you can add a field which enables you to add the recipient information. This is accomplished with a MacroButton field:

1. Select all the recipient mailing information.

2. Select Insert, Field to display the Field dialog as shown in Figure 1.19.

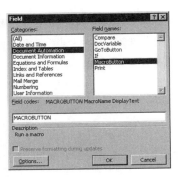

3. Select the Document Automation category and select MacroButton from the Field Names list.

4. Click after the MACROBUTTON keyword.

5. Type NoMacro [Click Here to Type Recipient Information] and click OK.

6. Delete the person's name after Dear and repeat these steps for another Click Here field.

7. Type : and press Enter.

8. Select the Body Text style.

9. Save and close the template.

After you have saved the template, it is ready to use. You can select File, New, and then select your template. When you click OK, Word will create a new document based on your template (see Figure 1.20).

> If you like using the Letter Wizard, you can make changes to one of the existing templates to add your letterhead text. Be sure that you do not change the name of the template or its fields. The template is referenced by that fixed name, and the fields are completed by the wizard. If the name or fields are missing, you may encounter errors.

With this overview of the automation tools, you can begin to fill in the third column on your Automation Needs document. In many cases, VBA macros will still be needed to speed up your work. Completing the list of tasks will help you determine which automation project to complete first.

FIGURE 1.20

The template is ready to use with the date completed and the MacroButton prompts.

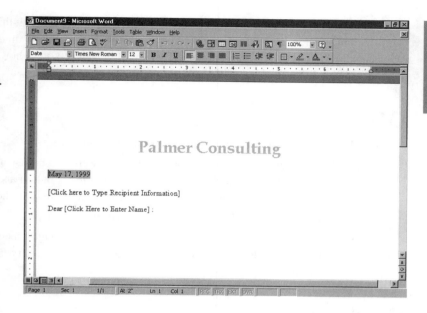

Summary

In this hour, you reviewed the process for automating your work in Word. You learned that all automation tools are stored in a template. There is a global template called Normal, which is a general document with standard margins and some prebuilt automation tools.

You learned that to automate your work, you can create your own templates or make modifications to the Normal template. You can add special page settings, styles, AutoText entries, boilerplate text, and fields. This hour provided an overview of these features. For more information, you can look up these topics in the online help.

This hour introduced a table that will help you track your automation needs. By listing the task, how often it is performed, and what will be needed to automate it, you can determine your priorities. Initially, it is a good idea to use the brainstorming techniques to get an idea of what needs automation. After this initial automation, it is a good idea to keep a running list of automation needs or take a little more time as you create a new document to automate as you work.

Finally, if you used one of your own letters as you worked through this hour, you have a working customized letter template. It will start saving you some time right away, but it can also be improved. The remaining hours will introduce you to how Visual Basic for Applications macros can speed up your work.

Q&A

Q Is there a way to move from one field to another?

A Yes, you can use the Browse buttons in the lower-right corner of the window to Browse by Field. You click the Select Browse Object button and select Browse by Field. Then use Ctrl+Page Down to move to the next field in the document.

Q Can I modify a style without using the Style dialog?

A Yes, you can apply a style to some text, make any changes needed, and reselect it from the Style drop-down list. You will be prompted to verify that you want to modify the style.

Workshop

Here are some questions and exercises to help you reinforce the material covered in this hour. The answers to the quiz questions can be found in Appendix A, "Quiz Answers."

Quiz

1. If I want access to an automated task from more than one type of document, where is the automation saved?
2. If I use a custom style in a global template, but the formatting is not displayed, what is wrong?
3. Can I include graphics in an AutoText entry?
4. Can the close of a letter be boilerplate text instead of an AutoText entry?

Exercises

1. Create a letter using your new template. Be sure to try out your new styles.
2. Finish brainstorming for automation ideas.

HOUR 2

Getting Started with VBA

The highlights of this hour include

- Planning your macro
- Recording your macro
- Maintaining your macro

In the first hour, you evaluated tasks that needed automation and reviewed the basic steps for creating templates. Sometimes, the basic automation tools don't do enough to simplify your work.

In those cases, you might want to create a macro. When you frequently complete a series of tasks that can't be saved as part of one of the other template elements, you might decide to record your actions so that they can be repeated on demand. This is accomplished with the Macro Recorder.

The Macro Recorder creates sub-procedures in Visual Basic for Applications (VBA). If you need to change the process, you can then use VBA to make the changes instead of re-recording the steps. This hour introduces the Macro Recorder and VBA.

Planning Your Macro

In the previous hour, you learned that creating a template for a document that you work with regularly can save time. Eliminating some of the steps for creating documents is a good start, but you can still add automation.

When you determine that a group of tasks needs to be automated with a macro, you need to put together a plan of in what sequence the steps need to be completed. This is important when you are going to use the Macro Recorder, because each action you complete is part of the new macro. To get the greatest timesavings, you don't want to record with a lot of unnecessary steps or steps that you later reverse with more steps.

To assist you with getting started with VBA, you will start with a simple project. Assume you have to create a memo every Friday to set up the Monday morning staff meeting. It is a regular occurrence, and all staff members are expecting a memo. You do not want an elaborate agenda such as the Agenda Wizard might create, but the memo does have some standard elements.

One approach is to use the Memo Wizard to create the memo and then add the additional custom elements. To create the memo this way, perform the following steps:

1. Launch Word and select File, New.
2. Select the Memo tab and double-click on the Memo Wizard.
3. Click Next to begin setting up the memo.
4. Select the Contemporary Memo and click Next.
5. Click Next to leave the heading alone.
6. Type `Weekly Staff Meeting` and click Next.
7. Type `All Staff Members`, de-select the Cc checkbox, and click Next.
8. Click Next twice to skip the closing items, and leave the default header and footer information.
9. Click Finish to create the memo (see Figure 2.1).

Because the Wizard will remember your selections, you have already saved some time, but there are still quite a few steps remaining to create the finished product. This is especially true for regularly created memos with similar content, like the weekly staff meeting memo. The remaining tasks can be simplified with VBA.

FIGURE 2.1

The memo is ready to have text entered.

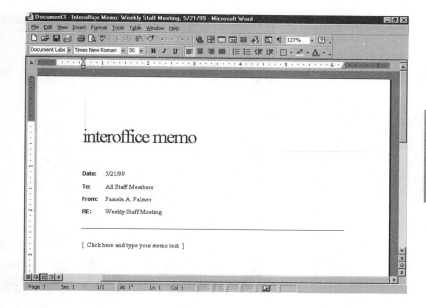

Walking Through the Steps

When you have located a task that needs to be automated, determine what steps are needed to do so. In this case, many of the steps are going to mimic what is done by the Memo Wizard.

When you are creating the memo, one of the first choices that you make is the style. If you use the Contemporary memo style every time, you can avoid a step by selecting this template directly. When you select File, New, and select the Contemporary memo template without the Memo Wizard, you will see a different version of the memo (shown in Figure 2.2).

Using this template just as it is creates more work for you. Therefore, you are going to customize the template. Look at its elements and determine what changes are needed in your memo template.

You don't have to use the Contemporary memo. If you want, you can select an existing memo you have already created and customize it.

FIGURE 2.2
The Contemporary memo uses fields and has some instruction as text.

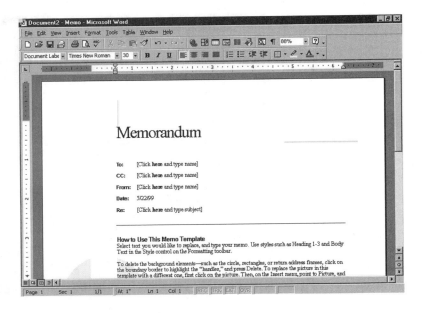

As you examine the introduction for the memo, you realize that the From field is always going to contain your name. That means that you can save time by replacing the Click Here field with your name. You also realize that you don't want to have to delete all the instruction text each time you use the template. To customize the template, perform the following steps:

1. Click on the Click Here field next to From and type your name.
2. Select the text below the line and press Delete.
3. Take the remaining paragraph mark and apply the Body Text style.
4. Select File, Save As.
5. Type Custom Memo as the File name.
6. Select Document Template as the Save As type.
7. Click Save and then close the template.

Creating the custom template saves some time when creating the Weekly Staff Meeting memo, but you can still automate part of the process even more. Within the Weekly Staff Meeting memo created with the Memo Wizard, all the fields are completed, as well as the headings for the text.

The reason for walking through the steps used in creating the document to be automated is to isolate those elements that never change and which become boilerplate text in a custom template. You also isolate the steps that will be a part of the VBA macro. The following are steps to create the Weekly Staff Meeting memo:

1. Select File, New.

2. Double-click on Custom Memo.

3. Select Browse by Field using the Select Browse Object button to highlight the first field.

4. Press Shift+Right Arrow to select the field.

5. Type `All Staff Members` and press Ctrl+Page Down to move to the next field.

6. Press Shift+Right Arrow and type `John Smith`.

7. Press Ctrl+Page Down twice to skip the date and move to the Re field.

8. Press Shift+Right Arrow and type `Weekly Staff Meeting`.

9. Press Ctrl+End to get to the bottom of the document.

10. Type the following paragraph:

    `The weekly staff meeting will begin promptly at 9:00 AM and end at 10:00 AM. We will get an update on the work of the group as a whole and you will need to bring updated information regarding your tasks.`

11. Press Enter and press Ctrl+Alt+1 to select the Heading 1 style.

12. Type `Project Status` and press Enter.

13. Notice the insertion point is ready to accept the project status items formatted with the Body Text style (see Figure 2.3). That style is selected as the style to follow for the Heading 1 style.

As you walk through the steps, you might notice that you are relying on the keyboard more than you might if you were just creating the document. When you are creating a VBA macro, you need to be careful with the mouse.

You can use the mouse to select commands, such as when you select the browse object or even when you change styles; but you can't use the mouse to select text. In the steps above, the Shift Right Arrow shortcut is used to select a field because you can't click on it with the mouse. Using the Ctrl+Alt+1 in step 11 isn't necessary, but it might save some time because you don't pick up the mouse.

If you aren't familiar with the Word shortcut keys, there is a special macro provided to print a list of the shortcut keys. If you enter *shortcut keys* in Help's search text, you will see that one of the choices is Print a List of Shortcut Keys. It gives you instructions on how to get a list.

FIGURE 2.3

*The memo is ready for
the agenda for the
meeting.*

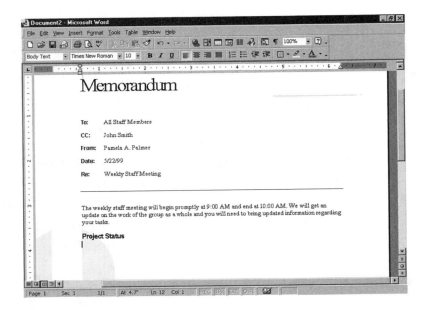

Determining the Location for the Macro

After you have determined the steps to be automated, you determine where you want to
save your macro. You can save a macro in a specific template like the Custom Memo
template. This approach is good if the macro is to assist with automating a process for a
particular type of document.

Another alternative is to store the macro in your Normal template or create a Global
template in which to store macros. This approach makes it accessible from any Word
document.

> For more information on Global templates, please refer to Hour 23,
> "Creating a Global Template or Add-In."

You can place all macros in your Normal template, but doing that has some disadvan-
tages. The first is response time. The more macros placed in the Normal template, the
longer any one macro will take to execute.

The second disadvantage is it is more difficult to share macros with others. The last disadvantage is the possibility for errors to arise. Unless you are creating a new document

as part of the macro, you take the risk of running a macro for a specific document without that document being open.

This decision hinges on the first step outlined above. The first step was select File, New. If you want to automate this step, you must use the second approach, and place the macro in the Normal template or a Global template. If the macro is placed in the Custom Memo template, you won't have access to the macro until you have completed the initial step.

Determining How to Access the Macro

You should also determine how you want to access the macro. When you create a macro, you can run it using four different techniques:

- You can use the Macro dialog to run macros.
- You can create a custom menu item or toolbar button.
- You can create a custom shortcut key combination.
- You can automatically execute a macro based on a document action such as creating a new document based on a template.

Using the Macro dialog is a good way to execute a macro that isn't used frequently. Creating a custom menu or toolbar button is good for macros you use frequently. Assigning a shortcut key is useful for macros you use more than once a day. An auto-executing macro is useful for actions that need to occur every time one of the specific events occurs.

> For more information on auto-executing macros, please refer to Hour 16, "Working with Auto Macros, Events, and Built-In Dialogs."

You next determine which approach you want to use. This macro isn't something you use every time you create a memo, so you don't want to automatically execute it. Also, it isn't used several times a day.

The Macro dialog, however, requires too many steps to be convenient. You conclude, therefore, that you need this macro frequently enough to warrant a menu item or toolbar button. After this decision is made, you are ready to create your macro.

Recording Your Macro

When you decide a macro is the answer to one of your automation problems, you have two methods for creating it. You can create a macro from scratch by writing a procedure in VBA, or you can record the automation steps with the Macro Recorder.

When you begin working with automation, recording a macro has its advantages. It enables you to get started without knowing the Visual Basic for Applications language. It is also very visual. As you complete steps, you can see the results to make sure you are producing the correct results.

After you have recorded the macro, you can edit it, if any changes are needed. To record a macro, you will define the macro, start the recorder, walk through the steps to automate, and stop the recorder.

Defining the Macro

The first step in recording a macro is to define the macro. This involves assigning it a name, setting up access (a menu item, toolbar button, or keystroke), indicating where to save the macro, and providing a description for the macro. To define a macro:

1. Select Tools, Macro, Record New Macro to display the Record Macro dialog (see Figure 2.4).

Figure 2.4

The Record Macro dialog defines the macro.

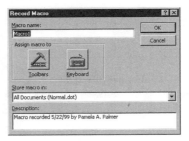

2. Type StaffMeeting as the Macro name.

> Notice there isn't a space between Staff Meeting in the macro name. You can't have any spaces in a macro name. If you added a space, you will get an error message. For more on naming macros, please see Hour 3, "Working with VBA and the Visual Basic Editor."

3. Verify the macro is to be stored in All Documents (Normal.dot).

4. Type the following as the description:

   Creates the Weekly Staff Meeting memo.

5. Click the Toolbars button to display the Customize dialog (see Figure 2.5).

FIGURE 2.5

The Customize dialog is used to create new toolbars and menus and add commands to them.

6. Select the Commands tab and notice that the only category is Macros.

7. Point to Normal, NewMacros, StaffMeeting macro and press the left mouse button.

8. Drag the macro to the Standard toolbar and release the mouse button.

9. Right click on the new button and select Name.

10. Press Ctrl+A to select the Contents, type Staff Meeting and press Enter.

11. Click Close to complete the macro's placement on the toolbar.

At this point, you are ready to record the macro. There are several visual clues that you are recording (see Figure 2.6).

When you begin recording, the Macro toolbar becomes visible to allow you to Stop or Pause the recording of your macro. The mouse pointer also changes to a pointer with a cassette tape to remind you to be careful with your mouse. You will also notice that REC is lit on the status bar.

Walking Through the Steps

After you have defined the macro, you are going to walk through the steps you outlined above. You need to be careful with the mouse when recording a macro. It can be used to select menu items, select toolbar buttons, change views, select browse objects, as well as work with the ruler.

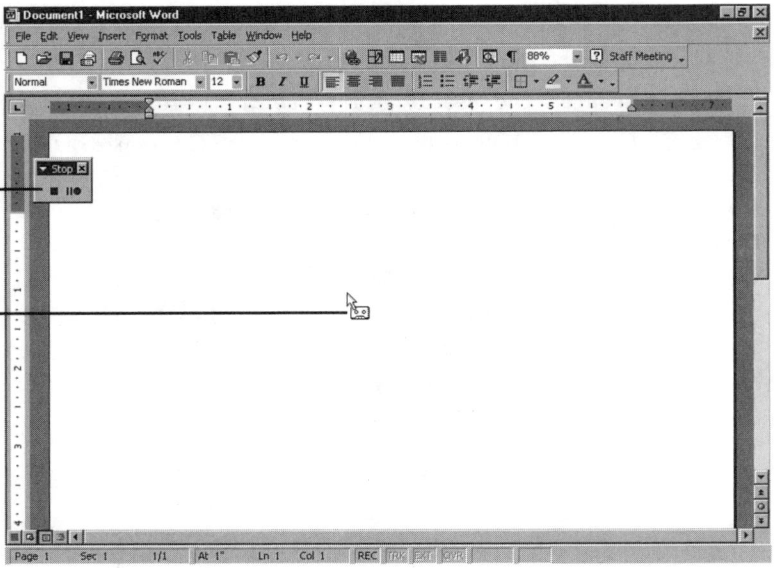

FIGURE 2.6

When you are recording a macro, the Macro toolbar is visible and the mouse pointer changes shape to include a tape.

Macro toolbar

Mouse pointer

You can't use it to do anything in the document window. You can't use it to move the insertion point or select text. You will need to use the keyboard shortcuts for those tasks. To complete the macro, perform the following steps:

1. Select File, New and double-click on Custom Memo.
2. Select Browse by Field, using the Select Browse Object button to highlight the first field.
3. Press Shift+Right Arrow to select the field.
4. Type All Staff Members and press Ctrl+Page Down to move to the next field.
5. Press Shift+Right Arrow and type John Smith.
6. Press Ctrl+Page Down twice to skip the date and move to the Re field.
7. Press Shift+Right Arrow and type Weekly Staff Meeting.
8. Press Ctrl+End to get to the bottom of the document and type the following paragraph:

   The weekly staff meeting will begin promptly at 9:00 AM and end at 10:00 AM. We will get an update on the work of the group as a whole, and you will need to bring updated information regarding your tasks.

9. Press Enter and press Ctrl+Alt+1 to select the Heading 1 style.

10. Type `Project Status` and press Enter.

11. Click the Stop button to stop the recording of the macro.

Maintaining Your Macro

After you click the Stop button, the macro is complete. It is ready for the next time you want to send the Staff Meeting memo. After you use the Macro Recorder and see how easy it is to get started with automation, you will begin to create more and more macros.

As you use those macros, you will discover that you will make mistakes as you record. You may also find that your needs for the macros will change as well. When that occurs, you don't have to rerecord the macro from the beginning. You can edit the macro with the Visual Basic Editor.

As you create macros, it is a good idea to test the macros immediately. This will enable you to check your work as you go while the steps you used and the desired results are still fresh in your mind.

Testing the Macro

Testing a macro is one of the most important steps because it makes sure the results match your expectations. To test the StaffMeeting macro, you can close the memo without saving and click the Staff Meeting button on the toolbar.

After you click the Staff Meeting button, Word will execute the macro. You will see the new document created and the fields completed, as well as the paragraph and heading entered at the bottom of the memo.

> As you test your macros, remember you have an Undo command, which can be an asset. If you click on the Undo drop-down list, you will see that you can roll back the macro's actions.
>
> With the StaffMeeting macro, the code creates a new document. Creating a new document or opening an existing file will reset the Undo list. Despite this restriction, the Undo command is still a valuable feature when creating a macro to review the steps after the new document is created.

Examining and Editing Your Macro

The StaffMeeting macro performs exactly as planned. Even with macros that work as expected, you might still need to make a change.

For example, you decide that you don't like the word "weekly" in the Subject and first paragraph. You do not want to have to re-record the macro from scratch. This is especially true for the paragraph.

When you need to make a change to a macro, you don't rerecord. You can use the Visual Basic Editor to correct the existing macro. To edit the StaffMeeting macro, perform the following steps:

1. Select Tools, Macro, Macros to open the Macros dialog (see Figure 2.7).

FIGURE 2.7

The Macros dialog enables you to run, edit, create, and delete macros.

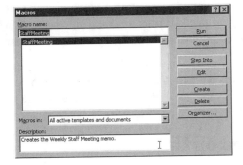

2. Select the StaffMeeting Macro and click Edit to open the Visual Basic Editor (see Figure 2.8).

FIGURE 2.8

The Visual Basic Editor is provided to maintain your macros.

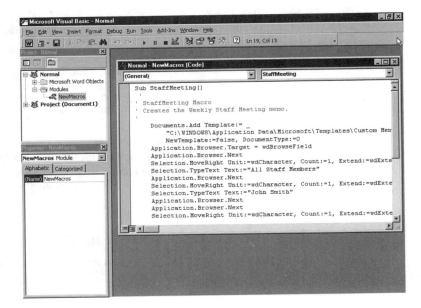

The Visual Basic Editor is a special application that provides a mechanism for editing your macros. When you select Edit from the Macros dialog, it automatically launches the editor and opens your macro in the Code window.

NEW TERM A *procedure* is a set of actions that can be executed as a unit. When you record a macro, Word is generating the Visual Basic for Applications language for each action you record. Each macro is stored in a procedure.

In this case, you created a new procedure called StaffMeeting, which was the name you entered in the Record Macro dialog. Notice that your description is displayed in green preceded by an apostrophe. By placing an apostrophe in front of the text, it is transformed into a comment, and it is disregarded as the macro executes.

> Comments in your code are very helpful when you need to edit your code later. In this case, the comment provides the purpose of the macro. As you begin working more with the Visual Basic Editor, you might want to add comments to describe different actions or sub-tasks in your procedures. To create a comment, you type an apostrophe, which tells the program that a comment follows, and then type your comment.

Each action you walked through when the recorder was active is represented by an action in the code. For example, the first step you recorded was to select File, New, and double-click on the Contemporary Memo template. These steps are recorded as

```
Documents.Add Template = _
  "C:\WINDOWS\Application Data\Microsoft\Templates\Custom Memo.dot", _
  NewTemplate:=False, DocumentType:=0
```

Although this is represented on three lines, it is still only one action. To make the code more readable, Visual Basic allows you to break a line of code across lines. This is accomplished by pressing the spacebar followed by the underscore.

This action indicates that you are adding a new document using your memo template as its template. Your macro may be shown with a different path for the template depending on how your machine is set up.

As you scroll down in the window, you will see each step represented. To change the subject for the memo, locate the line that inserts the text:

```
Selection.TypeText Text:="Weekly Staff Meeting"
```

This line takes the field that was selected and enters the text for you. The text to be entered is enclosed in quotations. If you make any changes to the text, make sure you don't disturb the quotations.

When you want to make a change to the macro, you have many techniques available to you. To remove the word *Weekly*, double-click on it and press Delete. You may have to press Delete one more time to remove the space.

Two lines below this line begin the paragraph. You can double-click on *Weekly* again and press Delete to remove it in these lines as well. After you have made any changes to a macro, it is important to save your macro and test it to make sure it behaves as you expect.

Saving Your Macro

After you have made your changes, save the macro. You can save your template from the Visual Basic Editor. You can click the Save button on the toolbar or select File, Save Normal from the menu. It displays the template name as part of the command on the menu.

After you have saved your macro, it needs to be tested. To test the macro, go back to the Word window. You can click the View Microsoft Word button on the toolbar or press Alt+Tab.

After you are back to Word, you can test the macro. Because you created a toolbar button, you can click the Staff Meeting button. It creates the new document with the changes you just made in the text (see Figure 2.9).

FIGURE 2.9

The word "Weekly" is no longer in the subject or the first paragraph.

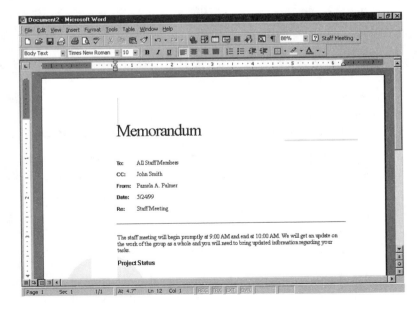

Do	Don't
Do leave the quotations intact when editing text in a macro. The quotations indicate where Word should begin and end inserting text.	**Don't** let the Visual Basic Editor scare you. Just remember each action you recorded is represented in your macro. Learning more about your macro code is what this book is all about.

Summary

This hour focused on getting started with Visual Basic for Applications (VBA). The easiest way to get started is to let Word do the work for you in the form of macros. By recording your macros, all you have to do is walk through the steps you want the macro to execute.

You also learned that you need to be careful about using the mouse as you walk through the steps for your macro. You can't use the mouse to do anything in the document window. You can't move the insertion point or select text with the mouse while recording a macro; you have to use the keyboard for those steps.

Editing macros was also introduced. If you make a mistake while recording a macro, don't get upset. You can edit the macro using the Visual Basic Editor. If you make changes to a macro, it is important to save the template and test the macro to make sure the changed macro performs as expected.

Finally, you may have your own custom memo template. Even if you don't need a staff meeting memo set up by macro, you have created the generic memo template using the Contemporary Memo template or one of your existing memos as a foundation. You can modify it to perform many tasks.

Q&A

Q What happens if I make a typographical error while recording macro?

A If you use the Backspace to remove the typographical error and then continue typing, the error isn't recorded.

Q What if I forget to select a field and begin typing?

A You can use the Backspace to remove what you typed and then select the field and try again. What you typed isn't recorded.

Q Can I use the mouse to select toolbar buttons while recording a macro?

A Yes, the toolbar isn't part of the document area.

Q Can I set tabs and adjust the Ruler settings?

A Yes, you can adjust the Ruler settings and set tabs because they are also not part of the document area.

Q What if I forget to assign a shortcut key or create a button on the toolbar as I record the macro?

A You can always select View, Toolbars, Customize, and use the Customize dialog to assign shortcut keys or place macros on the toolbar or menu.

Workshop

Here are some questions and exercises to help you reinforce the material covered in this hour. The answers to the quiz questions can be found in Appendix A, "Quiz Answers."

Quiz

1. Why is it a good idea to walk through the steps before recording the macro?
2. Why can't I just put all the macros in the Normal template?
3. What happens if I type in a name for the macro that is invalid?

Exercises

1. Develop a macro to create a new generic memo without the Staff Meeting text.
2. Develop a macro to create a new letter based on your letter template from Hour 1.

Hour 3

Working with VBA and the Visual Basic Editor

In Hour 2, "Getting Started with VBA," you learned to automate your work with Visual Basic for Applications (VBA) macros. You used the macro recorder to do most of the work. You will now learn how to edit a macro, using the VBA language and the Visual Basic Editor to make the changes.

The highlights of this hour include

- Examining the macro structure
- Introducing the Visual Basic Editor
- Examining the macro

To complete this hour successfully, you should have already completed the preceding hour in which you created a macro for the Staff Meeting memo. It should be in your Normal template.

Examining the Macro Structure

In Hour 2, you used the macro recorder to capture your actions as you created a simple memo for a staff meeting as shown in Figure 3.1. This document can now be created without any user input except to click the Staff Meeting Memo toolbar button.

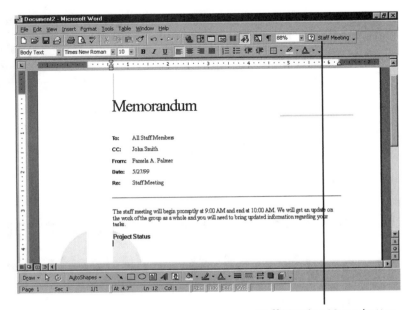

Staff Meeting Memo button

The macro recorder enables you to get started with your automation without having a great deal of knowledge of VBA. When you change a macro, however, knowledge of VBA will enable you to edit your macro without re-recording your steps.

Launching Visual Basic Editor

In the preceding hour, you learned that to make changes to your macro, you need to edit it. Microsoft Office has a central tool for maintaining macros. It is called the Visual Basic Editor. To launch Visual Basic Editor, perform the following steps:

1. Launch Microsoft Word.
2. Select Tools, Macro, Macros to display the Macros dialog (see Figure 3.2).
3. Select the StaffMeeting macro and click Edit.

FIGURE 3.2

The Macros dialog enables you to manage your macros.

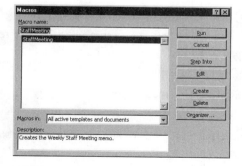

4. Notice that it launches the Microsoft Visual Basic Editor and displays your macro (see Figure 3.3).

FIGURE 3.3

The Visual Basic Editor is used to manage your VBA macros.

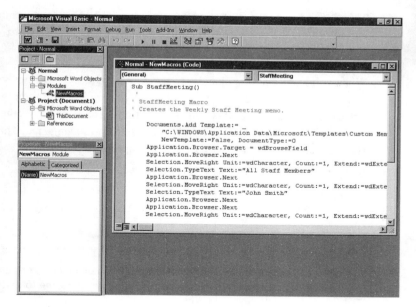

As discussed in Hour 2, the macro recorder has done a lot of the work for you. The recorder sets up the structure of your VBA code. Before you can begin enhancing the macro created by the Macro Recorder, you have to understand the structure of a VBA macro.

In this hour, you have launched the Visual Basic Editor to enable you to view the StaffMeeting macro to begin learning VBA. When a macro is recorded, it is stored as a VBA procedure.

Understanding Procedures

When you want to automate a set of actions to minimize the time required to create format and manage documents and text, you are going to create a macro. You can use the macro recorder, or you can enter the macro directly using the Visual Basic Editor.

When you created the StaffMeeting macro, you were actually creating a *procedure*, which is a group of programming statements and declarations executed as a unit.

In most cases, you can use the term's macro and procedure interchangeably. A macro, however, is really a *subprocedure,* defined as a group of statements that executes as a unit *to perform a specific task*. It is one of four types of procedures. For example, as you look at the macro in the Visual Basic Editor in Figure 3.3, you will see the first line is

```
Sub StaffMeeting()
```

This line indicates the start of a new procedure. When you are creating procedures, they will all follow the same format, more formally referred to as *syntax*.

Understanding Syntax

When you learn a new spoken language, you have to learn the new words and how the language goes together. It is the same when you are learning to program with a computer language, such as Visual Basic for Applications. The structure of the commands, statements, and instructions in your code is dictated by the language. This is referred to as the *syntax*. The following is the syntax for a subprocedure:

SYNTAX
```
[Public¦Private¦Friend][Static] Sub procedurename (arglist)
     statements
     Exit Sub
     Statements
End Sub
```

Learning the syntax or structure of a command can be a trying process, but each syntax presented in this book uses the same formatting to help you understand it quickly.

The syntax is represented in monospaced text to designate that it is code (programming language information). Special formatting and characters are used to indicate what each component represents:

- The regular text represents keywords you must type exactly. You don't have to worry about capitalization as you type them because VBA is not case sensitive. Depending on your Visual Basic Editor options, the editor may adjust the capitalization as you enter text.

- Italics indicate placeholders that you must replace with your own program's values.
- In many cases, there are some options that can be used with a command. In those cases, the optional keywords or placeholders will be presented in brackets.
- If there are multiple options with different keywords, the keywords will be separated by vertical bars referred to as *pipes*. If you don't specify one of the options, the default settings for the command will be used.

As you begin working with VBA and its various syntaxes, you will be able to read the syntaxes much easier. In this book, each syntax is explained in detail with many of the default settings shown.

3

A subprocedure can begin with `Public`, `Private`, or `Friend` to indicate where this can be used. This is known as the *scope* of a procedure. This is covered in greater detail in Hour 5, "Exploring VBA."

This can be followed by `Static`. This controls whether the values used in a procedure will retain their value in between uses of the procedure during one work session. This is also covered in greater detail in Hour 5.

In the macro you created, the line begins with `Sub`. This indicates that it is a subprocedure. The `Public¦Private¦Friend` as well as `Static` are omitted.

With the `Sub` procedure, Public and non-static are the defaults. Their omission means that the procedure is public and can be executed throughout the programming project and no values retain their value. This is followed by `StaffMeeting`, which is the name of the procedure.

When you are naming your procedures, you have to follow specific rules. There are also some guidelines to make writing and reading your VBA code easier to read.

When you name a macro, you adhere to the following:

- Use a letter as the first character.
- Do not exceed 255 characters.
- Do not use spaces, periods, exclamation marks, @, &, $, or # in the name.
- Do not repeat a procedure name within the same scope. This is covered in greater detail in Hour 5.

When you name a macro, you should

- Avoid using any names that match a Visual Basic function, statement, or object name. Although doing so isn't prohibited, it can lead to additional work.
- Consider using title case in the name. In StaffMeeting, the first letter of each word is capitalized. This has no effect on the execution of your code, but it does make it more readable.

The name of the procedure is followed by parentheses. These hold any arguments required by the procedure. An *argument* is a value that is needed by the procedure to complete its task.

If you use the scroll bar to scroll to the bottom of the StaffMeeting procedure, you will see that the last line is

```
End Sub
```

This line is called the *declaration*.

When you create a procedure, the last line must be End Sub. This indicates where the procedure ends and halts its execution. In between the Sub and End Sub statements, you will have statements to accomplish the task.

Each statement will execute a part of the task that is automated. They are usually on separate lines. If, for some reason, you need to stop executing your code before you have finished executing all the code (such as when you are trying to work with a table, but a table isn't selected), you can. To exit a procedure before executing all the lines of code, you can put in the Exit Sub statement.

Functions and Event Procedures

A *function* is a procedure that executes a series of steps, but also returns a value. Functions are often used to test the values of settings or perform calculations.

When you are working with Word, you don't automatically think of having to perform calculations, but there are times when functions are useful. For example, you are trying to automate document creation and add a date automatically that is ten days away. A standard function could be created and called from other procedures.

The syntax for a function is slightly different from that for the Sub procedure to accommodate the fact that the function returns a value:

▼ SYNTAX

```
Public¦Private¦Friend Function functionname (arglist) as Type
     statements
     functionname = value
     Exit Function
```

```
        statements
        functionname = value
 ▲   End Function
```

You can determine the scope and status of the values used in the function. You can also skip statements by using the Exit function statement. There are two differences between the syntax for a subprocedure and that for a function:

- The declaration line for a function can specify what type of value is returned.
- In a function syntax, there needs to be a line setting the function name equal to the value.

An *event procedure* is a special type of subprocedure that executes when a specific action is performed by the user—whether that user is you or someone else. These are often referred to as *auto-executing macros*.

There are two syntaxes for auto macros. One is to use a special name for the procedure. The syntax for an event procedure is

```
Sub autoname (arglist)
    statements
    Exit Sub
    statements
End Sub
```

The second approach is to use or create an event for a specific object. The syntax is slightly different:

```
Sub object_event (arglist)
    statements
    Exit Sub
    statements
End Sub
```

Here the object is followed by an underscore and the name of the event you want to use. This approach is more common when you are going to respond to an action on a UserForm.

There are specific event procedures you can create for a template or object. An example is a macro that will execute every time a new document is created based on that template. To do this, you create an event procedure called AutoNew. For more information on auto-executing macros, please refer to Hour 16, "Working with Auto-Executing Macros and Dialogs."

Understanding Templates and Modules

When you want to create a macro, you will have to decide where to store the macro. Macros are stored in templates. When you use the macro recorder to capture your actions for a macro, the macro recorder sets up the template to store your macro.

By default, a template doesn't have any procedures included, so Word doesn't include any place to store macros. When you create a macro, the macro recorder automatically creates a module for your macros in your template called NewMacros. A *module* is an object that stores the procedures and declarations.

If you are going to create a macro from scratch or you want to organize your macros, you can create additional modules as needed for your template. Within Visual Basic, your template or document is referred to as a *Project*. For more elaborate templates or documents that contain many procedures, you might consider having a module for each different category of procedures.

You might have a module for managing text procedures and another for procedures that format text. Because you are just beginning to create macros, this is less of a concern. This feature becomes more important as you create many and more complex macros and begin sharing your automation with others.

When a new module is needed, it can be inserted easily. You simple select the project and select Insert, Module from the menu. You will have a chance to use this feature as you complete some of the hours in this book.

Introducing the Visual Basic Editor

Regardless of what type of procedure you are creating, you will use the Visual Basic Editor to edit and manage the procedures. The Visual Basic Editor, which you launched at the beginning of this hour, is a separate application that is used by all the Microsoft Office applications. The Visual Basic Editor is designed to facilitate the writing and maintaining of your Visual Basic for Applications code.

When you first look at the Visual Basic Editor, its window may seem confusing. It isn't like Word. In Word, it is possible to work with more than one document at a time, and each document is shown in an identical window. Instead of displaying identical windows, the Visual Basic Editor's main window has separate windows to display different aspects of the management process.

The Visual Basic Editor has a title bar with a menu and toolbar. Inside the workspace, three windows are currently displayed (see Figure 3.3). There are additional windows that will be displayed as needed. It may take a little while until you feel comfortable working with these different windows. To optimize your use of the Visual Basic Editor, each window is described separately below.

Examining the Project Explorer

The first window on the left is the Project Explorer (see Figure 3.4). It assists with the management of the modules in your project. The Project Explorer lists all the documents and templates open at this time.

FIGURE 3.4

The Project Explorer shows what templates and documents are open.

The Project Explorer is organized in a tree structure similar to the Windows Explorer to facilitate navigation between projects. If you launch Word, and it creates the new document for you, the Project Explorer shows two projects, Normal is the default template and Project(Document1) is the open document.

For each project, there is a folder for Microsoft Word Objects. When you are automating your work, you do so by manipulating Word Objects such as a document or a field. There are also several other folders, including a Modules folder if you have recorded a macro, and a References folder if you have any templates attached or references to any other coding resources.

Under the Normal project, you see the Microsoft Word objects and Modules folders. The Modules folder is open and the NewMacros module is selected. The Project(Document1) has Microsoft Word Objects and a References Folder. If you open the References folder, you will see a Reference to the Normal template shown.

The Project Explorer has three buttons that become active depending on what is selected:

- The first button will be active when you have a module selected. This first button is the View Code button, and it opens the code window for the selected module. In your case, the code window is already open because you selected Edit from the Macros dialog.

- The second button is the View object button. It will display the selected object to you. If the object is a document, it will switch back to that document window. If the object is a user form, it will open the object in a window in the Visual Basic Editor. For more information on user forms, please refer to Hour 17, "Working with User Forms."

- The last button changes the view in the Project Explorer. By default, it organizes the contents using folders. If you prefer to see the list of objects, you can click the Toggle folders button. Now the objects are listed in alphabetical order with small icons used to differentiate the types of objects (see Figure 3.5).

FIGURE 3.5

The Project Explorer can list objects without folders.

Normally the Project Explorer is located (*docked*) at the far left of the window. You can move it to another location if you want.

Exploring the Code Window

The next window is the code window (see Figure 3.6). It is the one you began using in Hour 2. The code window, which lists the code in a module, is where you will complete all your coding.

FIGURE 3.6

The Code window is used to maintain your code.

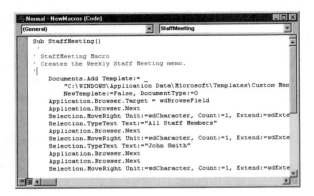

The Code window has its own title bar. It lists the name of the project followed by a hyphen and the name of the module followed by the word *Code*.

This window doesn't have a standard toolbar. It has two drop-down lists:

- The first list is the Object list. If you aren't adding code to a specific object like the document, this list will only display the word *General* in parentheses.
- The second list is the Procedure list. It can be used to select a specific procedure to view. It will have a list of the procedures in a module as well as the word *Declarations* in parentheses. The Declarations choice will display at the very top of the module where you can declare values that can be used by several modules.

Under the drop-down lists, you see the editing area. This is where your code will be displayed, and where you can make changes to the module. The editing area is very similar to the document window in Word. The code is displayed as text in the center, with an Insertion point indicating where text will appear as you type.

You have scroll bars on the right and bottom of the area to facilitate viewing. You have two small view buttons at the lower-left edge of the window. You can choose to view all the code in a module, which is the default. You can choose to view one procedure at a time by clicking the first button.

The gray bar at the left is the Breakpoint selection bar. This facilitates testing your code. Although it isn't visible, you also have a selection bar just to the right of it to enable you to select a line or more than one line at a time.

If you are accustomed to using the keyboard to move the insertion point and select text in Word, you will find that most of the Word navigation and selection techniques will work here as well.

One difference between Word's document area and the Code window is the use of color. As you examine the StaffMeeting macro, you will notice some words displayed in blue and others in green or black. Color is used to help you identify different VBA elements. For example, blue text indicates a VBA key word; green indicates that the text is a comment and, therefore, won't execute.

Introducing the Properties Window

The third window is the Properties window (see Figure 3.7). As you work with VBA, you will be manipulating objects. Each object's behavior and appearance is controlled with properties.

NEW TERM *Properties* are defined characteristics that can used and changed with your VBA code.

The Properties window will list the properties for an object selected in the Project Explorer.

FIGURE 3.7

The Properties window displays the attributes for an object.

If you select the `ThisDocument` object, you will see properties like `DefaultTabStop`. The Properties window has a drop-down list with the objects in a project. It also has two tabs. You can view the properties alphabetically or by category, as shown in Figure 3.8.

FIGURE 3.8

You can view the properties by category.

When you view the properties by category, you see them as a structured list with a minus button. If you click on that button, you will collapse that category. With some objects, this view is better. With the document object, it isn't as useful because there is only one category.

The Properties window is docked to the left side of the window like the Project Explorer, but you can move it anywhere in the window.

Examining the Immediate, Locals, and Watches Windows

There are three more windows that are not displayed when you open the Visual Basic Editor as you did. These windows are used when you are trying to track down a problem. To display them, you will select View and the window you want to use.

You cannot access these windows unless you have paused the execution of a macro. If you select View before pausing, these choices will appear disabled.

The Immediate window is shown in Figure 3.9. This window enables you to check values, set values, and interact with your code as it is running. When selected, it shows an insertion point where you can enter what you want to test.

FIGURE 3.9

The Immediate window enables you to interact with a procedure during execution.

The Immediate window is docked to the lower-right edge of the Visual Basic Editor. You can move it to another location if needed.

The second window that can be useful while testing your code is the Locals window as shown in Figure 3.10. There are times when you will want to view values set by your code. The Locals window can save you time by listing all active values specified by your code.

FIGURE 3.10

The Locals window tracks expressions set up in your procedure.

The last window that may be useful during testing is the Watches window shown in Figure 3.11. If you have many active values, it may be difficult to locate a specific value in the Locals window. You can set up Watch expressions to monitor specific values.

All three of these windows assist with the testing of your code only. These windows will be covered in greater detail in Hour 8, "Handling Problems in VBA."

3

FIGURE 3.11

The Watches window enables you to determine what you need to monitor.

Examining the Macro

Now that you have toured the Visual Basic Editor, you can begin to examine your macro and get started learning VBA. The StaffMeeting macro you created in Hour 2 is shown below in Listing 3.1.

The line numbers that precede each line of code in Listing 3.1 and much of the code in this book are not part of VBA, but are for reference only. Therefore, when working with VBA code, do not enter line numbers.

LISTING 3.1   The StaffMeeting Macro

```
 1: Sub StaffMeeting()
 2: '
 3: ' StaffMeeting Macro
 4: ' Creates the Weekly Staff Meeting memo.
 5:'
 6:    Documents.Add Template:= _
 7:     "C:\WINDOWS\Application Data\Microsoft\Templates\
       ➥Custom Memo.dot", _
 8:        NewTemplate:=False, DocumentType:=0
 9:    Application.Browser.Target = wdBrowseField
10:    Application.Browser.Next
11:    Selection.MoveRight Unit:=wdCharacter, Count:=1,
       ➥Extend:=wdExtend
12:    Selection.TypeText Text:="All Staff Members"
13:    Application.Browser.Next
14:    Selection.MoveRight Unit:=wdCharacter, Count:=1,
       ➥Extend:=wdExtend
15:    Selection.TypeText Text:="John Smith"
16:    Application.Browser.Next
17:    Application.Browser.Next
18:    Selection.MoveRight Unit:=wdCharacter, Count:=1,
       ➥Extend:=wdExtend
19:    Selection.TypeText Text:="Staff Meeting"
20:    Selection.EndKey Unit:=wdStory
21:    Selection.TypeText Text:= _
```

```
22:         "The staff meeting will begin promptly at 9:00 AM and "
23:     Selection.TypeText Text:= _
24:         "end at 10:00 AM. We will get an update
        ➥on the work of the gr"
25:     Selection.TypeText Text:= _
26:         "oup as a whole and you will need to bring
        ➥updated information"
27:     Selection.TypeText Text:="n regarding your tasks."
28:     Selection.TypeParagraph
29:     Selection.Style = ActiveDocument.Styles("Heading 1")
30:     Selection.TypeText Text:="Project Status"
31:     Selection.TypeParagraph
32: End Sub
```

The StaffMeeting creates a new document, fills in fields, adds text, and changes formatting for you. As you recorded the macro, Word was constructing the macro using VBA.

Visual Basic for Applications is the programming language used by most of the Microsoft Office applications to automate tasks. When Microsoft Office was introduced, automation was more complicated. Each product had its own macro language.

When switching applications, you had to learn how to develop a macro from scratch. This was a formidable obstacle for automating your work. Microsoft introduced VBA as the common macro language to minimize the learning curve.

VBA has a core set of language components that are available in each application. Because the features of each application are different, each application has a custom set of components. The theory is you can learn the core language features of VBA and, as you need to automate tasks in one of the applications, you have to learn only the language components for that application.

To make learning VBA even easier, each application's components share a common structure. After finishing this book, you will have a good foundation in using VBA, as well as a good start on mastering the Word components called objects.

The remaining sections are designed to introduce you to VBA; they don't cover the macro in detail. In Hour 4, "Understanding Objects," you will get a complete explanation of the Word objects.

Introducing Objects

As you work with VBA, you will master the shared elements that make up the core language. As you begin to automate in one of the applications, you will have to learn the components that are unique to that specific application. To make the task easier, these components are organized in a hierarchy, which is referred to as the *object model*.

As you automate tasks, you are going to manipulate objects. An *object* is a component in Word that can be manipulated with VBA. When there is more than one object available at a time, you can work with an *object collection*. A *collection* is a group of like objects.

In the StaffMeeting macro (refer to Listing 3.1), you work with one collection and manipulate several objects. You add a new document to the Documents collection. You manipulate the Word settings with the Application object, and you modify text using the Selection object.

When you work with objects, you can read and change attributes about the object, use built-in actions, or respond to events that affect the object. In this macro, you are setting properties and taking advantage of many of the built-in actions.

Introducing Methods and Arguments

For each object, there will be a set of built-in actions. These are referred to as *methods*. A method is a built-in procedure that takes action on (or with) a specific object.

In StaffMeeting (Listing 3.1), the first statement uses a method. You are using the Add method to create a new document (line 6). The Add method is used with collections to enable you to create new instances of a type of object. In this case, you are adding a new document to the Document collection.

Line 10 uses the Next method for the application's Browser object. This facilitates the move from field to field. The MoveRight method for the Selection object is used to select each field after you move to it on line 11.

The TypeText method for the Selection object is used to insert text beginning on line 12. Notice that there are several statements used to create the paragraph. That was done to make the code easier to read.

When you are using a method, there is a general syntax that is followed: You will have the object, followed by a period, followed by the method's name. In many cases, this will be followed by any arguments that are required by the method, as follows:

`object.method argumentlist`

Many of the methods need some additional information to perform the desired action. Any information required will be supplied with arguments. In the first statement beginning on line 6, the Add method is used. It requires information regarding what template to use, as well as some additional arguments.

When a method is expecting arguments, the arguments can be specified one of two ways:

- You can specify them in an expected order. The values are placed after the method separated by commas. Each argument has a space. If you are skipping an argument, you will have two commas side by side to indicate the default should be used. All arguments have a default value.

- You can also use the argument name. This is illustrated with the Add method. For the Documents collection, there can be up to four arguments. You can use Template, NewTemplate, DocumentType, and Visible.

The Template argument indicates which template will be used to create the new document. NewTemplate indicates whether you are creating a template. DocumentType indicates what type of file is created like a document, email message, Web page or frameset.

This last argument, Visible, isn't specified in the statement. The Visible argument is set to True by default, so it isn't needed.

When you are going to use the named-argument approach, you have to enter the name of the argument, followed by a colon, followed by the equal sign:

```
Object.method argumentname:=value
```

Introducing Properties

In addition to methods, you can also use and change settings that affect the appearance and behavior of objects. This are referred to as *Properties*. The second statement on line 9 sets a property value, the Target property, for the Browser object.

The Browser object lets you determine what object you want to use to scroll through your document. You changed this as you recorded the macro by selecting By Field from the Browse Object button's list.

When you want to use or set a property, you are building an expression. You will set the Property equal to a value. In this case, the Target property is set equal to wdBrowserField to indicate that you want to move from field to field in the document.

Introducing Constants

In the second statement, you are setting the Target property equal to wdBrowserField. This is a constant. A *constant* is a placeholder for a value that will not change as your macro executes.

You can declare your own constants, but in this case, you are using one of the built-in constants. Many of the arguments for methods, as well as properties, are stored as numbers. When you are writing your macros, it can be quite difficult to remember what number means what for each argument or property.

For example, you have to set the `DocumentType` argument in the first statement. It is set to `0`. Can you tell `0` means that you are going to get a new blank document?

Built-in constants make your code more readable. The `wdBrowseField` value for the `Target` property describes the setting much better than `6`, which is the numeric value.

Summary

This hour explored the Visual Basic Editor. When you need to make changes to the macros you record or want to create macros from scratch, you will use the Visual Basic Editor.

Unlike Word, it has several windows to accomplish your tasks. You can manage your code with the Project Explorer and view it with the Code window. You can use the Properties window to view the property values for a selected object.

There are also three windows that aren't available when you are editing your code. The Immediate, Locals, and Watches windows are used when you are testing your code.

You began to explore the structure of the code that was created by the Macro Recorder. You learned that as you were recording the steps, the recorder created a subprocedure for you. You also learned that there were different types of procedures.

As you explored the macro you created, you learned that VBA is designed to reduce the learning curve for programming throughout Microsoft Office. There is a core set of language components with specific application features accessed through an object model. In the StaffMeeting macro (refer to Listing 3.1), you used the object model using specific object's methods and properties to create the memo.

As you complete the remaining hours in this book, you will learn more of the specifics of the Word object model. You will also build a foundation of knowledge regarding the VBA core language.

Q&A

Q **What if the Visual Basic Editor appears while I am executing my macro?**

A This happens when you have an error in your macro. You see a message informing you there is a problem, and the Visual Basic Editor comes up for you.

You will be in Break mode. This enables you to repair the problem before continuing. For more information, please refer to Hour 8, "Handling Problems in VBA."

Q **How can I find out what settings are used for arguments and properties?**

A The Visual Basic Editor offers a complete help system. You can enter the name of the property, place your cursor in the word and press F1. There are also some additional resources. For more information on getting help, please refer to Hour 5, "Exploring VBA."

Q **What if I can't see one of the windows in the Visual Basic Editor?**

A Select View from the menu and you can select the window of your choice. If the window choice is gray, that window isn't available at that time.

3

Workshop

Here are some questions and exercises to help you reinforce the material covered in this hour. The answers to the quiz questions can be found in Appendix A, "Quiz Answers."

Quiz

1. What is an object?

2. What are properties, methods, and events?

3. Why are constants a better choice than entering the numeric settings for arguments and properties?

4. What window displays the list of documents currently active?

Exercises

1. Place your insertion point in the Target property in the second statement of your StaffMeeting macro and press F1 to view the Help topic. What is the constant to browse by tables?

   ```
   wdBrowseTable
   ```

2. Navigate in the Code window using the scroll bars and some of the keystrokes you are accustomed to using in your Word documents, such as End to move to the end of a line.

HOUR 4

Understanding Objects

In Hour 3, "Working with VBA and the Visual Basic Editor," you began exploring the structure of your macro, and you were introduced to several of the Word objects that were used in your macro. In this hour, you will get a more complete tour of the Word objects.

The highlights of this hour include

- Learning about object-oriented programming
- Working with objects
- Introducing the Word Object Model

Learning About Object-Oriented Programming

In Hour 3, you were introduced to many new terms. Most of them centered around working with objects. Objects speed up development of your macros. To get a better understanding of why objects are important, a short history lesson may be helpful.

When computers were first developed, the programmer or developer had to know everything about the hardware to get results. The developer needed a great deal of knowledge to perform even simple tasks.

As computers became more powerful, they also became easier to use. Computer languages changed to make it easier to access the computer's functions. A developer just needed to understand how to call a process. He or she was no longer required to understand how the computer completed the processing.

The Desktop Revolution

When computers moved to the desktop to assist with day-to-day operations like word processing, the first packages had the capability to manipulate and format text and data. Automation consisted largely of features built into the software. A good example of this is the capability to number lines and track revisions, features needed by the legal profession.

> The demand for additional features also made it difficult for developers. I worked for a company that made a word processing package. When a new printer was introduced, we had to know everything about that printer's internal language to print even the simplest document.

Soon users began to look for other ways of automating their work. That was when the macro was born. In older word-processing packages, macros were limited to working on an open document or a selected section of text.

Another major complaint for computer users was that the learning curve was very great. To run programs, or manipulate files, you had to learn a set of character-based commands. For example, copying files from one location to another required the copy command and remembering the source and destination of the files.

The learning curve was also a problem with automation. If you learned how to automate in your word processor, but wanted to use automation in your spreadsheet, you had to start learning from the very beginning. The two methods were completely different.

A New Look and Feel

Many people recognized the issues with working with a desktop computer. The first commercial solution was introduced with the Apple Macintosh. The Macintosh discarded all older methods for interacting with a desktop computer.

The Macintosh used a more user-friendly interface. It didn't rely on learning a set of character-based commands. It provided a graphical user interface where users could select what actions they wanted from a menu or select graphical icons representing different functions.

When the Macintosh was introduced, the philosophy of computers changed. One of its goals was to create universal methods for accomplishing standard tasks, thereby making the computer easier to use and minimizing the learning curve. A good example is the task of opening files. Applications that manipulate files now all have a File menu with an Open command.

The Macintosh provided more flexibility. Users could now run more than one application and switch between applications very easily. The problem with the Macintosh was that there were many of these older character-based computers, especially in businesses. Most businesses couldn't afford to abandon all those machines.

Microsoft Windows was introduced to bring the benefits of a graphical user interface to the standard desktop systems. It provided a great jump in productivity with its new interface, but not without a cost. This graphical approach to performing day-to-day tasks required the development of a new way of programming.

The older languages used procedural programming and were very restrictive. The languages were linear in design. The user could only do one thing at a time. With the many options provided by Windows, this programming philosophy no longer worked.

A new philosophy was developed. It is called *object-oriented programming*. Rather than being forced down a specified path in an application, the user can now choose from several paths. For example, think of how many paths are represented by the menu commands alone.

Because a developer can't predict what choice the user will make, each choice must be self-contained so that it can be called from several places. A good example is text on the Clipboard. It can be accessed with Cut, Copy, or Paste using the menu, the shortcut menu, the toolbar, or the keyboard.

Object-oriented programming is based on defining specific things (objects) that need to be manipulated. Manipulating these objects is accomplished by working with their properties, using their methods, and responding to their events.

Visual Basic for Applications is not considered a "true" object-oriented language, but it does use many of the object-oriented concepts. To accomplish many of your automation tasks, you will manipulate built-in objects.

4

It is possible to create your own objects with Visual Basic for Applications by developing *Classes*. The development of objects is outside of the scope of this book.

Working with Objects

The key to successful development with VBA is to learn how to work with objects. In Hour 3, you were introduced to objects. An object is a thing that can be manipulated. In object-oriented programming, an object can represent a physical object as well a conceptual one.

An example of a real world object is a stove. It is a self-contained entity that can be manipulated. An example of an object in Word is a document. It is also self-contained and can be manipulated.

To manipulate objects, there are five concepts to keep in mind. Objects can

- Have characteristics or attributes to define them that can be used and sometimes changed.
- Perform specific actions.
- Be affected by specific actions.
- Be part of a group of like objects.
- Be comprised of other objects.

Examining Properties

The first concept is that objects have characteristics or attributes to define them, and these characteristics can be used and sometimes changed. These characteristics are referred to as *properties*.

For the stove object, a property might be type, color, or self-cleaning capability. For the Word document, there are many properties like name, paragraphs in a document, words in a document, or capability to have styles updated when the document is opened.

Understanding the Types of Properties

Properties can be used two different ways. You can use them to retrieve information or to set information about an object. Some properties only allow you to retrieve information. These are referred to as *read-only properties*.

For the stove, type, color, and self-cleaning capability all represent read-only properties. For a particular stove, you can't change the model number, color, or its capability to self-clean. You can test to see the setting for this property, however.

For the document, the name of the document, number of paragraphs, or number of words are read-only properties. You can't directly affect the settings of these properties with VBA. Whether the styles can be updated is a property that can be changed.

Using Properties

When you want to set or use a property value, you create an expression. You code this expression with a value on one side of the expression and the property on the other:

```
x = object.property
```

or

```
object.property = y
```

When you refer to the property, you will specify the object first, followed by a period and the name of the property. Many properties are referred to with more than one word. In that case, the words are strung together with no space in between. They are shown with initial capitalization for each word, such as UpdateStylesOnOpen. You don't have to worry about typing in the capital letters; the Visual Basic Editor will automatically add the capital letters.

When you are working with properties, you will be retrieving or setting their values. Different properties have different types of values. For example, a document's Name property is stored as text, and its Words property is stored as a number.

NEW TERM   These different types are referred to as *data types*. Learning the data type for a variable is helpful. You may have problems with your code if you choose the wrong one. (For more information about data types, refer to Hour 5, "Exploring VBA.")

In many cases, the Visual Basic Editor provides some assistance. For many of the properties that are stored as values, there are built-in constants to represent the numbers. In Hour 3, for example, your StaffMeeting macro used the Target property for the Browser object. It has specific numeric settings. Instead of remembering the number 6, it is entered as wdBrowseField.

If you are typing that statement in the Visual Basic Editor instead of recording it, you have help. As you begin typing a value for a property, you see a list appears with the built-in constants for that property, as shown in Figure 4.1.

FIGURE **4.1**

*The built-in constants
are displayed as you
begin typing.*

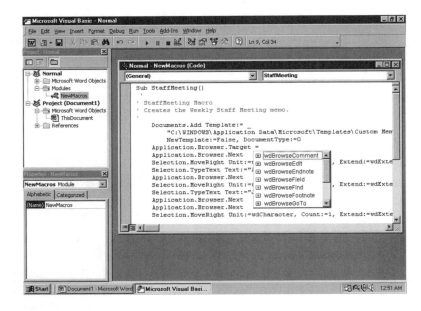

You can use your mouse to select one from the list, or you can type as many of the characters as needed to move to it in the list and press Tab. It will automatically insert the rest of the constant and move to the end of the constant.

Examining Methods

The second concept is that objects can perform specific actions. An object's actions are referred to as *methods*. The stove object has several methods. It can cook, bake, broil, and so forth. You can also use many methods with the document object, such as closing, saving, saving with a new name, and so on.

To use a method, you need to indicate which object you are working with and any arguments required. The syntax is

```
object.method argument1, argument2,..., argumentn
```

Many methods use arguments. Arguments provide instructions for completing the action. For the stove, baking is a method. Its arguments might include temperature, bake time, and rack position.

You just don't press a button on the stove that reads Bake; you have to give it more information. It is the same for Document methods. For example, the method to save a document with a new name is called SaveAs. It has eleven arguments including the filename and file type.

As discussed in Hour 3, arguments store data, and they expect a specific type of data—like properties. Sending the wrong kind of data can cause your macro not to run or to give you unexpected results.

There are also two methods for specifying arguments. In Hour 3, you examined the Add method for the Documents collection. Its arguments are specified using the named-argument approach. The argument begins with the argument name followed by a colon, an equal sign, and its value. Each argument is separated by commas.

The other technique is to specify arguments by position. This approach depends on the arguments appearing in a specific order. This approach requires less typing, but at the cost of readability because the argument name isn't shown.

The Visual Basic Editor provides help with the arguments similar to the help provided for constants. Type the object, the period, method name, and a space. The Visual Basic Editor will provide the syntax for the method with all the arguments, as shown in Figure 4.2.

FIGURE 4.2

The methods arguments are listed to assist with method use.

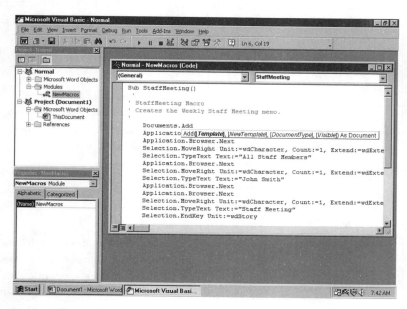

The argument in that position is highlighted in bold. It is like fill-in fields. To skip an argument, type a comma without specifying a value. The list of arguments will move to the next one.

Examining Events

The third concept is that objects are affected by outside actions called *events*. The object may have to take action based on those outside influences. For the stove object, there are many outside actions performed by the cook. The burner is turned on, the oven temperature is set, the timer is set, the timer goes off, etc. The document object is created, opened, saved, and closed.

To respond to an event, you are going to create an *event procedure*. The syntax for event procedures differs slightly from one Office application to another. In Word, you assign the procedure a special name. In other applications, the syntax is more complex. (Responding to events is covered in greater detail in Hour 16, "Working with Auto Macros, Events, and Built-In Dialogs.")

Examining Collections

The fourth concept is that there can be more than one of the same object accessible at a time. When it is possible to have more than one object accessible, the objects are part of a *collection*. The stove may not seem like it is part of a collection, but it is. In the world, there are many stoves. In Microsoft Word, it is possible to work with more than one file at a time.

When you work with collections, you must manage the collection. You will have to add, delete, and manage objects for the collection. When you have several objects in the collection, you may have to reference a specific object. In most cases, you can reference the object by its name or by an index value. The syntax is

```
collection.object("name")
```

or

```
collection.object(index)
```

If an object has a name, it needs to be enclosed in quotation marks. Another approach to working with objects is to take advantage of some collection properties. For example, the `Document` collection has an `ActiveDocument` property to work with the document that is currently active. This works well with generic macros that work with all documents. If you don't need to work with a specific document, this property lets you work with the document that is active.

Understanding Object Models

The last concept focuses on the fact that some objects contain other objects. Often you have to manipulate an object's components. For the stove object, there are many components or parts. You have the burner, oven door, timer, and temperature control. A document also has many component objects, and many of them have components of their own. For example, a document can have paragraphs, which can have sentences, which are constructed with words, which are constructed with characters. All these objects are part of collections.

To help you manage the collections and objects, there is a hierarchy of objects. This is referred to as an *object model*. An object model serves the same purpose as an organization chart for a company. An organization chart for a company or department maps out the roles and relationships of each person. It helps to explain who is responsible for each business function.

The object model also explains relationships. If you work with a sentence, for example, you must reference the document and paragraph where the sentence is stored.

When you are working with VBA and Microsoft Office, each application has its own object model. After you have learned the core language of VBA, beginning to automate your work in another application is a matter of learning the object model.

Introducing the Word Object Model

4

The Word object model is like the others. It breaks down the operations of the application using objects with properties, methods, and events. To get a feel for the organization of the model, Microsoft represents the object model as shown in Figure 4.3.

The object model represents the objects and collections that can be controlled with VBA. As you learned in Hours 2 and 3, it is not a requirement that you know everything about every object to get started automating your work. As you increase the amount of automation used in Word, your knowledge of the object model will increase as well.

There are some objects you will never use, just as there are some Word features you will never use. The remaining sections focus on three objects that are used frequently.

Understanding the Application Object

The first object you will find useful is the Application object. The Application object is the one that represents the entire Word application for your VBA code. The Application object acts as a storage area for information about the installation of Microsoft Word. It acts as a container for the other Word objects. Another purpose of the Application object is to provide access for other applications.

In Hour 20, "Working with Other Office Applications," you will see how to take advantage of other applications from Word. You can also use Word from those applications.

FIGURE 4.3

The Word object model provides the structure for automating Word commands.

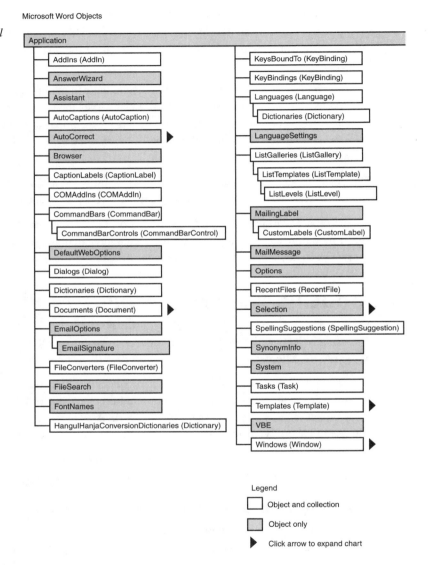

The `Application` object is the container for all the objects to control every aspect of Word. In the `StaffMeeting` macro, you used the `Browser` property for the `Application` object to access the `Browser` object to set it to browse by field.

As you complete this book, many of these objects will be covered in detail. Two of them have already been used in the `StaffMeeting` macro, and they happen to be two of the most common objects in Word: the Document object and the Selection object, both of which are described in the following sections.

Introducing the Document Collection and Object

In the StaffMeeting macro, you used the Document collection's Add method to create a new Document object. The Document collection and its Document objects are used frequently in VBA because they keep track of what files are currently open and active. With some macros, it is important to make sure a specific document is active before executing.

You will also use the Document collection and Document object to create new files, as shown in the StaffMeeting macro. You may also want to automate actions like saving, closing, or printing.

You can use the Document object to verify the contents of documents before the document is saved or closed. You can use it to check how many pages or words are in a document. These characteristics are stored in properties for the Document object. To perform specific actions on the contents of a document, you will use another frequently used object, the Selection object.

Introducing the Selection Object

The Selection object was also used in the StaffMeeting macro. The Application's Browser object was used to move the insertion point to the next field in the memo, but that wasn't enough. You wanted to replace the field with the text entered by the user. This required that you highlight or select the item in the document. In VBA, the highlighted or selected item is controlled and accessed with the Selection object.

The Selection object can be used to evaluate the contents of a selection, make changes to the contents, and even change the formatting for a selection. There are a great many possibilities.

A problem with working with the Selection object is that, while using it, you aren't allowed to use the mouse to select text and objects. If you click in one spot or select text using the mouse, the computer, unlike the keyboard, doesn't have a mechanism for telling where you were before you began. Remember that you must use the keyboard to navigate in the document when you are using the Selection object.

In Hour 2, this fact was mentioned, and it was suggested that you print a list of shortcut keys to familiarize yourself with how Word uses the keyboard. In Table 4.1, a list of the navigation keystrokes is provided. All these navigation shortcut keys can be combined with the Shift key to make them selection shortcuts.

4

TABLE 4.1 Navigation Keys

Keys	Action
Home	Move to the beginning of a line
End	Move to the end of a line
Ctrl+Home	Move to the top of the current view
Ctrl+End	Move to the bottom of the current view
← or →	Move left or right one character
↑ or ↓	Move up or down one line
Ctrl+← or Ctrl+→	Move left or right one word
Ctrl+↑ or Ctrl+↓	Move to the top or bottom of a procedure

Selecting objects other than text can also present some special problems. You may have to work with other collections to get the information necessary to select it before you can work with it. Throughout this book, you will be introduced to the collections and their special problems and how to work with them.

Summary

In this hour, you got an overview of what object-oriented programming is and how it is used in VBA. Many of the object-oriented concepts are used because the Word user has so many choices. You must take into account that the user can do something completely different from what you expect.

You learned the definition, as well as looked at some examples, of how objects work with their properties, methods, and events. You also got a chance to look at the object model for Microsoft Word.

As you complete the remaining lessons, you will get a chance to examine some of these objects in greater detail. You will also get to work more with the `Application`, `Document`, and `Selection` objects.

Q&A

Q How can I get more information about an object's property or method if I need more information after completing this book?

A Don't forget you have Help. In the Visual Basic Editor, you can place the insertion point in a Visual Basic keyword and press F1 to move directly to that Help topic.

Q When I want to work with a document, and I want to make sure I have the specific one using the `Documents` collection specifying a document name, does the document name include a file extension?

A Yes, you must have the .DOC included inside of the quotations.

Workshop

Here are some questions to help you reinforce the material covered in this hour. The answers to the quiz questions can be found in Appendix A, "Quiz Answers."

Quiz

1. What is a collection?

2. Why are all objects a component of the `Application` object?

3. Why is the `Selection` object so important in your automation?

4

HOUR 5

Exploring VBA

In Hour 4, "Understanding Objects," you learned more about working with objects and the Word Object model. In this hour, you will learn more about the statements and functions that are a part of the Visual Basic for Applications core language.

The highlights of this hour include

- Introducing general language features
- Experimenting with functions
- Getting help with VBA

Introducing General Language Features

As you have seen in the previous hours, you can get started with Visual Basic for Applications (VBA) with the Macro Recorder. It enables you to capture or record your actions within Word. Most actions are recorded as methods or property settings.

Recording macros will only get you so far when automating your work. In Hour 4, you examined the structure of the Word Object model to learn more about what the Macro Recorder generated. To make your macros more responsive during operation, you must use some of the general language components: statements, functions, variables, and constants. They make your code more responsive and, in some cases, more efficient.

Introducing Statements and Functions

The first language components to understand are statements and functions. In Hour 3, "Working with VBA and the Visual Basic Editor," you learned that you can create a sub-procedure or a function to accomplish your tasks. Statements and functions are very similar in definition.

A *statement* is defined as one complete action. Many statements are part of the language to facilitate programming your tasks. For example, you have seen two statements already:

```
Sub StaffMeeting
```

and

```
End Sub
```

The Sub statement indicates the beginning of a macro, and the End Sub statement indicates the point at which VBA should stop executing statements for a procedure.

A *function* (not to be confused with a function procedure) is different from a statement because it is rarely complete by itself. A *function* is a built-in routine that returns a value. When you use it, you will create an expression setting something equal to the function. You can set a property value, field, and bookmark equal to the results of a function. You can also set a variable equal to a function.

Examining Variables and Constants

When you are developing your code, you manipulate information. There are two types of information:

- *Variables*: Information that changes during the execution of your code
- *Constants*: Information that doesn't change during the execution of your code

Using Variables

To assist with information manipulation, you can store information in memory for quick access. If the information will change during execution, it can be stored in a variable.

A *variable* is a named storage location in the computer's memory to store data that can be modified during execution of code. Storing information in a variable can speed up the execution of your code, in many instances, as well as make your code more readable. It can be used to share information between procedures and modules, as well as to evaluate information in your code.

There are two approaches to using variables. The first approach is to just create the expression. If you put X = 2 + 2 in your code, you have created the variable, X, when the line is executed. This is known as an *implicit declaration*.

Declaring a variable with this approach is by far the easiest way, but there are drawbacks. When you place a value in memory, it is taking up space there and you are going to want to retrieve it later. An implicit declaration doesn't give you very much control over these two areas.

The first issue is the space in memory. When a variable is placed in memory, it is prepared to store a specific type of information. This is called the *data type*. There are thirteen different data types available in VBA. The different data types determine how much space is reserved for your value referenced by the variable name. Data Types are summarized in Table 5.1.

TABLE 5.1 Visual Basic Data Types

Type	Storage	Range
Byte	1 byte	0 to 255.
Boolean	2 bytes	True or False.
Integer	2 bytes	−32,768 to 32,767.
Long	4 bytes	−2,147,483,648 to 2,147,483,647.
Single	4 bytes	−3.402823E38 to −1.401298E-45 for negative values; 1.401298E-45 to 3.402823E38 for positive values.
Double	8 bytes	−1.79769313486232E308 to 4.94065645841247E-324 for negative values; 4.94065645841247E-324 to 1.79769313486232E308 for positive values.
Currency	8 bytes	−922,337,203,685,477.5808 to 922,337,203,685,477.5807.

5

continues

TABLE 5.1 continued

Type	Storage	Range
Decimal	14 bytes	+/-79,228,162,514,264,337,593,543,950,335 with no decimal point; +/- 7.9228162514264337593543950335 with 28 28 places to the right of the decimal; smallest non-zero number is +/- 0.0000000000000000000000000001.
Date	8 bytes	January 1, 1000 to December 31, 9999.
Object	4 bytes	Any Object reference
String (variable-length)	10 bytes + string length	0 to approximately 2 billion.
String(fixed-length)	Length of string	1 to approximately 65,400.
Variant(with numbers)	16 bytes	Any numeric value up to the range of a Double.
Variant(with characters)	22 bytes + string length	Same range as for variable-length String.
User-defined	Number required by elements	The range of each element is the same as the range of its data type.

You want to try to minimize the amount of space reserved for your data in memory because it might impact the performance of your code. The key is to use the smallest data type possible. For example, X = 2 + 2 can be stored as a Byte variable because the result of the equation doesn't exceed the 255 value range.

With this implicit declaration, you don't indicate which data type you want to use. This means you are using the default data type, Variant. The Variant is the most flexible data type because it can store any type of data, but it doesn't conserve your resources. The X variable in the sample equation can be stored as a Byte, which is the smallest data type, but as a Variant, it takes 16 bytes. You are wasting 15 bytes.

The second issue involves retrieving the information during the execution. You place data in memory, because you want to access it later. The challenge is making sure that necessary information is available when you need it, but unnecessary information is not left in memory. This issue can't be addressed with implicit declaration.

When you create a variable by setting up an equation, you are creating a variable that will hold its value only during the execution of that procedure. To make a variable available to more than one procedure, you have to use the second approach to declaring variables.

The second approach involves defining a variable before you use it. This is known as *explicit declaration*. It gives you the benefit of controlling access, as well as the storage space in memory, but at the expense of time. You will have to add a line of code for declaration.

> Explicit variable declaration is also preferable because it makes your code more readable and minimizes typographical errors.

To explicitly declare your variables, you must include an extra line of code. You will indicate the type of data, as well as what procedures can access the variable, as you declare it. The syntax is

```
[Dim¦Static¦Private¦Public] variablename As typename
```

The first component of the declaration statement is the keyword to indicate what procedures will have access to the variable. This is called *scope*. There are three levels of declaration.

If you use the `Dim` or the `Static` keyword, you are selecting a *local declaration*. That variable is now only available to you from within the procedure where it is declared. Its scope is the same as an implicit declaration. If you use the `Dim` keyword, the value placed in a variable is cleared when the procedure ends. If you use the `Static` keyword, the variable retains its value the next time the procedure is called while the project remains in memory. The value still isn't accessible by other procedures.

The next level is the *private scope*. If you choose the `Private` keyword, you are indicating that you want to share this variable among the procedures in one module. In addition to using the `Private` keyword, you also have to declare the variable in another location. You must select the `(General)` `Object` from the object list with `(Declarations)` selected from the procedures list (see Figure 5.1).

The last level is the *public or global* level. If you share a variable between modules, you define the variable in the `General Declarations` with the `Public` keyword.

After the declaration keyword, place the name of the variable. The goal of using variables is to make the code easier to read and to share data. When you name the variable, you want to make it easy to interpret, yet keep it easy to type. There are some naming rules and guidelines to assist you with this choice. The variable name can be up to 255 characters.

5

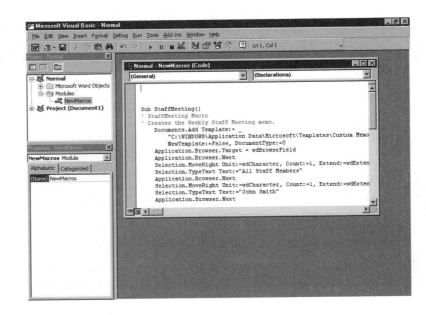

FIGURE 5.1

The General *object* Declarations *section is the location for module variables.*

Variable names

- Can include letters or numbers
- Must begin with a letter
- Can't be a Visual Basic keyword
- Must be unique within the same scope

There are also some recommendations to increase the readability of your variable names. In the sample procedures, the variable names illustrate these recommendations. The first recommendation is that you indicate the type of variable in the variable name with a prefix. In the example above, you can't tell what data type is used with the variable, X. If you had a variable to represent a discount rate, for example, you could name it sngDiscount. The sng prefix indicates that it is a Single data type. Table 5.2 lists the recommended prefixes for all the data types.

TABLE 5.2 Recommended Data Type Prefixes

Type	Naming Convention Prefix
Byte	b or byt
Boolean	f or bln
Integer	i or int
Long	l or lng
Single	sng

Type	Naming Convention Prefix
Double	d or dbl
Currency	c or cur
Decimal	dec
Date	dt or dtm
Object	o or obj
String	s or str
Variant	v or var

The variable name sngDiscount also illustrates the second recommendation. After the prefix, the identifier for the variable should be easy to understand. Again, with the example variable of X, you may not be able to tell what it is storing by looking at the name. With sngDiscount, you have the identifier of Discount, which is easier to interpret.

You can use up to 255 characters to name your variables, so the identifier can consist of more than one word. Because you can't use spaces in a variable name, it is recommended that you capitalize the first character of each word such as sngDiscountRate.

 Just because your variables can be 255 characters long doesn't mean you have to use all 255. The shorter the variable name is, the better. Remember, you are going to type the variable name into your code. If it is used frequently, you don't want to spend a lot of time typing it.

5

These recommendations are only guidelines. Some programmers also like to indicate the scope of the variable in the name with an additional prefix character. An *m* is used for a module-level variable and a *g* for a public variable. (It is a *g* rather than a *p* because public variables used to be referred to as global variables.)

After the variable name, you will use the As keyword with one of the data types to indicate the type of data that can be stored in the variable. If you don't include the As datatype clause, you will be defining the variable with the default data type of Variant.

You can also indicate the variable type with an implicit declaration with the type declaration character. For example, a string variable uses the dollar sign in an implicit declaration. Then you could enter Name$ = "Pam" and it will be saved as a string. For more information, please refer to VBA online help.

If you know that you will only have two characters stored in a string variable, you can conserve space by using a fixed-length string. This is declared by indicating the number of characters with an asterisk and a number such as

```
Dim strState As String * 2
```

This syntax is used for all your explicit variable declarations except for the user-defined type.

There are times when you want to store several values together because they are related. That is the purpose of the user-defined type. It enables you to create a combination data type by declaring a single variable with several components. The syntax combines elements of a variable declaration:

```
[Private ¦ Public] Type typename
    componentname As type
    componentname  As type
End Type
```

SYNTAX

It is placed in the General Declarations section with either the `Public` or `Private` keyword with the `Type` keyword. The name of the type is next. Declare each variable of the type on a separate line. The variable name is followed by the `As` keyword and the type. After all the components have been declared, it is completed with the `End Type` keywords.

Another type of variable that needs a special declaration is an array. An *array* is a variable that can store multiple values of the same data type. Setting up an array is very similar to defining any other variable. The syntax is

```
[Private¦Public] arrayname(NumberofElements) As Type
```

You place the declaration in the General Declarations area, and the declaration is the same as any other variable except that the number of elements follows the name. The number of elements indicates the number of individual values that will be stored under this array name. This can be followed by the `As` keyword and one of the data types to cut down on the space needed in memory.

To manage the array, the number of elements indicates how many values can be stored in the array. To place or retrieve information from an array, you will reference the variable name indicating a number in parentheses like `strName(3)`.

That number is a pointer to a specific value you want to work with. It is referred to as the *index number*. The number of elements and the corresponding index do have one confusing feature: Indexes begin with the number 0. That means that `strName(3)` is actually returning the fourth value.

If this is confusing, place the `Option Base 1` statement in the General Declarations sections. This indicates that indexing will begin with 1 so that, for example, `strName(3)` will reference the third value in the array.

VBA offers a great deal of flexibility with arrays. You can create and manage multidimensional arrays with up to 60 dimensions. You can also create an array without immediately specifying how many elements are needed. This is known as a *dynamic array*. For more information on these features, please refer to the Visual Basic Editor's Help.

Using Constants

A *constant* is also a named placeholder in memory, but it won't be modified during the execution of your code. It makes your code more readable and easier to maintain.

There are two types of constants used in VBA. The first type is the *built-in constant* introduced in Hour 3. When there are multiple settings for properties or arguments for methods, statements, or functions, VBA has provided some built-in constants.

For example, if you want to turn on underlining for some text, you have two alternatives:

```
Selection.Font.Underline = 11
```

or

```
Selection.Font.Underline = wdUnderlineWavy
```

There are many properties and arguments. Remembering what 11 means for one property or another can be quite vexing. Remembering `wdUnderlineWavy` is easier. It will minimize errors as you enter your code.

Throughout VBA, the built-in constants are designed to be easy to remember. They begin with a prefix:

- vb: Constants for functions and statements of the Visual Basic core language
- wd: The methods and properties of the Word object model

The second part is an identifier. In many cases, it will contain the name of the property or argument, or a form of the word, as well as a description of the setting.

The second type is a *user-defined constant*. The purpose is the same: You want to make your code easier to read and maintain.

5

If you saw an expression that had `curCommission = .15*curTotal`, you may have to think a little before you remember what `.15` was for. If you use a constant, there is much less guesswork. For example, in the following expression, you get better information to decipher it:

```
curCommission = curSTDCOMMRATE*curTotal
```

Examples of constants might include a commission rate, a tax rate, bonus rate, company name, or department name.

The key thing to remember about constants is that you will use this macro in the future and you might need to modify it. Even if you remember what `.15` is today, you may not remember what it represents a month or year from now.

Unlike the built-in constant, this constant must be declared in your code. To declare a constant, use the `Const` keyword. The syntax is as follows:

```
[Public ¦ Private] Const constname [As type] = expression
```

Constants also have a scope. You can use `Public` or `Private` or omit both, depending on the scope you want for the constant. A constant is followed by the `Const` keyword. The `Const` keyword is followed by the name of the constant.

You can use the same naming guidelines that are recommended for variables. You may have noticed that the identifier for the constant is in capital letters. Microsoft recommends that the constant identifier be placed in all capitals to assist you with determining whether it represents a constant or a variable. Another approach is to create your own constant prefix, such as `consngDiscount`, where `con` indicates that it is a constant.

After the name, you can indicate a data type. The last part of the declaration is to assign it a value. You place an equal sign before the value you want to assign to the constant.

Experimenting with Functions

To get a better idea of how statements and functions work, consider this scenario. In your documents, you use dates frequently. Often, you take today's date as a base for your new dates, such as a due date. To do this, take today's date, add 15 days to it, determine whether it is a weekday, adjust it if it isn't, and display it in a formal format. All this can be done with VBA.

To implement this scenario, you create a procedure called `AdjustedDate` in your Normal template:

1. Launch Word.

2. Select Tools, Macros, Visual Basic Editor.

3. Double-click on Normal in the Project Explorer to open the NewMacros module in the Code window (see Figure 5.2).

FIGURE 5.2

The NewMacros Module is open in the Code window ready for entry.

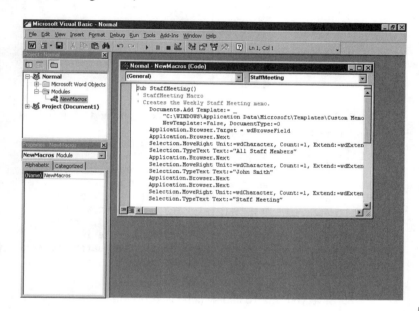

4. Select Insert, Procedure to open the Add Procedure dialog as shown in Figure 5.3.

5

FIGURE 5.3

The Add Procedure dialog is one method for creating a new procedure.

5. Type AdjustedDate as the Name and click OK.

6. Notice that the framework as shown in Figure 5.4 for the AdjustedDate procedure has been created for you.

FIGURE 5.4

The Public Sub *and*
End Sub *statements are
created for you.*

7. Press the Tab key to indent your code and add the following:

```
 1: Public Sub AdjustedDate()
 2:     Dim dtToday As Date, dtAdjusted As Date
 3:     dtToday = Now()
 4:     dtAdjusted = DateAdd("d", 15, dtToday)
 5:     If Weekday(dtAdjusted) = vbSunday Then _
 6:         dtAdjusted = DateAdd("d", 16, dtToday)
 7:     If Weekday(dtAdjusted) = vbSaturday Then _
 8:         dtAdjusted = DateAdd("d", 14, dtToday)
 9:     Selection.TypeText "The due date is "
10:     Selection.TypeText Format(dtAdjusted, "mmmm d, yyyy")
11:     Selection.TypeText "."
12: End Sub
```

8. Save your macro and switch back to Word.

After the procedure is entered, it is ready to use. Because you entered this procedure from the Visual Basic Editor, you didn't have a chance to create a toolbar button or key combination as you did with the StaffMeeting macro. You will have to add these manually:

1. Point on the toolbar area and right-click.

2. Select Customize from the menu.

3. Select the Commands tab from the Customize dialog.

4. Select the Macros category.

5. Point to the Normal.NewMacros,AdjustedDate macro and drag it to the toolbar next to the Staff Meeting button.

6. Right-click on the new button and select Name.

7. Enter Adjusted Date and press Enter.

8. Select Close and notice the new button on the toolbar (see Figure 5.5).

Newly created macro button ⸺

FIGURE 5.5
The new macro is now accessible from the toolbar.

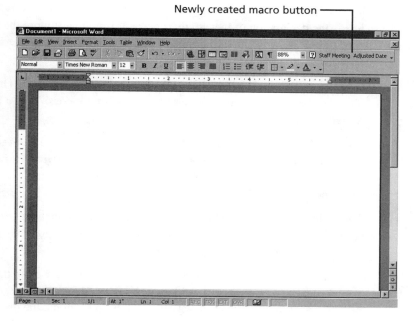

Now you can try out the new macro by clicking on its toolbar button. It looks at your system date and constructs the sentence as shown in Figure 5.6.

FIGURE 5.6
The current date was used to calculate the new date.

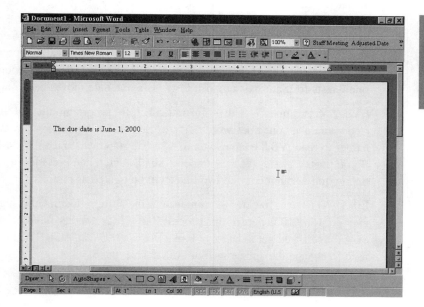

5

The due date is June 1, 2000.

This subprocedure takes advantage of four built-in functions and two variables. The first line is the declaration of the variables needed. If you have more than one variable you need to declare, you can use separate lines for each variable or place more than one variable declaration on one line separated by commas.

Line 2 sets the value for `dtToday`, which stores the current date. The current date is retrieved from the system using the `Now()` function. It doesn't have any arguments, and it actually retrieves the system date and time.

Line 3 calculates the new date with the `DateAdd` function. The `DateAdd` function enables you to add or subtract an interval from an existing date or time. It has three arguments. The `d` indicates that you want to add days to the existing date. It is a string that represents specific intervals.

The `15` in line 4 is the number of intervals to add. If the number is negative, subtract rather than add the intervals. The last argument is the date to modify. In this case, you are sending the date variable you just created.

Lines 4–8 are taking care of a potential problem. If 15 days from the current date falls on a weekend, the new date isn't valid. You should move to the nearest weekday. When you have to check the contents of a variable, you need to mimic the decision you would make manually. If the date is a Saturday, you move to the previous Friday. If the date is a Sunday, you move to the next Monday.

When you need to evaluate data in your code, you are going to take advantage of the decision statements in Visual Basic. In this case, you are using the `If` statement to test the variable. Line 5 uses the `Weekday` function to determine what day of the week the new date falls on, and then it tests this against a constant value representing Sunday. If the test is `True`, the `dtAdjusted` is moved one day ahead. The second `If` statement on line 7 tests for Saturday, and if it tests `True`, the date moves back one day.

Lines 5–6 and lines 7–8 also illustrate a helpful programming tool in Visual Basic. In the Code window, your lines won't wrap as they do in Word. This can make your code harder to read. VBA enables you to take one statement and split it across multiple lines. If you press a space, type the underscore character, and press Enter to move to the next line within a statement, the two lines will be treated as one.

Lines 9–11 begin to enter the sentence in the current document using the `TypeText` method. Line 10 is part of this process, but it uses another function. If you just used `dtAdjusted`, you get a date that looks like 5/17/99 12:54:56 PM. The Format function is used to change the appearance of the variable value.

This macro illustrates several functions that you might need in your development. There are many others. You may have to do some exploring to find the ones that are most valuable to you.

Introducing the **InputBox** Function

One drawback of the macro created to calculate a due date is the fact that it just pulls the system date for its calculations. To choose a date for the calculation, you can use the InputBox function.

The InputBox enables you to display a dialog box and ask for information. The user can type a date and press Enter. What was entered can be used as the basis for further processing. To see the InputBox in action, you can modify the AdjustedDate procedure by adding the code shown in bold in Listing 5.1.

LISTING 5.1 AdjustedDate Procedure with InputBox

```
 1: Public Sub AdjustedDate()
 2:     Dim dtToday As Date, dtAdjusted As Date
 3:     dtToday = InputBox("Please enter date.", "Set Date", _
 4:         Format(Now(), "mm/dd/yy"))
 5:     dtAdjusted = DateAdd("d", 15, dtToday)
 6:     If Weekday(dtAdjusted) = vbSunday Then _
 7:         dtAdjusted = DateAdd("d", 16, dtToday)
 8:     If Weekday(dtAdjusted) = vbSaturday Then _
 9:         dtAdjusted = DateAdd("d", 14, dtToday)
10:     Selection.TypeText "The due date is "
11:     Selection.TypeText Format(dtAdjusted, "mmmm d, yyyy")
12:     Selection.TypeText "."
13: End Sub
```

5

When you run the procedure, it no longer just prints the due date sentence. It displays a dialog asking the user to enter a date as shown in Figure 5.7.

FIGURE 5.7

The InputBox *asks the user for a date.*

The user can choose to use the date displayed or type a different one. When the user presses Enter or clicks OK, the due date is calculated, and the sentence is placed in the document.

The `InputBox` is very simple to set up. It has seven arguments, but many of them are optional. The syntax is

`InputBox(`*prompt*`[, `*title*`] [, `*default*`] [, `*xpos*`] [, `*ypos*`] [, `*helpfile, context*`])`

The first argument is the `prompt`. This is a string that stores the question for the user. It can be up to 1064 characters in length.

> When you are working with setting string values for arguments or variables, these values must be set off in quotations.

The `title` is the second argument. It indicates what title to use for the dialog box. If omitted, Microsoft Word will be displayed instead.

The third argument is the default. If this is omitted, no text will be shown in the entry area when the `Inputbox` is displayed. In this example, the `Format` and `Now` functions are used to format the system date for display as the default.

The `xpos` and `ypos` have been omitted from the example, but they enable you to control where the `Inputbox` is displayed on the screen. You can set a position from the top-left corner of the screen with these two arguments.

> Using these arguments can take a little experimenting because VBA has a special measurement unit. The `xpos` and `ypos` arguments are measured in twips. A *twip* is one-twentieth of a point. It gives you a lot more precision for placement, but it can take some getting used to. If you remember that there are 72 points in an inch, you'll know there are 1,440 twips in an inch. You can complete the math and begin placing the dialog. If these arguments are omitted, the dialog is centered.

The last two arguments enable you to set a custom help file and topic for the `Inputbox`. For more information about providing help, please refer to Hour 22, "Adding Help."

Introducing the `MsgBox` Function

Another function that is useful for getting information from the user is the `MsgBox` function. It can be useful for indicating when a process is finished, asking the user to confirm some information, or even providing a pause in the macro for the user to manually complete a task. Its syntax is very similar to the `InputBox`:

`MsgBox(`*prompt*`[, `*buttons*`] [, `*title*`] [, `*helpfile, context*`])`

The arguments are all the same except for the second argument. The `buttons` argument enables you to control the appearance and behavior of the `MsgBox`. You can choose an icon to display next to the message. You can choose what buttons are displayed for the user to choose from, and you can choose how `MsgBox` interacts with other applications on the system.

The `buttons` argument sets three different settings for the dialog. It can do this because it is a numeric argument. You will use the built-in constants and add them together in your code. If you want to ask a simple question of the user and have him respond, use `vbQuestion + vbYesNo`. If you don't specify this argument, the buttons argument defaults to `0`. This means that you won't have an icon displayed, there will only be an OK button and you won't control how the `MsgBox` works with other applications.

In the example, it might be useful to confirm the due date before placing it in the document. To use the `MsgBox`, complete the changes to `AdjustedDate` as shown in bold in Listing 5.2.

LISTING 5.2 The `AdjustedDate` Procedure with `MsgBox` Verification

```
 1: Public Sub AdjustedDate()
 2:     Dim dtToday As Date, dtAdjusted As Date, lResponse As Long
 3:     dtToday = InputBox("Please enter date.", "Set Date", _
 4:         Format(Now(), "mm/dd/yy"))
 5:     dtAdjusted = DateAdd("d", 15, dtToday)
 6:     lResponse = MsgBox("It calculated this due date " _
 7:         & dtAdjusted & _
 8:         ". Do you want to use it?", vbQuestion + vbYesNo, _
 9:         "Date Confirmation")
10:     If lResponse = vbNo Then Exit Sub
11:     If Weekday(dtAdjusted) = vbSunday Then _
12:         dtAdjusted = DateAdd("d", 16, dtToday)
13:     If Weekday(dtAdjusted) = vbSaturday Then _
14:         dtAdjusted = DateAdd("d", 14, dtToday)
15:     Selection.TypeText "The due date is "
16:     Selection.TypeText Format(dtAdjusted, "mmmm d, yyyy")
17:     Selection.TypeText "."
18: End Sub
```

5

When the macro is chosen from the toolbar, it displays the `Inputbox` for the date. The user can use the default or type a new one. After the user closes the `InputBox`, the date is calculated and the `MsgBox` is displayed as shown in Figure 5.8.

FIGURE 5.8

The MsgBox *confirms
the new due date.*

The change to line 2 declares a new variable to store the button the user selected. After the due date is calculated, the lResponse variable is set to the results of the MsgBox function on line 6. It has a prompt that indicates the due date. This is displayed by concatenating some text with the contents of the dtAdjusted variable.

The buttons argument is set to show a question mark with the Yes and No buttons. There is also a title given. After the user has selected either Yes or No, the response has to be tested.

The lResponse is tested with another If statement on line 10. If lResponse is equal to vbNo, which is the built-in constant for the No button in the Msgbox, it means that the user doesn't want to use the calculated date. Rather than placing it in the sentence, the Exit Sub statement is used to terminate the execution of the subprocedure. The user can begin again.

Getting Help with VBA

In this hour, you have been exposed to several functions and statements. When you are learning VBA, you won't remember all the settings for each statement, function, property, and method that you want to use. There are some special help features to help you get started.

> If these features don't seem to be working for you, they are optional features of the Visual Basic Editor. If you select Tools, Options, and the Editor tab, you can set the Auto Syntax Check, Auto List Members, and Auto Quick Info.

The first feature you will notice as you start to enter your code is the Auto Quick Info. You don't have to memorize all the arguments required for a keyword. As you finish typing the keyword, an information box will be displayed with the arguments listed for you as shown in Figure 5.9.

FIGURE 5.9

The Auto Quick Info setting lets you see the list of arguments.

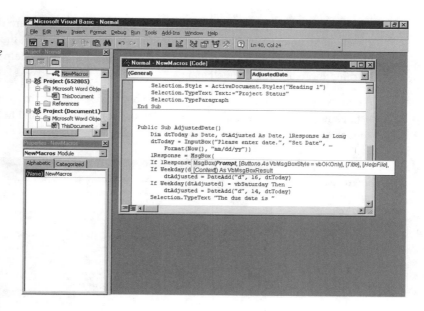

As you type each argument, it is highlighted in bold. When you are typing an argument that has built-in constants for the arguments, you will see a list of those constants (see Figure 5.10) if Auto List Members is turned on.

FIGURE 5.10

The Auto List Members lists built-in constants.

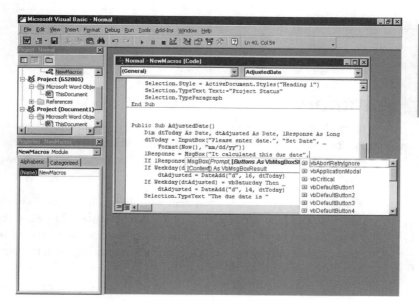

5

There are two additional tools to assist with code creation. They are the Auto Syntax Check and Context Sensitive Help. If you make a syntax mistake, the code line will be highlighted in red when you press Enter. The Context Sensitive Help will assist with learning more about a code element.

As an example, if you want to learn more about using the Msgbox, you can type in MsgBox and place the insertion point in the keyword. Press F1 and help will display the MsgBox topic as shown in Figure 5.11.

FIGURE 5.11

The Context Sensitive Help pulls up the help topic for a selected keyword.

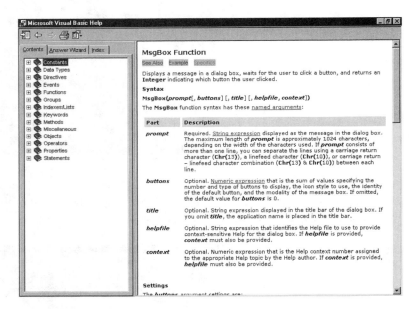

Summary

In this hour you had a chance to increase your general VBA knowledge. You learned the fundamentals of working with statements and functions. You learned that your code can be more readable and easier to work with if you represent values with variables and constants.

You also had a chance to experiment with several functions. The AdjustedDate procedure illustrated the use of several of the date functions, as well as introduced the InputBox and MsgBox functions. These two functions will be used frequently in your procedures because they are a quick means for interacting with the user.

Q&A

Q When would you want to use the Variant data type?

A The Variant data type is a part of VBA because there are times when you don't know what type of data you will need to store. This is especially true when you work with other applications.

Q Can I compare dates?

A Yes, you can use the DateDiff function to compare two dates.

Q Should I use the InputBox function when I have several questions for the user?

A When you get too many questions, the InputBox isn't practical. Using a User Form or a Word Form is a better choice. For more information please refer to Hour 15, "Working with Forms" and Hour 17, "Working with User Forms."

Workshop

Here are some questions and exercises to assist with your review of this hour's material. The answers to the quiz questions can be found in Appendix A, "Quiz Answers."

Quiz

1. Which keyword is used to declare a variable that needs to be shared between modules?

2. If you need to use a variable in several procedures, where does it need to be declared?

3. What does the WeekDay function do?

4. Why is the MsgBox so valuable?

Exercises

1. Change the icon in the MsgBox to the Exclamation mark icon in AdjustedDate.

2. Make a copy of your Custom memo template and create a macro to ask what the To, From, and Subject information is by using the InputBox. When the macro is complete, add code to indicate that it is finished with a MsgBox. (Hint: Use the StaffMeeting macro as a model for the completion of the text.)

5

HOUR 6

Understanding Decision Processing

In Hour 5, "Exploring VBA," you created a macro that adjusted a date. In that procedure, you used the MsgBox function to ask the user if the date was acceptable. The user could have selected Yes or No. The If statement was used to see what was selected. This hour will focus on adding decision making to your code.

The highlights of this hour include

- Examining the need for decision processing
- Using the If statement
- Learning about condition testing
- Using the If...Then...Else structure
- Using the Select Case structure

Examining the Need for Decision Processing

As you begin automating tasks, you will find that some tasks pose problems. You will find yourself saying, I could automate this task if only I didn't have to enter this text or perform these action. For example, you could automatically generate an entire marketing package if the material wasn't product specific. What you are really saying is that the task involves a decision.

As you perform the steps to accomplish this task, you are making a decision. That is where decision processing becomes important. Decision processing is accomplished with a group of statements that enable you to perform specific actions based on an evaluation of a *condition*. This is often referred to as *program control* or *conditional logic*.

In many cases, you will evaluate a setting for a field or property to make decisions. In some cases, you will need to interactively provide the information. You can use the `InputBox` or `MsgBox` introduced in Hour 5 to provide the condition or a `Form` or `User Form` introduced later in this book in Hour 15, "Working with Forms," and Hour 17, "Working with User Forms."

The capability to have code evaluate a condition and make decisions can greatly increase your automation potential. There are three basic decision-processing approaches:

- The `If` statement
- The `If...Then...Else` structure
- The `Select Case` structure

Using the `If` Statement

In Hour 5, you began experimenting with some core language features. You created a procedure called `AdjustedDate`. It added fifteen days to a given date, and then it evaluated to make sure that the date was a weekday. If not, the procedure added or subtracted a day to get to the closest weekday. After a date is generated, a `MsgBox` is used to confirm that the user wants to use that date, as shown in Figure 6.1.

This is an example of the `If` statement. It involves an evaluation of a user's button selection in the `MsgBox`, which is stored in a variable called `lResponse`:

```
lResponse = MsgBox("It calculated this due date " _
    & dtAdjusted & _
    ". Do you want to use it?", vbQuestion + vbYesNo, _
    "Date Confirmation")
If lResponse = vbNo Then Exit Sub
```

FIGURE 6.1

The message box gets the condition to test with the If statement.

ANALYSIS The If statement evaluates the condition of lResponse and, if the condition is True, takes an action. When you want to evaluate one condition and take one action, you will use the syntax illustrated in the AdjustedDate procedure in Hour 5:

```
If condition Then statement
```

You begin with the If keyword followed by the condition you want to test. That is followed by the Then keyword and the statement you want to execute.

If you need to take more than one action, you can separate each action with colons. In most cases, you will want to place the code on more than one line. Then the syntax is

SYNTAX

```
If condition Then

    Statements
End If
```

To take more than one action, you will place each action on a line by itself. All your statements are followed by the End If statement to indicate the end of this conditional logic block.

Also notice that the Statements line is indented. This isn't a requirement, but it can make your code more readable: You will be able to see more easily where the conditional logic block begins and ends.

When you are writing your code, adding indention is as easy as using the Tab key. After you type a conditional statement such as the If statement and press Enter, you can press the Tab key and Visual Basic will indent the line 4 characters.

As you enter each statement after that it will maintain that level of indention to eliminate the need to press the Tab key on every line. When you press Enter to move to the line for the end of the conditional code, you can press the Backspace or Shift+Tab to move back to the previous level of indention for the Exit If statement.

6

If you have to test multiple conditions, you can nest the If statements. When you nest the logic, the indention can really make the difference:

SYNTAX

```
If condition1 Then
    If condition2 then
        Statements
    End If
    statements
End If
```

The indentation visually highlights the logical sequence. In short procedures, such as the ones you have created, you can read most of the code in the window without scrolling. With longer procedures, this technique will help you track your code when you are trying to locate specific actions or decision processing.

Learning About Condition Testing

Getting the most from the If statement or any of the conditional logic structures is based on the construction of the condition being tested. With the If statement, you are indicating what actions need to be taken if the condition tested is true. The condition to be tested is any valid expression.

Examining Comparison Operators

In the example in Hour 5, the AdjustedDate Subprocedure shown in Listing 5.2, the value being tested is the value assigned to lResponse with the MsgBox. You can test the contents of variables, properties, or the results of functions. The general syntax is

```
Testitem operator value
```

Following the testitem, there is an operator. VBA supports a full list of comparison operators. You can perform a simple equal test, as shown in the example in Hour 5, or you can look for a range of values. You can use any of the operators in Table 6.1.

TABLE 6.1   The Comparison Operators

Operator	Symbol	Will Return a True Value When
Equals	=	Testitem and value match
Not Equals	<>	Testitem and value don't match
Greater Than	>	Testitem is greater than the value

Operator	Symbol	Will Return a True Value When
Less Than	<	`Testitem` is less than the value
Greater Than or Equal	>=	`Testitem` matches or is greater than the value
Less Than or Equal	<=	`Testitem` matches or is less than the value

If you are working with numeric values, these operators are very easy to use. For example, you have a variable `lTotalSales`, and it is equal to 100,000. You are testing the value with `lTotalSales > 100,000`. The condition would be returned `False`. If you used the greater than or equal operator instead, the condition would be returned `True`.

With text, the comparison is a little tougher. When text is stored in memory, the characters are represented by codes. This means that a capital `A` is stored as a different code than a lowercase `a`. It also means that the comparison might not meet your expectations. To see this problem in action, perform the following steps:

1. Switch to the Visual Basic Editor.
2. Select View, Immediate window.
3. Create the following subprocedure:

```
 1: Sub TextComparisonTest()
 2:     Dim x, y
 3:     x = "Chocolate"
 4:     y = "chocolate"
 5:     If x = y Then
 6:         Debug.Print "Chocolate is good!"
 7:     Else
 8:         Debug.Print "No Chocolate"
 9:     End If
10: End Sub
```

4. Make sure your insertion point is in the procedure.
5. Click the Run Sub/User Form button on the toolbar.
6. Notice that you have `"No Chocolate"` shown in the Immediate window as shown in Figure 6.2.

This short subprocedure illustrates the problem. If you have ever used the Find command with the Match Case option selected, you have seen this type of result. Even if all the letters are the same, the Find command will skip over the ones that don't match exactly.

6

FIGURE **6.2**
*The two words were
considered not equal.*

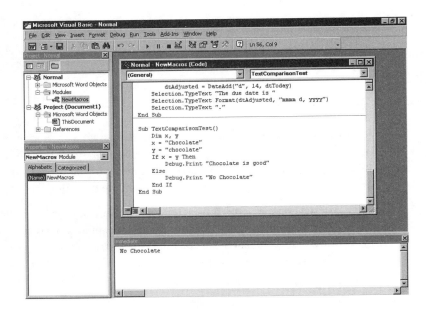

If you are going to use comparisons with text, and you want the comparison to ignore the case of the text, you must add one line of code to your module. By default, VBA uses a binary comparison of text. To compare the text without regard for capitalization, you need to use the Option Compare statement:

1. Press Ctrl+Home to move to the top of the module.

2. Enter Option Compare Text.

3. Click on the procedures list and select TextComparisonTest to move back to the procedure.

4. Click the Run Sub/User Form button on the toolbar to execute the procedure.

5. Notice that the Immediate window shows the words match this time (see Figure 6.3).

The Option Compare statement enables you to control the sort order. The default setting is Binary. This compares the characters based on its binary code.

The Text setting is case-insensitive. For example, it will treat an E as an e. You do need to consider this carefully because it also uses your computer's language settings when comparing characters. For example, all e's are treated alike. That means E = e = ë = è = é = ê.

FIGURE 6.3

The two words were compared and determined to be equal.

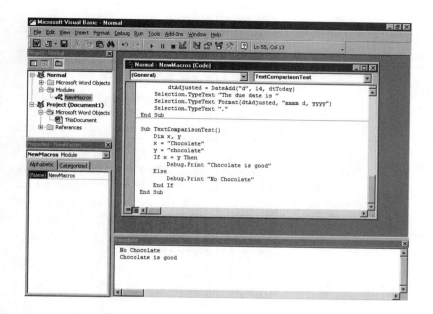

In this example, `TextComparisonTest`, VBA's Debug object is used. It has a `Print` method that enables you to print text to the Immediate window. This is often useful for testing a procedure that performs calculations and evaluations. For more information on using the Immediate window, please refer to Hour 8, "Handling Problems in VBA."

Understanding Logical Operators

In addition to the comparison operators, VBA also has logical operators that combine more than one comparison test. In many cases, this will enable you to use one structure instead of two. The logical operators that are used most frequently are listed in Table 6.2.

TABLE 6.2 The Logical Operators

Operator	Description
And	The And operator enables you to test multiple conditions. If each condition is True, the combined condition returns a True value. If any of the conditions are False, the entire condition is False.
Not	The Not operator enables you to return the opposite value from the results of the condition tested.

6

TABLE 6.2   continued

Operator	Description
Or	The Or operator enables you to test multiple conditions. If one of them is True, the value of the compound condition is True.
Xor	The Xor operator is similar to the Or operator. It evaluates each condition. If one and only one of the conditions is True, the compound condition is True. If more than one condition is True, the compound condition is False.

To view a logical operator at work, consider a procedure that creates a title and subtitle for a report. You might want to use the document's property settings. When you create a document, it has specific properties. The user can set them by selecting File, Properties to access the Properties dialog as shown in Figure 6.4.

FIGURE 6.4

The Properties window lets you set information to assist with managing the document.

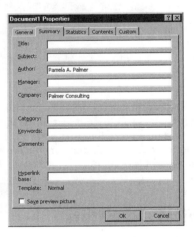

These properties can also be accessed with VBA. You might want to create a subprocedure to use the Title and Subject properties to create text. In that case, use an If statement with a compound condition, similar to the one in Listing 6.1, to make sure the user has completed those properties.

LISTING 6.1   An If Structure Using a Compound Condition

```
1: Dim strTitle As String, strSubTitle As String
2: strTitle = ActiveDocument.BuiltInDocumentProperties(wdPropertyTitle)
3: strSubject = _
4:     ActiveDocument.BuiltInDocumentProperties(wdPropertySubject)
5: If Len(strTitle) = 0 Or Len(strSubject) = 0 Then
```

```
6:     MsgBox _
7:         "The document properties are missing. please enter them.", _
8:         vbInformation, "Missing Information"
9: End If
```

ANALYSIS Line 1 starts by declaring two variables to hold the title and subject. After the variables are declared, they are populated by using the BuiltInDocumentProperties property to get the contents of the Title and Subject properties with lines 2–4.

The If statement tests a compound condition on line 5. The Len function is used to determine the length of each string. If any of the conditions are equal to zero, the user hasn't filled in the properties. The Or logical operator is used because if either one of the properties is blank, you don't want to continue processing. A MsgBox is used to indicate that the information is missing beginning on line 6.

> For additional information on using the document properties, please refer to Hour 9, "Working with Text."

Using the If...Then...Else Structure

The If structure is designed to test a condition and take action if it is True. There are times when you need to test a condition and take one set of actions if it is True or a second set of actions if it is False. In those cases, you will use the If...Then...Else structure. Its syntax can also be used to test multiple conditions:

▼ SYNTAX

```
If condition Then
    [statements]
[ElseIf condition-n Then
    [elseifstatements] ...
[Else
    [elsestatements]]
End If
```

The first part is identical to the If statement used above. You begin with the If keyword followed by the condition to test and the Then Keyword. It is followed by the statements to execute if the condition is True. The difference is its capability to take more than one set of actions and test more than one condition. If you want to test more than one condition, the If's True statements are followed by an ElseIf clause. The ElseIf keyword is followed by the next condition to test and its Then keyword.

6

Below the ElseIf line are the statements that should be executed if that condition is
True. You can have more than one ElseIf clause in your structure.

At the end of this structure, you will have an Else clause that has statements that will
execute if all the conditions are False. After those statements, the End If statement is
used to indicate the end of this conditional test.

> The following procedure is the longest procedure examined in this book so
> far. Please remember, you can download this hour's sample template along
> with the others from the companion Web site. If you prefer to enter this
> procedure instead, you can copy and paste many of the lines of code from
> the StaffMeeting procedure created in Hour 2, "Getting Started with VBA."

To get a better idea of how this structure works, consider the StaffMeeting macro
recorded in Hour 2. This macro creates a new document based on the Custom Memo
template and adds some text. If there are several types of memos, you can have several
macros; but you can also have one macro that can create several memos as illustrated in
the GeneralMemo procedure in Listing 6.2.

LISTING 6.2   The General Memo Procedure

```
 1: Sub GeneralMemo()
 2: ' General Memo can create more than one memo with one procedure
 3: ' instead of having separate macros for each type of memo.
 4:     Dim strMemoTitle As String
 5:     strMemoTitle = InputBox("Enter memo subject", "Memo Title")
 6:     Documents.Add Template:= _
 7:         "C:\WINDOWS\Application Data\Microsoft\Templates\Custom Memo.dot", _
 8:         NewTemplate:=False, DocumentType:=0
 9:     Application.Browser.Target = wdBrowseField
10:     Application.Browser.Next
11:     Selection.MoveRight Unit:=wdCharacter, Count:=1, Extend:=wdExtend
12:     If strMemoTitle = "Staff Meeting" Then
13:         Selection.TypeText Text:="All Staff Members"
14:         Application.Browser.Next
15:         Selection.MoveRight Unit:=wdCharacter, Count:=1, Extend:=wdExtend
16:         Selection.TypeText Text:="John Smith"
17:         Application.Browser.Next
18:         Application.Browser.Next
19:         Selection.MoveRight Unit:=wdCharacter, Count:=1, Extend:=wdExtend
20:         Selection.TypeText Text:=strMemoTitle
```

```
21:          Selection.EndKey Unit:=wdStory
22:          Selection.TypeText Text:= _
23:             "The staff meeting will begin promptly at 9:00 AM and "
24:          Selection.TypeText Text:= _
25:             "end at 10:00 AM. We will get an update on the work of the gr"
26:          Selection.TypeText Text:= _
27:             "oup as a whole and you will need to bring updated informatio"
28:          Selection.TypeText Text:="n regarding your tasks."
29:          Selection.TypeParagraph
30:          Selection.Style = ActiveDocument.Styles("Heading 1")
31:          Selection.TypeText Text:="Project Status"
32:          Selection.TypeParagraph
33:      ElseIf strMemoTitle = "Task Update" Then
34:          Selection.TypeText Text:="All Staff Members"
35:          Application.Browser.Next
36:          Selection.MoveRight Unit:=wdCharacter, Count:=1, Extend:=wdExtend
37:          Selection.TypeText Text:="John Smith"
38:          Application.Browser.Next
39:          Application.Browser.Next
40:          Selection.MoveRight Unit:=wdCharacter, Count:=1, Extend:=wdExtend
41:          Selection.TypeText Text:=strMemoTitle
42:          Selection.EndKey Unit:=wdStory
43:          Selection.TypeText Text:= _
44:             "During the staff meeting, these tasks were reviewed. "
45:          Selection.TypeText Text:= _
46:             "Each task is reviewed separately with the person "
47:          Selection.TypeText Text:= _
48:             "responsible, its status and due date."
49:          Selection.TypeParagraph
50:          Selection.Style = ActiveDocument.Styles("Heading 1")
51:          Selection.TypeText Text:="Task:"
52:
53:          Application.Browser.Next
54:          Application.Browser.Next
55:          Application.Browser.Next
56:          Selection.MoveRight Unit:=wdCharacter, Count:=1, Extend:=wdExtend
57:          Selection.TypeText Text:=strMemoTitle
58:          Selection.HomeKey Unit:=wdStory
59:          Application.Browser.Next
60:          Selection.MoveRight Unit:=wdCharacter, Count:=1, Extend:=wdExtend
61:      End If
62: End Sub
```

ANALYSIS The revised procedure, GeneralMemo, offers greater flexibility than the StaffMeeting procedure. It can create three types of memos instead of one (see Figure 6.5).

FIGURE 6.5

The staff meeting, task update, and generic memos can all be created with one procedure.

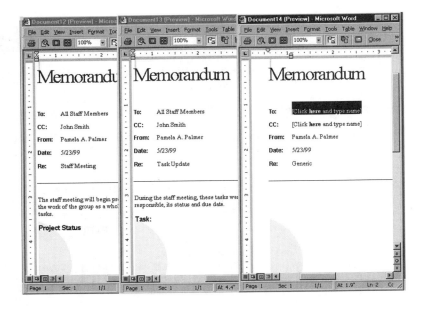

This is accomplished by having the user type in a title for the memo and evaluating it with an If...Then...Else structure. This can be expanded to include additional memos as the need increases or changes.

In Listing 6.3, you will see line numbers preceding the code. Unlike older forms of BASIC, line numbers aren't required in VBA. Line numbers have been added to the listing throughout this book to provide a reference point as you review the code. You will not need to include them as you type your code.

The GeneralMemo procedure takes the existing code of the StaffMeeting procedure, duplicates it, and edits it to support more than one memo type.

On line 4, the strMemoTitle variable is declared to store the entry from the InputBox function on line 5. This gets a subject for the memo that can be evaluated to determine how much of the memo is completed by the procedure. Lines 6–11 are copied straight from the StaffMeeting memo. They create the document using the Custom Memo template, set up the Browser object, move to the first field, and select it.

Line 12 is the beginning of the evaluation of the subject entered by the user in the InputBox. You begin with the If keyword followed by the expression to compare the variable to the string, "Staff Meeting". If is followed with the Then keyword. If this condition is True, lines 13–32 are executed. These lines are the remaining lines from the StaffMeeting procedure.

Line 33 is the next condition test. It begins with the ElseIf keyword to indicate there is another condition to evaluate. This is followed by the expression to compare the variable against the "Task Update" string. This is followed by the Then keyword.

If this condition is True, lines 34–51 are executed. These lines almost duplicate the lines for the Staff Meeting condition above it except that the text is different.

On line 52, you have the Else clause. When you have other possible conditions that can't be anticipated, you will need to include an Else clause. This clause will be executed if none of the conditions evaluated are True. The lines following it are slightly different because there is less information to fill in on the memo.

The Application.Browser.Next method is used three times to move to the subject field. Line 56 selects the field, and line 57 places the subject in the field. Line 58 moves to the top of the document, and lines 59 and 60 move to the first field and select it. The memo is now ready for the user to enter the person this memo is for on the To line.

Line 61 indicates the end of the If...Then...Else block. Line 62 indicates the end of the procedure.

If there are additional special memos that can be partially completed by the procedure, you can add additional ElseIf clauses to test the text for the subject.

> This procedure is not the easiest to maintain because of the TypeText method required to enter in the paragraph text. In Hour 9, you will learn some different methods for managing text.

6

Using the Select Case Structure

The last structure for decision processing is the Select Case structure. It is used to test one item for several values. In Listing 6.3, the If...Then...Else structure is used to evaluate the entry from the user in an InputBox in order to determine what could be automatically filled in by the procedure.

The `Select Case` structure can also be used to test the value. It is also easier to read. Its syntax is

SYNTAX

```
Select Case testexpression
    [Case expressionlist-n
        [statements-n]] ...
    [Case Else
        [elsestatements]]
End Select
```

The `Select Case` statement is a little cleaner in its construction and will eliminate some typing. It begins with the `Select Case` statement. The `Select Case` keywords are followed by the test expression. This is not a complete expression as is required by the `If...Then...Else` structure. It is only what is to be tested.

For each possible value, you will need a separate `Case` clause. It begins with the `Case` keyword followed by the value to test. When a value is the only thing after the `Case` keyword, it is an equal test. Is the test expression equal to this value? The code lines to be executed if the test expression matches that value follow this line.

The `Select Case` structure can perform more than an equal test. You can test a group of values or a value range. When you do this, the `Case` clause syntax changes. The syntax possibilities are summarized in Table 6.3.

TABLE 6.3   The Case Clause Syntax Choices

Syntax	Description
Case *value*	The test expression must equal the value.
Case *value1, valuen*	The test expression must equal one of the values listed.
Case *value1 to value2*	The test expression must be within the range of the values.
Case Is < value	The test expression must be less than the value.
Case Is <= value	The test expression must be less than or equal the value.
Case Is > value	The test expression must be greater than the value.
Case Is >= value	The test expression must be greater than or equal the value.

If there is a possibility of another value, you would include a `Case Else` clause. It is followed by the code lines to be executed if no value matches the test expression. This is not required when the test expression can only match a defined set of values.

The last line is the `End Select` statement. It indicates that the conditional logic structure is complete. The procedure called `SelectMemo` shown in Listing 6.3 is the `GeneralMemo` procedure rewritten with the `Select Case` statement.

LISTING 6.3   The Select Memo Procedure

```
 1: Sub SelectMemo()
 2: ' Select Memo can create more than one memo with one procedure
 3: ' instead of having separate macros for each type of memo.
 4:     Dim strMemoTitle As String
 5:     strMemoTitle = InputBox("Enter memo subject", "Memo Title")
 6:     Documents.Add Template:= _
 7:         "C:\WINDOWS\Application Data
           ➥ \Microsoft\Templates\Custom Memo.dot", _
 8:         NewTemplate:=False, DocumentType:=0
 9:     Application.Browser.Target = wdBrowseField
10:     Application.Browser.Next
11:     Selection.MoveRight Unit:=wdCharacter, Count:=1, Extend:=wdExtend
12:     Select Case strMemoTitle
13: Case "Staff Meeting"
14:         Selection.TypeText Text:="All Staff Members"
15:         Application.Browser.Next
16:         Selection.MoveRight Unit:=wdCharacter, Count:=1,
           ➥ Extend:=wdExtend
17:         Selection.TypeText Text:="John Smith"
18:         Application.Browser.Next
19:         Application.Browser.Next
20:         Selection.MoveRight Unit:=wdCharacter, Count:=1,
           ➥ Extend:=wdExtend
21:         Selection.TypeText Text:=strMemoTitle
22:         Selection.EndKey Unit:=wdStory
23:         Selection.TypeText Text:= _
24:             "The staff meeting will begin promptly at 9:00 AM and "
25:         Selection.TypeText Text:= _
26:             "end at 10:00 AM. We will get an update on the
               ➥ work of the gr"
27:         Selection.TypeText Text:= _
28:             "oup as a whole and you will need to bring updated
               ➥ informatio"
29:         Selection.TypeText Text:="n regarding your tasks."
30:         Selection.TypeParagraph
31:         Selection.Style = ActiveDocument.Styles("Heading 1")
32:         Selection.TypeText Text:="Project Status"
33:         Selection.TypeParagraph
34:       Case  "Task Update"
35:         Selection.TypeText Text:="All Staff Members"
36:         Application.Browser.Next
37:         Selection.MoveRight Unit:=wdCharacter, Count:=1,
               ➥ Extend:=wdExtend
38:         Selection.TypeText Text:="John Smith"
39:         Application.Browser.Next
40:         Application.Browser.Next
41:         Selection.MoveRight Unit:=wdCharacter, Count:=1,
               ➥ Extend:=wdExtend
42:         Selection.TypeText Text:=strMemoTitle
```

6

continues

LISTING 6.3 continued

```
43:                    Selection.EndKey Unit:=wdStory
44:                    Selection.TypeText Text:= _
45:                        "During the staff meeting, these tasks were reviewed. "
46:                    Selection.TypeText Text:= _
47:                        "Each task is reviewed separately with the person "
48:                    Selection.TypeText Text:= _
49:                        "responsible, its status and due date."
50:                    Selection.TypeParagraph
51:                    Selection.Style = ActiveDocument.Styles("Heading 1")
52:                    Selection.TypeText Text:="Task:"
53:              Case Else
54:                    Application.Browser.Next
55:                    Application.Browser.Next
56:                    Application.Browser.Next
57:                    Selection.MoveRight Unit:=wdCharacter, Count:=1,
                      ➥ Extend:=wdExtend
58:                    Selection.TypeText Text:=strMemoTitle
59:                    Selection.HomeKey Unit:=wdStory
60:                    Application.Browser.Next
61:                    Selection.MoveRight Unit:=wdCharacter, Count:=1,
                      ➥ Extend:=wdExtend
62:              End Select
63: End Sub
```

ANALYSIS The code that is executed is the same for both procedures, except the examination of the condition of the strMemoTitle is changed.

On line 12, the beginning of the If...Then...Else is changed to the Select Case statement. The Select Case keywords are followed by the variable name only. On line 13, the first string is tested. It has the Case keyword followed by the "Staff Meeting" string.

Line 34 is the revised ElseIf. It becomes another Case clause, and line 53 is the Else clause converted to the Case Else. The last change is line 62. The End If is converted to an End Select statement.

When you are creating decision processing, decide which case your users most often select. When your code is executed, it is executed in order. If you had a Select Case structure where each case was numbered between 1 and 5, the cases would be in order, with 1 being the value for the first Case statement. If what is now numbered 3 is the most common choice, make 3 the first Case clause. Doing so will require fewer lines of code to be processed on a regular basis.

Summary

In this hour, you have learned more about the VBA core language. What makes VBA so powerful is the capability to automate many document creation decisions.

You learned that the `If` statement is good for evaluating a condition and executing an action based on that condition. You learned that the `If...Then...Else` structure allows a greater flexibility. It can evaluate one or more conditions and take more than one set of actions based on its conditions.

You also learned that the `Select Case` structure may be easier to maintain than an `If...Then...Else` structure, if you have many conditions. You also learned that how you order your conditions can affect the execution time.

Last, but not least, you may have created a framework for a procedure for your own work. The `SelectMemo` procedure may be something you will be able to implement for your own work. You may want to wait to modify it for your own work until you look at Hour 9. It contains some alternative methods for handling text that might make your work easier.

Q&A

Q Must you use a variable for decision processing?

A No, you aren't required to set up a variable for decision processing. Setting up a variable is a good idea if you need to use a value more than once.

For example, the `GeneralMemo` and `SelectMemo` procedures use a variable to store the information entered into the `InputBox`. That information is used to determine which memo to create, and it is also used as the subject on the memo itself. The use of a variable eliminates the need to ask for that information twice.

Q Can you nest decision-processing structures?

A Yes, you can. One recommendation, if you are going to nest the structures, is to maintain the indention of each structure. That will make it easier to read in your code.

Workshop

Here are some questions and exercises to assist with your review of this hour's material. The answers to the quiz questions can be found in Appendix A, "Quiz Answers."

6

Quiz

1. What statement needs to be in the code to disregard a character's case when evaluating it, and where does it need to be placed?

2. Which logical operator would be used if you wanted to make sure that several conditions were met before executing your code?

3. What property holds the document properties?

4. How would the Case clause for a Select Case structure be worded to see if a value was less than or equal to 10?

Exercises

1. Review your list of tasks to automate and think about where you will need decision processing.

2. Edit the Automated Title to also check the Author property. (Hint: Place your insertion point in the property name and press F1 to see a list of index constants.)

Hour **7**

Understanding Repetitive Processing with Loops

In Hour 6, "Understanding Decision Processing," you explored the mechanisms that can be used to execute different actions based on the evaluation of an expression. Another valuable programming technique that will make your procedures more flexible is the capability to execute a group of actions more than once automatically.

There are times when you want to automate a process that is to be repeated a number of times. Rather than duplicating the code for each occurrence, you can use a programming loop.

In certain situations, you want to repeat actions a specific number of times. At other times, you want to repeat actions until a condition is True or while a condition is True. When you are creating your code, you will need to select the correct looping structure to meet your present need.

The highlights of this hour include

- Using the `For...Next` loop
- Using `Do` loops

Using the `For...Next` Loop

The first loop that you can use in your code is the `For...Next` loop. It is designed to repeat the actions a specific number of times. The syntax for the `For...Next` loop is

SYNTAX

```
For counter = start To end [Step step]
    [statements]
    [Exit For]
    [statements]
Next [counter]
```

The `For` keyword is followed by a counter. This counter is a variable that will be incremented automatically by the loop. It is followed by an equal sign to set the range of the counter.

The range of the counter is specified by a start value followed by the `To` keyword and an end value. By default, the `For...Next` loop counts by increments of one. If you want to change that, you can use the `Step` keyword and indicate a step value.

The `For` statement is followed by the statements that will be executed within the loop. If there is a reason not to complete the entire cycle specified by the start and end values, you can include the `Exit For` statement to terminate execution.

The last line is the `Next` counter line. This line automatically increments the counter. After the last line is executed, the processing will continue at the top of the loop. If the counter is still within the range specified, the code will be repeated.

In Hour 6, you modified the `StaffMeeting` procedure to accommodate different types of memos. One of these was a Task Update memo. It created the memo structure. The last step was to create a heading for the task with your insertion point on the line so you could enter the title of the task.

In your working environment, I would be willing to bet that there are more tasks than one on your list. It might be best to have a separate template (see Figure 7.1) and use a `For...Next` loop to generate several task-tracking lines.

Using a `For...Next` loop, you can generate a specific number of task entries. You can have fixed start and end dates, or you can get the range from the user utilizing one of the VBA tools, such as the `InputBox` function.

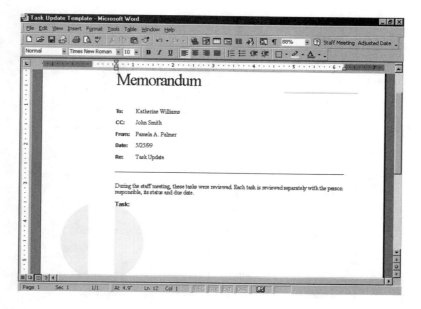

FIGURE 7.1
The Task Update Template has all the beginning memo information entered.

When you are creating a procedure that changes formatting and enters text, you can rely on the macro recorder to capture the exact settings to get the look you want. After the settings are captured, you can use the Visual Basic Editor to make the necessary changes to repeat these actions as many times as needed.

Recording the Basic Task Set Up Steps

To provide a template for each task, the name of the task, the due date, and the status should each appear on a separate line. You also want to have the information indented on any wrapped lines. To record the set up information, perform the following steps:

1. Press Ctrl+End to move to the end of the document.
2. Make sure the Normal style is selected.
3. Double-click on the REC in the status bar to open the Record Macro dialog (see Figure 7.2).
4. Enter `TaskSetUpRecorded` as the name.
5. Select Documents based on the Task Update Template to store the macro.
6. Enter `Set up template for tasks` as the Description and click OK to begin recording.
7. Place a tab at the 1.5 inch mark.
8. Drag the left indent marker to the 1.5 inch mark.

7

FIGURE 7.2

The Record Macro dialog enables you to specify information about the macro.

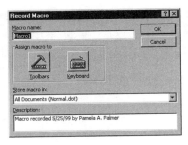

9. Press Ctrl+B to toggle Bold and type `Task:`

10. Press Ctrl+B to toggle Bold.

11. Press Tab and Enter.

12. Press Ctrl+B to toggle Bold and type `Due Date:`

13. Press Ctrl+B to toggle Bold.

14. Press Tab and Enter.

15. Press Ctrl+B to toggle Bold and type `Status:`

16. Press Ctrl+B to toggle Bold.

17. Press Tab and press Enter twice.

18. Click the Stop button on the macro toolbar to stop recording.

19. Delete all the text below tasks and press Enter.

20. Make sure that the Normal style is selected.

The macro has been recorded, and the document has been returned to its initial state. After the macro is recorded, you are ready to make changes.

Examining the Recorded Procedure

After the macro is recorded, you are ready to make it repeat. Access the Visual Basic Editor and open the module containing this macro. You should then perform the following steps:

1. Select Tools, Macro, Macros.

2. Select `TaskSetUpRecorded` and click Edit to open the Visual Basic Editor with the macro in view (see Figure 7.3).

3. Select the entire macro and copy it to the clipboard.

4. Press Ctrl+End to move to the bottom of the Code window.

5. Paste the macro from the clipboard.

6. Scroll up until you find the beginning of the second procedure.

7. Edit its name to be TaskSetUpwithFor.

Steps 3–7 aren't normally required when you've recorded a macro to edit, but for this example you are going to use this macro as the base for several macros to try out all the loops. You can now examine the TaskSetUpwithFor procedure shown in Listing 7.1.

FIGURE 7.3

The recorded macro is ready to be modified.

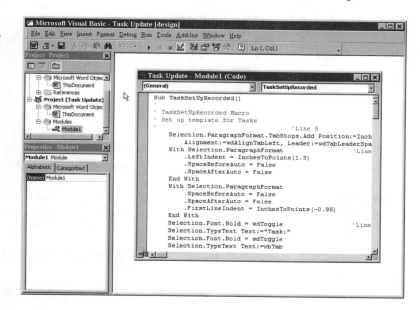

LISTING 7.1 The TaskSetUpwithFor Procedure Before Any Changes

```
 1: Sub TaskSetUpwithFor()
 2: '
 3: ' TaskSetUpRecorded Macro
 4: ' Set up template for Tasks
 5: '                                    'Line 5
 6:     Selection.ParagraphFormat.TabStops.Add Position:=InchesToPoints(1.5), _
 7:         Alignment:=wdAlignTabLeft, Leader:=wdTabLeaderSpaces
 8:     With Selection.ParagraphFormat                  'Line 8
 9:         .LeftIndent = InchesToPoints(1.5)
10:         .SpaceBeforeAuto = False
11:         .SpaceAfterAuto = False
12:     End With
13:     With Selection.ParagraphFormat
14:         .SpaceBeforeAuto = False
15:         .SpaceAfterAuto = False
16:         .FirstLineIndent = InchesToPoints(-0.95)
```

continues

7

LISTING 7.1 continued

```
17:      End With
18:      Selection.Font.Bold = wdToggle
19:      Selection.TypeText Text:="Task:"
20:      Selection.Font.Bold = wdToggle
21:      Selection.TypeText Text:=vbTab
22:      Selection.TypeParagraph
23:      Selection.Font.Bold = wdToggle
24:      Selection.TypeText Text:="Date Due:"
25:      Selection.Font.Bold = wdToggle
26:      Selection.TypeText Text:=vbTab
27:      Selection.TypeParagraph
28:      Selection.Font.Bold = wdToggle
29:      Selection.TypeText Text:="Status:"
30:      Selection.Font.Bold = wdToggle
31:      Selection.TypeText Text:=vbTab
32:      Selection.TypeParagraph
33:      Selection.TypeParagraph
34: End Sub
```

ANALYSIS The code in this recorded macro uses many new techniques. In this hour, you are focusing on the loops, not these techniques. These techniques are covered in more detail in later hours.

The `TabStops` collection stores the tabs for the selected text. On line 6, the `Add` method is used to add the left tab at the 1.5-inch mark.

The next step is to move the left line indent. When you modify a setting of indentation, you are adjusting the paragraph properties for the selection. This is accomplished by setting properties. When you are adjusting more than one property for an object, you can take advantage of the `With` statement used in lines 8–17. It enables you to set more than one property at a time. The syntax is

SYNTAX
```
With object
    [statements]
End With
```

The `With` keyword is followed by the object you are working with. The following lines will contain the settings you want to change. When you are working with properties, you will precede the property name with a period. The last line is the `End With` statement to indicate that you have completed working with the specified object.

You can see one drawback to using the recorder. There are some property settings included in the `With` statement that you didn't change like the `SpaceBefore` and `SpaceAfter`. You can delete the settings you didn't change. You will eliminate this extra code in the next section.

The code for setting up the task template begins on line 18. This is the code that must be repeated. You are ready to make changes.

Editing the Recorded Macro

You will now make several changes to the code in Listing 7.1 to make it meet the expectation of this procedure. The first step is to make some adjustments to the code that is not repeated to make it more efficient. Then you will add the code needed to repeat the task template. Perform the following steps:

1. Edit lines 8–17 in Listing 7.1 to match the following in order to minimize the number of code lines to be processed:

   ```
   With Selection.ParagraphFormat
       .LeftIndent = InchesToPoints(1.5)
       .FirstLineIndent = InchesToPoints(-0.95)
   End With
   ```

2. Move the insertion point to the end of the `End With` line and press Enter to get a new line.

3. Add the following lines of code to define the variables, get the end value with the `InputBox`, and initialize the `For...Next` loop:

   ```
   Dim lTask As Long, lNumberofTasks As Long
   lNumberofTasks = InputBox("How many tasks?", "Number of Tasks", "1")
   For lTask = 1 To lNumberofTasks
   ```

4. Select all the lines below except the `End Sub` line as shown in Figure 7.4.

5. Press the Tab key to indent the entire block to make the `For...Next` loop easier to read as shown in Figure 7.5.

6. Move to the end of the last `Selection.TypeParagraph` line and press Enter.

7. Press Shift+Tab to remove the indention from the line and type `Next lTask` to finish the `For...Next` loop.

> The Tab and Shift+Tab keystrokes can be used to indent or remove indention from a line or multiple lines of code.

FIGURE 7.4

The lines are ready to be indented as a block.

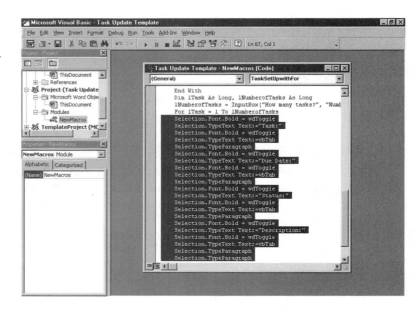

FIGURE 7.5

The lines are now indented to make the beginning and end of the For...Next *loop easier to read.*

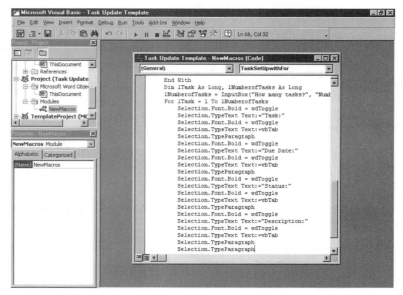

These are the only changes needed to make the task template code repeat as many times as indicated by the user. The completed code should match the code listed in Listing 7.2.

LISTING 7.2   The `TaskSetUpwithFor` Procedure Completed

```
 1: Sub TaskSetUpwithFor()
 2: '
 3: ' TaskSetUpRecorded Macro
 4: ' Set up template for Tasks
 5: '
 6:     Selection.ParagraphFormat.TabStops.Add
      ➥ Position:=InchesToPoints(1.53), _
 7:         Alignment:=wdAlignTabLeft, Leader:=wdTabLeaderSpaces
 8:     With Selection.ParagraphFormat
 9:         .LeftIndent = InchesToPoints(1.53)
10:         .FirstLineIndent = InchesToPoints(-0.95)
11:     End With
12:     Dim lTask As Long, lNumberofTasks As Long
13:     lNumberofTasks =
      ➥ InputBox("How many tasks?", "Number of Tasks", "1")
14:     For lTask = 1 To lNumberofTasks
15:         Selection.Font.Bold = wdToggle
16:         Selection.TypeText Text:="Task:"
17:         Selection.Font.Bold = wdToggle
18:         Selection.TypeText Text:=vbTab
19:         Selection.TypeParagraph
20:         Selection.Font.Bold = wdToggle
21:         Selection.TypeText Text:="Due Date:"
22:         Selection.Font.Bold = wdToggle
23:         Selection.TypeText Text:=vbTab
24:         Selection.TypeParagraph
25:         Selection.Font.Bold = wdToggle
26:         Selection.TypeText Text:="Status:"
27:         Selection.Font.Bold = wdToggle
28:         Selection.TypeText Text:=vbTab
29:         Selection.TypeParagraph
30:         Selection.Font.Bold = wdToggle
31:         Selection.TypeText Text:="Description:"
32:         Selection.Font.Bold = wdToggle
33:         Selection.TypeText Text:=vbTab
34:         Selection.TypeParagraph
35:         Selection.TypeParagraph
36:     Next lTask
37: End Sub
```

Using the Modified Code

Now that the changes are in place, you can use them to create your task memo. Save the
template, create a new document based on it, and try out the macro:

1. Click the Save button on the toolbar.

2. Switch to Word.

7

3. Close the template.

4. Select File, New to open the New dialog.

5. Select the General tab, if necessary.

6. Double-click the Task Update Memo icon to create the new document.

7. Press Ctrl+End to move to the end of the document.

8. Select Tools, Macro, Macros to open the Macros dialog.

9. Double-click on the `TaskSetUpwithFor` to start the macro and display the `InputBox` (see Figure 7.6).

FIGURE 7.6

The `InputBox` *asks for the number of tasks.*

10. Type 4 and press Enter to enter the task templates (see Figure 7.7).

FIGURE 7.7

The tasks are ready to be filled in.

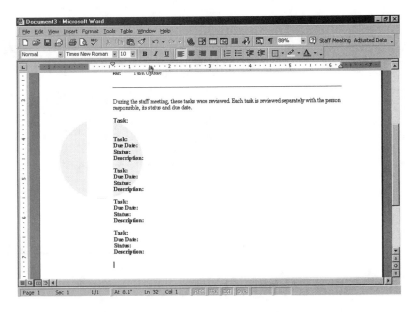

Now the user can move to the first task line and press the End key to move to the end of the line. After the task name is typed, the user can use the down arrow to move to the line below and enter the due date. The one drawback is that the user has to know how many tasks there are before calling this macro.

Using Do Loops

The `For...Next` loop enables the user to indicate how many tasks are needed and creates the templates. The drawback is that users must know how many task templates to create; otherwise, they have to run the macro more than once.

Another alternative to repeat actions in your code is to use a `Do` loop. There are several syntaxes available depending on your needs. The `Do` loop will repeat actions until the loop is manually exited, a condition is met, or while a condition is true.

There are two forms the syntax can take:

SYNTAX

```
Do [{While | Until} condition]
    [statements]
    [Exit Do]
    [statements]
Loop
```

SYNTAX

```
Do
    [statements]
    [Exit Do]
    [statements]
Loop [{While | Until}] condition
```

There are two forms of the syntax because the `Do` loop is very flexible. The `Do` loop can be executed until you exit the loop with code, or it can evaluate a condition to determine when to stop executing.

There are two types of condition testing possible with a `Do` loop:

- `Do...Until`: Your code can execute the loop *until a condition is met*.
- `Do...While`: Your code can execute the loop *while a condition is true*.

Use the `Until` and `While` keywords to determine which type of evaluation you are using. If you are going to use the `Until` or `While` keyword, you also have a choice about when the code performs the condition testing. You can place the testing at the top or bottom of the loop. If it is placed at the top of the loop, the condition must not be true with the `Until` keyword and must be true with the `While` keyword. If the testing is placed at the bottom of the loop, the code will be executed once.

If you want to test the condition at the top of the loop, the syntax begins with the `Do` keyword. This is followed by the `Until` or `While` keyword depending on the type of test. This is followed by the expression to test. You can use any of the tools discussed in Hour 6 to build your expression.

7

On the following lines, you will have the code to be executed. If at any time you need to exit the loop without meeting the condition test, you can use the Exit For statement. The last line is the Loop keyword to indicate that the code should begin repeating at the first line.

If you want to execute the lines of code once before testing the condition, you will use the second syntax. It begins with the Do keyword to begin the loop. The code lines to execute follow it. The last line begins with the Loop keyword. When there is a condition to test, the Until or While keyword is followed by the condition.

The Do...Until Loop

To get a better idea of how the Do...Until structure works, you can modify the task set up to use a Do...Until loop instead of the For...Next. Instead of initially determining the number of tasks to be performed, you can use the InputBox to prompt for a task description and continue to loop as long as text is entered into the InputBox.

This actually requires very few changes. Add the code found in Listing 7.3.

LISTING 7.3   The TaskSetUpwithUntil Procedure

```
 1: Sub TaskSetUpwithUntil()
 2: '
 3: ' TaskSetUpRecorded Macro modified to illustrate
 4: ' The Do...Until Loop
 5: '
 6:     Selection.ParagraphFormat.TabStops.Add
    ➥ Position:=InchesToPoints(1.53), _
 7:        Alignment:=wdAlignTabLeft, Leader:=wdTabLeaderSpaces
 8:     With Selection.ParagraphFormat
 9:        .LeftIndent = InchesToPoints(1.53)
10:        .FirstLineIndent = InchesToPoints(-0.95)
11:     End With
12:     Dim strprompt As String, strTitle As String, strTask As String
13:     strprompt = "Enter the task description and press Enter. "
14:     strprompt = strprompt & "Click Cancel when there aren't any tasks."
15:     strTitle = "New Task"
16:     strTask = InputBox(strprompt, strTitle)
17:     Do Until strTask = ""
18:        Selection.Font.Bold = wdToggle
19:        Selection.TypeText Text:="Task:"
20:        Selection.Font.Bold = wdToggle
21:        Selection.TypeText Text:=vbTab & strTask
22:        Selection.TypeParagraph
23:        Selection.Font.Bold = wdToggle
24:        Selection.TypeText Text:="Due Date:"
25:        Selection.Font.Bold = wdToggle
```

```
26:         Selection.TypeText Text:=vbTab
27:         Selection.TypeParagraph
28:         Selection.Font.Bold = wdToggle
29:         Selection.TypeText Text:="Status:"
30:         Selection.Font.Bold = wdToggle
31:         Selection.TypeText Text:=vbTab
32:         Selection.TypeParagraph
33:         Selection.Font.Bold = wdToggle
34:         Selection.TypeText Text:="Description:"
35:         Selection.Font.Bold = wdToggle
36:         Selection.TypeText Text:=vbTab
37:         Selection.TypeParagraph
38:         Selection.TypeParagraph
39:         strprompt = "Enter next task or click Cancel."
40:         strTask = InputBox(strprompt, strTitle)
41:     Loop
42: End Sub
```

ANALYSIS Very few changes are needed to modify the `TaskSetUpwithFor` procedure to use the `Do...Until` loop. The first change is on line 12. The user will have to be prompted for the first task. Line 12 sets up the variables for the `InputBox` and prompts the user for the first task (see Figure 7.8).

FIGURE 7.8

The `InputBox` asks for the first task.

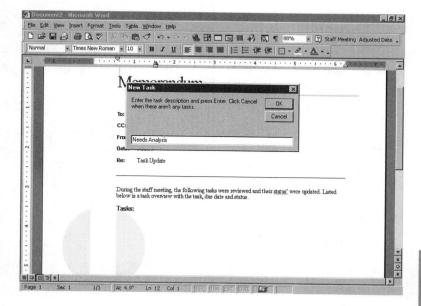

After the user enters a task, it is tested with the `Do...Until` loop. Line 17 sets up the `Do...Until` loop, testing the contents of the `strTask` variable. If the user clicks Cancel instead of entering text and pressing Enter, the variable contains an empty string.

If the user entered a string, the code inside of the loop executes. Because you asked for the task description, your code can do more of the work. On line 21, you'll notice that the `strTask` variable is concatenated into the text after the tab next to the Task label.

The rest of the code didn't change from the original until line 39. Line 39 resets the prompt variable and line 40 displays the `InputBox` again for the next task (see Figure 7.9).

FIGURE 7.9

The `InputBox` is ready for the next task.

If a task is entered, the code repeats beginning with the `Do` line. If the user clicks Cancel instead of entering a task, the `Do` line is `True` because the Cancel button returns an empty string. The loop would end and pick up executing with line 41, which in this case is the end of the procedure.

The `Do...While` Loop

The `Do...While` loop can also be used to perform the same task. The difference is the condition test. The `Do...While` test continues to process as long as a condition is `True`. The line that changes is line 17:

```
Do Until strTask = ""
```

The code should be executed if there is a valid task entered in the `InputBox`. This is testing to see when the task description is empty. For the `While` keyword, you must test to make sure you have a valid value. You could either use

```
Do While strTask <> ""
```

or

```
Do While Len(strTask) > 0
```

Either of these statements will give you the proper test of the variable. Both will execute as long as the user enters a task in the Input Box.

Examining the `While...Wend` Loop

The last loop is the `While...Wend`. It is like the `Do...While` structure. Just as you have inherited traits from your parents, VBA has inherited some statements from the older versions of BASIC.

The `While...Wend` is like a `Do...While` loop with the condition test at the beginning of the code block. Its syntax is

SYNTAX

```
While condition
    [statements]
Wend
```

This structure is included for backward compatibility. Its disadvantage is the fact that the testing is at the top only. There isn't a way to execute the loop once and then test the condition.

Summary

In this hour, you have learned another way to control the path of your code. You can use loops to execute a group of actions multiple times without having duplicate lines of code in your procedure. This will not only save typing time, it also makes code easier to maintain.

You learned that you can repeat a series of actions a specific number of times with the `For...Next` loop. You can also repeat the actions based on the state of a condition. You have the `Do...Until` loop to repeat *until* an expression is `True` and you have the `Do...While` loop that will repeat *while* an expression is `True`.

Q&A

Q Do you have to use an InputBox to get the counter range for the `For...Next` loop or as the entry for processing?

A No, you can use a fixed number or retrieve it from another source. Retrieving it from another source is useful when you are working with tables or an outside source like Excel or Access.

Q How do you decide which loop to use?

A Although the loops were illustrated with the same example, you will find that selecting the loop to use is easier with your own work.

7

The `For...Next` loop is best for those instances when the actions don't require user interaction. The `Do...Until` loop and the `Do...While` loops are tougher. You need to decide what you are testing. If the test expression is more likely to be `True` than `False`, you will probably select the `Do...While` loop.

Q While exploring VBA, I've seen the `For Each...Next` loop. What is it for?

A The `For Each...Next` loop is a special `For` loop designed to assist with object processing. You will use it with collections. This structure is discussed in Hour 11, "Working with Page Appearance and Printing."

Workshop

Here are some questions and exercises to assist with your review of this hour's material. The answers to the quiz questions can be found in Appendix A, "Quiz Answers."

Quiz

1. How can I increment the counter in the `For...Next` loop by more than one?
2. How do I decide whether to place the `While` or `Until` at the top or bottom of the loop?
3. Is there a time when the `While...Wend` is used?

Exercises

1. Examine your list of automation tasks to determine where you will be repeating tasks and determine which loop will be better for your purposes.
2. Create a procedure to create a list of goals for the week.

HOUR **8**

Handling Problems in VBA

As you automate more of your work, you are beginning to use more of the Visual Basic for Applications language and the Word Object model. As you learn, you will make some mistakes along the way. The key is to learn how to deal with those mistakes. You will also have to deal with circumstances you can't control that will generate errors.

The highlights of this hour include

- Examining errors
- Debugging your code
- Implementing error handling

Examining Errors

When you create a procedure using the Macro Recorder, you manually walk through the steps needed to automate a process. As you begin to create more complex procedures by writing your own code in the Visual Basic Editor, you are sure to make some mistakes along the way. If you include mechanisms for interaction with the macro, such as a MsgBox or InputBox, you will also encounter problems that you can't control—for example, a missing file.

When you begin writing code, you are taking on a role as a developer. Dealing with errors is part of that job, and you want to eliminate as many errors as possible as you develop your code. The first step is to understand what type of errors will occur. There are three types of errors:

- syntax errors
- runtime errors
- logic errors

The next step is learning how to address the errors in the code. Syntax errors and logic errors must be tracked down and corrected. Runtime errors can't be eliminated because you can't guarantee that your code will always have the external resources it needs to run. Instead, you have to plan for handling runtime errors. There are two techniques for correcting problems:

- Debugging: Testing your code to eliminate any errors that prevent the code from executing or that do not produce the correct output.
- Error Handling: Adding code to manage errors that cannot be eliminated.

This section focuses on defining errors. After that, you will learn the procedure for debugging your code and the statements used for error handling. With these techniques, you will be able to create clean code that runs effectively.

Examining Syntax Errors

The syntax error is basically a typographical error. When the code line is entered, a word may have been mistyped or an argument forgotten. As you worked with the Visual Basic Editor, you saw several features that can help you avoid these problems.

As with other Microsoft applications, the Visual Basic Editor enables you to control some of the behavior of the application with options. Select Tools, Options from the Visual Basic menu to display the Options dialog as shown in Figure 8.1.

FIGURE 8.1

The Options dialog enables you to control the appearance and behavior of the Editor.

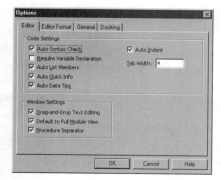

As you began working with the Visual Basic Editor, you became familiar with many of the features that help you avoid syntax errors:

- Auto Quick Info
- Auto List Members
- Auto Syntax Check
- Require Variable Declaration

Auto Quick Info provides a syntax guide as you type a statement or function, as shown in Figure 8.2. When entering the MsgBox function, as soon as you type the phrase MsgBox(, the Quick Info displays.

FIGURE 8.2

The framework for the function is displayed.

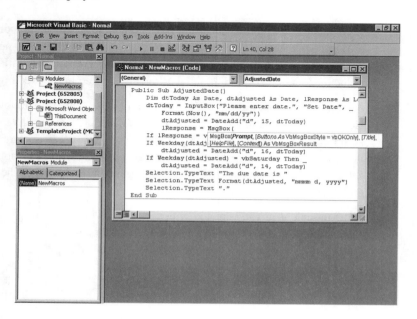

As you enter the arguments, they are highlighted in the Quick Info. If you are working on an argument that has built-in constants, the Auto List Members displays a list of the valid constants as shown in Figure 8.3. As you type, the selected constant will be highlighted. When you get to the one you want, you can press Tab to finish the entry.

FIGURE 8.3

The list of constants is displayed when you get to that argument.

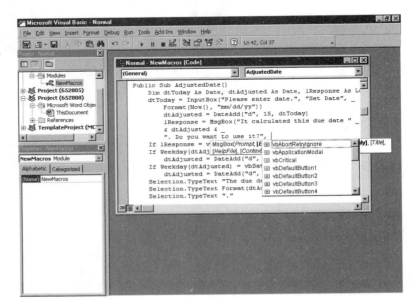

If you accidentally press Enter and move to another line without completing a statement, or if you make a typographical error, the Auto Syntax Check will notify you that the line has a problem. It will display a message such as the one shown in Figure 8.4. In addition to the message, the offending line will be highlighted in red (see Figure 8.5).

Another option that isn't turned on by default is the Require Variable Declaration. In Hour 4, "Understanding Objects," you were introduced to using variables. You can use an implicit declaration, which is quick and easy, or you can declare the variable before you use it. You can force yourself to declare variables using this option. If this option is selected, it will place the Option Explicit statement at the top of the module in the general declarations as the module is created.

If the module is already created, you can add this line manually. It will display a message when a variable name that hasn't been declared is entered.

FIGURE 8.4

The Auto Syntax Check validates each line as it is entered.

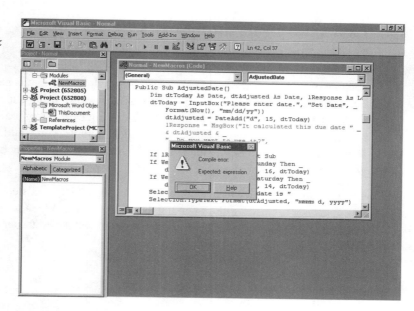

FIGURE 8.5

The line is highlighted to help you identify problems.

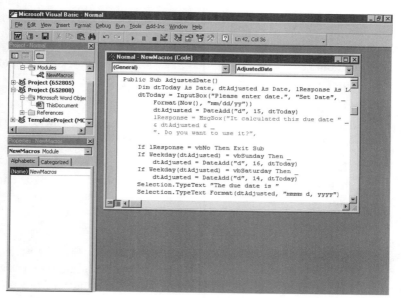

Examining Runtime Errors

Runtime errors stop the execution of your code. A runtime error can be a typographical problem, but it is different from a syntax error. It isn't a problem with the syntax of the command, it involves a typographical error or missing data that is needed by a command. For example, it can involve trying to open a document or using a template without referencing the name correctly (see Figure 8.6). A runtime error might also result from trying to work with a resource that isn't available. For example, you could try to access a file from a floppy with no floppy in the drive or access a file from a network drive that you don't have permission to access.

These errors aren't easy to deal with. In most cases, the file existed when you created the procedure, or there was a floppy in the drive at that time. When the procedure is used later, the file or floppy is no longer there, and that fact generates an error message.

FIGURE 8.6

The error is displayed, and the Visual Basic Editor is opened.

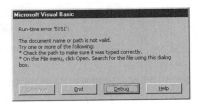

Runtime errors are more serious because they halt the execution of the code. Runtime errors may also cause some problems if you are sharing this procedure with another user.

When the problem occurs and this dialog is displayed, one of the options is to Debug the code. For you, dealing with the error is a nuisance. If others are using the procedure, you probably don't want others to edit your code.

Most runtime errors are resolved by adding error handling. You will have to do some brainstorming to create a list of possible problems and then determine what should happen if any occur.

Examining Logic Errors

A logic error can be harder to track down than the first two because it doesn't prevent or stop the execution. It appears to execute, but the results won't match your expectations. Logic errors are very common with calculations and conditional logic.

A logic error is easiest to deal with as you write the code. If you take a little time to verify the results as you try out your code, it will save a lot of time later. Now that you have been introduced to the types of errors, you are ready to explore some techniques to minimize their impact.

Debugging Your Code

The options that assist with entering code will cut down on errors, but they won't eliminate all of them. Testing your procedures is critical to make sure it gives you the results you expect.

When you identify a problem, track it down. The Visual Basic Editor has several tools to assist with this process called *debugging*. To examine the debugging process, you will now work with an error in a procedure you created in an earlier lesson.

Defining the Problem

To walk through this process, you have to have some code with problems. Listing 8.1 displays the code for a procedure called DueDateCalc. It is similar to the AdjustedDate procedure, but it has three errors.

 This procedure is located in the Hour8 template located on the companion Web site.

LISTING 8.1 The DueDateCalc Procedure

```
 1: Sub DueDateCalc()
 2: '    This is a revised version of the AdjustedDate to
 3: '    illustrate debugging and error handling.
 4:     Dim dtToday As Date, dtAdjusted As Date, lResponse As Long
 5:     dtToday = InputBox("Please enter date.", "Set Date", _
 6:         Format(Now(), "m/d/yy"))
 7:     dtAdjusted = DateAdd("d", 15, dtToday)
 8:     If Weekday(dtAdjusted) = vbSunday Then
 9:         dtAdjusted = DateAdd("d", 17, dtToday)
10:     ElseIf Weekday(dtAdjusted) = vbSaturday Then
11:         dtAdjusted = DateAdd("d", 14, dtToday)
12:     End If
13:     lResponse = MsgBox("It calculated this due date " _
14:         & dtAdjusted & _
15:         ". Do you want to use it?", vbQuestion + vbYesNo, _
16:         "Date Confirmation")
17:     If lResponse = vbNo Then
18:         Selection.TypeText "The due date is "
19:         Selection.TypeText Format(dtAdjusted, "mmmm d, yyyy")
20:         Selection.TypeText "."
21:     Else
22:         Selection.TypeText "The due date is "
23:     End If
24: End Sub
```

ANALYSIS   Rather than try to figure out what is wrong in the code, you want to focus on the debugging and error-handling techniques. To help you concentrate on the process instead of on the errors, they are defined below:

The first error is in line 17. After the due date is calculated, it is displayed in a MsgBox to be confirmed. The button the user selected is stored in the variable, lResponse. Line 17 tests that variable and then adds the appropriate text. The problem is that the code to execute is backwards. If the response is vbYes, it should create the entire sentence. If the No button is selected, the beginning of the sentence should be entered instead of the entire sentence. The constant, vbNo, needs to be replaced by vbYes.

When you execute the procedure, the first step is that the InputBox appears (see Figure 8.7). The user can enter a date or use the default.

FIGURE 8.7

The InputBox *asks for the date.*

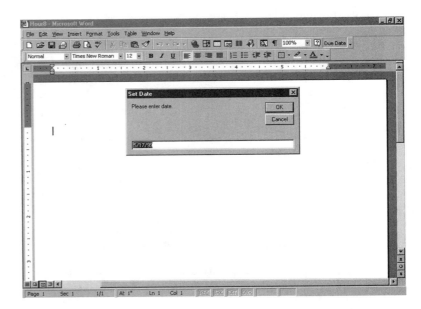

The date is used in the calculation and the MsgBox is displayed to confirm the new due date (see Figure 8.8). The user can click Yes or No.

If the user clicks No, the error is evident in the document (see Figure 8.9). The date is used despite the choice.

FIGURE 8.8

The MsgBox *confirms the date choice.*

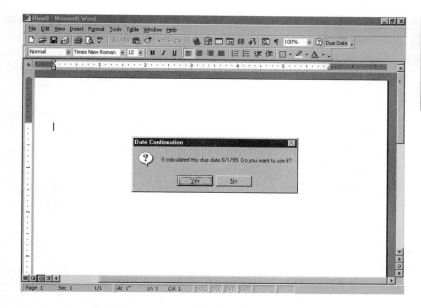

FIGURE 8.9

The document shows the date anyway.

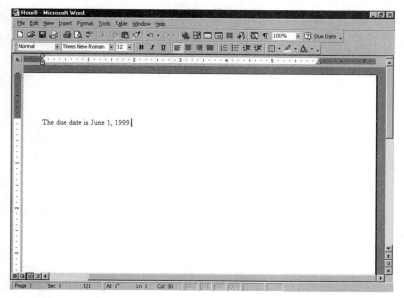

The second error is on line 9. This error is more subtle than the MsgBox problem because there isn't a visual sign that there is a problem. If the new date is a Sunday, the code is adding too many days in an attempt to move the date to the next weekday. If you use 5/15/99 as the date, and click No to accommodate the first error, the result is one day off. The code returns the 6/1/99 date when the date should be 5/31/99.

This error is trickier than the first because the procedure appears to work. You get a date when you enter one. This means that you are going to have to think of all the possible things that can be entered.

The last error is much more severe. It is one that, after you locate it, you can't fix it by correcting a mistake. You can't eliminate it. You will have to add code to determine what to do when it occurs. If you enter letters in the InputBox or click the Cancel button, the procedure can't continue to process.

When this happens, the execution of the procedure is paused, and the Visual Basic error message appears, as shown in Figure 8.10. When you, yourself, are the user, it isn't a serious problem. You click End to stop the execution and move on.

FIGURE 8.10

The Visual Basic Message Box can lead to bigger problems.

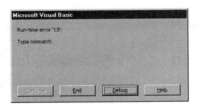

If someone else is the user, this occurrence might cause a bigger problem. The first issue is that it is going to startle the user. He might panic and destroy part of the document. The second issue is that it pulls up the Visual Basic Editor, and the user might try to fix the error himself.

These three problems illustrate the need for debugging and error handling. With runtime errors, you will have a clear picture where the problem is because the procedure can't continue to execute. It pauses, and you can click Debug to see what is wrong.

With logic errors, the process is more difficult because the error doesn't cause the procedure to stop running. It finishes executing, but the results are wrong.

For logic errors, you will have to make sure to test different entries and verify the results match your expectations. The Visual Basic Editor has several tools to help test your code. To begin experimenting with debugging, you must correct the problem with the MsgBox first.

The rest of this section shows you how to fix the first two problems by debugging. The third problem is addressed in the following section, "Implementing Error Handling."

Adding a Breakpoint

With the `MsgBox` problem, the procedure runs. What you must do is force the code to stop so you can watch what is happening. This is referred to as *stepping* or *walking through*.

There is a `Stop` statement to halt the execution of the code, but it is a carry-over from older forms of BASIC. The problem with this approach is that after you have tracked down the problem, you have to remove the code line. This can cause more problems.

With the Visual Basic Editor, you have another method for stopping the code. It is called a *breakpoint*. Adding a breakpoint is very easy in the Visual Basic Editor. When you encounter the `MsgBox` problem, you might begin by saying, the `MsgBox` is displayed, but the button isn't being handled correctly. The line that evaluates the `MsgBox` button might make a good place to begin checking the code.

In this case, you know that it is a problem with the test of the variable returned by the message box. You might want to set the `If  1Response  =  vbNo` line as a breakpoint.

Setting a breakpoint is simple. Point in the gray bar to the left of the code and click. If you prefer to use the menu, place the insertion point in the code line and select Debug, Toggle Breakpoint. It will highlight the line and place a dot next to it in the gray bar as shown in Figure 8.11.

FIGURE 8.11

The breakpoint indicates where to pause the execution of the code.

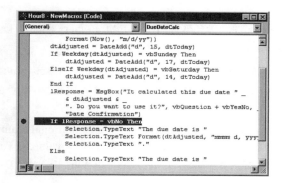

Using the Breakpoint

After the breakpoint is in place, you are ready to test your code. You will need to switch back to Word.

1. Press Alt+F11 to switch to Word.
2. Click the Due Date button on the toolbar.

3. Click OK to accept the default date in the InputBox.

4. Select Yes in the MsgBox.

5. Notice that instead of getting the correct sentence in the document, the breakpoint has paused the execution of the procedure (see Figure 8.12).

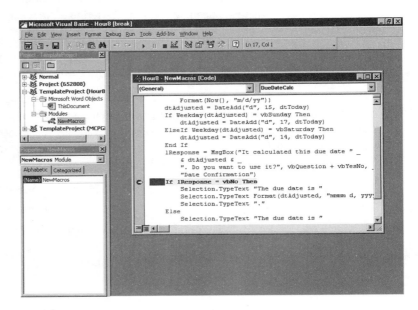

The breakpoint occurs, and the Visual Basic Editor enters what is known as *break mode*. The procedure is paused to enable you to locate the problem.

You can check out the contents of variables and constants, set values, and gather other kinds of information. When you are having trouble with a variable, you have an easy way to see what it is storing.

The Options dialog, shown in Figure 8.1, offers one additional feature that can be useful. The AutoData Tips give you quick access to a variable's value. If you point to lResponse in the highlighted line, you will get a balloon displaying its value (see Figure 8.13).

In this case, lResponse is equal to 6, which is the value stored by vbYes. If you point to vbNo, it will show you its value as 7. After you have located and resolved the error, you must clear the breakpoint.

Simply changing the vbNo to vbYes will correct this problem. After you correct the prob-lem, you can click in the gray bar on the dot to remove the breakpoint or select Debug,

Toggle Breakpoint from the menu. If you don't want to continue executing, you can select the End button on the toolbar.

FIGURE 8.13

The AutoData Tips let you see a variable's current value.

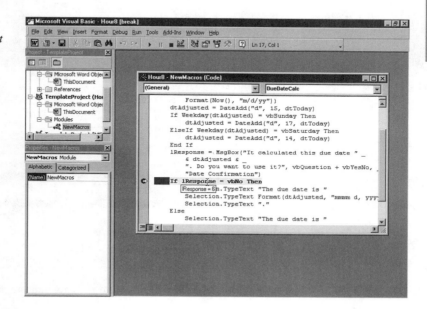

Other problems will probably be more complex and break points might not be enough to track the errors. The Visual Basic Editor has several other tools that may be beneficial for the more difficult problems, which are described in the following sections.

Examining the Locals Window

When you are in the Break mode, the Locals window may make examining variables easier. For example, you want to determine why the procedure isn't returning the correct date. You can set another breakpoint and then use the Locals window.

If you set a breakpoint for the first dtAdjusted code line, switch to Word and run the macro again. You can enter a date like 5/15/99 in the InputBox and click OK. The procedure breaks at the specified code line, and the Visual Basic Editor is displayed.

In this case, there are several possible problem areas. You might not want to point to all of them separately to determine their values. The Locals window eliminates this task by displaying all active data elements (see Figure 8.14). If it isn't already displayed, you need to select View, Locals Window to open it.

FIGURE 8.14

The Locals window displays all active data elements.

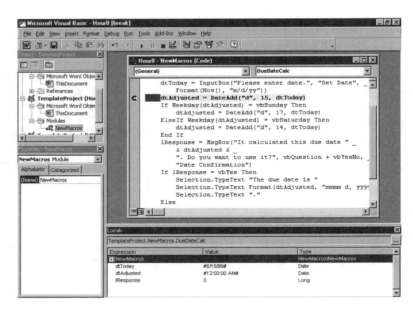

Remember, the pound signs (#) around the date indicate that it is stored as a date.

The Locals window provides a hierarchical list of those data elements that have been declared in the code. In this case, it is listing dtToday which was populated with the date from the InputBox. dtAdjusted is currently set to #12:00:00 AM# because it currently is set to 0, and lResponse has no value.

Tracking Down the Problem

Now that the code is in the Break mode you can watch as it executes. At this point, all three variables are correct. The line that is highlighted hasn't been executed yet. You are now ready to step through the code.

The Run, Pause, and End commands are all located on the menu and toolbar to make them accessible. The step through function isn't on the toolbar. It can be used by selecting Debug, Step Into. You can also press F8.

The F8 key is the way you will step through most of the time. If you press F8 now, the line with the breakpoint is executed, and the following line becomes active. Notice that the dtAdjusted is now set to #5/30/99# (see Figure 8.15).

FIGURE 8.15

The dtAdjusted *variable has changed.*

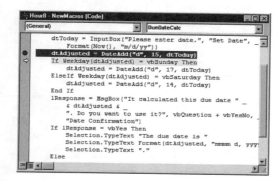

Given the code line, the variable is still correct. Press F8 again, and the editor is ready to test to see if dtAdjusted is Sunday. Press F8 and the editor finds that the variable is a Sunday. When you press F8 again, you will notice the variable changed; it is now set to #6/1/99#.

In this case, you should make sure that you have tried out data for each possible type of entry. In this case, the date should be set to #5/31/99#.

Using the Immediate Window

Now that you have isolated the line that is causing the problem, you might want to test the rest of the code before you make the change. Use the Immediate window to make sure the variable isn't affected by any of the remaining lines.

You can select View, Immediate Window to open it (see Figure 8.16). This window enables you to interact with your code in the break mode. You could type ?dtAdjusted to see the current setting, or change the setting by entering dtAdjusted = #5/31/99#. Then you could continue to run the code to verify that it is correct. Continue to step through the code or select Run to finish it. F5 will also run the code.

Adding a Watch Variable

The Data Info Tips, Locals window, or the Immediate window do enable you to use breakpoints and the step though command to explore your code when there is a problem;

but, you may find this tedious. When there are many variables, or your code is longer
than this small procedure, you may want to use a *watch variable*.

FIGURE 8.16

*The Immediate window
enables you to interact
with the code.*

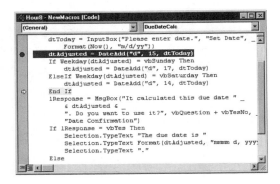

A watch variable is an expression identified to the Visual Basic Editor to be monitored.
You can set a watch variable to break the run of your code when an expression changes
or becomes True. To use a watch variable, perform the following steps:

1. Select Debug, Add Watch to view the Add Watch dialog (see Figure 8.17).

FIGURE 8.17

*The Add Watch dialog
enables you to set up a
watch expression.*

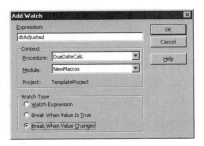

2. Type in dtAdjusted as the Expression.
3. Make sure the Watch Type is Break when value changes and select OK.
4. Notice the Watches window opens, and the variable is set (see Figure 8.18).
5. Switch back to Word and run the procedure.
6. Notice the procedure begins to execute. You complete the InputBox.
7. The line that sets dtAdjusted is executed, the code is halted, and the Visual Basic
   Editor is displayed.

8. Check the value of `dtAdjusted` and press F5.

9. Notice the code to change the value is executed, and the `End If` line is about to be executed.

FIGURE 8.18

The Watches window doesn't display all variables as the Locals window does.

```
Hour8 - NewMacros (Code)
(General)                              DueDateCalc
  Sub DueDateCalc()
  '    This is a revised version of the AdjustedDate to
  '    illustrate debugging and error handling.
      Dim dtToday As Date, dtAdjusted As Date, lResponse As l
      dtToday = InputBox("Please enter date.", "Set Date", _
          Format(Now(), "m/d/yy"))
      dtAdjusted = DateAdd("d", 15, dtToday)
      If Weekday(dtAdjusted) = vbSunday Then
          dtAdjusted = DateAdd("d", 17, dtToday)
      ElseIf Weekday(dtAdjusted) = vbSaturday Then
          dtAdjusted = DateAdd("d", 14, dtToday)
      End If
      lResponse = MsgBox("It calculated this due date " _
          & dtAdjusted & _
          ". Do you want to use it?", vbQuestion + vbYesNo, _
          "Date Confirmation")
      If lResponse = vbNo Then
```

With watch expressions, you avoid a lot of keystrokes and save time. You don't have to press F8 to execute every line. You can let the Visual Basic Editor do the work of monitoring changes.

After you have located the error, you can correct it and select Debug, Edit Watch to delete the watch expression. In this case, after you determine that the day is Sunday, the line that sets `stAdjusted` needs to add 16 instead of 17.

If you take the time to check each procedure as you create it, you will have a much easier time tracking down any problems that you find. The code's goal will be fresh in your mind.

> When you begin developing longer procedures, you may also benefit from the use of comments. By placing a small note about what specific lines of code are for, you will also cut down the confusion when you try to determine what some code is doing. You first saw comments used in Hour 2. The Macro Recorder adds comments for the information entered in the Record Macro dialog.

Implementing Error Handling

The debugging process is only part of the process. There are times that, even when you track down the problem, it isn't a solvable typographical or logical error.

Some errors are the result of availability. For example, the first Subprocedure you created was one that made a new file from a template. What if the template gets deleted or moved accidentally? When you created the macro the template was there, but you can't guarantee that it will be there later. When you create procedures, you need to anticipate possible problems. Error handling is a method for doing this.

There are three general steps to creating an error handler:

1. Initialize (that is, turn on) the error trap.
2. Write code to deal with the error.
3. Indicate how to proceed after the error is taken care of.

In the DueDate procedure, the InputBox can be a error waiting to happen. Line 7 assumes that there was a valid date entered in the InputBox. If someone enters letters or symbols or deletes the default value, the code fails. You want to add error handling to protect against its failure.

Initializing the Error Trap

Visual Basic has some built-in error handling. When an error occurs, it displays its error message and provides an opportunity to end the execution or debug it. You should indicate that you want your code to handle any errors. You use the On Error statement to indicate this preference. The syntax is

```
On Error [GoTo line | Resume Next | GoTo 0]
```

The On Error statement sets up the error trapping. Its three choices determine what happens when an error occurs by one of the other statements that follow it.

- Goto line label: This choice indicates that, if an error occurs, the code should pick up in a specific location indicated by the line label.
- Resume Next: This indicates that the error handling will occur in the following statement.
- GoTo 0: This choice disables error handling to enable you to have more than one set of error-handling routines in one procedure.

The On Error line is entered above the code that could generate the error. You can add it on the line directly above the InputBox line or at the beginning of this procedure as follows:

1. Place the insertion point at the beginning of the InputBox line.
2. Type On Error GoTo ErrInput and press Enter.

The error trap is set and indicates that the code under the line label ErrInput needs to be executed. Now you have to add that code.

Setting Up the Error Handler

When you use the GoTo choice for the error trap, you indicate that the code should branch to another location to deal with the problem. This is often at the bottom of the procedure. You have to separate that code from the regular code that performs the tasks.

You place an Exit Sub statement after the code, and add the line label for the error handler below:

1. Place the insertion point after the End If line and press Enter to get a blank line.
2. Type Exit Sub and press Enter.
3. Press Shift+Tab to remove the indent.
4. Type ErrInput: and press Enter.
5. Press Tab to indent your code.

Now you have the framework to tackle the error. You must next add code to deal with possible problems. When an error occurs in Visual Basic, it is returned using the Err object. This enables you to test to see what error was returned.

The Err object has properties like other objects. Two of them give the information needed to handle the problem. You have the Number property to give you the error number, and the Description is the text explaining the error number.

The InputBox is used to populate a date variable. No information or letters can be used to populate this type of variable. When the wrong type of information is used, the number of the error is 13 and the Description is Type Mismatch. At a minimum, you might want to display this message in a better form, not giving the user an opportunity to get at your code.

Most developers prefer to use a Select Case structure for error handling. You can test the Error number and have different cases for different problems.

You are going to include code to handle each error. The code might do nothing more than repackage the Number and Description using the MsgBox. You can also use the Case Else to handle any unforeseen problems.

The code which follows indicates what you want to do to resolve the problem. In it, you indicate how to proceed with statements. You have several choices:

- The Resume statement indicates that you want to try executing the line of code that generated the error again.

- The `Resume Next` statement indicates that you want to pick up the execution with the line below the line that generated the error.
- The `Exit Sub` line indicates that you want to terminate the run of the procedure. If this is the last case in the `Select Case`, you can place nothing in the case and the `End Sub` will perform the same task.

In this case, error 13 doesn't need any processing. You can inform the user of the problem with a `MsgBox`, and then let him give it another try. The revised code would be similar to the code shown in Listing 8.2.

LISTING 8.2   Using the `Select Case` Statement for Error Handling

```
 1: Sub DueDateCalcComplete()
 2: '   This is a revised version of the AdjustedDate to
 3: '   illustrate debugging and error handling.
 4:     Dim dtToday As Date, dtAdjusted As Date, lResponse As Long
 5:     On Error GoTo ErrInput
 6:     dtToday = InputBox("Please enter date.", "Set Date", _
 7:         Format(Now(), "m/d/yy"))
 8:     dtAdjusted = DateAdd("d", 15, dtToday)
 9:     If Weekday(dtAdjusted) = vbSunday Then
10:         dtAdjusted = DateAdd("d", 16, dtToday)
11:     ElseIf Weekday(dtAdjusted) = vbSaturday Then
12:         dtAdjusted = DateAdd("d", 14, dtToday)
13:     End If
14:     lResponse = MsgBox("It calculated this due date " _
15:         & dtAdjusted & _
16:         ". Do you want to use it?", vbQuestion + vbYesNo, _
17:         "Date Confirmation")
18:     If lResponse = vbYes Then
19:         Selection.TypeText "The due date is "
20:         Selection.TypeText Format(dtAdjusted, "mmmm d, yyyy")
21:         Selection.TypeText "."
22:     Else
23:         Selection.TypeText "The due date is "
24:     End If
25:     Exit Sub
26: ErrInput:
27:     Select Case Err.Number
28:         Case 13          'Type Mismatch
29:             Dim lError As Long
30:             strMessage = "You have entered an invalid date. "
31:             strMessage = strMessage & "Do you want to try again?"
32:             strTitle = "Error Occurred"
33:             lError = MsgBox(strMessage, vbQuestion & vbYesNo, strTitle)
34:             If lError Is vbYes Then
```

```
35:                    Resume
36:                Else
37:                    Exit Sub
38:                End If
39:            Case Else
40:                strMessage = "An unexpected error, " & Err.Number
41:                strMessage = strMessage & ", " & Err.Description
42:                strMessage = ", has occurred. This procedure can't continue."
43:                MsgBox strMessage, vbExclamation, "Unexpected Error"
44:                Exit Sub
45:        End Select
46: End Sub
```

ANALYSIS   Now when you run this procedure and delete the default date, you see the error message displayed, and you get to choose whether you want to try again. If you choose Yes, the InputBox redisplays.

Line 5 initializes the error handler indicating that if an error occurs, Visual Basic should pick up the execution with the ErrInput line label. The code is identical to the code before, until you reach line 25.

Line 25 is the Exit Sub statement. This is the last line executed if everything runs fine. Line 26 is the ErrInput line. This is where Visual Basic will begin executing if an error occurs.

Line 27 sets up the Select Case structure to test any error. Line 28 has the first Case clause. If no data or incorrect data is entered in the InputBox, line 8 will generate an error, error 13. Lines 29–33 set up and display a MsgBox to ask the user what should happen. If she selects the Yes button, the variable, lError is set to vbYes.

The If structure evaluates this variable. If it is set to vbYes, the Resume keyword will indicate that Visual Basic should attempt to execute the line that generated the error again. In this case, line 8 would be attempted again.

If the user chose No and the variable is set to vbNo, the procedure is exited. In reality, this line could be eliminated because the next line to be executed if this error was generated is line 45, which is the end of the Select Case structure.

The Case Else clause just displays the error in a MsgBox. This lets the user determine what needs to happen next.

This procedure is not complex. It accomplishes one task. As your procedures grow in size and complexity, the need for error handling will grow as well.

Summary

In this hour, you were introduced to some of the tools for tracking down problems in your code. These were referred to as the debugging tools. You can pause the execution of your procedure to see the state of your processing and watch it as you step through each line. You can use the Data Tips, Locals Window, Immediate window, and Watches to track changes in your data.

When you track down a problem that can't be eliminated because you can't guarantee the health and contents of a user's machine, you learned that you need to add code to prevent the procedure from halting and possibly exposing the procedure for editing. This is known as error handling.

In this hour, the example for error handling is very straightforward. As you continue to complete the remaining hours, you will see more examples of error handling.

Q&A

Q Can I change the appearance of my code?

A Yes. If you find that reading your code is difficult when you are debugging, you can change its appearance with the Options dialog.

Q What are some other instances where error handling is important?

A Error handling is important whenever you are getting information while you execute your procedure. It can be information from the user or from his system or network. If there is a possibility that you won't get what you need to continue processing, you should add error handling to avoid a halt in execution.

Q When would you use the `Resume Next`?

A An example might be when you have added code to create another `InputBox` informing the user that the last date he entered was invalid and asking him for another date. In this case, you would use the `Resume Next` statement. You should always test the value from the new `InputBox`.

Q What errors do you need to watch for?

A There are many errors that might occur in you code. There is a list of trappable errors available in online help. If you view the `On Error` statement in help and select the See Also choice, it will open a dialog with other topics. You can then select the "Trappable Errors" topic.

Workshop

Here are some questions and exercises to assist with your review of this hour's material. The answers to the quiz questions can be found in Appendix A, "Quiz Answers."

Quiz

1. How can I halt the execution of my procedure for debugging?

2. If you have the Locals window to view the values for the variables, why would you want to use the Immediate window?

3. What is the first step for error handling?

Exercises

1. Examine your list of tasks to automate to determine where you might need error handling.

2. Rewrite the DueDateCalc using a MsgBox to ask if the user wants to use the current date and skip the InputBox line.

8

HOUR 9

Working with Text

Given that Microsoft Word is a word processor, many of the tasks you will want to automate will involve inserting text into a document.

The highlights of this hour include

- Adding text
- Using AutoText
- Inserting files
- Adding fields

Adding Text

When you want to work with text, one of the first methods for automating the placement of text in a document is one that was illustrated in Hour 2, "Getting Started with VBA." You can use the TypeText method.

In addition to inserting plain text, you will also be required to manage special text codes like paragraph marks and tabs. You may even work with special characters and symbols.

Inserting Text

First, you will learn to enter plain text. The `TypeText` method for the `Selection` object enables you to insert text at the insertion point or replace text if an area is selected. Its syntax is

```
expression.TypeText Text:=Text
```

The expression represents the `Selection` object that is going to receive the text. It is followed by the `TypeText` method separated by a period. The `TypeText` method has one argument: `Text`. It is the text to be inserted. For example, the following line of code inserts a sentence:

```
Selection.TypeText Text:= "Thank you for your order."
```

The `Text` argument can be a string as shown in this example. If you are using a string, it must be enclosed in quotation marks. You can also insert the value of a string variable as shown below. For more information on using variables, please refer to Hour 5, "Exploring VBA."

```
Dim strThanks
StrThanks = "Thank you for your order."
Selection.TypeText Text:=strThanks
```

The text is put in at the insertion point, but very little checking occurs as the text is inserted. If you are getting information from users, you might want to check the information before using the `TypeText` method.

Processing User Entries

When you are getting information from the user for the completion of text, you can use an `InputBox`, `Form`, or `User Form`. You normally will use variables to store that information from the user. At times, you will want to verify the data and possibly change the position of the information.

In those instances, you can rely on the text functions. These built-in functions assist with verifying the contents of data, as well as manipulating it.

Verifying text can be as simple as the test that was used in Hour 7, "Understanding Repetitive Processing with Loops." You can use the `Len` function to make sure a string isn't empty. Its syntax is

```
Len(string)
```

Another function that you might want to take advantage of is the Trim function. It will remove any extra spaces entered before or after the text. Its syntax is also very straight-forward:

```
Trim(string)
```

Four additional functions are useful for working with only part of a string. You can use the Instr function to locate a character in a string. You can use the Left, Right, or Mid functions to retrieve a substring from a string.

With these functions, you can reorder a string if needed. As an example, when you ask the user for a full name with an InputBox, you can use this function to flip the first and last names. The code might resemble Listing 9.1.

LISTING 9.1   The ReverseName Procedure

```
 1: Sub ReverseName()
 2:     Dim strName As String, lSpace As Long, strFirst As String,
           ➥ strLast As String
 3:     strName = InputBox("Please enter your full name.", "Name Entry")
 4:     If Len(strName) = 0 Then Exit Sub
 5:     lSpace = InStr(1, Trim$(strName), Chr$(32))
 6:     If lSpace <> 0 Then
 7:         strFirst = Left$(strName, lSpace - 1)
 8:         strLast = Right$(strName, Len(strName) - lSpace)
 9:         Selection.TypeText Text:=strLast & ", " & strFirst
10:     Else
11:         Selection.TypeText Text:=strName
12:     End If
13: End Sub
```

ANALYSIS In ReverseName, variables are declared to facilitate the task of swapping positions. The variable, strName, is assigned the entry in the InputBox. Line 4 uses the Len function to make sure that the variable isn't empty.

Line 5 is where the swapping process begins. The Instr function is used to locate the space entered in the string. Its syntax is

InStr([*start,*]*string1, string2*[, *compare*])

The Instr keyword is followed by its arguments in parentheses:

- The start argument is the character position in the string where you will begin searching.

- String1 is the argument that points to the string to be searched.

- `String2` is the string to locate.
- `Compare` enables you to control how the strings are compared.

In this example, you are hunting for a space. When you are creating code, you might know exactly what you are writing, but when you go back to look at it later, the meaning might not be clear. The `Chr$` function can be helpful in this case. Instead of having " " to indicate a space, the `Chr$` function returns the code for a space.

To locate a tab marker, you don't have to use the `Chr$` function. In some cases, there is a built-in constant, such as `vbTab`, which you can use to look for a tab marker.

The last argument has been omitted from this code sample. It enables you to control how the strings are compared. It isn't needed here because the space is a special character that has no case.

The `lSpace` variable will store a numeric value indicating the position in the string for the space. If it is set to `0`, there is no space in the string.

If there is a space, line 7 begins breaking the string into two pieces. The variable, `strFirst`, is set using the `Left` function. The `Left` function returns a specific number of characters from a string. In this case, it is taking the position of the space and subtracting `1` to get the characters to the left of the space.

Line 8 does the same thing in reverse. It is using the `Right` function to return a specific number of characters from the right of the string. It takes the length of the string and returns only the characters to the right of the space represented by `lSpace`.

Then line 9 uses the `TypeText` method to switch the first and last name. The ampersands indicate that you want to concatenate the strings. The comma and space are enclosed in quotations rather than being represented by a variable.

NEW TERM   To *concatenate* strings means taking each string and creating a larger string. The first string is the first part of the larger string. Its last character is followed by the first character of the second string, and so on.

If a space isn't found, the `Else` clause takes the entire string and inserts it into the text.

Here is what you will do to see the results of this procedure:

1. Run the `ReverseName` macro.
2. Type a name in the `InputBox` (see Figure 9.1) and press Enter.

FIGURE 9.1

The InputBox with a two-word name.

3. Notice the first name is placed after the last name, separated by a comma and a space as shown in Figure 9.2.

FIGURE 9.2

The name is now reversed in the document.

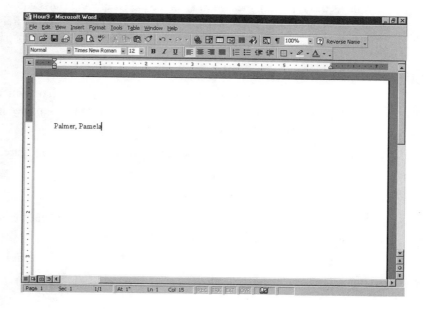

This is a very simple example of swapping a first and last name to illustrate the use of these functions. It doesn't have any elaborate code to deal with names, such as Mary Jo Harris or Kristen Van Hope, which have more than two words in them.

In cases where you deal with two-word names, you are better off switching from an `InputBox` to a `Form` or `User Form`. These enable you to solicit each part of the name separately.

Inserting Paragraph Marks

In addition to inserting text, you may want to add additional text markers such as the end of a paragraph mark. You don't do this with the `TypeText` method.

In the `SelectMemo` macro, you used the captured macro from Hour 2 as the base for the text. It included text that used the Enter key to produce a paragraph mark. In the code, you have the following:

```
Selection.TypeParagraph
```

The `TypeParagraph` method is the equivalent of pressing the Enter key. You have the `Selection` object followed by a period and the `TypeParagraph` method. If this method follows the `TypeText` method, it ends the paragraph and starts a new line. This is very useful when you are going to create several paragraphs of text or a list with a procedure. If text is selected, it will delete the text and replace it with a blank paragraph.

Inserting Symbols

Another task that you may want to automate is the insertion of symbols. If you frequently use a symbol in your work, you can eliminate the steps needed to add it from one of the fonts available on your machine:

1. Select Insert, Symbols to open the Symbols dialog (see Figure 9.3).
2. Select a font and a symbol.
3. Select Insert and select Close.

To insert a symbol in your procedure, you use the `InsertSymbol` method. It enables you to indicate the font and symbol needed. Its syntax is

```
expression.InsertSymbol(CharacterNumber, Font, Unicode, Bias)
```

The expression represents the `Selection` object to use followed by a period. It is followed by the `InsertSymbol` keyword. There are four named arguments:

- `CharacterNumber` is the code for that specific symbol.
- `Font` is the name of the font to retrieve the symbol.
- `Unicode` indicates whether to insert a regular text character or a Unicode symbol.
- `Bias` is used when you are working with other languages.

FIGURE 9.3

The Symbols dialog enables you to insert a symbol from one of the fonts or a special character.

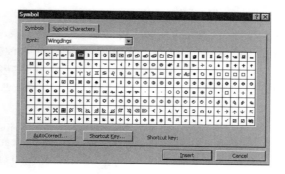

9

One thought that might cross your mind as you look at the Symbols dialog is using the AutoCorrect button to turn the symbol into an AutoCorrect entry.

If you plan to share your template with others, this isn't the best solution. AutoCorrect entries aren't stored in the template. The user who receives the template will not have that entry, so the procedure will not produce the desired results.

Using AutoText

Using the `TypeText` and `TypeParagraph` methods, as discussed above, is one way to automate text creation, but it isn't the easiest method to use when editing text. When you revised the text of the `StaffMeeting` macro to produce the `GeneralMemo` subprocedure, you might have found it difficult to keep track of the flow of the paragraph because of the coding.

In Hour 1, "Introducing Automation Fundamentals," you reviewed how to create and use AutoText entries. AutoText entries enable you to create your text in the document and save it as an AutoText entry to be used at a later time. You can include text, paragraph marks, formatting, tables, graphics, etc. Anything that can be placed in the document can be stored as an AutoText entry.

Combining Visual Basic and AutoText entries can give you the best of both features. You can save the text you need as an AutoText entry and use Visual Basic to insert it into your document. To insert an AutoText entry, use the `Insert` method for the `AutoTextEntries` collection from the template. The syntax is

```
expression.Insert(Where, RichText)
```

The expression indicates the chosen template's `AutoTextEntries` collection item. It is followed by a period and the `Insert` method. It has two arguments. The `Where` argument indicates the location to place the information and `RichText` indicates whether it maintains its original formatting or adopts the formatting of the location. By default, it keeps its formatting.

The procedure created in Hour 5 to create a task template can be simplified by using AutoText entries. The original code was very tedious to create because you switched the formatting on and off. If the text block were saved as an AutoText entry, the code is much simpler. Instead of the procedure shown in Listing 9.2, you could use the code in Listing 9.3.

LISTING 9.2   The Original `TaskSetUpwithFor`

```
 1: Sub TaskSetUpwithFor()
 2: '
 3: ' TaskSetUpRecorded Macro
 4: ' Set up template for Tasks
 5: '
 6:     Selection.ParagraphFormat.TabStops.Add Position:=InchesToPoints(1.53), _
 7:         Alignment:=wdAlignTabLeft, Leader:=wdTabLeaderSpaces
 8:     With Selection.ParagraphFormat
 9:         .LeftIndent = InchesToPoints(1.53)
10:         .FirstLineIndent = InchesToPoints(-0.95)
11:     End With
12:     Dim lTask As Long, lNumberofTasks As Long
13:     lNumberofTasks = InputBox("How many tasks?", "Number of Tasks", "1")
14:     For lTask = 1 To lNumberofTasks
15:         Selection.Font.Bold = wdToggle
16:         Selection.TypeText Text:="Task:"
17:         Selection.Font.Bold = wdToggle
18:         Selection.TypeText Text:=vbTab
19:         Selection.TypeParagraph
20:         Selection.Font.Bold = wdToggle
21:         Selection.TypeText Text:="Due Date:"
```

```
22:         Selection.Font.Bold = wdToggle
23:         Selection.TypeText Text:=vbTab
24:         Selection.TypeParagraph
25:         Selection.Font.Bold = wdToggle
26:         Selection.TypeText Text:="Status:"
27:         Selection.Font.Bold = wdToggle
28:         Selection.TypeText Text:=vbTab
29:         Selection.TypeParagraph
30:         Selection.Font.Bold = wdToggle
31:         Selection.TypeText Text:="Description:"
32:         Selection.Font.Bold = wdToggle
33:         Selection.TypeText Text:=vbTab
34:         Selection.TypeParagraph
35:         Selection.TypeParagraph
36:     Next lTask
37: End Sub
```

LISTING 9.3   The Revised TaskSetUp Procedure

```
1: Sub RevisedTaskSetUp()
2: ' TaskSetUp procedure using an AutoText entry.
3:     Dim lTask As Long, lNumberofTasks As Long
4:     lNumberofTasks = InputBox("How many tasks?", "Number of Tasks", "1")
5:     For lTask = 1 To lNumberofTasks
6:         ActiveDocument.AttachedTemplate.AutoTextEntries("TaskSetUp") _
7:             .Insert Where:=Selection.Range, RichText:=True
8:     Next lTask
9: End Sub
```

ANALYSIS   The original procedure has 37 lines compared to the 9 lines of the new one using the AutoText entry. You eliminated all the formatting for the paragraph before you began adding tasks.

The lines that create the text are also reduced because you aren't building the text character by character with all the formatting. These lines are replaced by one Insert statement. You indicate which entry you want to insert with the location for the text. You must, however, use the RichText argument so that the entry retains all the formatting saved with the text in the AutoText entry.

Inserting Files

Another mechanism for bringing existing material into your document is to insert an existing file into it. Manually, this is accomplished by selecting Insert, File and using the resulting Insert File dialog to locate the file to insert. To automate the process, you use the `InsertFile` method. With this method, you can control the way the file is inserted into your current file. The method's syntax is

```
expression.InsertFile(FileName, Range, ConfirmConversions, Link, Attachment)
```

The expression represents the range or selection you are using. It is followed by a period and the `InsertFile` keyword. There are five arguments that can be set for this method:

- `FileName`: This argument is required because it represents the file name and path for the file to be inserted. If the path is omitted, the current folder is assumed.

- `Range`: This argument is optional, but it does give you a greater control over the placement of the inserted file. The `Range` argument can indicate a bookmark where the text to insert is located in the document. A *bookmark* is a placeholder in your document. (For more information about creating and using bookmarks, please refer to Hour 14, "Working with Large Documents.")

- `ConfirmConversions`: The `InsertFile` method can insert many types of files into your Word document. The `ConfirmConversions` arguments can be set to `True` to confirm a conversion.

- `Link`: You can use this argument to indicate that, rather than insert the file, you want to reference it. This method insures you will always see the most current version of the file.

- `Attachment`: This argument is used if you are automating actions to create email messages.

> If you are using the Macro Recorder to capture the insertion of a file, make sure that you check whether a path was included for the `FileName` argument. In most cases, you will want to include a path for the file name and not depend on the current path. You can't guarantee what the current path will be when your procedure is run.

Working with Folders

When you automate the insertion of a file, finding that file can be a problem. If you don't include a path, the `InsertFile` method assumes the file is in the current folder. Unfortunately, the current folder used while you create a procedure may not be the current folder when the file is called.

The first thing to consider is where to place the file. You may want to designate a special folder for files you insert on a regular basis. After you have decided to place the file to be inserted in a special folder, you enter the path and file name as a string. If you plan to share the procedure with others, however, you cannot guarantee that the folder will exist on their systems.

One alternative is to use one of the folders specified in the user Options. When a user sets up Word, several folders are referenced for specific files. If you select File, Options and select the File Locations tab (see Figure 9.4), several folders are specified. You might store the file to insert in one of these folders for easier access.

FIGURE 9.4

The Options enable you to set specific folders for Word information.

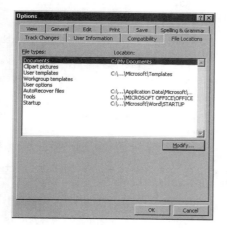

If you use one of the folders listed in the File Locations tab, you don't have to know the name of the document's folder when you create the procedure. There is a property, `DefaultFilePath()`, that enables you to retrieve that information as needed. It is an array that stores all the file paths listed in the Options dialog.

For example, you create a special folder for inserted files. It is placed in the Documents folder listed in the Options dialog. You can build a string storing the path using that property:

```
Dim strFilePath as string
StrFilePath = Options.DefaultFilePath(wdDocumentsPath) _
    & "\Insert Files\Development Cycle.doc"
```

This eliminates the problem of locating the file, but it isn't the end of all possible problems. You still can't guarantee that the file will exist. You need error handling.

Inserting a File

After you determine what file you are going to insert and where you are going to place it, you are ready to automate its insertion. The code might resemble the code outlined in Listing 9.4.

LISTING 9.4 The `InsertDevCycle` Procedure

```
 1: Sub InsertDevCycle()
 2: '   This procedure inserts the Development Cycle Document
 3:     On Error GoTo DevError
 4:     ActiveDocument.AttachedTemplate.AutoTextEntries("Automate") _
 5:         .Insert Where:=Selection.Range, RichText:=True
 6:     Dim strFilePath As String
 7:     strFilePath = Options.DefaultFilePath(wdDocumentsPath) _
 8:         & "\Insert Files\Development Cycle.doc"
 9:     Selection.InsertFile FileName:=strFilePath, Range:="", _
10:         ConfirmConversions:=False, Link:=False, Attachment:=False
11:     Exit Sub
12: DevError:
13:     Dim strMessage As String, strTitle As String
14:     Select Case Err.Number
15:         Case 5273       'Path or File not valid
16:             strMessage = _
17:             "Please verify the Insert Files folder exists and try again."
18:             strTitle = "Invalid Folder or File Name"
19:         Case 5174       'File Couldn't be found
20:             strMessage = _
21:             "Please verify the Development Cycle file is in the folder."
22:             strTitle = "Missing File"
23:         Case Else
24:             strMessage = "Error " & Err.Number & "," & _
25:             Err.Description & "has occurred. Processing was halted."
26:             strTitle = "Unexpected Error"
27:     End Select
28:     MsgBox strMessage, vbOKOnly + vbExclamation, strTitle
29: End Sub
```

ANALYSIS The `InsertDevCycle` procedure illustrates the combination of using AutoText entries and separate files to add information to a document automatically. The first step on line 3 is to initialize the error handler. Given that this procedure is interacting with an outside resource, take into account that there may be problems with that resource. Here the error handler is instructed to use the code in `DevError` if anything fails to execute.

Lines 4–8 insert the AutoText entry and set up the string for the file path using the document path from the Options dialog. Line 9 inserts the file. This step is the one most likely to fail. It is followed by the Exit Sub command to indicate that if the procedure functions properly, execution should stop here.

Line 12 is the line label for the error handling code. It has a standard Select Case to test the `Err.Number` property.

The first case begins on line 15. It is responding to error `5273`. This error is generated if there is a problem locating or accessing the path or file indicated. If this error is generated, a message and title for the message box is assigned.

Line 19 is the case to respond to error `5174`, which is generated if the file is missing. It also sets up a message and title variable.

> If the document you are attempting to insert has a password, you will be prompted to enter this password, just as you would if you were inserting manually. You may want to consider making the files to be inserted read-only instead of using passwords.

Line 23 is just a `Case Else` for any unforeseen errors. It sets up a message and title as well. Regardless what error occurs, the error is displayed in a `MsgBox`, and the procedure ends.

Adding Fields

Another document element you might like to add to your document is a Word field. This is done manually by selecting Insert, Field. It displays the Field dialog (see Figure 9.5).

FIGURE 9.5

Using the Insert Field dialog gives you access to information without having to enter it each time in your document.

When you want to automate the addition of fields, you will use the Add method for the Fields collection for selection. The syntax is

```
expression.Add(Range, Type, Text, PreserveFormatting)
```

The expression indicates the Fields object followed by a period. The Add method is followed by parentheses with the arguments needed to add to the Fields collection:

- Range: This is the first argument. It is required because it indicates where you want to add the field.
- Type: Range can be followed by the Type argument. It indicates the kind of field you want to insert. There are constants for the field types to make them easier to set.
- Text: This is an optional argument for those fields that have text to work with.
- PreserveFormatting: This argument saves the current formatting of the field as it is updated.

Using Fields can minimize the amount of editing needed for information that changes each time the document is accessed. For example, add the following code to display the date the document was last saved:

```
Selection.TypeText Text:="The document was last saved on: "
Selection.Fields.Add Range:=Selection.Range, Type:=wdFieldSaveDate, Text:= _
    "SAVEDATE \@ ""MMMM d, yyyy""", PreserveFormatting:=True
```

The beginning of the sentence is entered into the document with the TypeText method. It is followed by the Add method to add the save date field.

There are 88 fields that can be inserted into the document. In the dialog, they are separated into categories. Two categories, that you will use more than the others, might need special handling.

Taking Advantage of User Information

The first category of fields that can require more than just inserting the field is the User Information category. The User information fields include information that is entered by the user in the Options dialog. This includes the user's name, initials, and address. To enter them automatically, you can use Listing 9.5.

LISTING 9.5   The InsertUser Procedure

```
1: Sub InsertUser()
2:     Selection.TypeText Text:="For more information, please contact:"
3:     Selection.TypeParagraph
4:     Selection.Fields.Add Range:=Selection.Range, Type:=wdFieldUserName
```

```
5:      Selection.TypeParagraph
6:      Selection.Fields.Add Range:=Selection.Range, Type:=wdFieldUserInitials
7:      Selection.TypeParagraph
8:      Selection.Fields.Add Range:=Selection.Range, Type:=wdFieldUserAddress
9: End Sub
```

This code will generate the text you want, unless the user hasn't filled in one of the options. When the procedure is called, a missing field will be shown as an empty field as shown in Figure 9.6.

FIGURE 9.6

The field can't display the address because there isn't one.

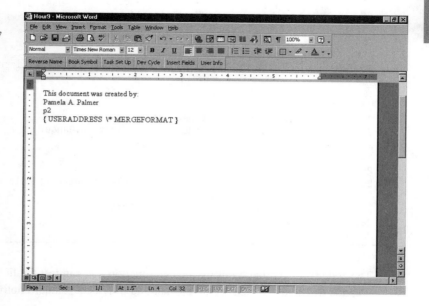

To remedy this, first check to see if the information exists. This can be done with properties. The `Application` object has three properties to provide access to these options.

You have the `UserName`, `UserInitials`, and `UserAddress` properties. You can use these properties in conjunction with some condition testing to prevent this problem, as shown in Listing 9.6.

LISTING 9.6   The Revised `InsertUser` Procedure

```
1: Sub InsertUser()
2:      Selection.TypeText Text:="For more information, contact:"
3:      Selection.TypeParagraph
4:      If Len(Application.UserName) > 0 Then
```

continues

LISTING 9.6 continued

```
 5:          Selection.Fields.Add Range:=Selection.Range,
            ➡Type:=wdFieldUserName
 6:          Selection.TypeParagraph
 7:      Else
 8:          MsgBox _
 9:            "The name is missing, please enter it into the document.", _
10:            vbInformation, "Missing Data"
11:      End If
12:      If Len(Application.UserInitials) > 0 Then
13:          Selection.Fields.Add Range:=Selection.Range, _
14:              Type:=wdFieldUserInitials
15:          Selection.TypeParagraph
16:      Else
17:          MsgBox _
18:              "The initials are missing, please enter it into
                ➡the document.", _
19:              vbInformation, "Missing Data"
20:      End If
21:      If Len(Application.UserAddress) > 0 Then
22:          Selection.Fields.Add Range:=Selection.Range, _
23:              Type:=wdFieldUserAddress
24:      Else
25:          MsgBox _
26:              "The address is missing, please enter it into
                ➡the document.", _
27:              vbInformation, "Missing Data"
28:      End If
29: End Sub
```

The code is longer, but by using the Len function you can test the field contents before you add the field. The results are cleaner and provide a standard notification that something is wrong (see Figure 9.7).

> If you want, you can prompt the user for the entry and set the option, or you can open the Options dialog for them. These two processes are covered later in Hour 21, "Working with Microsoft Outlook, the Internet, and Windows," and Hour 16, "Working with Auto Macros, Events, and Built-In Dialogs."

FIGURE 9.7

The message box notification is standard and won't upset the user.

Taking Advantage of Document Information

The second category you will use frequently is the document information field. It enables you to add information stored in the built-in document properties or custom properties. These are listed in the Properties dialog (see Figure 9.8).

FIGURE 9.8

The Properties dialog displays the statistics about the file.

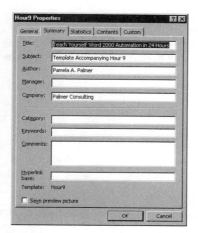

All the properties displayed on the first three tabs are part of the built-in properties. They have fields that will automatically pull the information. If you want to verify the data, you use the `BuiltinDocumentsProperties` property.

The last tab is the Custom tab. It enables you to create your own properties. Do this with a special field called `DocProperty`. You have to include the `Text` argument with the name of the property. To verify contents, you use the `CustomDocumentProperties` property.

To add the author, title, subject, and the custom property, use both methods. The code might look like that in Listing 9.7.

LISTING 9.7   The `InsertDocumentPages` Procedure

```
1: Sub InsertDocumentProps()
2:     Selection.TypeText Text:="This document titled, "
3:     Selection.Fields.Add Range:=Selection.Range, Type:=wdFieldTitle
4:     Selection.TypeText Text:=", concerning "
5:     Selection.Fields.Add Range:=Selection.Range, Type:=wdFieldSubject
6:     Selection.TypeText Text:=". It was prepared by "
7:     Selection.Fields.Add Range:=Selection.Range, Type:=wdFieldAuthor
8:     Selection.TypeText Text:=" and typed by "
```

continues

LISTING 9.7 continued

```
 9:     Selection.Fields.Add Range:=Selection.Range, Type:=wdFieldEmpty,
        ➥Text:=
10:        "DOCPROPERTY ""Typist"" "
11:     Selection.TypeText Text:="."
12: End Sub
```

The document properties are very useful for creating headers and footers. For more information on creating headers and footers with VBA, please refer to Hour 11, "Working with Page Appearance and Printing."

Summary

In this hour, you have explored different methods for inserting information into a document with VBA. In addition to the `TypeText` method (used to insert text a character at a time) and the `TypeParagraph` (used to get a new paragraph), you examined how you can use Symbols, AutoText entries, separate files and fields.

You learned that the `Insert` method for the `AutoTextEntries` collections was much easier to use than the `TypeText` method for longer text strings because you could get the text organized as needed and then insert it anytime. To change the text, use the AutoText entry instead of the code.

You learned that inserting a file is a good way to integrate lengthier text from different documents. You also learned it has one disadvantage. You need error handling to deal with that possibility that the file may not be accessible when a user wants to insert it.

You also learned that there is a lot of information readily available by using fields. These fields can be inserted by using the `Add` method for the `Fields` collection for the document. If you haven't worked with fields, you might want to review the field settings with on-line help.

Q&A

Q What is the purpose of the `TypeParagraph`, `InsertParagraph`, `InsertParagraphAfter`, and `InsertParagraphBefore` methods?

A The insert methods give you more control when you are working with larger documents and using the Outline view. For more information, please see Hour 14.

Q **Why are there properties and fields for some of the options and properties?**

A With VBA, you need both, depending on what you are trying to accomplish. Using the fields enables you to display the information in the document. If you want to just retrieve, evaluate, or set the options or properties, you will work with the specific properties.

Workshop

9

Here are some questions and exercises to help you review the information covered in this hour. The answers to the quiz questions can be found in Appendix A, "Quiz Answers."

Quiz

1. What argument is needed to make sure that the formatting is inserted in the document with the text of an AutoText entry?

2. Why is error handling needed when inserting a file?

3. How would you access the Company property (another one of the document properties) and place it in the document?

4. How would you access the Checked by property (another one of the custom properties) and place it in the document?

Exercises

1. Review your list of tasks to automate and record where you are going to use the techniques discussed in this hour.

2. Modify the InsertDocumentProps procedure to check to see if the property has anything in it before inserting the field.

HOUR 10

Adjusting Text Appearance

In Hour 9, "Working with Text," you explored different approaches to adding text to a document with VBA. After the text is in place, you often add formatting. Now, you will explore different methods for formatting text automatically.

The highlights of this hour include

- Applying formatting
- Working with paragraph formatting
- Using tabs, borders, and lists
- Working with styles

Applying Formatting

In Hour 7, "Understanding Repetitive Processing with Loops," you were experimenting with loops to generate a framework for task reporting. In that framework, you had a label at the beginning of the line followed by a tab and the description of that label. The labels were bold to set them apart from the rest of the text. This format was accomplished with the following line of code:

```
Selection.Font.Bold = wdToggle
```

There are times when you must apply formatting directly to the text in a procedure. You have access to all the text formatting that is available from the Format menu with Visual Basic for Applications (VBA). When you want to work with the text formatting, you work with the Font object for the selected text. The Font object is accessible through the Font property as shown in the line above.

To control various aspects of character formatting, the Font object has a group of properties. They duplicate the choices represented in the Font dialog. In the example above, you set the Bold property. It can be turned on with a setting of True or turned off with a setting of False. In this case, a special constant is used. It is wdToggle. This constant reverses the current setting of the property.

There are 23 Font properties that you will use on a regular basis to adjust the text's appearance. To get a better idea of what is possible, you are going to use the Macro Recorder to make a font change:

1. Create a new document and type in a phrase such as Need Time? and press Enter.
2. Select the phrase.
3. Double-click on Rec on the status bar to open the Record Macro dialog.
4. Enter FormatLead as the name and press Enter to begin recording.
5. Select Format, Font to open the Font dialog as shown in Figure 10.1.

FIGURE 10.1

The Font tab in the Font dialog enables you to format text in one action.

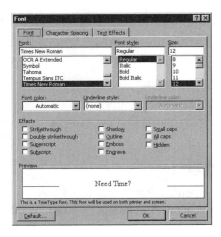

6. Select Arial as Font, Bold as the Font Style, and 24 as the Size.

7. Select the color of your choice such as Blue.

8. Select Small Caps for Effects.

9. Click on the Character Spacing tab.

10. Select Expanded in the Spacing drop-down list and enter 10 pts in its By text box. Select Raised from the Position drop-down list and enter 3 pts in its By text box.

11. Click OK to accept the changes and click the Stop button on the Macro toolbar to stop recording.

12. Click somewhere on the document to release the highlight.

Now the text appears as shown in Figure 10.2. It is beginning to look like a banner on a flyer, and you have created a new macro that will enable you to duplicate this formatting again.

10

FIGURE 10.2

The text formatting has been applied to the phrase.

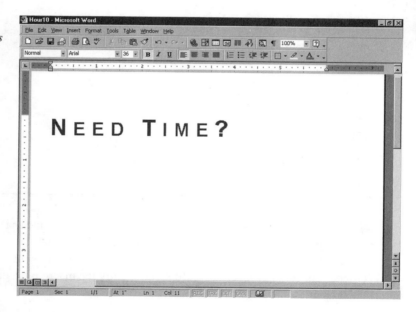

All the specified formatting has been stored in a macro so you can call on it in the future. The procedure that was created is shown in Listing 10.1.

LISTING 10.1   The FormatLead Procedure

```
 1: Sub FormatLead()
 2: '
 3: ' FormatLead Macro
 4: ' Macro recorded 5/18/99 by Pamela A. Palmer
 5: '
 6:     With Selection.Font
 7:         .Name = "Arial"
 8:         .Size = 36
 9:         .Bold = True
10:         .Italic = False
11:         .Underline = wdUnderlineNone
12:         .UnderlineColor = wdColorAutomatic
13:         .StrikeThrough = False
14:         .DoubleStrikeThrough = False
15:         .Outline = False
16:         .Emboss = False
17:         .Shadow = False
18:         .Hidden = False
19:         .SmallCaps = True
20:         .AllCaps = False
21:         .Color = wdColorDarkBlue
22:         .Engrave = False
23:         .Superscript = False
24:         .Subscript = False
25:         .Spacing = 10
26:         .Scaling = 100
27:         .Position = 3
28:         .Kerning = 0
29:         .Animation = wdAnimationNone
30:     End With
31: End Sub
```

ANALYSIS   All the formatting for the phrase has been set using the With...End With structure. Despite the fact that you only adjusted seven attributes, the Macro Recorder sets all 23 properties. This makes them easy to review, but this method isn't the most efficient for setting properties. Before you modify the macro procedure, you can review the properties that are set in Table 10.1.

TABLE 10.1   The Font Properties as They Appear in the Font Dialog

Property	Description
The Font Tab	
Name	It sets the font name. It must have a valid font name enclosed in quotations.

Property	Description
Bold	It sets the font weight with True, False, or wdtoggle to switch between the two states.
Italic	It sets the slant of the characters with True, False or wdtoggle to switch between the two states.
Size	It sets the size of the characters measured in points.
Color	It sets the color of the text using built-in constants for the color choice such as wdColorDarkBlue.
Underline	It sets the style of underline using built-in constants such as wbUnderlineNone.
UnderlineColor	It sets the color of the underline using built-in constants such as wdColorAutomatic.
StrikeThrough	It indicates whether the characters have a line through them with True, False, or wdtoggle to switch between the two states.
DoubleStrikeThrough	It indicates whether the characters have a double line through them with True, False, or wdtoggle to switch between the two states.
Superscript	It determines whether the characters are shown raised from the base line in a smaller text rather than plain text.
Subscript	It determines whether the characters are shown lowered from the base line in a smaller text rather than plain text.
Shadow	It determines whether the characters have a shadow behind the text.
Outline	It determines whether the characters are shown in outline rather than solid text.
Emboss	It determines whether the characters are shown embossed rather than plain text.
Engrave	It determines whether the characters are shown engraved rather than plain text.
SmallCaps	It determines whether the characters are shown in capital letters with the lower case letters smaller than the true capital letters.
AllCaps	It determines whether the characters are shown in all capital letters rather than plain text.
Hidden	It determines whether the characters aren't visible when document marks aren't shown.

The Character Spacing Tab

Spacing	It determines whether the characters are farther apart or closer together than normal text. It is set using points.

10

continues

TABLE 10.1   continued

Property	Description
Scaling	It determines if the text is scaled from the default text size.
Position	It determines whether the text is raised or lowered from the base line.
Kerning	It sets the minimum point size that can be kerned. Kerning is the adjusting of the space between pairs of letters. For example, the letter *w* takes more space than the letter *i*; therefore, Kerning adjusts the amount of space between other letters and the *i* to avoid large gaps of white space.
	The Animation Tab
Animation	It sets the animation type for the text using built-in constants such as wdAnimationNone.

When you are entering your own code to set the Font properties, include only the ones you need.

If you use the Macro Recorder, you can delete the ones you didn't set to make the code run faster. In this small example, this deletion won't make much of a difference. Larger procedures can definitely benefit from any time savings you can include. The revised macro, shown in Listing 10.2, is much more compact.

LISTING 10.2   The FormatLead Procedure with Changes

```
 1: Sub FormatLeadRevised()
 2:     With Selection.Font
 3:         .Name = "Arial"
 4:         .Size = 36
 5:         .Bold = True
 6:         .SmallCaps = True
 7:         .Color = wdColorDarkBlue
 8:         .Spacing = 10
 9:         .Position = 3
10:     End With
11: End Sub
```

Working with Paragraph Formatting

In addition to setting the appearance of the text, you might want to adjust the formatting for the paragraph. The formatting for the paragraphs is handled by more than one dialog.

The first method for adjusting the appearance of the paragraph is to use the Format, Paragraph command to open the Paragraph dialog (see Figure 10.3).

FIGURE 10.3
The Paragraph dialog enables you to control the behavior of the selected paragraph.

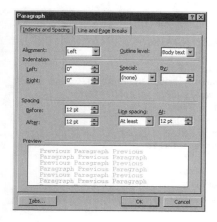

It can be used to control the indention of a paragraph or the amount of space before or after the paragraph. It can also be used to control how the line and page breaks will be handled if this paragraph is at the bottom of the page.

Just as with the Font settings, you have more than one method for setting the properties. You can use the Font dialog and set everything at once, or you can use the buttons on the toolbar. With Paragraph settings, you can use the Paragraph dialog or use the toolbar or adjust the ruler.

If you use the Macro Recorder, the buttons on the toolbar and any adjustments to the ruler will each be listed as separate actions. If you use the dialog, it will record the settings using the With structure. Regardless, you will be setting properties.

To get a better feel for setting the paragraph properties, you want to create a macro to center the Need Time? phrase and add some white space below. Turn on the Macro Recorder and use the dialog. It generates the code shown in Listing 10.3.

LISTING 10.3   The LeadParagraph Procedure Created by the Macro Recorder

```
1: Sub LeadParagraph()
2: '
3: ' LeadParagraph Macro
4: ' Macro recorded 5/18/99 by Pamela A. Palmer
5: '
```

continues

LISTING 10.3 continued

```
 6:     With Selection.ParagraphFormat
 7:         .LeftIndent = InchesToPoints(0)
 8:         .RightIndent = InchesToPoints(0)
 9:         .SpaceBefore = 0
10:         .SpaceBeforeAuto = False
11:         .SpaceAfter = 12
12:         .SpaceAfterAuto = False
13:         .LineSpacingRule = wdLineSpaceSingle
14:         .Alignment = wdAlignParagraphCenter
15:         .WidowControl = True
16:         .KeepWithNext = True
17:         .KeepTogether = False
18:         .PageBreakBefore = False
19:         .NoLineNumber = False
20:         .Hyphenation = True
21:         .FirstLineIndent = InchesToPoints(0)
22:         .OutlineLevel = wdOutlineLevelBodyText
23:         .CharacterUnitLeftIndent = 0
24:         .CharacterUnitRightIndent = 0
25:         .CharacterUnitFirstLineIndent = 0
26:         .LineUnitBefore = 0
27:         .LineUnitAfter = 0
28:     End With
29: End Sub
```

To change the paragraph settings, you can adjust the properties for the `ParagraphFormat` object, which is represented by the `Selection`'s `ParagraphFormat` property in line 6. The Macro Recorder has used the `With...End With` structure to set all the properties, despite the fact you only changed the alignment and spacing.

If you enter this macro without relying on the recorder, the code can be much shorter. This procedure can be revised as shown in Listing 10.4.

LISTING 10.4 The `LeadParagraph` Procedure with Changes

```
Sub LeadParagraphRevised()
    With Selection.ParagraphFormat
        .SpaceAfter = 12
        .SpaceAfterAuto = False
        .Alignment = wdAlignParagraphCenter
    End With
End Sub
```

The key to setting the paragraph properties is to understand what each setting does for you. Each property is introduced in Table 10.2.

TABLE 10.2 The Paragraph Properties as They Appear in the Dialog

Property	Description
The Indents and Spacing Tab	
Alignment	This sets the alignment of the selection using built-in constants such as `wdAlignParagraphCenter`.
OutlineLevel	This sets the outline level for this paragraph for display in Outline view. It is set with built-in constants such as `wdOutlineLevelBodyText`.
LeftIndent	This sets the indention from the left margin for the selection. It is measured in points.
RightIndent	This sets the indention from the right margin for the selection. It is measured in points.
FirstLineIndent	This sets the indention of the first line from the left margin for the selection. It is measured in points. It is used to create an indented first line or a hanging indent.
SpaceBefore	This sets the amount of white space above the paragraph for the selection. It is measured in points.
SpaceBeforeAuto	This indicates that the spacing before a selection is automatically set by Word. If you want to set a specific amount of space above a paragraph, you must set this property equal to `False`.
SpaceAfter	This sets the amount of white space below the paragraph for the selection. It is measured in points.
SpaceAfterAuto	This indicates that the spacing after a selection is automatically set by Word. If you want to set a specific amount of space above a paragraph, you must set this property equal to `False`.
LineSpacingRule	This sets how much white space there should be in between lines using built-in constants such as `wdLineSpaceSingle`.
The Line and Page Break Tab	
WidowControl	If it is set to `True`, this property indicates that the first and last lines of a paragraph must remain on the same page as the rest of the paragraph.

10

continues

TABLE 10.2   continued

Property	Description
KeepWithNext	If it is set to True, this property indicates that the paragraph must remain on the same page as the following paragraph.
KeepTogether	If it is set to True, this property indicates that all the lines of the paragraph must stay on the same page.
PageBreakBefore	If it is set to True, this property will force a new page before the selected paragraph.
NoLineNumber	If it is set to True, this property indicates that the paragraphs should not be numbered.
Hyphenation	If it is set to True, this property indicates that the paragraph can be adjusted by automatic hyphenation.

There are five additional properties listed in the code generated by the Macro Recorder that aren't listed in the dialog. They are the Language Specific Properties to support east Asian languages, which are used in place of their regular counterparts:

```
CharacterUnitLeftIndent

CharacterUnitRightIndent

CharacterUnitFirstLineIndent

LineUnitBefore

LineUnitAfter
```

As you examine the code generated by the Macro Recorder, you may have noticed the function InchestoPoints used to populate several of the properties. There are several instances where a property is expecting a measurement in points. For example, lines 7–8 of Listing 10.3 set properties that require a measurement in points where you most likely are used to working with inches.

Most people are familiar with setting font size using points, but they are not accustomed to calculating actual measurements in points. You may be more comfortable thinking in inches. The InchestoPoints function takes a measurement specified in inches and converts it to points automatically. It eliminates the need to do conversions in your head.

One area that benefits from this function is working with indention. Indention is one of the trickier features to set with properties because there is the LeftIndent, RightIndent and the FirstLineIndent. For example, in the Task Update template, you create a macro to get a task set up. You want your text to have the label at the left and the text indented at a specific position on the ruler. The code used is as follows:

```
With Selection.ParagraphFormat
    .LeftIndent = InchesToPoints(1.58)
    .FirstLineIndent = InchesToPoints(-0.95)
End With
```

When you look at the results in the enlarged view shown in Figure 10.4, you will notice that the First Line Indent marker on the ruler is slightly past the .5 inch mark and the Left Indent marker is at the 1.58 inch mark.

FIGURE 10.4

The indention markers format the text as needed, but the code looks different.

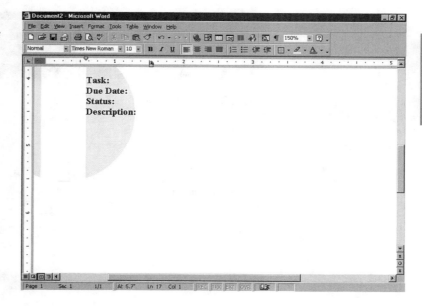

10

When you think of indenting code, think of where you want the left indention to be and then decide how much to subtract or add to that mark to get the Left Indent mark.

Using Tabs, Borders, and Lists

The paragraph properties enable you to control many of the appearance attributes of your paragraphs, but there are three additional formatting features that can be automated. You can add tab stops, borders, and bullets or numbers to your text with VBA.

Adding Tabs

There are times when you want to place text at specific positions in the margins. That is the purpose of tabs. In Microsoft Word, you can set a tab stop to control the alignment of the text at that tab and whether there are any preceding characters called *leaders*. For example, if you frequently use call lists, such as the one shown in Figure 10.5, you want to automate the placement of tabs to clean up the text alignment.

 A *leader* is a row of characters, usually dots or dashes, that provides a path for the eye to follow across a page, often used between columns separated by tabs.

FIGURE 10.5

The items shown here don't line up.

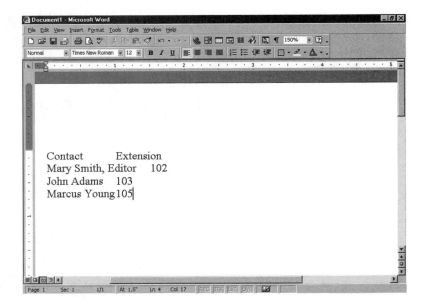

To add tabs, you need to work with the `TabStops` collection for the `ParagraphFormat` object. You will use the `Add` method to add a new tab stop. The syntax is

```
expression.Add(Position, Alignment, Leader)
```

It starts with the expression representing the selection, followed by the period. This is followed by the `Add` keyword. When you are setting up the new tab stop, you need to set three arguments. The `Position` argument sets the position of the tab on the ruler. In most cases, you will find it easier to use the `InchestoPoints` function to be able to work with the standard ruler.

The `Alignment` argument indicates what type of tab will be added. This is set using built-in constants such as `wdTabRight`. It can be omitted if you want a left tab. That is the default.

The last argument is the `Leader` argument. It sets a leader for the tab stop if desired. It is set with built-in constants. It can also be omitted if a leader isn't needed because the default setting is `wdTabLeaderSpaces`.

The code to set the leader tab for the Call List requires six lines of code as shown in Listing 10.5. Line 2 uses the `ClearAll` method to clear any previous tab stops. Line 3 uses the `Add` method to create the new tab stop.

LISTING 10.5 The `FormatCallList` Procedure

```
1: Sub FormatCallList()
2:     Selection.ParagraphFormat.TabStops.ClearAll
3:     Selection.ParagraphFormat.TabStops.Add _
4:         Position:=InchesToPoints(6), _
5:         Alignment:=wdAlignTabRight, Leader:=wdTabLeaderDots
6: End Sub
```

10

Select the list that needs the format and execute the procedure. The document will have the extensions lined up at the right margin with the new tab and its leader as shown in Figure 10.6.

FIGURE 10.6

The new tab cleans up the list's appearance.

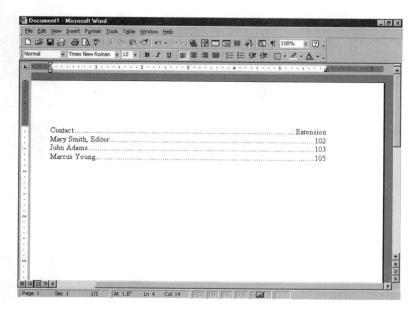

Adding Borders

You may also want to automate the inclusion of borders for your text. To add borders manually, you will use the Borders and Shading dialog (see Figure 10.7). It gives you many customization options.

FIGURE 10.7

The Borders and Shading dialog gives you many options.

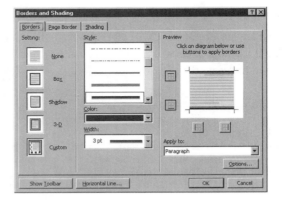

If you select your text and open this dialog, you can use the mouse to choose your custom settings. If you have some settings you rely on, you can develop a macro to automatically add them to your text. For example, the Need Time lead paragraph might look better with a light gray background and top and bottom borders as shown in Figure 10.8.

FIGURE 10.8

The lead paragraph now looks more like a newsletter banner.

This can be automated with a macro, such as the LeadBorders macro in Listing 10.6. It uses the ParagraphFormat object's Borders collection and Shading object to adjust the appearance.

LISTING 10.6   The LeadBorder Macro

```
 1: Sub LeadBorders()
 2:     With Selection.ParagraphFormat
 3:         With .Borders(wdBorderTop)
 4:             .LineStyle = wdLineStyleThinThickSmallGap
 5:             .LineWidth = wdLineWidth300pt
 6:             .Color = wdColorDarkBlue
 7:         End With
 8:         With .Borders(wdBorderBottom)
 9:             .LineStyle = wdLineStyleThickThinSmallGap
10:             .LineWidth = wdLineWidth300pt
11:             .Color = wdColorDarkBlue
12:         End With
13:         With .Shading
14:             .Texture = wdTextureNone
15:             .ForegroundPatternColor = wdColorAutomatic
16:             .BackgroundPatternColor = wdColorGray125
17:         End With
18:     End With
19: End Sub
```

The Borders collection enables you to control the appearance of each border separately if needed. You specify the Border you want with the appropriate index constant and then set its properties. In this example, you are adding borders to the top and bottom. For each, you have to set three properties. You need to set the line style, line width, and line color. All these properties have a built-in constants to save time.

After the borders are set, the shading settings take up the rest of the code. The Shading object has several properties that control the appearance. You have the Texture property to control the pattern or texture selected for the text. You have the ForegroundPatternColor and the BackgroundPatternColor properties to select the color choice for the text.

There are two more properties that aren't listed. You can use the ForeGroundPatternColorIndex and BackgroundPatternColorIndex properties if you prefer, but they are more restrictive than the ones used by the Recorder.

The color properties are more flexible than the index properties. With the ForegroundPatternColor and BackgroundPatternColor properties, you can use the built-in color constants or use the RGB function to create a custom color for the shading. The index properties restrict you to using the constants.

Adding Bullets and Numbering

Other types of formatting include bullets and numbering. On the Formatting toolbar, you have bullets and numbering buttons. These buttons are great for simple bullets or basic numbering. You also have the AutoFormat command to automatically add the bullets or numbers as you type the first entry. If you need special numbering or bullets, you might want to consider VBA.

To create a custom bullet or numbering style, use the ListGalleries collection. It stores the templates for the bulleting numbering and outline numbering styles provided in the Bullets and Numbering dialog. For example, you can create a procedure called CustomBullets (see Listing 10.7) to use the book symbol used earlier as a bullet symbol. The procedure works with the BulletGallery to set your custom style.

LISTING 10.7   The CustomBullets Procedure

```
 1: Sub CustomBullets()
 2:     With ListGalleries(wdBulletGallery).ListTemplates(7).ListLevels(1)
 3:         .NumberFormat = ChrW(61478)
 4:         .TrailingCharacter = wdTrailingTab
 5:         .NumberStyle = wdListNumberStyleBullet
 6:         .NumberPosition = InchesToPoints(0.25)
 7:         .Alignment = wdListLevelAlignLeft
 8:         .TextPosition = InchesToPoints(0.5)
 9:         .TabPosition = InchesToPoints(0.5)
10:         With .Font
11:             .Color = wdColorDarkBlue
12:             .Size = 13
13:             .Name = "Wingdings"
14:         End With
15:     End With
16:     Selection.Range.ListFormat.ApplyListTemplate
ListTemplate:=ListGalleries( _
17:         wdBulletGallery).ListTemplates(7), ContinuePreviousList:=False,
ApplyTo:= _
18:         wdListApplyToWholeList, DefaultListBehavior:=wdWord9ListBehavior
19: End Sub
```

To create custom bullets, you have to set up characteristics and apply them to your current selection. You use the ListLevels collection for the ListTemplate in the ListGalleries collection in a With structure. Set the symbol you want to use with the ChrW function to send the specific character code to the NumberFormat property. You set the TrailingCharacter property to automatically follow the bullet with a tab. You set the TextPosition and TabPosition to specify the position of the tab and the placement of the text.

A nested With structure is used to store the font information. After the bullet is defined, it needs to be applied. The Selection's Range object is used. Its ListFormat is set with the ApplyListTemplate method using the new settings.

If you are using one of the predefined styles, you can eliminate the With structure. You only need the number of the style to use in the ListTemplate property. The same is true for numbering. If you wanted to have a procedure that sets up numbering using the capital Roman numerals, the code is simpler (as shown in Listing 10.8).

LISTING 10.8 The CustomNumbering Procedure

```
Sub CustomNumbering()
    Selection.Range.ListFormat.ApplyListTemplate ListTemplate:=ListGalleries( _
        wdNumberGallery).ListTemplates(3), ContinuePreviousList:=False,
    ➥ApplyTo:= _
        wdListApplyToWholeList, DefaultListBehavior:=wdWord9ListBehavior
End Sub
```

10

As with bullets, you have complete control with numbering. You can define a custom style using VBA as shown in Figure 10.9. You can set each property to get the look you want. There may, however, be an even easier approach.

FIGURE 10.9

The numbering has been changed from the default.

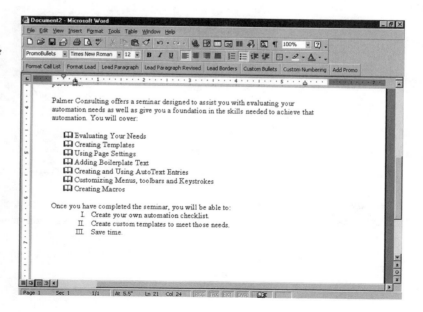

Working with Styles

When you begin working with text formatting, you tend to do everything manually. Every setting requires a new set of steps to get the formatting you want. If you are considering using procedures to automate formatting, don't forget you can utilize styles. You can add font settings, paragraph settings, tabs, language specifics, borders, frames, or bullets and numbering to a style.

After the style is created, you can turn it on. Again, you don't want to do more than you have to. You can put a style right on the toolbar. If you are creating only one style, adding VBA just to turn it on isn't worth the effort. You must, however, be able to turn on styles if you are formatting text as you add it in a macro.

For example, you have specific formatting for promotional material. You might create the AddPromo procedure shown in Listing 10.9.

LISTING 10.9   The AddPromo Procedure

```
 1: Sub AddPromo()
 2:     Selection.Style = ActiveDocument.Styles("PromoText")
 3:     ActiveDocument.AttachedTemplate.AutoTextEntries("Imagine").Insert
        ➥Where:= _
 4:         Selection.Range, RichText:=False
 5:     Selection.TypeParagraph
 6:     Selection.TypeParagraph
 7:     ActiveDocument.AttachedTemplate.AutoTextEntries("Seminar").Insert
        ➥Where:= _
 8:         Selection.Range, RichText:=False
 9:     Selection.TypeParagraph
10:     Selection.Style = ActiveDocument.Styles("PromoBullets")
11:     ActiveDocument.AttachedTemplate.AutoTextEntries("Topics").Insert
        ➥Where:= _
12:         Selection.Range, RichText:=False
13:     Selection.Style = ActiveDocument.Styles("PromoText")
14: End Sub
```

ANALYSIS   The Selection object has a Style property. In your code, you will set this property on lines 2 and 10. In this case, you use the ActiveDocument property to point to the active file, and you are accessing a specific style in that document. This line of code is used in conjunction with the AutoTextEntries and TypeParagraph to create the text on lines 3–9 and lines 11–12.

Notice line 13 sets the style back to PromoText. **Don't** forget to reset the style to the one you want for the text you are entering. Otherwise, you will have to reset it manually.

Summary

This hour has focused on how to format your text automatically with VBA. You have learned how to adjust all aspects of paragraph formatting. You have learned how to set font and paragraph settings.

You have also learned how to add tabs, bullets, and numbers. The last topic introduced was how to work with styles in VBA. If there is some formatting you use regularly, you may be better off creating a style, which you can access without VBA. Created styles are also easier to modify in the future.

Q&A

Q What happens if you attempt to set a font that isn't loaded on the system?

A The procedure will run. It will leave the initial font in place, but you will see the specified font name in the toolbar.

Q Can I use the new formatting designed for Web pages?

A Yes, you can automate the special Web page formatting with VBA. Please refer to Hour 20, "Working with Other Office Applications."

Q Can I set page borders with VBA?

A Yes, you can set page borders with VBA. Please refer to Hour 11, "Working with Page Appearance and Printing," for more information.

Workshop

Here are some questions and exercises to help you review the material covered in this hour. The answers to the quiz questions can be found in Appendix A, "Quiz Answers."

Quiz

1. To change the indention of the first line of a paragraph, what properties do you need to set?

2. What method is used to clear the tab stops for a selection?

3. What collection stores the different numbering and bullet styles?

Exercises

1. Create a procedure to add three tabs for a selection at the 2-inch, 4-inch, and 6-inch marks. After the tabs are created, create a border around the paragraph and build a call list similar to the one in the earlier example.

2. Create a procedure that applies the square bullet style and adds a list.

3. Review your own automation list to indicate where you will need to use the formatting techniques outlined in this hour.

HOUR 11

Working with Page Appearance and Printing

In addition to changing the way the text is formatted, you may also regularly change the appearance of the page, such as changing its orientation or margins. You may also use specific settings when you print documents like a specific page range. This feature can be automated with Visual Basic for Applications just like the text formatting features.

The highlights of this hour include

- Setting up the page
- Automating page borders
- Working with stories
- Automating printing

Setting Up the Page

When you are creating a document, you often have to change the page setup to accommodate specific limitations of your selected output medium. You can automate the process of changing the page settings with Visual Basic for Applications (VBA).

In this hour, you are going to experiment with adjusting the page setup and controlling the printing of a document. To get the most from this hour, you need a longer document to work with.

Go to the companion Web site at www.samspublishing.com/product_support, and type the ISBN of this book: 0-672-31652-8. The Hour11 template contains 10 pages of text to give you pages to manipulate. You can use a document of your own and place the macros in the Normal template, or you can work with the template provided.

When you are creating a template for a specific purpose, normally, your first step is to create your page settings. You adjust the page settings by selecting File, Page Setup and using the Page Setup dialog as shown in Figure 11.1.

FIGURE 11.1

The Page Setup dialog enables you to adjust the page settings manually.

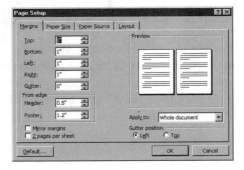

You can work with page margins, paper sources, and header and footer settings, as well as line numbers. These features enable you to control the appearance of all the pages or a group of pages. If you change the appearance of a group of pages, you automatically create a section. (For more information regarding the use of sections, please refer to Hour 14, "Working with Large Documents.")

In every case, you will be setting the properties for the selected section. Even if you don't have multiple sections, the document still contains at least one section.

Adjusting Page Margins

When you are creating documents, you often adjust the margins on a document-by-document basis rather than relying on a template. For example, if you change printers or paper, you adjust the margins for the best look for a specific printer or paper. To adjust the settings for the choices represented on the Margins tab of the Page Setup dialog, use the properties listed in Table 11.1.

TABLE 11.1 The Margins Properties

Property	Description
TopMargin, BottomMargin, LeftMargin, and RightMargin	These properties set the amount of white space around the page. They are measured in points, but you can use the InchestoPoints function to convert.
Gutter	This property sets the extra white space amount needed for binding. It is also measured in points.
GutterPos and GutterStyle	Although not visible in the Page Setup dialog. These properties control how a gutter is treated for languages that read right to left.
HeaderDistance and FooterDistance	These properties control the placement of the header and footer on the page. They are also measured in points.
MirrorMargins	This property indicates whether the left and right margins need to be reversed for binding.
TwoPagesonOne	This new property determines whether two pages are printed on one page. It is used to support some of the additional features for different languages.

VBA can be useful if you sometimes, but not always, use duplex printing. You can create a macro to set up your document for duplex printing by mirroring the margins. You can then add another macro to change the settings back when you are printing normally. Using these macros gives you correct settings for duplexing when needed, without requiring constant manual resetting of margins.

NEW TERM   Duplex printing is printing on both sides of the page with an odd-numbered page on the front and an even-numbered page on the back; that is, the left and right pages face one another when the document is bound.

Your two macros can be called `DuplexPrinting` and `NonDuplexPrinting`. Both of these are shown in Listing 11.1.

LISTING 11.1   The Duplex Switching Macros

```
 1: Sub DuplexPrinting()
 2: '   Create mirror margins for duplexing and binding
 3:     With ActiveDocument.PageSetup
 4:         .TopMargin = InchesToPoints(1.25)
 5:         .BottomMargin = InchesToPoints(1.25)
 6:         .LeftMargin = InchesToPoints(1.25)
 7:         .RightMargin = InchesToPoints(1)
 8:         .HeaderDistance = InchesToPoints(0.5)
 9:         .FooterDistance = InchesToPoints(0.5)
10:         .MirrorMargins = True
11:     End With
12: End Sub
13:
14: Sub NonDuplexPrinting()
15: '   Create regular margins
16:     With ActiveDocument.PageSetup
17:         .TopMargin = InchesToPoints(1.25)
18:         .BottomMargin = InchesToPoints(1.25)
19:         .LeftMargin = InchesToPoints(1)
20:         .RightMargin = InchesToPoints(1)
21:         .HeaderDistance = InchesToPoints(0.5)
22:         .FooterDistance = InchesToPoints(0.5)
23:         .MirrorMargins = False
24:     End With
25: End Sub
```

ANALYSIS   Both procedures use the exact same structure except that the settings for the `LeftMargin`, `RightMargin` and `MirrorMargins` change. The `MirrorMargins` property is set to `True` on line 10 to indicate that you want to prepare the document for duplexing. The `LeftMargin` and `RightMargin` set the amount of white space on lines 6–7.

The hardest part in creating these macros is that you don't have the assistance of the dialog. When you click the Mirror Margins check box, the dialog changes the labels from Left and Right to Inner and Outer as shown in Figure 11.2.

FIGURE 11.2

The Page Setup dialog changes the headings for the left and right margins.

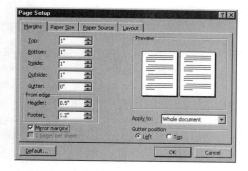

When you are writing the VBA, you have to remember that the `LeftMargin` property stores the inner edge margin when the `MirrorMargins` is set to `True`. The `RightMargin` stores the outer margin.

As you run the macros, the changes to the text are subtle. You will notice the text will shift slightly to the right when you run the `DuplexPrinting` macro. The text will shift back as you run the `NonDuplexPrinting` macro.

Choosing the Paper Size and Source

The second two tabs in the Page Setup dialog give you control over paper size, the paper's location, and the orientation of the printing on the paper. When you are creating a template, you use the dialog to create your base settings for paper size and source.

Use VBA when you have to accommodate more than one set of circumstances. As with the margin settings, the paper size and paper source settings have corresponding properties as listed in Table 11.2.

TABLE 11.2   The Paper Size and Paper Source Properties

Property	Description
PaperSize	This property enables you to pick one of the standard sizes of paper. You indicate your choice with a built-in constant.
	The most common settings are wdPaperLetter or wdPaperLegal. If you are using a size of paper that isn't standard, you set the next two properties, and Word will automatically change this property to wdPaperCustom.

continues

11

TABLE 11.2 continued

Property	Description
PaperHeight and PaperWidth	If you are using a custom paper setting, set the paper's height and width with these two properties. They are specified using points, but you can use the InchestoPoints function as you did with margins.
Orientation	This property determines if the printing will be portrait or landscape.
FirstPageTray and OtherPageTray	These properties indicate where the paper for the document is placed in the printer.

VBA can be especially valuable if you have several sources for paper. For example, you often print the first page of documents on letterhead. You can create a macro to adjust the properties to support letterhead and set it back again for plain paper. I do this in the macros LetterheadPrompt and NoLetterheadPrompt shown in Listing 11.2.

LISTING 11.2 LetterheadPrompt Macro

```
 1: Sub LetterheadPrompt()
 2:     With ActiveDocument.PageSetup
 3:         .FirstPageTray = wdPrinterManualFeed
 4:         .OtherPagesTray = wdPrinterDefaultBin
 5:     End With
 6: End Sub
 7:
 8: Sub NoLetterHeadPrompt()
 9:     With ActiveDocument.PageSetup
10:         .FirstPageTray = wdPrinterDefaultBin
11:         .OtherPagesTray = wdPrinterDefaultBin
12:     End With
13: End Sub
```

Automating Header and Footer Settings

The last tab in the Page Setup dialog is the Layout tab. It is designed to give you control over headers and footers, section starts, and vertical alignment. Its settings also have corresponding VBA properties. They are listed in Table 11.3.

TABLE 11.3   The Layout Properties

Property	Description
SectionStart	This property sets the point at which new sections should start. It is set with built-in constants.
OddEvenPagesHeaderFooter	This property determines if odd and even pages have different headers and footers. It can be set to True or False.
DifferentFirstPageHeaderFooter	This property determines whether the first page of a section has a different header and footer. It is also set to True or False.

There are also three properties that support settings for other languages:

    SectionDirection

    CharsLines

    LayoutMode

These aren't represented in the dialog. This dialog also has buttons to access the Line Numbering settings in the Page Borders tab of the Borders and Shading dialog.

Automating Line Numbers

Line numbering is one of the features that you might not have worked with if you aren't working with legal documents. The line numbering feature lets you place numbers in the margin before a line. It can be set up to indicate the line number for the document or the line number for the page.

If you haven't used line numbering in the past, you might want to consider using it for proofing or discussion purposes. If you frequently review documents in meetings, having numbered lines might facilitate locating material in a document.

You can also have macros that turn settings on and off. You have already created two macros for paper tray settings; but doing that isn't the only approach. With conditional logic, you can test a property setting and then take action based on its value. This is illustrated in ChangeLineNumbering shown in Listing 11.3.

11

LISTING 11.3 The ChangeLineNumbering Macro

```
 1: Sub ChangeLineNumbering()
 2:     If ActiveDocument.PageSetup.LineNumbering.Active <> True Then
 3:         With ActiveDocument.PageSetup.LineNumbering
 4:             .Active = True
 5:             .StartingNumber = 1
 6:             .CountBy = 10
 7:             .RestartMode = wdRestartContinuous
 8:             .DistanceFromText = InchesToPoints(0.25)
 9:         End With
10:     Else
11:         ActiveDocument.PageSetup.LineNumbering.Active = False
12:     End If
13: End Sub
```

ANALYSIS   To work with line numbering, you use five properties. There is a LineNumbering object represented by the LineNumbering property for the PageSetup object shown in line 2 that controls all the line numbering settings.

The Active property on line 4 is the most important property. It indicates whether line numbering is displayed and printed. It can have one of three settings. It can be undefined, True or False. In this procedure, this property is tested to see if it is equal to False or undefined.

Unless the Active property is set to True, the line numbering is turned off, and you must turn it on. This is done by means of a With structure on lines 3–9. If the Active property is not first turned on, the other properties' settings won't be recognized, and you will end up with the default settings.

This is followed by the properties that determine how line numbering will be used. The StartingNumber indicates the number you will use to start the line numbering. The CountBy enables you to set the line interval to number. These properties are both set with numeric values.

The RestartMode is the next setting. It enables you to set the line numbers to begin over at the document level, page level, or section level. This property is set with built-in constants.

When you run this macro to place line numbers in the document, you probably don't want line numbers on the title page. In most cases, you will solve this problem by using a separate section for the title page. Working with sections is discussed in Hour 14.

The last property is the `DistanceFromText` property which is adjusted on line 8. It controls the placement of the numbers in the margin. When you run this macro, the line numbers are only visible if you are in Print Layout mode. If you are afraid that Print Layout will not be the view mode selected, you can add a line of code to shift the view.

```
ActiveWindow.View.Type = wdPrintView
```

Another approach would be to use the `MsgBox` function to ask the user if he wants to see line numbers even if it means changing the view. You could use the `If` statement to exit the subprocedure before changing the view and adding line numbers.

Automating Page Borders

The last setting in the Page Setup dialog is a button to open the Borders and Shading dialog with the Page Borders tab selected. You can customize the look of the document by adding a border around the page. It is very similar to the techniques used to add borders to a text selection. You can use all the same properties, except you use the Sections collection to affect the entire section or document.

You also have the capability to add artwork as a border instead of just lines. If you are going with this approach, you will work with several different properties. You might also want to make a distinction between printing in color versus printing in black and white. The `AddPageBorder` procedure shown in Listing 11.4 illustrates this technique.

11

LISTING 11.4 The AddPageBorder Procedure

```
 1: Sub AddPageBorder()
 2:     Dim lColor As Long, lGraphic As Long
 3:     lColor = MsgBox("Do you want color?", vbQuestion + vbYesNo)
 4:     If lColor = vbYes Then
 5:         lGraphic = wdArtPeopleHats
 6:     Else
 7:         lGraphic = wdArtPeopleWaving
 8:     End If
 9:     With Selection.Sections(1)
10:         With .Borders(wdBorderLeft)
11:             .ArtStyle = lGraphic
12:             .ArtWidth = 15
13:             .ColorIndex = wdAuto
14:         End With
15:         With .Borders(wdBorderRight)
16:             .ArtStyle = lGraphic
17:             .ArtWidth = 15
18:             .ColorIndex = wdAuto
```

continues

LISTING 11.4   continued

```
19:            End With
20:            With .Borders(wdBorderTop)
21:                .ArtStyle = lGraphic
22:                .ArtWidth = 15
23:                .ColorIndex = wdAuto
24:            End With
25:            With .Borders(wdBorderBottom)
26:                .ArtStyle = lGraphic
27:                .ArtWidth = 15
28:                .ColorIndex = wdAuto
29:            End With
30:            With .Borders
31:                .DistanceFrom = wdBorderDistanceFromText
32:                .AlwaysInFront = True
33:                .SurroundHeader = True
34:                .SurroundFooter = True
35:                .JoinBorders = True
36:                .DistanceFromTop = 12
37:                .DistanceFromLeft = 12
38:                .DistanceFromBottom = 12
39:                .DistanceFromRight = 12
40:                .EnableFirstPageInSection = True
41:                .EnableOtherPagesInSection = True
42:                .ApplyPageBordersToAllSections
43:            End With
44:        End With
45:        With Options
46:            .DefaultBorderLineStyle = wdLineStyleSingle
47:            .DefaultBorderLineWidth = wdLineWidth050pt
48:            .DefaultBorderColor = wdColorAutomatic
49:        End With
50: End Sub
```

ANALYSIS   This procedure uses a MsgBox on line 3 to determine if the user wants the border in color. The lColor variable is tested with an If structure beginning on line 4, and the correct constant is assigned to lGraphic.

Regardless of whether color is selected or not, the process for setting the borders is the same. The Borders collection for the selected section is set on lines 9–29 using three properties:

- ArtStyle is a built-in constant to indicate which graphic will be used. This is set with the constant assigned to lGraphic.
- ArtWidth sets the size of the graphic using points.
- ColorIndex indicates what color to use for printing the border.

In all cases, the `wdAuto` is used to select the default colors for the style chosen. The remainder of the code beginning with line 30 sets the additional properties associated with placing the border a specific distance from the text. If you are always going to use the default settings, these lines can be omitted.

When this code is run, it asks the question about color. If the user selects Yes, a color border is added such as the one shown in Figure 11.3. Otherwise, the black and white border is used. In this case, the graphics are very similar. Unfortunately, most of the borders don't have two versions. For those borders, you can work with the `ColorIndex` to get the effect you want.

FIGURE 11.3

The border has been added for the page.

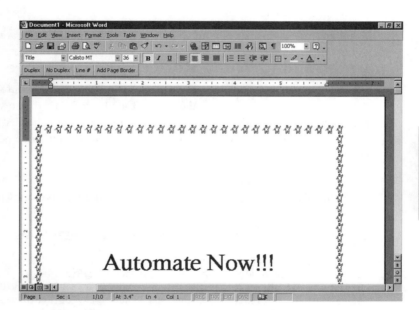

11

Working with Stories

In addition to adding borders for a page, a common addition to a multipage document is the addition of a header or footer. If you add nothing else, you will probably add a page number to your document to help you keep the pages in order when you print the file.

The header and the footer are treated separately from the document text. With VBA, they are classified as Story objects. A *story* is specific range of text in a document that is treated differently from the rest of the text. In a document, there are 11 types of stories:

Comments	Even page footer
Footnotes	First page header
End notes	First page footer
Odd or primary page header	Frame text
Odd or primary page footer	Main text
Even page header	

There are times you are going to want to add or manipulate these areas with your code.

Determining What Stories Exist

When you create a document in regular text, you don't worry about stories. To work with the main text, you normally use the Selection object. You will use stories to add other document elements with your code. When you want to add a header, footer, or other element, the first step is to determine if it already exists in your document. To see if an element exists, use the StoryType property.

As an example, you want to have a macro build the header and footer for a document automatically. To determine if one already exists, use the code shown in Listing 11.5.

LISTING 11.5   Determining Whether a Header or Footer Exists

```
 1:    Dim bHeaderFooter As Boolean, objTestStory
 2:    For Each objTestStory In ActiveDocument.StoryRanges
 3:        If objTestStory.StoryType = wdPrimaryHeaderStory Or _
 4:            objTestStory.StoryType = wdPrimaryFooterStory Or _
 5:            objTestStory.StoryType = wdEvenPagesHeaderStory Or _
 6:            objTestStory.StoryType = wdEvenPagesFooterStory Or _
 7:            objTestStory.StoryType = wdFirstPageHeaderStory Or _
 8:            objTestStory.StoryType = wdFirstPageFooterStory Then
 9:            bHeaderFooter = True
10:        End If
11:    Next
12:    If bHeaderFooter = True Then
13:        MsgBox "This document already has a header/footer.", _
14:            vbInformation, "Header/Footer Exists"
15:        Exit Sub
16:    End If
```

ANALYSIS This code sets up two variables on line 1. One tests the document's StoryRanges collection and the other collects the results. The For Each...Next structure on lines 2–11 is a special type of loop that is designed to work with collections. You begin with the For Next keywords followed by the variable you set up to represent each object in the collection. It is followed by the In keyword and the name of the collection. In this case, you are using the ActiveDocument property to access the active document's collection.

An If structure on lines 3–10 is used to test the StoryType property for each story in the collection. The test statement is longer than some, because each type of header and footer has its own built-in constant. If any of these stories exist, the Boolean variable is set to True.

After all the stories are tested, the Boolean variable is tested on lines 12–16 to see if it is True. If it is, a message box is displayed informing the user that headers and footers exist, and the subprocedure exits.

In this simple example, if any header and footer exists, you want to cancel the execution. In a more complex example, you can set up a Select Case structure to test the StoryType and build the headers or footers that are missing. This can dramatically reduce the amount of time it takes to create multiple headers and footers for longer documents.

Adding and Modifying a Story

After you have determined whether a story exists, you can take action. Adding a story isn't as simple as it is when working with other collections. You can't simply use the Add method to add the story and then set its properties. You must use other methods to create the story that you need.

Creating your header and footer automatically is one of the more complex stories to create. You have to check the view to make sure you are in Print view. Then you create the header/footer and the text. The complete macro might resemble the one listed in Listing 11.6.

LISTING 11.6   The AddHeaderFooter Procedure

```
1: Sub AddHeaderFooter()
2: '    Test to see if a Header or Footer exists
3:     If ActiveWindow.ActivePane.View.Type = wdNormalView Or ActiveWindow. _
4:         ActivePane.View.Type = wdOutlineView Then
```

continues

LISTING 11.6   continued

```
 5:          ActiveWindow.ActivePane.View.Type = wdPrintView
 6:      End If
 7:      Dim bHeaderFooter As Boolean, objTestStory
 8:      For Each objTestStory In ActiveDocument.StoryRanges
 9:          If objTestStory.StoryType = wdPrimaryHeaderStory Or _
10:              objTestStory.StoryType = wdPrimaryFooterStory Or _
11:              objTestStory.StoryType = wdEvenPagesHeaderStory Or _
12:              objTestStory.StoryType = wdEvenPagesFooterStory Or _
13:              objTestStory.StoryType = wdFirstPageHeaderStory Or _
14:              objTestStory.StoryType = wdFirstPageFooterStory Then
15:              bHeaderFooter = True
16:          End If
17:      Next
18:      If bHeaderFooter = True Then
19:          MsgBox "This document already has a header/footer.", _
20:              vbInformation, "Header/Footer Exists"
21:          Exit Sub
22:      End If
23:
24: '   Build Header and Footer
25:      ActiveWindow.ActivePane.View.SeekView = wdSeekCurrentPageHeader
26:      Selection.TypeText Text:="Automate Now!" & vbTab & vbTab _
27:          & "Prepared by: Pamela A. Palmer"
28:      ActiveWindow.ActivePane.View.SeekView = wdSeekCurrentPageFooter
29:      Selection.TypeText Text:=vbTab
30:      Selection.Fields.Add Range:=Selection.Range, Type:=wdFieldPage
31:      Selection.TypeText Text:=" of "
32:      Selection.Fields.Add Range:=Selection.Range, Type:=wdFieldNumPages
33:      ActiveWindow.ActivePane.View.SeekView = wdSeekMainDocument
34: End Sub
```

ANALYSIS   Lines 2–22 have the code introduced above to determine whether headers and footers already exist and exit the procedure if they do. Then, you are ready to build the header and footer.

When you want to write a procedure to automate the addition of headers and footers, the first step is to activate headers and footers. This is accomplished with the SeekView method on line 25. The TypeText method is used to add the text for the header on lines 26–27; then the SeekView method is used again on line 28 to switch to the footer.

On lines 29–32, the TypeText method and the Add method are used to add the number of pages. Line 33 activates the main document story so the user can continue editing.

This is a simple example of adding a header and footer. Depending on how flexible you want the procedure to be, you can test each type of header and footer and add any that are missing. If you are going to use any of the header and footer properties for page layout, you will also need to make sure that those properties are set up correctly before you write the code to create the headers and footers. (An additional example is provided in Hour 14 in the discussion of longer documents.)

Automating Printing

In addition to controlling the page appearance when a paper source is included, you might also want to control how a document is sent to the printer. With VBA, you can automate printing to handle special circumstances like choosing a printer, setting its options, and adjusting your print parameters. You can also create a batch print job to tackle printing more than one document with one command.

> If you want to save resources for this section, you might want to pause your printers to enable you to print without actually sending the document to the printer.

Selecting a Printer

One of the first things you might want to control about printing is the capability to switch to a specific printer. There is an `ActivePrinter` property that indicates what printer is currently selected. You can put that fact into an expression, specifying the printer's identifier in quotations. For example, I have a color printer:

```
ActivePrinter = "Color Printer on LPT1:"
```

Controlling Print Options

After the printer is selected, you can control your print options. As we did previously, you will use the `Options` collection and reference the printing options. You can adjust any of the properties that you see in the Options dialog shown in Figure 11.4.

You can set each property individually or use the `With` structure to set more than one at a time. For example, `PrintReverse` property is very helpful with my color printer.

```
Options.PrintReverse = True
```

> You can set options with VBA, but you can't change a printer's properties with VBA. This is because a printer's properties aren't stored in Word. They are a part of the printer definition for your computer.

FIGURE 11.4

The Print tab proper-
ties give you some
control over your
printing.

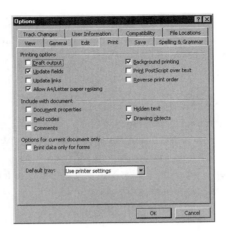

Automating Print Settings

After the printer is selected and any options are chosen, you can begin to modify the settings for this specific printing of your document. This is accomplished with the application's PrintOut method. If you are setting up a document to print two copies of the first
two pages, the code line is

```
Application.PrintOut FileName:="", Range:=wdPrintRangeOfPages, Item:= _
    wdPrintDocumentContent, Copies:=2, Pages:="1-2", PageType:= _
    wdPrintAllPages, Collate:=True, Background:=True, PrintToFile:=False, _
    PrintZoomColumn:=0, PrintZoomRow:=0, PrintZoomPaperWidth:=0, _
    PrintZoomPaperHeight:=0
```

There are 15 arguments that can be used to print your document. They are named arguments, so you can omit the ones that you won't change from the default value. In this
case, you can reduce the code to

```
    Application.PrintOut Range:=wdPrintRangeOfPages, Item:= _
        wdPrintDocumentContent, Copies:=2, Pages:="1-2", PageType:= _
        wdPrintAllPages
```

Automating Batch Printing

Another valuable automation tool is the capability to print more than one document at a
time with VBA. You may find that you print several documents as a group, such as a
marketing package. It might contain a letter, brochure, proposal, and so on. You create a
batch printing procedure so that you don't have to open each document and print it separately. VBA does all the work.

If you need to prompt for special paper to be loaded for a document such as the
brochure, a procedure can save wasted paper. An example is shown in Listing 11.7.

LISTING 11.7   The MarketingPrint Procedure

```
Sub MarketingPrint()
    MsgBox "Make sure letterhead is placed in the printer", vbInformation
    Application.PrintOut FileName:="C:\My documents\Sample Letter.doc"
    MsgBox "Make sure the brochure paper is loaded in the printer.",
vbInformation
    Application.PrintOut FileName:="C:\My Documents\Sample Brochure.doc"
End Sub
```

This code can speed up the process of printing multiple documents because you don't have to open each document, load paper, and print. You are prompted for the correct paper and then the procedure prints the document.

If you are going to implement this type of procedure, you can make it more elaborate by adding some error handling to deal with a missing file or inaccessible folder. You can add code similar to the code for inserting files found in Hour 9, "Working with Text."

Summary

In this hour, you have explored different properties and methods for controlling the appearance of the page and printing. Automation can greatly cut down on time spent creating custom layouts and special printing circumstances.

You learned how to control the settings adjusted in the Page Setup dialog with the corresponding properties. You also learned how to add line numbers and dress up your document with page borders.

You can add different document elements like headers and footers using stories, but the process can be vary greatly depending on what type of element is needed.

Last of all, you learned that you can automate many of the settings necessary to control printing. You can create procedures to customize the printing of one document or automate the printing of more than one document.

Q&A

Q   What is the function of the Gutter property?

A   It indicates the amount of space to add to a margin for binding.

Q   What is the benefit of the InchestoPoints function?

A   It allows you to think in inches, yet send information to VBA as points.

11

Q What settings can't you control while printing?

A You can't adjust a printer's properties because those are set for the computer in the operating system instead of within Word.

Workshop

Here are some questions and exercises to help you review the material covered in this hour. The answers to the quiz questions can be found in Appendix A, "Quiz Answers."

Quiz

1. How can you add a page border to the first page only?

2. How would you add a comment to the document?

Exercises

1. Set up a procedure to print pages 5–8 of this document. You want to duplex the pages to create a handout with a .25-inch border for binding.

2. Evaluate the items on your list to determine where you might use the techniques covered in this hour.

Hour **12**

Working with Tables

If you use tables frequently in your documents, you might often spend time creating tables that are very similar to each other. Visual Basic for Applications (VBA) can speed up the creation of these tables.

You may find that you frequently create weekly schedules or price lists using tables. You can use VBA to add a table with the proper number of columns and rows. Insert the standard text and add the selected formatting. It can greatly reduce the time you spend formatting special tables you use frequently.

You can also automate the creation of tables from standard text. This can be very helpful, if you receive information in text format and need to convert it into a table and format it regularly.

The highlights of this hour include

- Creating tables
- Converting text to tables
- Formatting tables

Creating Tables

There are several steps you take each time you create a table. The first step is to insert the table structure. Next you add text to your table. In some cases, you insert rows or columns dynamically as you work.

After you review the techniques for creating tables with VBA, make sure that these techniques are what you need in your project.

If the table is a stable element, you might instead be able to create the table as an AutoText entry and then use VBA to insert the AutoText entry.

A table is a good candidate for insertion as an AutoText entry if there are no issues that have to be decided each time it is used. It has the same structure, formatting, and text. An example of a table that is best stored as an AutoText entry would be a department abbreviation list or the editorial team of a newsletter.

The techniques shown in this hour are better used when the text changes each time. You can use an InputBox function to populate the table or you can use the techniques for converting standard text to get the text into the table.

There isn't a right or wrong choice, you can even combine the techniques in the hour with the use of AutoText entries. Each situation is different. For more information on using AutoText entries, you can review Hour 9, "Working with Text."

Inserting a Table

When you determine that the best option is to use VBA to create a table, the first step is to insert a table into your document. This is accomplished with the Add method to add a new table to the Tables collection for the active document. The syntax is

```
ActiveDocument.Tables.Add Range, NumRows, NumColumns, _
    DefaultTableBehavior, AutoFitBehavior
```

When the Add method is used with the Tables collection, you have five arguments to work with. The Range argument indicates the placement of the new table in the document. The insertion point can be set using the Selection.Range argument or you can use a bookmark to indicate the placement.

The NumRows and NumCols are numeric arguments to indicate how many rows and columns are expected. You will always specify how many columns you want, but you might consider using 1 as the NumRows.

If you are creating a table with a set number of rows, you simply enter that number. If the number of rows can vary each time you run the macro, however, you might begin by creating only one row. As you add text with VBA, you will have code to move to the next cell as you would use the Tab key manually. Just as it would happen manually when you are in the last cell and move to the next cell, an additional row is created automatically. This eliminates constant checking to see if there are a sufficient number of empty rows.

The purpose of the DefaultTableBehavior feature is to enable you to indicate how the AutoFit feature will be used for this table. In previous versions of Word, AutoFit was disabled by default. When the default was selected, the cells of the table did not automatically resize to fit the text placed in them. In Word 2000, the opposite is true. The AutoFit feature is enabled by default, and cells automatically resize when text is input. You can set this argument to use either approach with built-in constants.

The last argument, AutoFitBehavior, is only used when you choose to use the Word 2000 approach for AutoFit. This argument indicates what the table will AutoFit to. It is set with built-in constants like wdAutoFitContent to size the table around the content.

For example, if you are creating a table to track task assignments, you want one column for the task, one for the date assigned, and one for the date completed. The lines of code are

```
ActiveDocument.Tables.Add Range:=Selection.Range, NumRows:=1, _
    NumColumns:= 3, DefaultTableBehavior:=wdWord9TableBehavior, _
    AutoFitBehavior:= wdAutoFitFixed
```

This code uses the Selection.Range to indicate the insertion point of the new table. It sets NumRows to 1. This means that rows will be added as needed. The NumCols is set to 3. The DefaultTableBehavior is set to AutoFit and the AutoFitBehavior is set to make the columns a fixed width.

Inserting Text

After the table is created, you can add text or go straight to formatting, depending on your needs. If you preset the text with VBA, use the TypeText method just as you would with any text in Word.

As you are creating the code to insert text into a table, keep in mind how to navigate. When you insert the table, the code places your insertion point in the first cell, and you can begin with the TypeText method. After the text for that cell is entered, you must navigate within the table.

When you are working within a table to enter text manually, you can use the Tab, Shift+Tab, or the arrow keys to move through it. When you are creating your code, you

12

use one of the following methods: MoveRight, MoveLeft, MoveUp, and MoveDown. In most instances, you use the Tab key to move from cell to cell for text entry, so you will find that you use the MoveRight method the most when developing your code. The MoveRight method uses the following syntax:

expression.MoveRight(*Unit, Count, Extend*)

The *expression* indicates the object you are navigating through. It is followed by a period and the MoveRight keyword. If you need to move back to a cell, use the MoveLeft keyword instead.

There are three arguments expected. The unit indicates how far you want to move. When you are working with tables, this is frequently set to wdCell to indicate you want to move to the next cell. These methods can be used in the document as a whole. There are other built-in constants to support movement in the document itself as well.

The count argument indicates how many units to move. In this case, set it to 1. The last argument is the Extend argument. This can be set to wdMove or wdExtend depending on whether you are moving between units or selecting the units.

Given the example of building a task list to create a brochure, you might create a procedure similar to CreateTaskTable. This is shown in Listing 12.1.

LISTING 12.1   The CreateTaskTable Procedure

```
 1: Sub CreateTaskTable()
 2:     ActiveDocument.Tables.Add Range:=Selection.Range, NumRows:=1, _
 3:         NumColumns:=3, DefaultTableBehavior:=wdWord9TableBehavior, _
 4:         AutoFitBehavior:=wdAutoFitFixed
 5:     Selection.TypeText Text:="Task"
 6:     Selection.MoveRight Unit:=wdCell
 7:     Selection.TypeText Text:="Assigned"
 8:     Selection.MoveRight Unit:=wdCell
 9:     Selection.TypeText Text:="Completed"
10:     Selection.MoveRight Unit:=wdCell
11:     Selection.TypeText Text:="Create layout for brochure"
12:     Selection.MoveRight Unit:=wdCell
13:     Selection.TypeText Text:="5/16/99"
14:     Selection.MoveRight Unit:=wdCell, Count:=2
15: End Sub
```

ANALYSIS   This procedure adds the table on lines 2–4 and then lines 5–13 moves through the table adding text. Line 14 uses the MoveRight method with a count of 2. It moves to the last column, but doesn't fill it in. The count of 2 moves it again. Because there isn't another row, one is automatically created when the insertion point is in the last column. The resulting table is ready to have additional tasks entered as shown in Figure 12.1.

FIGURE 12.1

The table is created with the headings in place ready for more tasks.

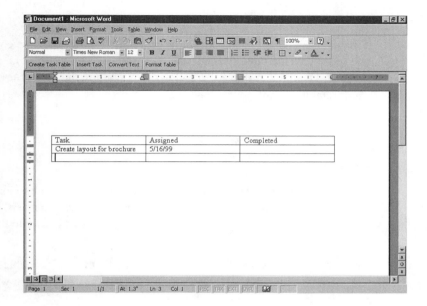

This approach can be used to redo the task macros that you created earlier. You can create a loop to ask for the task description, and then give the task an assigned date, which is the current date.

Inserting Rows and Columns

Another procedure you will frequently perform is inserting a row, column, or a number of rows and columns into a table. With the task list you have been creating, you might need to insert another task above an existing one. Another time when you may need to insert rows or columns is when you're converting text into a table. If you get a marketing mailing list from another source as a text file, you will want to convert it into a table, which is illustrated later in this hour. When it is converted, it might not have all the columns you want. You could add rows or columns to track additional information.

To insert rows or columns, you can use one of three methods: `InsertRowsAbove`, `InsertRowsBelow`, or `InsertColumnsRight`. The syntax is

expression.insertmethod

The `expression` is the selection object to affect. To function, these methods mentioned above require that you have selected a row or column. This expression is followed by a period and the appropriate insert method.

12

When you want to use these methods, you must indicate what part of the table you want to affect. You can indicate this with the `Selection.Range,` as shown above, if desired. You have to be careful when you are selecting cells in a table. If you select only one cell, you will affect only that cell's column or row.

It may be beneficial to add code to the procedure to make sure the complete row is selected. There are three selection methods you can use: `SelectRow`, `SelectColumn`, and `SelectCell`. In the example that follows, you will use the `SelectRow` method. Your code will resemble the procedure shown below:

```
Sub InsertTask()
    Selection.SelectRow
    Selection.InsertRowsBelow 1
    Selection.HomeKey Unit:=wdLine
End Sub
```

The `Selection` object is used to select the row. When you want to insert just one row, the `InsertRowsBelow` method is used with 1 as the number to insert. The last line of code uses the `HomeKey` method to release the highlight and move to the first cell in that row.

To try this out, move your insertion point to the first row of the table which is the row containing the headings. After you run the `InsertTask` macro, you will see a blank line above the first task as shown in Figure 12.2.

FIGURE 12.2

The new row is waiting for the new task.

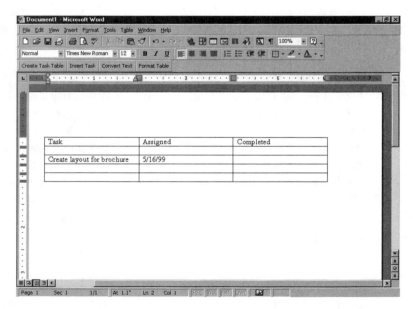

Adding columns requires a similar approach, but adding columns requires some additional coding to adjust the column widths. Setting column widths is covered in the "Formatting Tables" section later in this hour.

Converting Text to Tables

When you need to create a table, inserting one and adding text isn't the only approach. You can convert plain text into a table. Many older word processors didn't have a table feature; you created a table using tab stops in your standard text. There are also many other applications that generate what is referred to as a *delimited file*.

 NEW TERM   *Delimited file*: A file in which the separate elements (such as names and the parts of the addresses) are delineated by commas, tabs, or spaces.

Microsoft Word provides a command that enables you to open the existing file with the tabbed text or insert the text file into a document and convert it into a table by selecting Table, Convert, Text to Table. If this process sounds familiar and the structure of the text that is converted is the same, you can automate the process of converting text to tables. The VBA required to perform the conversion is minimal.

To convert text to a table using VBA, you use the `ConvertToTable` method for the `Selection`. You can control the conversion with arguments that represent the choices you see in the Convert Text to Table dialog (see Figure 12.3).

FIGURE 12.3

The Convert Text to Table dialog gives you control over the conversion.

The ConvertToTable method has seventeen arguments. Some of them are the same arguments used in the `Add` method for the `Tables` collection. The syntax is

```
Selection.ConvertToTable(Separator, NumColumns:=4, NumRows, Format, _
    ApplyBorders, ApplyFont, ApplyColor, ApplyHeadingRows, ApplyLastRow, _
    ApplyFirstColumn, ApplyLastColumn, AutoFit, AutoFitBehavior)
```

The Selection object is followed by a period and the method name. Then there is a list of the arguments used for the conversion.

NumColumns, NumRows, DefaultTableBehavior, AutoFit and AutoFitBehavior behave in the same way as they do when they are arguments for the Add method for the Tables collection. Creating a table is part of what this method does for you.

The Separator argument indicates what character is separating each entry in the list and thereby creating the columns. This character is set with built-in constants such as wdSeparateByTabs.

The remainder of the arguments set the formatting characteristics that you apply to the new table. The first formatting argument is Format. It enables you to select one of the predefined formats supplied by Table AutoFormat, using built-in constants such as wdTableFormatClassic2.

After you have selected a format style, you can use the other arguments to indicate which of the format's characteristics should be applied. These arguments mimic the check boxes that are shown in the dialog.

When you are converting text to a table, this method assumes you have text selected. If this isn't the case, the macro will generate the error 4605. This error indicates the method or property isn't available because the object is empty. You can add error handling to make this procedure execute cleaner. The procedure might resemble the one shown in Listing 12.2.

LISTING 12.2   The ConvertTasks Procedure

```
 1: Sub ConvertTasks()
 2:     On Error GoTo NoText
 3:     Selection.ConvertToTable Separator:=wdSeparateByTabs, NumColumns:=4, _
 4:         NumRows:=5
 5:     Selection.HomeKey Unit:=wdLine
 6:     Exit Sub
 7: NoText:
 8:     Dim strMsg As String, strTitle As String
 9:     Select Case Err.Number
10:         Case 4605    'No Text Selected
11:             strMsg = "There isn't any text selected, "
12:             strMsg = strMsg & "please select your text and try again."
13:             strTitle = "No Text Selected"
14:         Case Else
15:             strMsg = "An unexpected error, " & Err.Number
16:             strMsg = strMsg & ", " & Err.Description
17:             strMsg = ", has occurred. This procedure can't continue."
18:     End Select
19:     MsgBox strMsg, vbExclamation, strTitle
20: End Sub
```

ANALYSIS   Line 2 initializes the error handler to deal with the fact that this macro can be called with no text selected. Lines 3–5 are the lines that perform the conversion. Line 6 indicates this is the end of the code to execute if everything runs correctly.

Line 7 is the line label for the error handler. In this case, you display the problem in a message box and give the user a chance to select the text or take whatever action is needed to resolve the issue.

The number of the error is tested with a `Select Case` structure. For this method, you need to test specifically for error 4605. This error is generated when you attempt to convert text to table without having any text selected. The `Case Else` clause is there to display any unexpected errors.

Formatting Tables

The last arguments for creating a table from text affect the formatting of that table. When you create a table, either manually or using text as a base, you can add formatting. You might want borders around the table or in between cells, or the text in a special color or the alignment changed for the entire table.

You can add formatting two different ways. You can use the Table `AutoFormat` function or you can add your own custom formatting.

Selecting a Table `AutoFormat` Style

The first method for formatting a table is using the Table `AutoFormat` feature. If you are formatting manually, you select Table, Table AutoFormat to display the dialog as shown in Figure 12.4.

12

FIGURE 12.4

The Table AutoFormat enables you to select a predefined style.

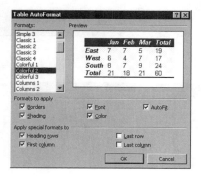

With Table AutoFormat, you select a predefined style and select the formatting elements you want to use. This enables you to use standard formatting for your tables.

To automate the application of one of the formats with VBA, you will use the
AutoFormat method. Its syntax is

SYNTAX

```
expression.AutoFormat Format, ApplyBorders, ApplyShading, ApplyFont, _
    ApplyColor, ApplyHeadingRows, ApplyLastRow, ApplyFirstColumn, _
    ApplyLastColumn, AutoFit
```

To apply a format, you must select the table. The *expression* represents the active selection. It is followed with the AutoFormat method after a period. The AutoFormat method
has nine arguments that represent the choices made in the dialog.

The Format argument is the style you choose from the list in the dialog. The styles are
built into Word, and they are represented with built-in constants such as
wdTableFormatColorful2.

The remainder of the arguments indicate whether you want to apply various characteristics of the table style. They are all True/False arguments.

As with many of the methods, the arguments have a default value. If you wanted to apply
this Colorful2 style with all the default settings to a table, the code is

```
Selection.Tables(1).AutoFormat Format:=wdTableFormatColorful2
```

The AutoFormat method with the Format argument is set to the correct style. None of the
other arguments are needed when you are using the default. If you run the macro to format
the table created from text above, the results will resemble the table shown in Figure 12.5.

FIGURE 12.5

*The table is formatted
with the* Colorful2
style.

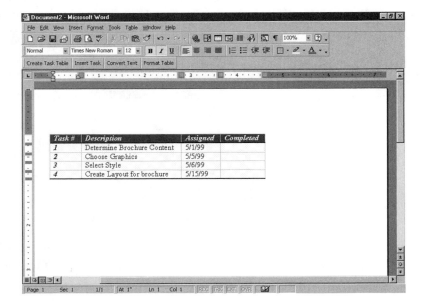

Adding Custom Formatting

Using the AutoFormat style to format the table is a great way to get a coordinated look for your table without a lot of work. There are times, however, when none of the AutoFormat table styles completely meets your needs. This is when you use custom formatting for your table.

For example, you like the Colorful2 style, but you want to adjust the column widths, column alignment, add column borders, and center the table on the page. These adjustments require some additional code.

Adjusting Column Width

When a table format is applied, there are specific column widths defined for each column, based on your choices. If you want to customize them, you can use each column's Width property.

To set a column width, you must indicate the table and the column you want to adjust. If you are recording this macro, you use the Table Properties dialog as shown in Figure 12.6 to adjust the width because you can't drag the column edge to a new position.

FIGURE 12.6
The Column tab is used to adjust the column width.

In VBA, you use the Width property for each individual column. This requires a separate command for each column using the Columns collection. To adjust the four columns of the tasks table, you include the following lines of code:

```
Selection.Tables(1).Columns(1).Width = InchesToPoints(0.75)
Selection.Tables(1).Columns(2).Width = InchesToPoints(3)
Selection.Tables(1).Columns(3).Width = InchesToPoints(1)
Selection.Tables(1).Columns(4).Width = InchesToPoints(1)
```

12

`Selection.Tables(1)` indicates that you want to work with the selected table. `Columns(index).Width` indicates you want to set the width for a column specified by the index number. In this case, the `InchestoPoints` function is used to convert the measurement to points.

Adjusting Column Alignment

After the column width is set, you can adjust the alignment of the text in a specific column. When you adjust the alignment of the text in a column, you are affecting the text, not the column or row. Select the column and then set the `Alignment` property. If you want to center the text in the Assigned and Completed columns in the converted text table, use the following lines of code:

```
Selection.Tables(1).Columns(3).Select
Selection.ParagraphFormat.Alignment = wdAlignParagraphCenter
Selection.Tables(1).Columns(4).Select
Selection.ParagraphFormat.Alignment = wdAlignParagraphCenter
```

The `Select` method is used to select a specific column in the `Columns` collection. The `Alignment` property for the selection's `ParagraphFormat` is set to Centered with the built-in constant.

Adding Borders to Tables

Another aspect of formatting you can adjust is the border for the table or for a specific element of the table. For example, you like the `Colorful2` style, but you decide that you want a border around the table and lines between each column in the same color this style uses for the rest of the table.

To add borders to a table, you use code that is similar to that which adds borders to paragraph text. There are, however, four additional settings. In addition to the top, bottom, left, and right borders, you can also adjust the diagonal down, diagonal up, horizontal, and vertical. To add the formatting discussed, you use the code shown in Listing 12.3.

LISTING 12.3   Code to Add Borders to the Table and Between Columns

```
 1: With Selection.Tables(1)
 2:     With .Borders(wdBorderLeft)
 3:         .LineStyle = wdLineStyleSingle
 4:         .LineWidth = wdLineWidth150pt
 5:         .Color = wdColorDarkRed
 6:     End With
 7:     With .Borders(wdBorderRight)
 8:         .LineStyle = wdLineStyleSingle
 9:         .LineWidth = wdLineWidth150pt
10:         .Color = wdColorDarkRed
11:     End With
```

```
12:        With .Borders(wdBorderTop)
13:             .LineStyle = wdLineStyleSingle
14:             .LineWidth = wdLineWidth150pt
15:             .Color = wdColorDarkRed
16:        End With
17:        With .Borders(wdBorderBottom)
18:             .LineStyle = wdLineStyleSingle
19:             .LineWidth = wdLineWidth150pt
20:             .Color = wdColorDarkRed
21:        End With
22:        With .Borders(wdBorderVertical)
23:             .LineStyle = wdLineStyleSingle
24:             .LineWidth = wdLineWidth025pt
25:             .Color = wdColorDarkRed
26:        End With
27: End With
```

ANALYSIS The `With` structure is used with a selected table to set its borders. Each border is set with the `LineStyle`, `LineWidth`, and `Color` properties using built-in constants.

Centering a Table

Another frequent formatting change is the alignment of the table in relation to the page. In a preceding section, the Alignment property was used for the `ParagraphFormat` for two columns. In that case, you weren't affecting the columns, just the text within the column. If you want to affect the alignment of the table on the page, you will use the `Alignment` property for the rows of a selected table. This requires one line of code, if the table is selected:

```
Selection.Tables(1).Rows.Alignment = wdAlignRowCenter
```

You now have all the components to create your custom table style. The completed procedure listed in Listing 12.4 can complete all the special formatting with one click on a toolbar button.

12

LISTING 12.4   The `FormatTaskTable` Procedure

```
1: Sub FormatTaskTable()
2:      On Error GoTo FormatError
3:      Selection.Tables(1).Select
4:      Selection.Tables(1).AutoFormat Format:=wdTableFormatColorful2
5:      Selection.Tables(1).Columns(1).Width = InchesToPoints(0.75)
6:      Selection.Tables(1).Columns(2).Width = InchesToPoints(3)
7:      Selection.Tables(1).Columns(3).Width = InchesToPoints(1)
8:      Selection.Tables(1).Columns(4).Width = InchesToPoints(1)
9:      Selection.Tables(1).Columns(3).Select
```

continues

LISTING 12.4 continued

```
10:        Selection.ParagraphFormat.Alignment = wdAlignParagraphCenter
11:        Selection.Tables(1).Columns(4).Select
12:        Selection.ParagraphFormat.Alignment = wdAlignParagraphCenter
13:        With Selection.Tables(1)
14:            With .Borders(wdBorderLeft)
15:                .LineStyle = wdLineStyleSingle
16:                .LineWidth = wdLineWidth150pt
17:                .Color = wdColorDarkRed
18:            End With
19:            With .Borders(wdBorderRight)
20:                .LineStyle = wdLineStyleSingle
21:                .LineWidth = wdLineWidth150pt
22:                .Color = wdColorDarkRed
23:            End With
24:            With .Borders(wdBorderTop)
25:                .LineStyle = wdLineStyleSingle
26:                .LineWidth = wdLineWidth150pt
27:                .Color = wdColorDarkRed
28:            End With
29:            With .Borders(wdBorderBottom)
30:                .LineStyle = wdLineStyleSingle
31:                .LineWidth = wdLineWidth150pt
32:                .Color = wdColorDarkRed
33:            End With
34:            With .Borders(wdBorderVertical)
35:                .LineStyle = wdLineStyleSingle
36:                .LineWidth = wdLineWidth025pt
37:                .Color = wdColorDarkRed
38:            End With
39:        End With
40:        Selection.Tables(1).Rows.Alignment = wdAlignRowCenter
41:        Exit Sub
42: atError:
43: Dim strMsg As String, strTitle As String
44: Select Case Err.Number
45:        Case 5941    'No Table Selected
46:            strMsg = "There isn't a table selected, "
47:            strMsg = strMsg & "please select a table and try again."
48:            strTitle = "No Table Selected"
49:        Case Else
50:            strMsg = "An unexpected error, " & Err.Number
51:            strMsg = strMsg & ", " & Err.Description
52:            strMsg = ", has occurred. This procedure can't continue."
53: End Select
54: MsgBox strMsg, vbExclamation, strTitle
55: Sub
```

ANALYSIS The code shown in listing 12.4 uses the same code that was introduced in the section "Formatting Tables" earlier in this hour to create a custom format for tables.

Line 2 sets up error handling for the formatting and line 3 uses the `Select` method to select the entire table to make sure the formatting is applied to the entire table and not only the cells selected by the user. Then the formatting can begin.

Line 4 applies one of the AutoFormat styles to act as a base for the custom style. Lines 5–8 adjust the column width for each column. When you are creating your own procedure, you need to make the changes manually to the table and use the Table Properties dialog to see what widths were chosen. Lines 9–12 adjust the alignment of the text in columns 3 and 4.

Lines 13–39 set the borders for the table using a `With` structure for the table, which is set up on line 13 and nested with structure for each border like the one shown on lines 14–18 which sets the appearance of the left border.

Line 40 centers the table between the margins and line 41 terminates the execution of the procedure if everything executed correctly. The one area that could cause problems is the fact that the user might not have the insertion point inside of a table. That is why you needed an error handling structure, which has been added on lines 42–54.

If you attempt to format a table that isn't active, Microsoft Word will generate error 5941: `No Table Selected`. This error number is the generic number for any missing object. The error handling structure displays an error message and exits the routine to enable the user to select a table and try again.

12

Summary

In this hour, you explored how to use VBA when you work with tables. You learned that you can automate the creation of tables, as well as the conversion of text to tables.

In addition to creating tables, VBA can also be used save time when formatting a table. You learned that you can use one of the built-in styles applied by the `Table AutoFormat`, or that you can also apply the same style with VBA.

If you find that none of the styles match your needs, or if you just want to add some special formatting to one of the existing styles, you can custom format by setting properties for the table as a whole or specific elements such as a column or row.

Q&A

Q Can I use the Draw Table command in a macro?

A No, the Draw Table command can't be recorded. It depends on the placement and movement of the mouse. Mouse motion can't be recorded. You can use this command to design a table and then save it as an AutoText entry. You can also use this command to get the specifications needed to control the properties to write the VBA that will adjust a standard table.

Q Can I use VBA to convert a table into text?

A Yes, converting a table into text can be done with VBA. Instead of using the `ConvertToTable` method, you need to use the `ConvertToText` method.

Q Can I merge cells with VBA?

A Yes, there is a Merge method. You would select the cells manually or add a line of code to select the cells and then use the Merge method. Its syntax is

```
Selection.Cells.Merge
```

Workshop

Here are some questions and exercises to help you review the material covered in this hour. The answers to the quiz questions can be found in Appendix A, "Quiz Answers."

Quiz

1. What is the advantage of setting the `NumRows` argument as 1 for the `Add` method when inserting a table?

2. Where are columns inserted?

3. Can you save time in formatting when converting text to a table?

Exercises

1. Review your automation needs list to determine where you need tables.

2. Review the built-in Table AutoFormat styles to determine if there is one style that meets your formatting needs.

3. Create a table to list regular tasks for each day of the week similar to the one shown in Figure 12.7.

Figure 12.7

The weekly task list lists regular tasks and provides room for unique tasks.

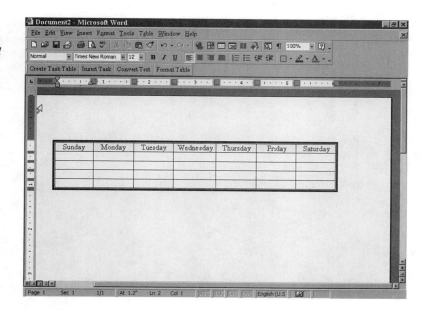

HOUR 13

Working with Graphics

If you use graphical elements in your document on a regular basis, look over your work to see how you can automate your graphics. You might find that you are using the same graphic often (such as your company logo, a graphic design on your personal stationery, or a favorite piece of clip art), or you are frequently formatting a number of graphics in exactly the same manner.

The highlights from this hour include

- Working with pictures
- Working with shapes
- Adding drop caps

Working with Pictures

One way of adding visual interest to your documents is to include pictures. When you examine your work, you might find that you insert the same picture (such as your company logo) in several places in your text. You might also find that you are inserting different pictures that require consistent formatting (such as the pictures of the screen shown in this book). Inserting and formatting graphics will rank high on your list of tasks to automate because they are time-consuming.

In this section, you will examine the different approaches to inserting pictures, as well as horizontal lines, with VBA. You will also learn how to automate the formatting of graphics, including their placement, wrapping properties, background, and borders.

Inserting Clip Art and Pictures

When you insert pictures into your document manually, whether from the clip art collections shipped with Microsoft Office or from an outside source, you use the menu choices and then have to format the picture manually, often with the mouse. When you automate this process, you must know what you are going to do with the image after it is in your document. This will save steps during the process and ensure that the picture is placed in the document correctly.

Whether you realize it or not, there are multiple layers to your document. There is the layer that contains the text, as well as drawing layers to support graphical images and other objects. When you insert a picture with VBA, you can choose to place the image in the text layer or to place it in one of the drawing layers.

When you insert a graphic manually, you aren't choosing the layer. Microsoft Word is choosing it for you. When you automate the insertion of a graphic, you are the one who determines where the graphic will be placed,

If you want your graphic to be treated as text—which means that as text is added to the document the graphic will flow with the text—you add the image to the `InlineShapes` collection.

The advantage to placing the object in the `InlineShapes` collection is that the text controls where the graphic is placed in the document. If a graphic is placed next to a paragraph, and later you add three pages of text above it in the document, the graphic will automatically move to the new page with the paragraph.

The drawback to using the `InlineShapes` collection is that it imposes some restrictions. An object must be a picture, OLE Object, or ActiveX control to be added to the `InlineShapes` collection. You can't attach the object to a page, nor can you control its size as it is added.

If you want to have greater control over the image as it is inserted and greater control over its formatting, you can, instead, add it to the `Shapes` collection. The `Shapes` collection contains the objects that reside in the drawing layer. An object in that layer can be an AutoShape, freeform, OLE object, ActiveX control, or picture.

Placing an object in the Shapes collection also provides a wider range of formatting choices. The greatest benefit is that the object can be sized as it is added to the document. It can also be placed in relation to a page rather than a paragraph.

Regardless of which collection you work with, you will be adding the picture to the document. To accomplish this task, you will always use the AddPicture method. Depending on which collection you are going to use, the syntax varies. Each instance is covered separately in the following sections.

Adding a Picture as an Inline Shape

Adding a picture to your document as an object in the InlineShapes collection is ideal in certain circumstances. It is a good approach when the picture is accurately sized for use in the document, and it is also a part of the text. To accomplish this in your code, use the syntax for the AddPicture method for the InlineShapes collection:

SYNTAX

```
expression.AddPicture(FileName, LinkToFile, SaveWithDocument, Range)
```

The AddPicture keyword follows an *expression* representing the current document's InlineShapes collection separated by a period. This syntax has four arguments:

- FileName: This argument is required. It stores the name and path of the file that stores the picture. If a path isn't included, the active folder is assumed.

- LinktoFile: This argument is optional, and it controls whether a copy of the file is inserted into the document or whether the picture maintains its connection to the original file. If this argument is set to False the picture is an independent copy of the file. False is the default value.

- SaveWithDocument: This argument is optional and indicates whether the picture is saved with the document. If it is set to True, the linked picture is saved when the document is saved. If this argument is omitted, the default value (False) is used.

- Range: This argument is also optional. The Range indicates the location of the inserted picture in the document. If the Range argument references a selected range of text, that text will be replaced. The location of the insertion point is used if no range is entered.

13

To test this approach, you can create a procedure to insert a box picture as shown in Listing 13.1. This procedure is a perfect candidate to put on the toolbar or to be assigned a shortcut key. It is something you will use frequently.

LISTING 13.1 The InsertBox Procedure

```
1: Sub InsertBox()
2:     Selection.InlineShapes.AddPicture FileName:= _
3:     "C:\Program Files\Common Files\Microsoft Shared\Clipart
       ➥\themes1\bullets\bd10254_.gif" _
4:     , LinkToFile:=False, SaveWithDocument:=True
5: End Sub
```

This procedure requires that you place your insertion point and click the toolbar button. It will place the box clip art image. You can use this procedure at the beginning and end of the line as shown in Figure 13.1 to accent a heading.

FIGURE 13.1

The box picture accents the heading text at the beginning and end of the line.

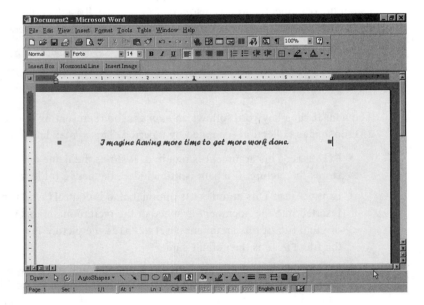

This procedure is fairly straightforward. The only area that might cause difficulty is the `FileName` argument. If the file or path doesn't exist or can't be accessed, the code will generate an error. You might consider adding some error handling. If you create an error handler and test for error 5152 (which is the invalid file error), you can avoid this particular problem.

Adding Horizontal Lines

In addition to inserting a graphic in the `InlineShapes` collection, you can also add horizontal lines. The horizontal line command is available from the Borders and Shading dialog. You can choose to add a horizontal line to your document to act as a separator between text sections. To automate this process, you use the `AddHorizontalLine` method.

The `AddHorizontalLine` method inserts a new object into the `InlineShapes` collection. It also uses the `Filename` and `Range` arguments. To add one of the horizontal styles, create an `InsertHorizontalLine` procedure such as the one shown in Listing 13.2.

LISTING 13.2   The `InsertHorizontalLine` Procedure

```
1: Sub InsertHorizontalLine()
2:     Selection.InlineShapes.AddHorizontalLine FileName:= _
3:         "C:\Program Files\Common Files\Microsoft
           ➥Shared\Clipart\themes1\lines\bd14996_.gif"
4: End Sub
```

If you execute this procedure on a line above and below the text shown in the Figure 13.1, you create a custom box. This technique is shown in Figure 13.2.

FIGURE 13.2

The custom box is created with four graphics.

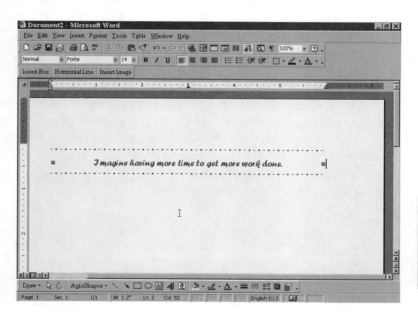

If you combine the code to insert a box image and the code to insert the horizontal line with some navigation code, you can turn any line into a boxed heading. The `PictureBox` procedure in Listing 13.3 turns a line into a boxed header at the insertion point.

13

LISTING 13.3   The PictureBox Procedure

```
 1: Sub PictureBox()
 2:     Selection.HomeKey Unit:=wdLine
 3:     Selection.TypeParagraph
 4:     Selection.MoveUp Unit:=wdLine, Count:=1
 5:     Selection.InlineShapes.AddHorizontalLine FileName:= _
 6:         "C:\Program Files\Common Files\Microsoft Shared\Clipart" & _
 7:         "themes1\lines\bd14996_.gif"
 8:     Selection.MoveDown Unit:=wdLine, Count:=1
 9:     Selection.HomeKey Unit:=wdLine
10:     Selection.InlineShapes.AddPicture FileName:= _
11:         "C:\Program Files\Common Files\Microsoft Shared\Clipart" & _
12:         "\themes1\bullets\bd10254_.gif", _
13:         LinkToFile:=False, SaveWithDocument:=True
14:     Selection.EndKey Unit:=wdLine
15:     Selection.InlineShapes.AddPicture FileName:= _
16:         "C:\Program Files\Common Files\Microsoft Shared\Clipart" & _
17:         "\themes1\bullets\bd10254_.gif", _
18:         LinkToFile:=False, SaveWithDocument:=True
19:     Selection.MoveDown Unit:=wdLine, Count:=1
20:     Selection.InlineShapes.AddHorizontalLine FileName:= _
21:         "C:\Program Files\Common Files\Microsoft Shared\Clipart" & _
22:         "\themes1\lines\bd14996_.gif"
23: End Sub
```

Adding a Picture as a Shape

Adding a picture as a shape is the best procedure to use when the graphic is not the size you need for your work or when you want to place the graphic relative to the page instead of to a paragraph. You will still use the AddPicture method, but the syntax is different:

SYNTAX

```
expression.AddPicture(FileName, LinkToFile, SaveWithDocument, _
    Left, Top, Width, Height, Anchor)
```

The arguments used when adding a picture as a shape are the same used in previous procedures except for Range argument. The Range argument isn't used with the Shapes collection. Instead, there are five other arguments that give you more control over placement.

The Left, Top, Width, and Height arguments enable you to control the placement and dimensions of the graphic as it is added to your document. These arguments expect a value measured in points. You can use the InchestoPoints function to perform the conversion.

The last argument is Anchor. This argument is very similar to the Range argument in that it indicates what the new object will be bound to. If it is omitted, the object will be set relative to the upper-left corner of the page.

For example, you are creating a document giving tips to save time when creating documents in Microsoft Word. You want to use a piece of clip art to illustrate your text, but there will be many steps to formatting the image because the clip art isn't the size you need. This over-sized art is illustrated in Figure 13.3.

FIGURE 13.3
The clock clip art is too big for your text.

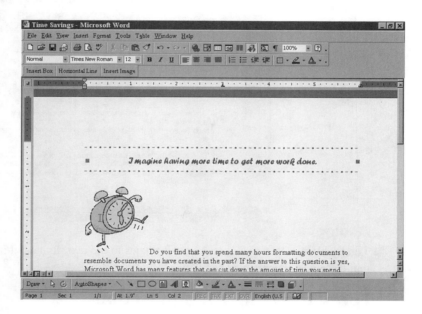

You can create a procedure that takes care of placing the art for you, using the AddPicture method. For example, you can place the clock in your document with the InsertImage procedure shown in Listing 13.4.

13

LISTING 13.4 The InsertImage Procedure

```
1: Sub InsertImage()
2:     ActiveDocument.Shapes.AddPicture FileName:= _
3:         "E:\PFiles\MSOffice\Clipart\standard\stddir1\bd05032_.wmf", _
4:         LinkToFile:=False, SaveWithDocument:=True, _
5:         Left:=InchesToPoints(0.5), Top:=InchesToPoints(2), _
6:         Width:=InchesToPoints(0.75), Height:=InchesToPoints(0.7)
7: End Sub
```

When the procedure is executed, the picture is inserted at the location specified by the Left and Top arguments. Its size has been altered by the Width and Height arguments. The resulting picture has the right dimensions, but it isn't perfect as shown in Figure 13.4.

FIGURE 13.4

The picture is in the right place and is the right size, but there is still work to be done.

The problem with the picture is how it relates to the text. Its layout must be changed so that the clock appears next to the text.

Formatting Clip Art and Pictures

To alter the formatting of a picture, you select it and adjust its properties. You can adjust any of the settings that are available in the Format Picture dialog (see Figure 13.5).

The first step is to identify the object you want to format. When you insert an object using the AddPicture method, the object isn't automatically selected. The insertion point is to the right of the inserted object. You have two ways to deal with this problem. You can work with the Shapes collection, or you can adjust the way the picture is added.

To set a property for an object in the collection, you will have to indicate which object you want to format. The general syntax is

```
expression.collection(index).property
```

The *expression* identifies the container you are working with. In many cases, you will use the ActiveDocument property to indicate you are working with the current document. The second part is the name of the collection. In this case, it is the Shapes collection.

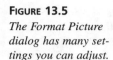

FIGURE 13.5

The Format Picture dialog has many settings you can adjust.

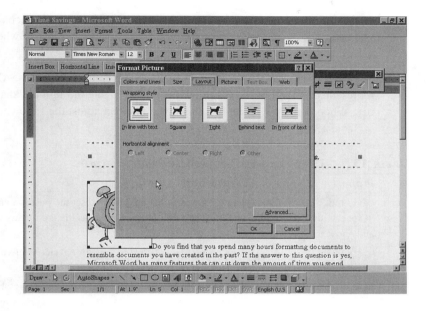

The individual shape is referenced by an index number. When you insert shapes, the shape you just inserted is the last one in the collection. This means you can use the Shapes collection to work with your picture. You might add the following lines of code:

```
Dim lShapeCount As Long
lShapeCount = ActiveDocument.Shapes.Count
```

The lShapeCount can now be used as the index. You can now set any of the properties for the object. This approach, however, is cumbersome.

A second approach is to use an object variable. An *object variable* is a special variable that can be set to enable you to reference a specific programming object. You can create an object variable as you add the picture to the document. Add a line of code and modify the AddPicture line:

```
Dim objectvariable as Shape
Set objectvariable = expression.AddPicture(FileName, _
    LinkToFile, SaveWithDocument, Left, Top, Width, _
    Height, Anchor)
```

The additional line of code declares the object variable in memory. Most of the objects available through VBA can be set up as an object variable and specified to be a certain type. In this case, the variable is defined as Shape.

The AddPicture line must be modified to assign the new picture to the variable. You begin with the Set keyword followed by the name of the object variable. You use the

13

equal sign to set up an expression. The remainder of the line is unchanged, except that you must use the parentheses around the arguments, regardless of whether you are using named arguments or not.

After the object variable is set up, you can begin setting properties. All of the settings represented in the Format Picture dialog are available through the Shape object's properties. When you are working with pictures, you can adjust the following properties listed in Table 13.1.

TABLE 13.1   The Shape Properties Used with Pictures

Property	Description
Left, Top, Height, Width and Anchor	These properties enable you to reset the position and dimensions of the picture. They use the same rules as the arguments for the AddPicture method.
Visible	This property can be set to True or False. It determines if a shape can be seen.
Line	This property represents the shape's LineFormat object. This object has properties like Style, DashStyle, and ForeColor to control the appearance of a border around the shape.
PictureFormat	This property represents the picture's PictureFormat object. It has properties to control contrast, brightness, and cropping instructions.
WrapFormat	This property represents the WrapFormat object for the shape. It has properties like Type to control how the text wraps around the shape.

In the case of the clock picture, the problem is text wrapping. To correct the placement of the picture, you can change the InsertImage procedure as shown in Listing 13.5.

LISTING 13.5   The Modified InsertImage Procedure

```
1: Sub InsertImage()
2:     Dim objPicture As Shape
3:     Set objPicture = ActiveDocument.Shapes.AddPicture(FileName:= _
4:         "E:\PFiles\MSOffice\Clipart\standard\stddir1\bd05032_.wmf", _
5:         LinkToFile:=False, SaveWithDocument:=True, _
6:         Left:=InchesToPoints(0.5), Top:=InchesToPoints(2), _
7:         Width:=InchesToPoints(0.75), Height:=InchesToPoints(0.7))
8:     objPicture.WrapFormat.Type = wdWrapTight
9: End Sub
```

When the procedure is executed, it takes care of the text wrapping automatically as shown in Figure 13.6. The graphic is now next to the first paragraph.

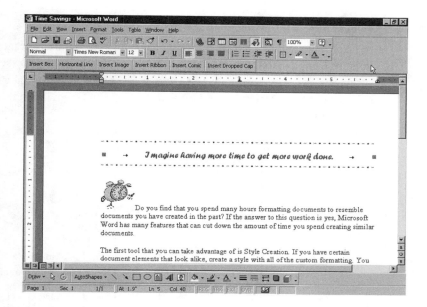

FIGURE 13.6
The first paragraph is now next to the picture.

The wrapping is taken care of automatically because of the change in how the picture is inserted. The `object` variable, `objPicture` is declared and then it is set to the result of the `AddPicture` method. Then `objPicture` is used to set the `WrapFormat`'s `Type` property.

If you are setting more than one property for the picture, you should use the `With` structure. You can add a border to the image by inserting the following additional code under the `Set` statement in the `InsertPicture` procedure:

```
With objPicture.Line
    .Style = msoLineThickThin
    .Weight = 2
    .Visible = msoTrue
End With
```

The `Line` property represents the `LineFormat` object for an object. It has properties to control the appearance of the border of an object. The `Style` property controls the appearance of the line using built-in constants. You will notice that the constant has a prefix of `mso`. This indicates that this feature is shared across all of the Office products.

You also control the thickness of the line with `Weight`. You specify the desired weight with points. Last, but not least, the `Visible` property is used to make the border visible in the document.

13

Working with Shapes

In addition to adding pictures to your document, you can take advantage of some of the other drawing objects available in Word from the Drawing toolbar (see Figure 13.7). Adding shapes from the Drawing toolbar is one of the features that can't be recorded effectively by the Macro Recorder because it relies too heavily on the mouse when you add it to the document.

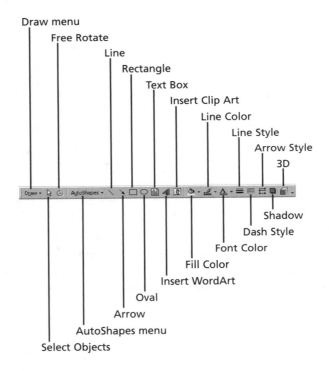

FIGURE 13.7
The Drawing toolbar offers many shapes for inclusion in your document.

To work with shapes you must add the shape to the Shapes collection and then work with its properties to control its appearance. You might want to walk through the steps to create the shape before you try to write code to automate it.

 Don't forget you can create the shapes using the toolbar and save the shapes as AutoText entries. This can be a great time saver if the shapes don't change as you add them.

Adding Shapes

The first step is to add the shape to your document. You use the AddShape method. Its syntax is

```
expression.AddShape(Type, Left, Top, Width, Height, Anchor)
```

This method is very similar to the AddPicture method you use when adding a picture to the Shapes collection. The AddShape keyword follows an expression representing the Shapes collection. Because you are going to work with the shape after it is added, you will assign it to an object variable as it is created.

The AddShape method has six arguments. The first argument is Type. It needs to be set to one of the built-in constants to indicate what type of shape is being created. For example, you use msoShapeCurvedUpRibbon to create the shape shown in Figure 13.8.

FIGURE 13.8

An example of the curved up ribbon Autoshape.

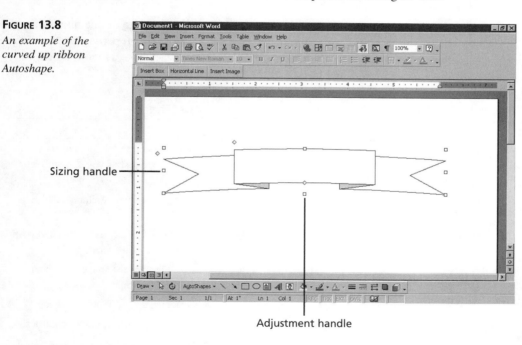

The Left, Top, Width, Height, and Anchor properties are the same as those for the AddPicture method. They control the placement and dimension of the shape. To create the shape shown in Figure 13.8, you can run the code shown in Listing 13.6.

13

LISTING 13.6   The `insertRibbonHeader` Procedure

```
1: Sub InsertRibbonHeader()
2:    Dim objRibbon As Shape
3:    Set objRibbon = ActiveDocument.Shapes.AddShape _
4:        (Type:=msoShapeCurvedUpRibbon, _
5:        Left:=InchesToPoints(1.25), Top:=InchesToPoints(1), _
6:      Height:=InchesToPoints(1), Width:=InchesToPoints(6))
7: End Sub
```

The object variable, objRibbon is declared to identify the new shape on line 2. Lines 3–6 use the AddShape method to add the shape to the Shapes collection for the active document. Again, the InchestoPoints function is used to convert the measurements.

Formatting Shapes

After the shape has been added to the collection, you can make any formatting changes needed. This is accomplished with properties. In addition to the properties listed in Table 13.1, there are also some other properties you might use when you are working with AutoShapes. These are listed in Table 13.2.

TABLE 13.2   The Additional Properties Used with AutoShapes

Property	Description
Adjustments	This property represents the Adjustments collection for some of the AutoShapes. They enable you to adjust a shape just as you can with an Adjustment handle.
AutoShapeType	This property stores the type of shape. It enables you to change the shape after it is added, if necessary.
Shadow	This property represents the shape's shadow object. It has associated properties to control the color, depth, and direction of the shadow.
TextFrame	This property represents the TextFrame object for the shape. You can add text to many of the shapes, as well as set their formats.
TextEffect	This property represents the TextEffect object for a Word Art shape.
ThreeD	This property represents the ThreeD object that enables you to control the three-dimensional properties of a shape.

With these properties, you can make any formatting changes to the shape as needed. If you wanted to adjust the ribbon and add text to it (for example, for announcing top performers), you can modify the InsertRibbonHeader procedure as shown in Listing 13.7.

LISTING 13.7 The Modified `InsertRibbonHeader` Procedure

```
 1: Sub InsertRibbonHeader()
 2:    Dim objRibbon As Shape
 3:    Set objRibbon = ActiveDocument.Shapes.AddShape _
 4:        (Type:=msoShapeCurvedUpRibbon, _
 5:        Left:=InchesToPoints(1.25), Top:=InchesToPoints(1), _
 6:        Height:=InchesToPoints(1), Width:=InchesToPoints(6))
 7:    With objRibbon
 8:        .Adjustments.Item(1) = 0.2
 9:        .Adjustments.Item(2) = 0.6
10:        .Shadow.Type = msoShadow2
11:        With .TextFrame.TextRange
12:            .Bold = msoTrue
13:            .Font.Name = "Ariel"
14:            .Font.Size = 24
15:            .ParagraphFormat.Alignment = wdAlignParagraphCenter
16:            Dim strtitle As String
17:            strtitle = InputBox("What title do you want?")
18:            .Text = strtitle
19:        End With
20:    End With
21: End Sub
```

ANALYSIS Lines 1–6 are the same as in the original procedure. They set up the object variable and add the shape to the collection. The formatting of this object begins on line 7 using a `With` structure.

The first property setting controls the adjustments. When you add shapes manually, you can use the Adjustment handles shown in Figure 13.8. When you want to control different components of a shape with VBA, you use the `Adjustments` collection.

Each Adjustment handle is represented in a collection. Some AutoShapes have no `Adjustments` and others have several. This object has three. You assign a value to each `Adjustment` using the `Item` property indicating the index of one of the `Adjustments`. For the most part, the handles are represented in order from top to bottom and left to right.

Adjustment handles control different things for each shape. Some control the width or height of an aspect of the shape. Others control the radius or the angle of an aspect of the shape. For dimension and radius, you indicate a position within the entire object. This is done by specifying a number between 0 and 1. With angles, you indicate up to 180 degrees.

In this procedure, you are adjusting two of the handles on lines 8–9. One controls the width of the ribbon loop and the second its tilt. Both of these use a setting between 0 and 1. It may take several tries before a number gives you the exact result you want. With practice, your estimation skills will get better.

13

Line 10 selects a shadow format for the object. The Shadow property represents the Shadow object for the Shape. It has different properties to control the appearance of the shadow. In this case, the Type property is set to one of the built-in constants representing one of the built-in styles represented on the Shadow palette accessed from the Drawing toolbar.

Lines 11–19 finish the formatting by setting up the text for the ribbon. A nested With structure is used to work with the TextFrame object's TextRange object. The TextFrame represents the TextFrame object for the Shape. The TextRange property represents the text that will be placed in the frame.

With the TextRange, you can modify any of the properties for the text and its display. This is identical to the formatting techniques shown in Hour 10, "Adjusting Text Appearance." Setting the format for the text in any Shape is different from the TextEffect property. It is used only with Word Art objects.

In the code to set the TextRange properties, lines 16–18 illustrate the power of VBA. At the beginning of this hour, I pointed out that you could create your shape and save it as an AutoText entry. This is great if the shape or group of shapes do not change. In this case, an input box is used to solicit the title to be placed on the ribbon each time the procedure is run, enabling you to change the image for every use.

Grouping Shapes

There are times when you want more than one shape to be treated as one entity, or as a compound shape. In these cases, you can manually select the shapes and the use the Group command to achieve your goal.

With VBA, you can use the ShapeRange collections to select the shapes and then use the Group method. The procedure, InsertComic, shown in Listing 13.8, illustrates this collection and method. It creates two objects, a happy face and a cloud callout. After setting their properties, the two shapes are added to the ShapeRange collection and grouped.

LISTING 13.8　The InsertComic Procedure

```
 1: Sub InsertComic()
 2:    Dim objFace As Shape, objCloud As Shape
 3:    Set objFace = ActiveDocument.Shapes.AddShape _
 4:        (Type:=msoShapeSmileyFace, _
 5:        Left:=InchesToPoints(1.75), Top:=InchesToPoints(1.5), _
 6:        Height:=InchesToPoints(0.75), Width:=InchesToPoints(0.75))
 7:    objFace.Name = "Face"
 8:    Set objCloud = ActiveDocument.Shapes.AddShape _
 9:        (Type:=msoShapeCloudCallout, _
```

```
10:        Left:=InchesToPoints(2.75), Top:=InchesToPoints(0.75), _
11:        Height:=InchesToPoints(0.9), Width:=InchesToPoints(1.5))
12:    objCloud.Name = "Cloud"
13:    With objCloud.TextFrame.TextRange
14:        .Bold = msoTrue
15:        .Font.Name = "Arial"
16:        .Font.Size = 14
17:        .ParagraphFormat.Alignment = wdAlignParagraphCenter
18:        .Text = "Wow"
19:    End With
20:    ActiveDocument.Shapes.Range(Array("Face", "Cloud")).Group
21: End Sub
```

ANALYSIS When this procedure is executed, the two shapes are added and formatted. The last step is the one that will enable you to treat them as one object as shown in Figure 13.9.

FIGURE 13.9

The face and callout are now treated as one shape.

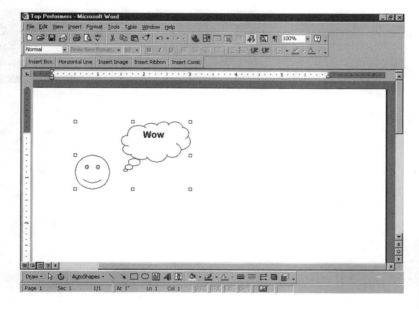

The first part of the code is similar to that in the InsertRibbonHeader procedure. Line 2 declares two object variables to reference the new shapes. Lines 3–6 creates the face shape with the AddShape method. Line 7 is new. Here you are setting the Name property for the new object so you can group it later in the procedure.

Lines 8–11 add the cloud callout shape to the collection. Line 12 assigns a value to its Name property as well. Lines 13–19 set its formatting properties.

Line 20 is the line that enables you to treat these objects as one. Here you are using the Range property to represent the Range object for the Shapes collection. The Array function is used to list the objects that you want to work with. Here you are using the Name properties for the objects to include them in the list of items to group.

The Range is followed with the Group keyword which enables you to create the compound object. There is also an Ungroup method if you want to break an object into its original shapes.

Adding Drop Caps

In addition to working with pictures and shapes, you can also add a dropped cap as the first character of a paragraph for the effect shown in Figure 13.10. This technique is frequently used in magazine articles.

FIGURE 13.10

This first letter of the first paragraph is double the size of the rest of the text.

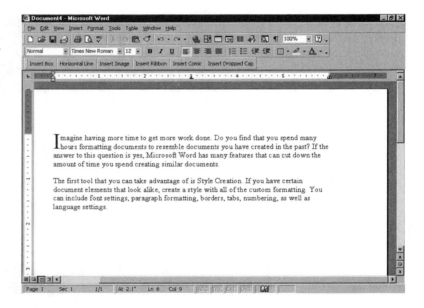

The dropped cap effect acts as a graphical header for a new topic. When you want to automate this effect, you will use the DropCap object for the selected text.

In this case, you aren't adding an object to the document as much as you are adjusting the formatting of one of the characters. The DropCap object has four property settings that control the appearance of this initial character as illustrated in the InsertDroppedCap procedure in Listing 13.9.

LISTING 13.9   The `InsertDropCap` procedure

```
1: Sub InsertDroppedCap()
2:     With Selection.Paragraphs(1).DropCap
3:         .Position = wdDropNormal
4:         .FontName = "Times New Roman"
5:         .LinesToDrop = 2
6:         .DistanceFromText = InchesToPoints(0)
7:     End With
8: End Sub
```

ANALYSIS These properties mimic the settings in the dialog. The `Position` property can be set on line 3 using built-in constants to represent no-dropped appearance, a normal drop below the line of text, or a drop in the margin.

`FontName` enables you to change the font of this one character on line 4. On line 5, `LinesToDrop` determines the size of the character. It will maintain its proportion to the font size of the paragraph text.

The last property is `DistanceFromText` on line 6. It determines how much whitespace there is between the character and the rest of the text.

Summary

In this hour, you have been introduced to some of the ways you can automate the integration of graphics in your documents. You looked at different approaches for inserting pictures into your document, as well as how to format them.

You learned how to integrate shapes from the drawing toolbar into your document automatically and control their formatting with properties. You also looked at automating a dropped cap formatting for a paragraph.

Q&A

Q Do you have to use clip art images?

A No, you can add any picture as long as it is stored in one of the supported formats such as the Windows Metafile format.

Q Can you automate the placement and formatting of Curves, Free Forms, and Scribbles?

A Yes, the creation of all the shapes is possible, but it can be very time-consuming to work with these objects because you have to determine where each small segment of the object will be placed.

13

Q Can you automatically insert charts in your document?

A Yes, charts can automatically be inserted using the InsertOLEObject method. This enables you to insert the chart, but not format it. To format charts, you have to use VBA with the Microsoft Graph object model. More information concerning charts is in Hour 20, "Working with Other Office Applications."

Workshop

Here are some questions and exercises to help you review the material covered in this hour. The answers to the quiz questions can be found in Appendix A, "Quiz Answers."

Quiz

1. What is the method for inserting pictures into your document?

2. What is the difference between placing the picture in the Shapes collection or InlineShapes collection with the AddPicture method?

3. Why are object variables so important when you are working with shapes?

Exercises

1. Create a procedure that inserts one of the cartoon clip art images and adds one of the callout shapes with text in it. Make sure they are grouped within the procedure.

2. Evaluate your automation checklist to see where you need to incorporate these graphic techniques.

Hour 14

Working with Large Documents

When you begin working with larger documents, there are many management tasks. In many cases, you will find that you are attempting to create large documents with similar formatting. In this hour, you are going to explore various automation techniques to make managing large documents easier.

The highlights of this hour include

- Speeding up navigation with bookmarks
- Working with sections
- Adding columns
- Creating indexes and tables of contents

To give yourself material to work on in this hour, you can make a copy of one of your large documents, or you can use the sample template from the companion Web site. It is called Hour14.dot.

When you are creating a template for a large document from an existing document, one of the steps involves deleting any text that will change from document to document. This text should not be part of the template. This step must still be completed in Hour14.dot. The majority of the material after section 5.1 is specific to a particular proposal. It was left in place to provide additional pages for use in the later sections of this book. Delete this material in preparation for creating the template. Likewise, if you are working with your own document, delete any information that is specific to that particular document and replace it with bookmarks for later automation.

Speeding Up Navigation with Bookmarks

As stated previously, when you begin working with large documents, you might find that you're creating documents that are basically very similar to each other except for several items of text that make each document unique. A good example is a sales proposal. The general content and structure of the proposal stays the same, but specific items in the document must be tailored to the specific sale.

To automate the process of altering the changeable areas of the document, you can use the standard navigation methods including keystrokes and the Goto command. Unfortunately, most changes won't fall at the specific points that commands and keystrokes take you to (such as the end of the document or the top of the page). For changes in other parts of the document, you can use bookmarks to make navigation easier, as well as to add text automatically.

A *bookmark* is a placeholder in your document that won't print. It normally isn't seen when you are working on the document, unless you have it selected from the Options dialog. Bookmarks not only mark places, they can also store data for automatic insertion in the document.

When you are creating a template for a large document, you usually begin with an existing document. What needs to be automated will be easy to spot. If you often find yourself opening an existing document and changing just a part of the text to create a new document, you have a prime candidate for automation.

Examine a standard sales proposal or job specification. In a proposal, certain items will be changed and certain items added each time it is used, depending on the circumstances.

An example of this variable information might be the company history. If you are sending your tenth proposal to a client, you already have a personal history with him, and he is well acquainted with your company. In that case, you don't need to include a history. If the company history section is bookmarked, it can be easily located to be added or deleted as you wish.

When you want to create a template for a large document, the first step is to open it and save it as a template. Then you are ready to make it generic.

Adding Bookmarks

After the template is created, you are ready to begin adding bookmarks that you will use in your procedure. An example of an area you will bookmark is the line where the company name appears on the title page (see Figure 14.1).

FIGURE 14.1

The company name is specific to each document.

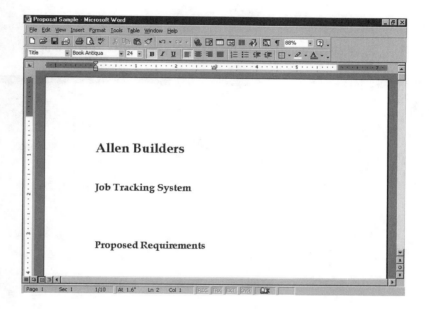

In the template, you are going to use VBA to fill in the company name throughout the document. To add a bookmark for the company name manually, complete these steps:

1. Select the company name on the title page.
2. Replace the name with Company.
3. Select the word Company.
4. Select Insert, Bookmark to display the Bookmark dialog shown in Figure 14.2.
5. Enter Company as the Bookmark name and click the Add button.
6. Click somewhere outside of the company name in the document to release your highlight.
7. Select Tools, Options to display the Options dialog.
8. Select the View tab, check the Bookmarks check box, and click OK.

14

FIGURE **14.2**
*The Bookmark dialog
is used to add and nav-
igate bookmarks
manually.*

9. Notice the thinner brackets surrounding the word Company (see Figure 14.3).

FIGURE **14.3**
*The bookmark is now
in place with text
inside of it.*

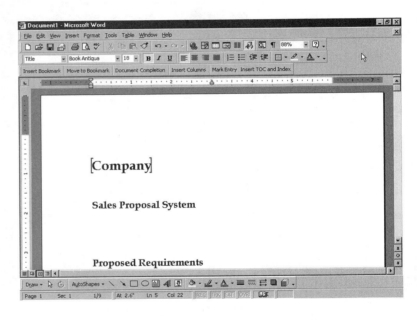

You do the same thing with the system name in this example. Although it isn't as common, you might also add a bookmark with VBA. To do so, you will use the Bookmarks
collection and the Add method. To insert a bookmark for the system, use the procedure
shown in Listing 14.1.

LISTING 14.1   The InsertSystemBookmark Procedure

```
1: Sub InsertSystemBookmark()
2:     With ActiveDocument.Bookmarks
```

```
3:            .Add Range:=Selection.Range, Name:="System"
4:            .DefaultSorting = wdSortByName
5:            .ShowHidden = False
6:       End With
7: End Sub
```

ANALYSIS This procedure is quite simple. It uses a `With` structure beginning on line 2 to work with the `Bookmarks` collection for the active document.

Line 3 adds the new bookmark to the collection. The `Add` method has various arguments depending on what collection you are working with. The `Bookmarks` collection needs two arguments to add a bookmark. You must supply a range and a name. In this case, the `Range` argument is set to the text that is currently selected. The name can be set to any valid string following the naming guidelines for VBA.

Lines 4–5 set some properties for the `Bookmarks` collection. These options are shown in the dialog, but they can be omitted in this case because you didn't change them. In the Bookmarks dialog, you can choose to sort the list by name or by location within the document.

You can also show any bookmarks that have been hidden in the document. This property controls those bookmarks in the text that have the hidden attribute applied, not bookmarks that can't be seen because of your Options settings.

Moving to a Bookmark

After the bookmark is in place, you can write code that moves to that bookmark. To move to a specific bookmark, use the `Goto` method. It can be used to move to a bookmark or other elements in your document. The syntax is

SYNTAX

```
expression.GoTo(What, Which, Count, Name)
```

The `Goto` keyword follows an expression and a period. The expression defines the object to move in. It can be a document, a range, or a selection. The `Goto` method can have up to four arguments:

- `What`: The first argument indicates what type of object you can search for. It is set to one of its built-in constants. For bookmarks, you use `wdGotoBookmark`.
- `Which`: The second argument indicates a fixed object to move to. Don't use this argument with bookmarks. Bookmarks are indicated with the `Name` argument.

14

- Count: The Count argument indicates an increment of an object to move to. For example, if you are using the Goto method to move by page, you can enter a 5 to move five pages forward from your location.

- Name: The last argument is used with bookmarks. Here you indicate which bookmark you want to move to with a string such as "Company".

If you want a procedure to move to the Company bookmark you placed in the file, the code will resemble the code shown below.

```
Sub MovetoBookmark()
    Selection.GoTo What:=wdGoToBookmark, Name:="Company"
End Sub
```

Moving to bookmarks is great when you want to end a procedure by placing the user in the exact spot to begin her typing. In this case as in most cases, you will want to retrieve information or place information by using a bookmark.

> Please don't forget that you can use a Fill-in or Macro Button field to add placeholders in your document. They are great for simple prompts for the user. For more information, please refer to Hour 1, "Introducing Automation Fundamentals."

Getting and Placing Information Using Bookmarks

When you use bookmarks for retrieving information or placing new information, you use the Bookmarks collections, the Range property, and its Text property. To reference a bookmark's contents, you use the bookmark syntax which follows:

SYNTAX

expression.Bookmarks(*Bookmarkname*).Range.Text

The expression represents the document or selection you want to work with. It is followed by the Bookmarks keyword. Because this is a collection, it has parentheses with an argument indicating the index of the bookmark you want to use. It can contain an index number or, as shown above, the bookmark name. In that case, the name must be enclosed in quotations.

The Bookmarks collection is followed by a period and the Range property. The Range Property represents the Range object for the collection. It is followed by a period and the Text property.

The previous syntax isn't used by itself. You are going to make it a part of an expression. To set the text property for the bookmark, put it on the left side of an expression followed by an equal sign and a value as shown below:

```
expression.Bookmarks(Bookmarkname).Range.Text = value
```

If you are going to use the contents of a bookmark, the equation is reversed as shown in the following code:

```
variable = expression.Bookmarks(Bookmarkname).Range.Text
```

The Bookmarks collection gives you a great deal of flexibility in completing the document. In the DocumentCompletion procedure listed in Listing 14.2, you use the InputBox and MsgBox functions to get information from the user. You use the bookmarks placed in the document to complete the needed information.

LISTING 14.2   The DocumentCompletion Procedure

```
 1: Sub DocumentCompletion()
 2: '    Define varaibles for fill in information
 3:     Dim strCompany As String, strSystem As String
 4:     Dim strEnvironment As String, strProduct As String
 5:     Dim lPhases As Long
 6: '    Get information using Input and Msg Boxes
 7:     strCompany = InputBox("What is the company name?", _
 8:         "Company Name")
 9:     strSystem = InputBox("What is the system name?", _
10:         "System")
11:     strEnvironment = InputBox("What is the operating system?", _
12:         "Operating System")
13:     strProduct = InputBox("What product will be used?", _
14:         "Product")
15:     lPhases = MsgBox("Is this a new customer?", vbYesNo + _
16:         vbInformation, "New Client")
17: '    Test and place information
18:     If ActiveDocument.Bookmarks.Exists("Company") Then
19:         If ActiveDocument.Bookmarks("Company").Range.Text = _
20:         "Company" Then _
21:             ActiveDocument.Bookmarks("Company").Range.Text = _
22:         strCompany
23:     End If
24:     If ActiveDocument.Bookmarks.Exists("System") Then
25:         If ActiveDocument.Bookmarks("System").Range.Text = _
26:         "System" Then _
27:         ActiveDocument.Bookmarks("System").Range.Text = _
28:         strSystem
```

14

continues

LISTING 14.2   continued

```
29:        End If
30:        If ActiveDocument.Bookmarks.Exists("System1") Then
31:            If ActiveDocument.Bookmarks("System1").Range.Text = _
32:            "System" Then _
33:            ActiveDocument.Bookmarks("System1").Range.Text = _
34:            strSystem
35:        End If
36:        If ActiveDocument.Bookmarks.Exists("Environment") Then
37:            If ActiveDocument.Bookmarks("Environment").Range.Text = _
38:            "Environment" Then _
39:            ActiveDocument.Bookmarks("Environment").Range.Text = _
40:            strEnvironment
41:        End If
42:        If ActiveDocument.Bookmarks.Exists("Product") Then
43:            If ActiveDocument.Bookmarks("Product").Range.Text = _
44:            "Product" Then _
45:            ActiveDocument.Bookmarks("Product").Range.Text = _
46:            strProduct
47:        End If
48:        If ActiveDocument.Bookmarks.Exists("Phases") Then
49:            Selection.GoTo What:=wdGoToBookmark, Name:="Phases"
50:            If lPhases = vbYes Then
51:                ActiveDocument.AttachedTemplate _
52:                    .AutoTextEntries("FullPhases") _
53:                    .Insert Where:=Selection.Range, RichText:=True
54:        Else
55:                ActiveDocument.AttachedTemplate _
56:                    .AutoTextEntries("SimplePhases") _
57:                    .Insert Where:=Selection.Range, RichText:=True
58:            End If
59:        End If
60:        Selection.GoTo What:=wdGoToBookmark, Name:="Purpose"
61: End Sub
```

ANALYSIS   When you execute this procedure from the toolbar, it begins by using the InputBox function to gather information (see Figure 14.4), and it stores this information in local variables.

After the procedure gathers some information for inclusion in the document, it uses a MsgBox to ask if it is a new client. This information will be used to insert an AutoText entry later in the procedure.

After all the information is gathered with the InputBox and MsgBox functions, the information is put into the document using those bookmarks. the last step uses the Goto method to move the insertion point to the Purpose bookmark where you will begin typing as shown in Figure 14.5.

FIGURE 14.4

The first InputBox *prompts for the company.*

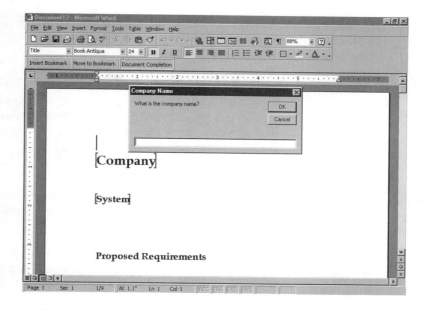

FIGURE 14.5

The Purpose section is selected and ready for your entry.

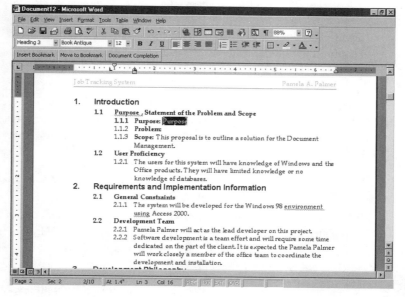

Lines 2–5 declare five variables that will store the information while processing. Lines 6–14 are the InputBoxes to gather the information that will be placed in the bookmarks, and in lines 15–16, the MsgBox function determines if the client who will receive this

document is new client. In this example, there isn't any error handling to make sure the user enters information in the Inputboxes. In your procedure, you want to make sure the user enters valid information in the Input Boxes.

 In this example, several InputBoxes are used to get information from the user. This is very tedious. In Hour 17,"Working with User Forms," you will learn how to develop and use User Forms. They are a better method to gather information from the user.

Beginning on line 17, you are placing the information in the bookmarks. The process isn't as simple as using the Text property to set the contents of the bookmark. You must do some error handling using an If structure.

The Exists method, shown for the first time on line 18, enables you to test whether the bookmark exists. If you try to place information in a bookmark that doesn't exist, you will generate an error.

The nested If structure tests to see the current contents of the bookmark. In this document, you entered some dummy text for the company. The bookmark contents are tested against this dummy text, and only if the bookmark contents match will the dummy text be replaced with the contents of the appropriate variable. Notice that the contents of the variable strSystem are used twice for two different bookmarks.

 Please remember that you can define custom document fields. If there is information used throughout a document, you can insert the information in a specific document property, such as Subject or Client, and then insert it into your document using a field.

The last bookmark that is completed is the Phases bookmark with lines 48—59. It is completed dependent on the user's answer in the MsgBox. In this template, there are two AutoText entries—one that has information especially for new clients, and one that has a reference to another document.

When you want to take advantage of an AutoText entry with bookmarks, you use the GoTo method as shown in line 49. This moves you to the bookmark. Then you use the Insert method introduced in Hour 9, "Working with Text," for inserting the AutoText entry.

Line 60 moves the user to the first spot in the document that needs custom input to start the manual completion of the document. Line 61 is the end of the procedure.

Although the use of the `InputBox` function is a tedious way to get information, using bookmarks to fill in unique information in a standard document makes automatic document completion attainable in your own work. Remember, you will see a better method for gathering information in Hour 17.

Working with Sections

In addition to completing text automatically, you can also adjust the formatting of larger documents automatically. For example, in this sample template for a system proposal, the header and footer on the first page is blank. The header and footer on the second page has information including the page number, 2, in the footer.

In larger documents, you might not want a cover page to be part of the page count. Another option you might want is a different type of page numbering in a certain part of a document. Adjusting the page count can be as simple as changing the starting number. If you want to change the styles of page numbering in a document, you can use sections.

A *section* is a break in the document similar to a page break, except that it has a greater impact on document formatting. Each section has its own page settings, headers, and footers.

To insert a section, use the `InsertBreak` method. The `InsertBreak` method enables you to insert any one of the available breaks: a page break, column break, text wrapping break, or section break. Its syntax is

SYNTAX

expression`.InsertBreak(`*Type*`)`

The `InsertBreak` keyword follows an expression that represents the object you are working with. It can be a document or a selection. It is followed by an argument in parentheses. The `Type` argument indicates what type of break you want to insert. If you wanted to automate adding page numbering to a new section, the code is

```
Selection.InsertBreak Type:=wdSectionBreakNextPage
```

After the section is inserted, you can add any custom formatting to that section as needed. If you want to have page settings apply to this section only, you can add two section breaks. One will separate the new section from the previous one, and one will separate the new section from the following one.

14

Adding Columns

One special circumstance that requires a new section is the inclusion of columns in your document. Although you may not have realized it, adding columns to your document is adjusting the Page Setup—even though you use a different dialog. When you choose to have more than one column in your document, these columns must be put in a separate section so the margin settings can be customized. The fact that you are adjusting the page Setup is clearer when you automate the process with VBA.

To set up columns, make sure you are in the Print view and use the PageSetUp object to adjust the columns. To create a three-column portion of text, use the InsertNewspaperColumns procedure shown in Listing 14.3:

LISTING 14.3   The InsertNewspaperColumns Procedure

```
 1: Sub InsertNewspaperColumns()
 2:     If ActiveWindow.ActivePane.View.Type <> wdPrintView Then
 3:         ActiveWindow.ActivePane.View.Type = wdPrintView
 4:     End If
 5:     With Selection.PageSetup.TextColumns
 6:         .SetCount NumColumns:=3
 7:         .EvenlySpaced = True
 8:         .LineBetween = False
 9:         .Width = InchesToPoints(1.47)
10:         .Spacing = InchesToPoints(0.29)
11:     End With
12: End Sub
```

ANALYSIS   Lines 2–4 test what view is selected for the document. If the view selected isn't the Print view, the view is switched automatically. This is done so you can see the text in columns.

Lines 5–11 adjust the TextColumns object for the PageSetUp object for the selected text. Line 6 uses the SetCount method to indicate that you want three columns. Line 7–8 sets the EvenlySpaced property to True and the LineBetween property to False for no line. The LineBetween line could be omitted because the default setting for this property is False indicating no line.

Lines 9–10 set up the attributes for the columns. Because the EvenlySpaced property is set to True, only one set of values needs to be given.

When you want different widths for each columns, each column is set up separately. The settings for the first column are completed as shown in this example except the SetCount is set to 1. Then you use the Add method to add columns to the TextColumn collection. If you want three columns—with a large column and then two smaller columns—the code would be as listed in Listing 14.4.

LISTING 14.4 The Revised `InsertNewspaperColumns` Procedure

```
 1: Sub InsertNewspaperColumns()
 2:     If ActiveWindow.ActivePane.View.Type <> wdPrintView Then
 3:         ActiveWindow.ActivePane.View.Type = wdPrintView
 4:     End If
 5:     With Selection.PageSetup.TextColumns
 6:         .SetCount NumColumns:=1
 7:         .EvenlySpaced = False
 8:         .LineBetween = False
 9:         .Width = InchesToPoints(2.822)
10:         .Spacing = InchesToPoints(0.29)
11:         .Add Width:=InchesToPoints(1.22), Spacing:= _
12:             InchesToPoints(0.37), EvenlySpaced:=False
13:         .Add Width:=InchesToPoints(1.22), Spacing:= _
14:             InchesToPoints(0.37), EvenlySpaced:=False
15:     End With
16: End Sub
```

These statements are all that is needed to set up the columns. Notice that there are no statements to add sections to the document. The sections are already added when you view the results as shown in Figure 14.6.

FIGURE 14.6

The three even columns are formatted and the section breaks are inserted automatically.

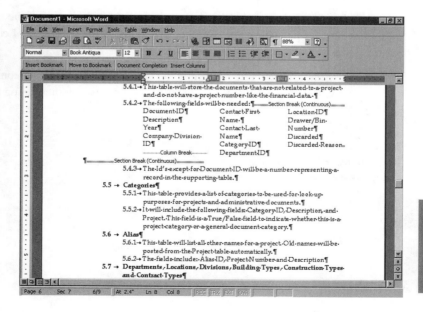

14

Please remember that setting up the newspaper columns adjusts the page setup. If you adjust any of the other page settings (such as Orientation) for a part of a document, those settings will add the sections for you automatically as well.

Creating Indexes and Tables of Contents

In addition to adding special sections for different parts of the document, you might also assist your reader with locating items in the document. Microsoft Word enables you to automatically create an index, table of contents, table of figures, and table of authorities.

Microsoft Word also tries to assist you with setting up what is needed to compile these lists. To create the table of contents and the table of figures, you can designate that any text formatted with specific styles should be included in a specific table. You can also mark items for inclusion manually. This enables you to create several tables for different purposes. For example, many books have a quick table of contents that gives major topics, and they also include a detailed table of contents with subtopics.

Take a look at how you insert custom marks with VBA, as well as how you insert the tables in your document. You will work with the table of contents and the index.

Inserting Marks

In addition to using styles to select items for inclusion in one of the lists, you can also mark entries manually. This is done with fields. To make a table of contents entry, you use the TC field. To mark an index field, you use the XE field.

You use the Fields dialog illustrated in Hour 1 to mark a table of contents entry. With index entries, because of the special settings, you use another dialog as shown in Figure 14.7.

FIGURE 14.7
The Mark Index Entry dialog is used to set up your choices.

For both sets of marks, you place your insertion point next to the text you mark. Access the dialog, enter the text for the reference, and enter any switches. You can automate the insertion of these marks with VBA.

For example, you could create the `InsertSpecialTOCandIndex` procedure as shown in Listing 14.4 to use some selected text for the entries. Using selected text does have certain problems you must work around.

LISTING 14.4 The `InsertSpecialTOCandIndex` Procedure

```
 1: Sub InsertSpecialTOCandIndex()
 2:     Dim strText As String
 3:     strText = Selection.Text
 4:     Selection.MoveRight Unit:=1
 5:     Selection.Fields.Add Range:=Selection.Range, Type:=wdFieldEmpty, _
 6:         Text:="TC """ & strText & """ \l 2", PreserveFormatting:=False
 7:     ActiveDocument.Indexes.MarkEntry Range:=Selection.Range, _
 8:         Entry:=strText, CrossReference:="", CrossReferenceAutoText:="", _
 9:         BookmarkName:="", Bold:=False, Italic:=False
10: End Sub
```

ANALYSIS When you insert a Table of Contents field or an Index mark, you replace what is selected. This means that you have to preserve what was selected by the user, and then clear the selection before inserting the mark. Preserving the information is accomplished on lines 2–3. A variable is declared and then the `Text` property for the selection is stored in it. After the information is preserved, the `MoveRight` method is used to move the insertion to the right of the text on line 4.

Lines 5–6 actually place the Table of Contents entry next to the text. It uses a standard field specifying the correct settings for a table of contents field as the text argument. Inside of the string, you are using the TC to indicate it's a table of contents mark. The TC is followed by a space and quotations, as well as by the variable with the text. This is followed by quotations to surround the text and the switch \l to indicate a level.

Each field has specific switches that can be used. There are three switches that can be used with the TC field. You can also set multiple Table of Contents support, as well as suppressed page numbers if desired. You can also use the MarkEntry method. It is similar to the format shown below for indexing.

Lines 7–9 insert the Index mark. Indexing can be inserted as a standard field, or you can work with the `Indexes` collection directly which gives you more control over the entry.

When using the `Indexes` collection, you use the `MarkEntry` method to place the field. With it, you specify a `Range` for the entry. The `Entry` argument stores the text. For

14

AutoEntries, there is also an AutoEntry argument (not shown) similar to that used with figures.

The CrossReference and CrossReferenceAutoText are used when you are referring the reader to another index entry. You can also use the Bookmark entry, if you are using another page reference. The Bold and Italic arguments indicate formatting for the reference.

When you select some text and execute the procedure, the marks are placed to the right of the text as shown in Figure 14.8. The text is preserved.

FIGURE **14.8**

The fields are automatically inserted.

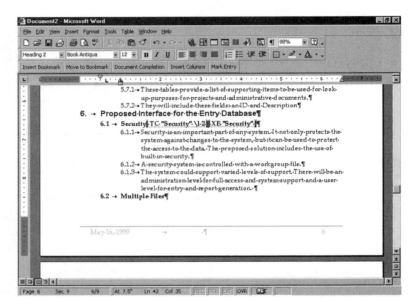

Inserting Tables

VBA can also be used to insert the table of contents and index themselves. If you want to complete your document and then automatically insert the tables, you can create the InsertTOCSection procedure shown in Listing 14.5.

LISTING **14.5**   The Procedure to Insert a Table of Contents and Index

```
1: Sub InsertTOCSection()
2:     Selection.GoTo What:=wdGoToPage, Which:=wdGoToNext, Name:="2"
3:     Selection.MoveLeft Unit:=wdCharacter, Count:=2
```

```
 4:     Selection.TypeParagraph
 5:     Selection.TypeParagraph
 6:     Selection.InsertBreak Type:=wdSectionBreakNextPage
 7:     Selection.Style = ActiveDocument.Styles("Subtitle")
 8:     Selection.TypeText Text:="Table of Contents"
 9:     Selection.TypeParagraph
10:     Selection.TypeParagraph
11:     Selection.Style = ActiveDocument.Styles("Normal")
12:     ActiveWindow.ActivePane.View.SeekView = wdSeekCurrentPageHeader
13:     If Selection.HeaderFooter.IsHeader = True Then
14:         ActiveWindow.ActivePane.View.SeekView = wdSeekCurrentPageFooter
15:     Else
16:         ActiveWindow.ActivePane.View.SeekView = wdSeekCurrentPageHeader
17:     End If
18:     Selection.HeaderFooter.LinkToPrevious = False
19:     With Selection.HeaderFooter.PageNumbers
20:         .NumberStyle = wdPageNumberStyleLowercaseRoman
21:         .HeadingLevelForChapter = 0
22:         .IncludeChapterNumber = False
23:         .ChapterPageSeparator = wdSeparatorHyphen
24:         .RestartNumberingAtSection = True
25:         .StartingNumber = 1
26:     .Add PageNumberAlignment:= _
27:         wdAlignPageNumberRight, FirstPage:=False
28:     End With
29:     ActiveWindow.ActivePane.View.NextHeaderFooter
30:     Selection.HeaderFooter.LinkToPrevious = False
31:      With Selection.HeaderFooter.PageNumbers
32:         .NumberStyle = wdPageNumberStyleArabic
33:         .HeadingLevelForChapter = 0
34:         .IncludeChapterNumber = False
35:         .ChapterPageSeparator = wdSeparatorHyphen
36:         .RestartNumberingAtSection = True
37:         .StartingNumber = 1
38:         .Add FirstPage:=True
39:     End With
40:     ActiveWindow.ActivePane.View.SeekView = wdSeekMainDocument
41:     Selection.GoTo What:=wdGoToPage, Which:=wdGoToNext, Name:="i"
42:     Selection.MoveDown Unit:=wdLine, Count:=1
43:     Selection.TypeParagraph
44:     With ActiveDocument
45:         .TablesOfContents.Add Range:=Selection.Range, _
46:             RightAlignPageNumbers:=True, UseHeadingStyles:=True, _
47:             UpperHeadingLevel:=1, LowerHeadingLevel:=1, _
48:             IncludePageNumbers:=True, AddedStyles:="", UseFields:=True, _
49:             UseHyperlinks:=True, HidePageNumbersInWeb:=True
50:         .TablesOfContents(1).TabLeader = wdTabLeaderLines
51:         .TablesOfContents.Format = wdIndexIndent
52:     End With
```

14

continues

LISTING 14.5 continued

```
53:     Selection.EndKey Unit:=wdStory
54:     Selection.TypeParagraph
55:     Selection.InsertBreak Type:=wdPageBreak
56:     Selection.Style = ActiveDocument.Styles("Subtitle")
57:     Selection.TypeText Text:="Index"
58:     Selection.TypeParagraph
59:     Selection.TypeParagraph
60:     Selection.Style = ActiveDocument.Styles("Normal")
61:     With ActiveDocument
62:         .Indexes.Add Range:=Selection.Range, HeadingSeparator:= _
63:             wdHeadingSeparatorLetter, Type:=wdIndexIndent, _
64:             RightAlignPageNumbers:=True, NumberOfColumns:=2, _
65:             IndexLanguage:=wdEnglishUS
66:         .Indexes(1).TabLeader = wdTabLeaderSpaces
67:     End With
68: End Sub
```

ANALYSIS In lines 2–43 set up the section for the table of contents, as well as modify the headers and footers for different page numbers.

Lines 44–52 set up the With structure to insert the table of contents field. You are working with the ActiveDocument property to indicate at what range you want to insert a table of contents. Then you are using the TableofContents property to represent the TableofContents collection for the document.

The Add method is used to add a new table to the collection. With the Tables of Contents, you can specify up to ten arguments. The Range indicates where the table should be placed. The UseHeadingStyles, UpperHeadingLevel and LowerHeadlinLevel indicate whether the paragraph styles are used for formatting the table and which of the Heading 1–Heading 9 styles are used as table of contents entries automatically. In this case, you are using the Heading 1 paragraphs only.

IncludePageNumbers indicates whether the page numbers are included in the list. The AddedStyles gives you a chance to specify any additional styles to be included in the list, with their levels.

The UseFields indicates whether any TX fields will be used when the table of contents is created. The UseHyperlinks and HidePageNumbersInWeb enable you to create special formatting for a table of contents for a Web page. There are also a TableID and RightAlignPageNumbers to allow more than one table of contents and to adjust the page number placement manually.

After the table of contents is in place, you can move to the end of the document to place the index. Lines 53–60 move to the end of document and format the title for the page.

Lines 61–67 insert the index using a `With` structure. The `Indexes` collection for the `ActiveDocument` is used with the `Add` method to add the new index. In this case, there are eight arguments.

You set the location of the new index with the `Range` argument. Whether you have a separator between index entries with specific letters is controlled with the `HeadingsSeparator`. The `Type` argument enables you to select a style for the index from a predefined list of styles.

The `RightAlignPageNumbers` and `NumberofColumns` indicate additional formatting. The `IndexLanguage` indicates how the index will be treated during spell and grammar check to support multiple languages.

The `TabLeader` property indicates what separates the text from the page numbers. You can also set the `AccentedLetters` property to control the treatment of accented letters as well as the `SortBy` argument to control sorting in other languages.

This procedure automatically adds these document elements to help you maintain consistent formatting in these tables. When the procedure is executed, you get a standard table of contents (see Figure 14.9) and index each time.

FIGURE 14.9

The table of contents is formatted as desired.

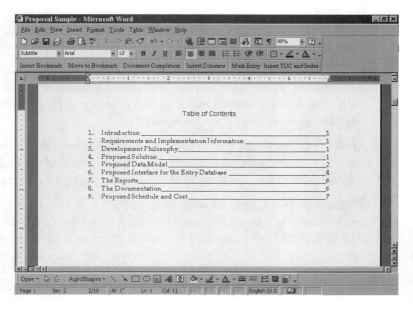

If desired, you can insert the following lines of code before line 53 to add testing before the insertion of the index. It checks for any index marks. If there are none, you can skip the insertion of the index. This eliminates having a table with nothing in it.

```
1:    Dim objField As Field, bIndexEntry As Boolean
2:    For Each objField In ActiveDocument.Fields
3:        If objField.Type = wdFieldIndexEntry Then
4:            bIndexEntry = True
5:            Exit Loop
6:        End If
7:    Next
8:    If bIndexEntry = False Then Exit Sub
```

Line 1 declares two variables. One is to represent an individual field in the `Fields` collection, and the second is set to `True` if there are index entry fields in the document.

Lines 2–7 use a `For each Next` loop to test each field in the active document. The `Type` property is evaluated using a built-in constant. If any of the fields is an index entry, the Boolean variable is set to `True` and the loop is terminated.

Line 8 tests the Boolean variable, and if it is False the procedure is terminated without an index. Otherwise, the remainder of the code is executed, the index page is formatted, and the index is inserted.

Summary

In this hour, you explored some of the techniques for working with larger documents. You explored how to use bookmarks to navigate within the document, as well as to retrieve and place information in a document.

You explored how to insert sections in your document automatically to facilitate special formatting. You also learned that when you apply special page settings to range, it automatically adds the needed section breaks.

In addition to exploring how to automate tasks with larger documents, you also created procedures to insert the table of contents and index, as well as to mark those entries for selected text. You can apply these same techniques with the other tables as well.

As you look ahead, there are some other techniques for working with larger amounts of text in Hour 19, "Managing Large Documents." That hour explores how to break larger documents into smaller ones and re-assemble them as needed. It also looks at how to take advantage of AutoCaptioning, referencing, summaries, and revisions with VBA.

Q&A

Q **Should placing the Table of Contents in the document with VBA be the last procedure you perform?**

A It isn't required that placing the Table of Contents in the document is the very last procedure, but doing so makes sure that all the items are there when the table is generated. If you are going to insert the Table of Contents first, you must have a procedure that recalculates the contents of the Table of Contents field before you save the file. You can use the ReCalc method.

Q **What is the advantage of bookmarks over fields?**

A The advantage is that instead of using the Browser object to move from field to field, you can use a bookmark to move directly to a named location.

Ideally, you would want to combine the two techniques. At the end of the DocumentCompletion procedure, you move to the Purpose bookmark. If you use a fill-in field and you include code similar to the code in one of the memo procedures, you can use a combined technique.

If you place a MacroButton field for the Purpose topic in the document, you can move to the bookmark and set the Browser's Target property to Field. This causes the user to see the first field selected and ready for typing. Once the Purpose is entered, the user can also access the remaining changeable fields with the Browse Object buttons.

Workshop

Here are some questions and exercises to help you review the material covered in this hour. The answers to the quiz questions can be found in Appendix A, "Quiz Answers."

Quiz

1. What property stores the text in a bookmark?
2. How do you create columns with different widths?
3. Why is the Bookmarks collections Exists method important?
4. Why would you use the MarkEntry method for inserting an index item instead of a standard field?

14

Exercises

1. Modify the Hour 14 template to use fill-in fields and modify the DocumentCompletion procedure to set the Browser object to look for fields in the document through the document.

2. Evaluate your automation list to see where you can use these large document techniques.

HOUR 15

Working with Forms

In Hour 1, you were introduced to the built-in fields that make it easier to fill in information in a document. You created on-line forms that could prompt you for missing information.

Although we, as a society, haven't completely made the transition from paper based forms to online forms, we are moving in that direction. Microsoft Word speeds the journey by providing some additional tools for you to create your own online forms.

Highlights from this hour include

- Creating a form
- Completing actions based on a form

When you begin implementing the VBA for working with online forms, the procedures might be longer than some of the other procedures you have created. Remember, there is a sample template and supporting files available on the companion web site.

In addition to copying the template, Hour15, into your template directory, copy the Seminar Evaluation Tracking Document into your workgroup template directory. Also, check your Options, File Locations tab. Make sure that the Workgroup Templates choice points to the location of this file.

Creating a Form

Although you took advantage of some of the built-in fields in the previous hours, you did not create a standard form. When you think of forms, you frequently think of a page or two with boxes where you enter simple answers to questions. An example is an evaluation for a seminar or a customer survey. Usually, neither of these forms exceed one page. If they did, no one would take the time to fill them out.

When you create a form, complete these three steps.

1. Create a template with the generic text of the form.
2. Add any fields to assist in the completion of the form with any automation.
3. Turn on protection for the template and save it.

Creating the Form Template

The first step is to create a framework for your form. On a blank template file, adjust all the settings that you would normally adjust for a template.

After the general settings of the template are set, add the framework for the form. Although it isn't required, you may find that creating a table will make formatting much easier than formatting free form text.

If you are creating a template for seminars, your base template might resemble the one shown in Figure 15.1. Notice that there are statements with a blank cell next to each for entering text or a rating. That is where you place your fields.

Adding Fields

After the template layout is complete, you are ready to turn it into an online form. This is accomplished by inserting special fields.

When you are creating a form, you use a special toolbar to facilitate the construction. If you right-click on the toolbar and select Forms, the Forms toolbar will display, as shown in Figure 15.2.

FIGURE 15.1

The template has a table and is ready for fields.

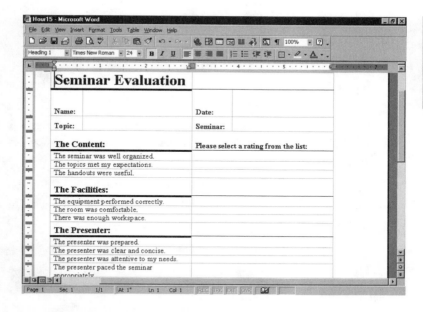

FIGURE 15.2

The Forms toolbar has the form fields as well as some management tools.

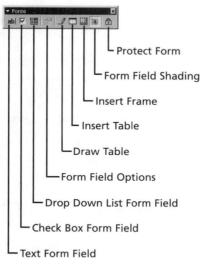

Protect Form

Form Field Shading

Insert Frame

Insert Table

Draw Table

Form Field Options

Drop Down List Form Field

Check Box Form Field

Text Form Field

This special toolbar provides quick access to the three form fields that can be used to automate data entry. There is a text form field, check box form field, and a drop-down list form field. The remaining buttons provide access to other tools you might need when creating forms.

Using the Text Form Field

The first field you will use is the text field. It is designed for basic entry such as plain text, dates, or numeric data.

To add a text field, move your insertion point to the correct location and click on the toolbar button. After the button is in place, you can set its properties with the fourth toolbar button. To get a better idea of how this works, set up the Name text field.

1. Move to the cell to the right of the word *Name*.

2. Click on the Text Form Field button on the toolbar to insert the field as shown in Figure 15.3.

FIGURE 15.3

The field is shown in the second cell in the second row.

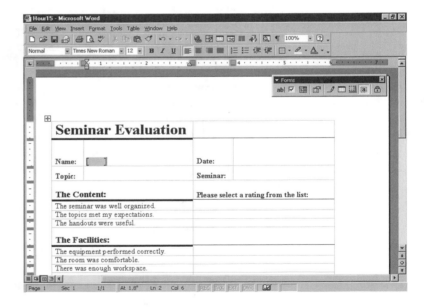

3. Click on the Form Field Options button on the toolbar to display the Text Form Field Options dialog as shown in Figure 15.4

4. Change the Bookmark to txtName and click OK.

With the options, you can set characteristics of the field. You can set the type of data to be entered, how long the entry should be, a default value, and a format. You can also indicate any macros that should run as the field is entered or exited.

FIGURE 15.4

Each type of field has its own Options dialog.

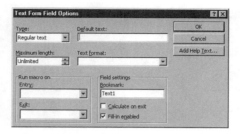

15

If you are going to write a procedure to use the form fields, you should change the Bookmark. By default, as each field is inserted it is assigned a bookmark. This is created from the type of field and the next available number. This bookmark can make it very hard to work with in VBA. In step 4, you change the bookmark to txtName. The txt is a prefix to indicate it is a text field and the Name is a repeat of the text to the left to make it easier to remember.

To finish the text fields for this form, just add text form fields for the Date entry. You can specify a format in the same way as you set a format with the Format function in the memo procedures created in Hour 2, "Getting Started with VBA."

Working with a Check Box Form Field

The second type of form field is a check box. This is very useful for indicating a Yes or No entry without having to type the words. The process is similar to inserting a text box except for a few properties.

For example, to include a field that indicates whether or not the seminar lasted only one day, insert a check box field by completing the following steps:

1. Move the insertion point to the top right cell.
2. Click the Check Box Form Field button on the Forms toolbar.
3. Click on the Form Field Options button on the toolbar to open the Check Box Form Field Options dialog, as shown in Figure 15.5.
4. Select Checked, enter a Bookmark of chkOneDay, and click OK.
5. Press the right arrow to unselect the check box.
6. Press a Space and type One Day Seminar for the check box text.

Selecting Checked is setting a default for the check box. It is similar to typing in default text. The bookmark shows the chk prefix to indicate its type.

FIGURE **15.5**

Check box field options.

Working with a Drop-Down List

The last type of field is the drop-down list. When you want to restrict the user's input to one of several choices, you use this field. It enables you to specify a list of choice for users to choose from.

For example, you want the user to enter the topic of the seminar, but you don't want creativity. If the seminar is concerns Microsoft Word, a user could type Microsoft Word, Word, Word 2000, and so forth. A drop-down list will simplify entry, as well as simplify your code that interprets the information. To insert a drop-down form field for Type, complete the following:

1. Move the insertion point to the cell at the right of the word Type.
2. Click the Drop-Down Form field button.
3. Click the Form Field Options button to open the Drop-Down form Field Options dialog as shown in Figure 15.6.

FIGURE **15.6**

For a drop down field you need to indicate what you want on the list.

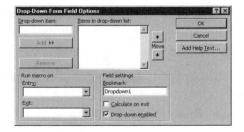

4. Type Word 2000 and press Enter. Notice these words are now on the list.
5. Add Excel 2000 and Access 2000 to the list with the same steps.
6. Change the Bookmark to cboType and click OK.

The drop-down list is now ready for the user to select from. With the options, you can make any changes as needed in the list by removing items or moving them into a new order.

15

If you wonder why the bookmark began with cbo instead of dd or something similar, the cbo stands for *combo box*. When you begin working with other Office applications, you will notice they don't have form fields. They have controls. One of these is a combo box. One of its types is a drop-down list. If you learn to use cbo now, it will make it easier to make the transition into other applications.

Protecting the Template

After the fields are placed in the template, make sure that the users are restricted to filling in only the information requested. They should not have the capability to alter the form. In most cases, making a document a template protects the document from harm by the user. With forms, you are going to add additional protection to facilitate the use of the form.

To protect the form, you can click on the Tools, Protect Document to open the Protect Document dialog as shown in Figure 15.7. you have to select forms and add a password if desired. Now the form can be used.

FIGURE 15.7

The Protect Document dialog is used to complete the form.

As you work on the template, refining the form and its fields, it is best not to set a password. Doing so will slow you down when you are making changes. You will be required to click the Unprotect button on the toolbar for each change. If you create a password, you will have to enter it each time you make a change.

Completing Actions Based on a Form

Now that you have reviewed the basics of setting up a form, you are ready to begin adding functionality with VBA. VBA can be used to add information to and retrieve information from a form. You will experiment with both.

Populating Fields Based on Entry

On the Evaluation form you created, there is a one spot left to add a field to before you get to the statements themselves. You could add another drop-down list with a set of Seminars, but you can make it even easier to use.

Rather than list all the possible seminars, you could only display those seminars for the type selected in the first drop-down list. This can be done by adding a macro procedure to execute when the user leaves that field.

To get started, add a drop-down list form field in the appropriate cell and change its bookmark to cboSeminar. After the field is in place, open the Visual Basic Editor.

In this case, you are creating the procedure from scratch. When you open the Visual Basic Editor without first creating a macro for the template, you don't have a module. You will have to add a module manually, as follows:

1. Click on the template in the Project Explorer.
2. Right-click on the template and click Insert or select Insert from the menu to open the menu.
3. Select Module from the Insert menu to create a new module.
4. Select the Name property in the Properties window and type modManagement.
5. Click the Save button to save the template.

The module is now ready for procedures. To populate a list for a drop-down form field with VBA, work with the FormFields collection. You first remove the current contents and then insert the new items. The procedure shown in Listing 15.1 performs this task.

LISTING 15.1 The SeminarChoice Procedure

```
 1: Sub SeminarChoices()
 2: '    Get selected department
 3:      Dim strType As String
 4:      lType = ActiveDocument.FormFields("cboType").Result
 5: '    Clear the contents of the seminar list.
 6:      ActiveDocument.FormFields("cboSeminar") _
 7:          .DropDown.ListEntries.Clear
 8: '    Evaluate the type and build the list of seminars in the array.
 9:      Select Case lType
10:          Case "Word 2000"
11:              With ActiveDocument.FormFields("cboSeminar") _
12:                  .DropDown.ListEntries
13:                  .Add Name:="Creating Documents"
14:                  .Add Name:="Using Merging"
15:                  .Add Name:="Working with Large Documents"
16:                  .Add Name:="Working with VBA"
17:              End With
18:          Case "Excel 2000"
19:              With ActiveDocument.FormFields("cboSeminar") _
```

```
20:                    .DropDown.ListEntries
21:                    .Add Name:="Creating a Workbook"
22:                    .Add Name:="Getting More with Functions"
23:                    .Add Name:="Using Charting"
24:                    .Add Name:="Working with VBA"
25:             End With
26:         Case "Access 2000"
27:             With ActiveDocument.FormFields("cboSeminar") _
28:                    .DropDown.ListEntries
29:                    .Add Name:="Creating a Database"
30:                    .Add Name:="Understanding Relational Databases"
31:                    .Add Name:="Using Queries"
32:                    .Add Name:="Working with VBA"
33:             End With
34:     End Select
35: End Sub
```

ANALYSIS Lines 2–4 retrieve the selected type from the Type drop-down list form field. A string variable is declared, and then it is assigned the contents of the drop-down list. When you want to work with a form field, use the FormFields collection. To reference a specific field, you will use the syntax shown as follows:

Expression.Formfields("*bookmark*")

The expression will represent the document or selection you are working with. In the example above, the ActiveDocument keyword is used to represent the current form.

A specific form field can be accessed in one of two ways:

- You can place its index number inside of parentheses.
- You can specify the bookmark name you assigned when you created the field.

Using bookmarks makes your code more readable.

In the case, of line 4, you want to use the type that was selected with the drop-down list. Each form field has a Result property. It stores what is entered, checked, or selected. Line 4 places the result in the variable.

The next step is to clear the current list of seminars. This is taken care of with lines 5–7. For a form field that is a drop-down list, there is a Dropdown property to represent its DropDown object.

Each DropDown object has a ListEntries collection that stores the text that has been added to the list. To remove these current items, use the Clear method.

If you want to remove one item from the list, you won't use the `Clear` method. You will use the `Delete` method.

The remainder of this procedure, beginning with line 8, evaluates the `strType` variable and rebuilds the list for the Seminar drop-down list. For each value that `lType` could be assigned, you are going to write a `Case` structure such as the one shown on lines 10–17.

Each case is handled with a `With` Structure working with the `cboSeminar` drop-down list. Instead of using the `Clear` method to remove all the entries, use the `Add` method to add each item to the list. You are going to use the `Name` argument to provide the string for the list text.

Now when the form is protected and you are entering values in the fields, the list will change each time you exit the `cboType` field.

Retrieving Information from a Form

In the last section, you learned how to retrieve a form field value using the `Result` property. This gives you an individual field value. When you are working with forms, you have the ability to set your save options so that you save only the data from forms in a text file. You can the import that text file to Word or another Office applications.

With the `Result` property, you can write VBA to arrange and format the information as you need it. You can place that information in a table. To complete the template, you can create drop-down lists for the responses to the statements. You will create eleven additional drop-down lists, as well as a text field for the comments. The lists are as follows:

CboContent1	CboPresenter1
CboContent2	CboPresenter2
CboContent3	CboPresenter3
CboFacility1	CboPreenter4
CboFacility2	cboOverall
CboFacility4	

If you create the first one and copy it to the clipboard, you can paste it in the other cells and change its bookmark.

The drop-down list needs to have six list choices with these bookmarks in order:

0—Not Selected

5—Strongly Agree

4—Agree

3—Neutral

2—Disagree

1—Strongly Disagree

After these layout changes, the form will be complete and ready for a user to fill in. It should resemble Figure 15.8.

FIGURE 15.8

The remaining drop-down lists are in place.

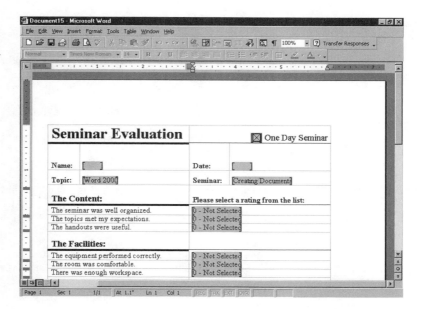

You are now ready to enter the code. The TransferResponses procedure listed in Listing 15.2 illustrates this process of transferring the information to another table.

LISTING 15.2   The TransferResponses Procedure

```
1: Sub TransferResponses()
2: '   Store the name of the active document.
```

continues

LISTING 15.2   continued

```
 3:     Dim strEval As String
 4:       strEval = ActiveDocument.Name
 5:  '   Open the Tracking document and move to the last row.
 6:       Documents.Open _
 7:          FileName:=Application.Options _
 8:          .DefaultFilePath(wdWorkgroupTemplatesPath) & "\" & _
 9:          "Seminar Evaluations Tracking.doc", _
10:          ConfirmConversions:=False, ReadOnly:=False, _
11:          AddToRecentFiles:=False, PasswordDocument:="", _
12:          PasswordTemplate:="", Revert:=False, _
13:          WritePasswordDocument:="", WritePasswordTemplate:="", _
14:          Format:= wdOpenFormatAuto, Visible:=True
15:  '   Enter the data in the table
16:       Dim lRows As Long
17:       lRows = Selection.Tables(1).Rows.Count
18:       With Documents("Seminar Evaluations Tracking").Tables(1)
19:           .Cell(lRows, 1).Range.Text = _
20:               Documents(strEval).FormFields("cboType").Result
21:           .Cell(lRows, 2).Range.Text = _
22:               Documents(strEval).FormFields("cboSeminar").Result
23:           .Cell(lRows, 3).Range.Text = _
24:               Documents(strEval).FormFields("txtName").Result
25:           .Cell(lRows, 4).Range.Text = _
26:               Documents(strEval).FormFields("txtDate").Result
27:           .Cell(lRows, 5).Range.Text = _
28:               Documents(strEval).FormFields("chkOneDay").CheckBox.Value
29:           .Cell(lRows, 6).Range.Text = _
30:               Left(Documents(strEval).FormFields("cboContent1").Result, 1)
31:           .Cell(lRows, 7).Range.Text = _
32:           Left(Documents(strEval).FormFields("cboContent2").Result, 1)
33:           .Cell(lRows, 8).Range.Text = _
34:           Left(Documents(strEval).FormFields("cboContent3").Result, 1)
35:           .Cell(lRows, 9).Range.Text = _
36:               Left(Documents(strEval).FormFields("cboFacility1").Result, 1)
37:           .Cell(lRows, 10).Range.Text = _
39:               Left(Documents(strEval).FormFields("cboFacility2").Result, 1)
40:           .Cell(lRows, 11).Range.Text = _
41:           Left(Documents(strEval).FormFields("cboFacility3").Result, 1)
42:           .Cell(lRows, 12).Range.Text = _
43:               Left(Documents(strEval).FormFields("cboPresenter1").Result, 1)
44:           .Cell(lRows, 13).Range.Text = _
45:               Left(Documents(strEval).FormFields("cboPresenter2").Result, 1)
46:       .Cell(lRows, 14).Range.Text = _
47:           Left(Documents(strEval).FormFields("cboPresenter3").Result, 1)
48:     .Cell(lRows, 15).Range.Text = _
49:           Left(Documents(strEval).FormFields("cboPresenter4").Result, 1)
50:       .Cell(lRows, 16).Range.Text = _
51:           Left(Documents(strEval).FormFields("cboOverall").Result, 1)
```

```
52:     .Cell(lRows, 17).Formula Formula:="=(SUM(LEFT))/11", NumFormat:=""
53:     .Rows(lRows).Select
54:  End With
55:    Selection.InsertRowsBelow
56:    ActiveDocument.Save
57:    ActiveWindow.Close
58: End Sub
```

ANALYSIS The TransferResponses takes the information entered into the fields and transfers it to a table. The first step is to identify the evaluation document before you begin. On lines 2–4, the strEval variable is declared and is assigned the Name property for the ActiveDocument.

The next step is to open the tracking document. When you summarize the entries into a form, you need a central location for the data. That can be a Word document, as illustrated here, an Excel spreadsheet, or an Access database table, as illustrated in Hour 20, "Working with Other Office Applications."

Lines 6–14 use the Open method to open the document. The Open method is similar to the Add method for creating a new document. There are several arguments that control how the file is accessed. The syntax is

SYNTAX

```
expression.Open(Filename, ConfirmConversions, ReadOnly, _
    AddToRecentFiles, PasswordDocument, PasswordTemplate, Revert, _
    WritePasswordDocument, WritePasswordTemplate, Format, _
    Encoding, Visible)
```

The expression points to the Documents collection, which is followed by the Open keyword. Then there are twelve arguments that can be used:

- FileName: The first argument indicates what file you want to open. It must include a path if you don't want to look in the current directory.

- ConfirmConversions: This must be set to True if you want the user to confirm when the file isn't in Word format.

- ReadOnly: This property controls whether the file can be edited.

- AddtoRecentFiles: This indicates that it will appear on the File menu. It is automatically set to True, but when you are doing the work behind the scenes, you probably want to set this to False.

- PasswordDocument, PasswordTemplate, WritePasswordDocument, WritePasswordTemplate: These arguments can be used to pass the corresponding passwords to the document if needed.

- `Revert`: This controls what should happen if the document is already open. If it is set to `True`, which is the default, all changes would be lost. In most cases, you are going to set this to `False`.
- `Format`: This argument is used when you know the file you are working with isn't a Word document. You can specify the conversion tool to use with a built-in constant, such as `wdOpenFormatAutoRTF`.
- `Encoding`: This argument indicates a character set to use with the document if there is a special one needed to support an alternate language. This is set with built-in constants.
- `Visible`: The last argument determines whether the user will see the document. It is set to `True` by default, but if you are doing all the work with VBA, set it to `False`.

With this procedure, you want to open a document called Seminar Evaluations Tracking (see Listing 15.2). If users will be accessing this template from various locations, you need to place this document in a shared location.

A possible location for the document is in the workgroup templates directory or a shared network drive. In this code, the `DefaultfilePath` property is used to look for the document in the work group on line 8. It is concatenated with the document name to fill the `FileName` argument.

The next step is to transfer the information from the form to the table. This is completed with lines 15–55. The first step is to locate the spot for the new information. On lines 16–17, the `lRows` variable is declared and set to the `Count` property for the `Rows` collection for the first table of the `Tables` collection for the Selection. You can assume the table you want to work with is the first because it is the only table in this document.

Lines 18–54 set up a `With` structure to populate each cell in the last row for the table. That is accomplished with the `Cell` method and its corresponding `Range` object for the Table. The syntax is

SYNTAX

`Expression.Cell(Row,Column)`

The expression indicates a valid table followed by the `Cell` keyword. It has two arguments that indicate the row and column you want to work with. With this method, you point to the cell and then you can adjust its properties (such as the `Range` property shown on lines 19–20).

15

The Text property for all the ranges is set to the Result property for the field, except the check box. In that case, you are setting the text property to the CheckBox property's value.

You aren't placing the entire choice from Results in the table. All you want is the number because you want to calculate an average. The Left function is used to retrieve the first character only.

Line 52 fills the last cell, not with a field value, but with a formula. Instead of setting the Range's text property, you use the Formula method to place an equation. You have to provide a Formula argument with the equation and a NumFormat argument with any formatting in a string.

> Notice the equation uses the sum function. It is using the word LEFT to add all the values to the left of this cell. You can use standard formatting.

After the text is place in the cells, the row is selected with line 53. It isn't a requirement to fill the table; it is to set up the table for the next time.

On line 55, the InsertRowBelow method is used to add a new row. Lines 56–57 save and close the tracking document. This leaves the user looking at his evaluation. You could add a message box telling the user that the transfer was complete if desired.

This preceding procedure is fine for trying out techniques, but when you are creatiang a form you will really use in the business world, you must add error handling. Error handling would detect a missing file (5174) or a file opened by another user.

Summary

In this hour, you have explored the process of setting up online forms and adding code to automate the manipulation of the form. When you want to create an online form, you must complete three steps:

1. Create a template with the formatting and structure of the form. It is advantageous to use a table because it lends itself easily to creating different boxes for data.

2. Add form fields. These are fields in which the user fills in the information requested. You can also add VBA code to fill in information or extract information from the form at this step.

3. Turn on document protection. When you are creating a form template, saving it as a template isn't enough. You must also protect it by locking it so that users can only access the form fields.

After this review of the basic process of creating a form, you explored some uses for VBA with forms. You explored how to create a dynamic drop-down list based on information in another field. You also looked at how to use VBA to extract the information from the form into a table.

If you use surveys or evaluations in your work, you may be one step closer to crossing off an item from your automation checklist. This hour showed you how to create an evaluation. You can modify this example to meet your needs.

Q&A

Q With the Text Form Field, what kind of calculations can be used?

A Microsoft Word offers many of the same functions offered with Excel. There is a wide range of functions. These include mathematical, statistical, logical, and financial functions.

Q Can I add option buttons for multiple choice questions such as the ones in the Print dialog for page range?

A No, there isn't an option button field for forms, but you can add option buttons on User Forms. For more information about User Forms, please refer to Hour 17, "Working with User Forms."

Q If I want to save a form as the field data only, what code do I need?

A You use the `SaveAs` method with the document. You just set the `SaveFormsData` argument to True to save only the data.

Workshop

Here are some questions and exercises to help you review the material covered in this hour. The answers to the quiz questions can be found in Appendix A, "Quiz Answers."

15

Quiz

1. Why is it important to change Bookmark text for a field?
2. How do you access the contents of a field with VBA?
3. What collection do you manipulate when you want to change a drop-down list's choices?
4. Why wasn't a fixed path added for the Open method in lines 6–14 of Listing 15.2?

Exercises

1. Change the Seminar Evaluations Tracking document so the One Day column is 1 Day/ Comments. Modify the `TransferResponses` procedure to test the comments field. You should change what is sent for the One Day field to a Y and send a Y if the comments field has anything in it. Send Ns if the answer is no for either field. (Hint: You can see if a string has anything in it with the Len function.)

2 Review your automation checklist to see if you can use the form fields to perform some of your tasks.

Hour 16

Working with Auto Macros, Events, and Built-In Dialogs

In the previous hours, you created various procedures to facilitate the completion of documents. To execute these procedures, you used the Macros dialog or added a menu, button, or keystroke shortcut.

In some cases, you designed the code to be executed at a specific point in the editing process of the document. In this hour, you are going to explore the different approaches to executing code automatically.

The highlights of this hour include

- Executing code automatically for documents
- Executing code automatically for Word
- Accessing built-in dialogs

In this hour, you will be adding code to your Normal template that will automatically execute at certain times. It is recommended that you back up your Normal template to another folder so you can restore it after this hour.

The sample code is included in a sample template, Hour16, from the companion Web site. Follow the instructions in Appendix B, "Using the Templates from the Companion Web Site," to move this code to your Normal template. There are comments in the module that instruct you concerning which procedures must be moved to execute correctly.

Executing Code Automatically for Documents

As you begin automating your tasks with Visual Basic for Applications, you will see an advantage to executing code automatically at specific times in the life of a document. You might want to execute code when a new document based on a specific template is created or when a document opens or closes. A good example of code executing automatically is the procedure created to generate memos.

To create custom memos, you created the StaffMeeting procedure, changed it to the GeneralMemo procedure, and later to the SelectMemo procedure In all these cases, you had to take some action to run the code. A better approach is to automate the selection of a memo type when the document is created from a template. When you make the assessment to automate, you have to decide the best way to automatically execute your code.

Comparing Auto Macros and Events for Documents

When you want to execute code automatically, you have two choices. You can use an auto macro or an event procedure:

- An *auto macro* or automatic macro is a subprocedure that has a specific name that is recognized by Word, making it respond to an action.
- An *event procedure* is a special procedure placed in a special module that is executed when specific events are triggered in Word.

As you read the two definitions above, you might conclude the two procedures are very similar, but there are some differences, which are rooted in the history of the Microsoft Word development.

When Microsoft Office was released initially, each package had its own language for automating actions. Microsoft Word had Word Basic. Word Basic had only the auto macros for executing code at specific times. For document processing, you had the following auto macros:

- The `AutoNew` macro, which executes when a document is created from a template.
- The `AutoOpen` macro, which executes as a document is opened.
- The `AutoClose` macro, which executes as a document is closed.

When Office 95 was released, Microsoft started to integrate the method for automation across all the Microsoft applications with Visual Basic for Applications. VBA's new approach of using objects was slowly integrated into the other Microsoft applications. Because of Word's complexity, however, it couldn't be upgraded with Office 95.

The concept of developing code to respond to specific actions by the user or the system was referred to as event-driven programming. When VBA was integrated into Word with Office 97, the object model included events for some of the objects. You might, for example, create the following event procedures.

- The `New` event which executes when a document is created from a template.
- The `Open` event which executes as a document is opened.
- The `Close` event which executes as a document is closed.

As you compare the list of macros with the list of events, you will notice that there is an exact match. When you decide to automatically execute code, you also decide which approach to use.

In most cases, when you have a choice between the older Word Basic approach and the new VBA approach, you should choose the VBA approach. Normally, it is more flexible and has greater speed of execution. That isn't true in every case, however. There are some times when the older method is best. These instances are discussed in greater detail later in this section.

The key to deciding which approach to use is whether you are creating more than one procedure to support an action. You can create an Auto Macro in a document, a template, or the Normal template. You can also create an auto macro in all three.

The capability to have more than one auto macro or event procedure recognized and executed at the same time illustrates the first difference between auto macros and event procedures. When one of these actions is triggered, such as when a document is opened, Word begins searching for any code that is required to respond. It begins looking in the closest object. It checks the document to see if there is an `AutoOpen` macro.

If it exists, Word stops looking and executes the code. If it does not find the code, it looks in the document's attached template. If it finds no the code there, it looks in the Normal template. Then it will search any other global templates.

If you created a New procedure instead, the process would be different. Event procedures handle procedures with the same names (but stored in different locations) in sequence.

If Word found an Open event in the document, it would execute the procedure and then look at the document's Normal and global templates in that order. If it found a New event in either template, these events would also be executed.

Another difference is the placement of the two types of procedures. When you are creating an auto macro, you write the procedure in a module (as you have been doing in the previous hours). Event procedures require a special type of module.

Event procedures must be created in a class module. A *class* module is a special module that stores not only procedures and declarations, but also class definitions, custom properties, and methods.

Although it is outside of the scope of this book, it is possible to create your own objects in Word using VBA. When you create a new object with code, it is referred to as a class. You can set up properties and methods for your classes.

To get a better idea of how this will affect your development, you will work with both AutoOpen and the Open event. Doing so will also give you an opportunity to create a class module.

Using AutoOpen Macro Versus Using the Open Event

To experiment, you will now add procedures to the Normal template and create a new document. To create an AutoOpen macro, complete these steps:

1. Open the Visual Basic Editor to begin adding code.

2. Right-click on the Normal object in the Project Explorer and select Insert, Module to create standard module.

3. Add the following code to the new module.

```
Sub AutoOpen()
    Selection.TypeText Text:="Document AutoOpen"
    Selection.TypeParagraph
End Sub
```

4. Click Save.

These steps create a macro that will be executed when a document is opened. It places the phrase in the document. Now, you can move on to creating the Open event procedure.

This requires the class module. To create the Open event, complete these steps.

1. Double-click on the ThisDocument object shown in Figure 16.1 for the Normal template in the Project Explorer to create its class module.

FIGURE 16.1

The ThisDocument object gives you access to different objects for the file.

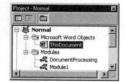

16

2. Select Document from the Object drop-down list in the code window and select Open from the Procedures drop-down list to create the framework for the procedure as shown in Figure 16.2.

FIGURE 16.2

You now have two procedures.

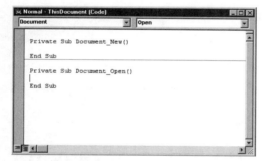

3. Delete the Document_New procedure.

4. Enter the following lines of code:

```
Selection.TypeText Text:="Document Open Event"
Selection.TypeParagraph
```

5. Save your work and switch back to Word.

6. Save the empty document and close it.

7. Open the document.

When the document opens in Word, there are two lines of text as shown in Figure 16.3. Notice that both procedures executed. You can choose which approach you want to use. If you are planning on developing in Word as well as some of the other Office applications, you might want to use events because they can be used in the other applications.

FIGURE 16.3

The lines indicate which procedure executed first.

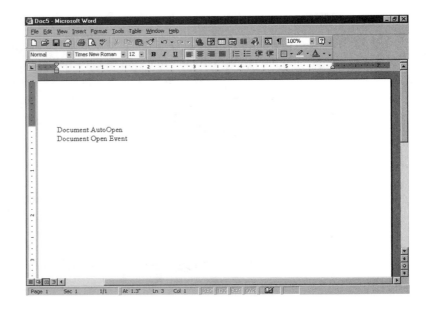

 You need to comment out or delete the AutoOpen and Document_Open events before continuing with the next section.

Executing Code Automatically for Word

In addition to executing code based on actions that help you work with documents, you can also create procedures based on actions used for working with Word as a whole. In many cases, you will combine auto macros and procedures to accomplish your tasks.

Comparing Auto Macros with Events for Word

In addition to the document-specific auto macros, two auto macros can affect the behavior of Word as a whole. You have AutoExec and AutoQuit. The AutoExec macro is executed anytime you launch Word or load a global template. The AutoQuit macro is executed when you quit Word or unload a global template.

These macro procedures are created using the same process discussed above when you created the AutoOpen procedure. The AutoExec procedure can be created in the Normal template or a template that will be loaded globally. The AutoQuit macro can be placed in these two locations, as well as in any template.

If more than one procedure has the same name, the same rule applies to determine which will be executed. The procedure that is closest to the document will be executed. For example, if you have an AutoQuit in your template and another AutoQuit in the Normal template, the one in your template is the one that executes.

You can also work with events for the Word application. There are times you want to take action based on the user's action rather than on what document is active. To do this, you will to set up a document event. There are twelve events (shown in Table 16.1) that you can add to a template.

16

TABLE 16.1   The Application Events

Event	Description
DocumentBeforeClose	This event is executed before any open document is closed. It occurs after the document is checked for changes and the user is prompted to save those changes. It won't execute if the user cancels the Save As dialog.
DocumentBeforePrint	This event is executed before any document is printed. If you are using the Print dialog, it occurs before the dialog is displayed.
DocumentBeforeSave	This event is executed before a document is saved. If the document hasn't been saved before, it will execute before the Save As dialog will be displayed.
DocumentChange	This event is executed when a new document is created, a document is opened, or when a switch is made to another open document.
DocumentOpen	This event occurs when an existing document is opened.
NewDocument	This event occurs when a new document is created.
Quit	This event executes when Word is exited or a global template is unloaded.
WindowActivate	This event executes when a document is activated.
WindowBeforeDoubleClick	This event executes before the default double-click action is completed (such as a word select, when you double-click on a word).
WindowRightClick	This event executed before the default right-click action is completed, such as when displaying a shortcut menu.
WindowDeactivate	This event executes when a document is deactivated.
WindowSelectionChange	This event executes when the selection area changes.

When you begin working with application events, you must be sure you choose the correct event to accomplish your goal. Trying to choose the correct event can be trickier that it looks because certain actions will trigger more than one event.

For example, when you create a new document, you aren't just triggering the NewDocument event. If another document is open when you create a new document, the first event that will occur is the Deactivate event. It is followed by the Activate event and the DocumentChange event for the new file. Finally, the NewDocument event executes. This is referred to as the order of events. As you begin creating events, keep in mind the order of events. It will help you decide which event to use.

After you establish the event to use, you write it. There are, however, some extra steps you must also take to get it to work. Creating events for the application requires the following steps:

1. Create a class module.
2. Create an object variable to represent the Word application.
3. Create your event procedures.
4. Initialize the object variable in another procedure.
5. Save your work.
6. Execute the Initialization code.

Using the AutoExec Macro and Event Procedures

To get a better understanding of the event procedure development process, you will now create a simple event procedure. In Hour 11, "Working with Page Appearance and Printing," you examined the VBA methods and properties to automate printing. During that discussion, you learned that there was one area that couldn't be controlled with VBA. You can't directly modify a printer's properties with VBA. An example was discussed in Hour 11 where you had to set the properties for your color printer to get a specific print quality. Consider creating a DocumentBeforePrint event to prompt the user not to forget to set the properties if they are needed.

The first step is to complete a class module for the events and create an object variable for the Word application. The process is similar to creating a standard module. Follow these steps:

1. Open or switch to the Visual Basic Editor.
2. Right-click on the Normal template in the Project Explorer.
3. Select Insert, Class Module to create the new class module.

4. Change the `Name` property for the new module in the `Properties` window to `modEvents`.

5. Enter the line of code below at the top of the new module to create an object variable to reference the Word applications.

```
Public WithEvents objWord as Word.Application
```

Now the new module is prepared to store the events for the application. The next step is to create the event procedure. To create the `DocumentBeforePrint` procedure:

1. Select `objWord` from the Object list in the `modEvents` code window and notice it creates the `Quit` event framework.

2. Click on the Procedures list and notice that all the procedures are listed for you in plain text as shown in Figure 16.4.

FIGURE 16.4

After the object variable is declared, you can select it and the procedures.

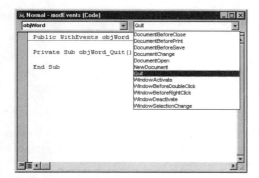

3. Select `DocumentBeforePrint` from the list to create the frame for the procedure.

4. Notice that the procedure automatically sets up two variables, `Doc` to reference the current document and `Cancel` to allow you to cancel the process of printing based on actions taken in your code.

Don't forget to change the printer's name for your printer on line 5 in the code that follows. If you don't know the name of your printer, you don't have to leave the Visual Basic Editor to find out.

Select View, Immediate Window from the menu. In the Immediate Window, type `?ActivePrinter` and press Enter. Your printer name will be displayed on the line below.

5. Add the following lines of code:

```
 1: Private Sub objWord_DocumentBeforePrint(ByVal Doc As Document, _
 2:     Cancel As Boolean)
 3: '  Don't forget to change Color Printer on LPT1: below to your
 4: '  printer name.
 5:     If ActivePrinter = "Color Printer on LPT1:" Then
 6:         Dim strMsg As String, lResponse As Long
 7.         strMsg = "Your active printer is the " & ActivePrinter
 8:         strMsg = strMsg & "." & vbCrLf & "Please adjust the "
 9:         strMsg = strMsg & " properties as needed. " & vbCrLf
10:         strMsg = strMsg & "If you clicked the Print button on the "
11:         strMsg = strMsg & "toolbar and need to access the "
12:         strMsg = strMsg & "Print dialog," & vbCrLf
13:         strMsg = strMsg & "select Cancel and click File, Print. "
14:         strMsg = strMsg & vbCrLf & "If you are happy with the "
15:         strMsg = strMsg & "settings or you have already selected "
16:         strMsg = strMsg & "File, Print, select OK."
17:         lResponse = MsgBox(strMsg, vbInformation + vbOKCancel, _
18:             "Printer Properties")
19:         If lResponse = vbCancel Then Cancel = True
20:     End If
21: End Sub
```

6. Delete the Quit event framework.

7. Save your template.

The code added to the DocumentBeforePrint event creates a message string by concatenating several strings together with the ActivePrinter contents. This message is displayed in a message box.

This message reminds the user to set any printer properties if the color printer is used. The user will select OK unless she accessed this message from the toolbar button. If that is the case, the document won't be sent to the printer, and the user will be left in the document window to enable the selection of File, Print. This is accomplished by setting the built-in argument, Cancel equal to True.

You can see this procedure in action when you print. Before you attempt to do so, however, you must complete the last step in the process. The code for the event procedures must be initialized with another procedure. The code required to initialize can be located on the AutoExec macro that executes when Word is launched or on a global template. To initialize the code, complete these steps:

1. Click on Modules for the Normal template in the Project Explorer.

2. Double-click on the modAutoProcs module to open it.

3. Press Ctrl+Home to move to the top of the module and the General Declarations area.

4. Enter the following code to declare an object variable to reference the class module with the event procedures.

```
Dim objApp As New modEvents
```

5. Press Ctrl+End to move to the bottom of the module.

6. Enter the following lines to initialize the events.

```
Sub AutoExec()
    Set objApp.objWord = Word.Application
End Sub
```

7. With your insertion point in the AutoExec code, click the Run button on the toolbar to initialize the events to test them.

8. Save your work and switch back to Word.

9. Click the Print button on the toolbar to display the new message as shown in Figure 16.5

FIGURE 16.5

The message is lengthy, but it gives the user a way to adjust the settings without having to cancel a print job.

10. Click Cancel.

Accessing Built-In Dialogs

With the DocumentBeforePrint event procedure you created, you solved the problem. You are alerting the user to the possibility that printer properties need to be adjusted, but you left the user to his own devices to access the Print dialog.

You don't have to leave it to the user to open the Print dialog. You can display Word's built-in dialog boxes with VBA for the user, or you can display a dialog to gather information for actions you will program.

If you just want to open a built-in dialog to save steps for the user, you use the Show method. That opens the dialog and enables the user to take whatever action he wants.

If you want to open a built-in dialog and make sure that information is gathered by the user, you can use the Display method. It opens the dialog for the user to make choices and then allows you to control what happens to the choices.

Using the Show Method

In order to make the response programmed for the DocumentBeforePrint event better, it might be nice to ask if the user is printing a final copy. If the answer is Yes, you can open the Print dialog for her. To open the dialog, you use the Show method. Its syntax is

SYNTAX

expression.Show(*TimeOut*)

The expression represents the Dialogs collection object with the dialog indicated. This is done with the Dialogs collection and a built-in constant to indicate which dialog. It is followed by the Show keyword. The Show keyword can be followed by parentheses containing the number of time units for which you want the dialog displayed before it automatically closes. A unit is .001 of a second.

In most cases, when you show a dialog, you want the user to make any choices needed. You probably won't want to limit the time the dialog is shown. If you don't, you can omit the argument described in the last paragraph.

When you use the Show method to open a dialog, you can adjust the dialog's settings before you display it. For example, you can adjust the FontName property for the Font dialog by using a With structure.

The DocumentBeforePrint method has a long message and doesn't really save time for the user if he needs to change the print settings. By using the Show method, you can simplify the message and require fewer steps from the user. If you modify the event as shown in Listing 16.1, it will work more efficiently.

LISTING 16.1 The Revised DocumentBeforePrint

```
 1: Private Sub objWord_DocumentBeforePrint(ByVal Doc As Document,
    ➥Cancel As Boolean)
 2: '    Please substitute your printer name in the line below.
 3:      Static bPrintSetAlready as Boolean
 4:      If ActivePrinter = "Color Printer on LPT1:" and _
 5:         bPrintSetAlready <> True Then
 6:         Dim strMsg As String, lResponse As Long
 7:         strMsg = "Your active printer, " & ActivePrinter
 8:         strMsg = strMsg & ", allows you to adjust the print quality "
 9:         strMsg = strMsg & "with its Properties. " & vbCrLf & vbCrLf
10:         strMsg = strMsg & "Is this your final version?"
11:         lResponse = MsgBox(strMsg, vbQuestion + vbYesNoCancel, _
12:             "Printer Properties")
13:         Select Case lResponse
```

```
14:             Case vbYes
15:                 bPrintSetAlready = True
16:                 Cancel = True
17:                 Dialogs(wdDialogFilePrint).Show
18:             Case vbNo
19:                 'No action needed
20:             Case vbCancel
21:                 Cancel = True
22:          End Select
23:       End If
24: End Sub
```

16

ANALYSIS This listing doesn't have fewer lines of code than the previous one, but it is much simpler for the user to interpret quickly. Line 3 declares a static variable to see if this procedure has been run before in this editing session. Lines 4–12 still create the message and display it to the user in a MsgBox. Lines 4–5 show a change to test this new variable as well. If it isn't True, the rest of this process is skipped because the setting has been altered. Line 11 shows that the buttons argument was changed to display three buttons instead of OK and Cancel.

The biggest change is made in the testing of 1Response. In lines 13–22, the testing of 1Response is completed with a Select Case structure.

If the user selects the Yes button, she tells you this is the final draft, and the property settings must be adjusted. Line 15 sets the static variable so that the user won't be prompted again during the editing session. Line 16 sets the Cancel argument to True to terminate the execution of the Print function called by the user. This means that if Print is issued from the toolbar button, it is canceled so that the user can open the dialog.

Line 17 opens the Print dialog so the user can make any changes. You can't open the Properties window because that is outside of Office.

If the user clicks No, the print settings are immaterial, and you don't need to do anything. If the user clicks Cancel, this message was displayed by mistake. In that case, the Cancel argument just needs to be set to True to cancel the print altogether.

After you have made the changes shown in Listing 16.1, you will need to re-initialize the events module by running the AutoExec macro again. When you place your insertion point in the AutoExec macro in the modAutoProcs module, click the Run button on the toolbar.

When you are debugging your code, using the Run button is much easier than exiting Word and relaunching it. After the event procedure is reinitialized, you are ready to try it out. Switch back to Word and click the Print button on the toolbar. The new message is displayed, as shown in Figure 16.6. If you click Yes, you will find the Print dialog displayed and ready for new settings.

FIGURE 16.6

The message is displayed to remind the user about print quality.

Using the `Display` Method

The other method for opening a built-in dialog box is the Display method. Like the Show method, it opens the built-in dialog to enable the user to make choices. The difference is what happens when the user is finished making choices.

By itself, the `Display` method doesn't accept the choices of the user. It gives you a chance to evaluate those choices and determine what to do with them. After you have choices that meet your criteria, you use the `Execute` method to lock those choices in place.

An example of how this approach can pay off in your development is file summary information. In Hour 14, "Working with Large Documents," you examined how to use bookmarks to fill in information in longer documents. You were reminded that you could use built-in fields, such as the document property fields, to get some of that information completed automatically.

You can set up your save options to display the properties dialog as you save the document, but it would also be useful to prompt for the summary information as a new document is created. You can also force the completion of specific fields. Listing 16.3 lists a `NewDocument` event to display a built-in dialog to get the needed information. This event also ensures that the information is completed.

LISTING 16.3   The NewDocument Event

```
 1: Private Sub objWord_NewDocument(ByVal Doc As Document)
 2:     Do
 3:         With Dialogs(wdDialogFileSummaryInfo)
 4:             .Display
 5:             .Execute
 6:             If .Title = "" Or .Subject = "" Or .Author = "" Then
 7:                 MsgBox _
 8:                     "You to have a title, subject and author completed.", _
 9:                     vbInformation + vbOKOnly, "Missing Information"
10:             Else
```

```
11:                 Exit Do
12:              End If
13:           End With
14:        Loop
15: End Sub
```

To make sure you get the needed information, the code is placed in a Do loop on line 2. Line 3 sets up the With structure to manipulate the dialog. To specify a title, subject, and author, you use the File Summary Information dialog. Its use is indicated with a built-in constant.

On line 4, the Display method opens the Summary Info dialog, as shown in Figure 16.7. Line 5 uses the Execute method to save any entries. The Execute method locks in those choices to prevent the user from having to retype any entries. If you comment this line of code out and place the Execute line before line 11, you can see that any entries are discarded and not stored in their respective properties.

FIGURE 16.7

The Summary Info Dialog is a subset of what is shown in the Properties dialog.

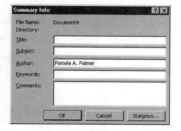

Lines 6–14 test the three settings to be completed. If any one of them is left empty, a Msgbox is used to notify the user of what must be filled in, as shown in Figure 16.8. If anything is missing, the code will loop to display the dialog again. After everything is complete the Exit Do on line 11 will end the execution by moving to the Exit With and then the Exit Sub statement.

FIGURE 16.8

The message will be displayed if one of the properties isn't completed.

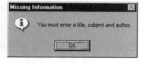

This code doesn't give the user any way out except to answer the necessary questions. If you want the user to be able to get out of this without filling in the information, you can keep track of what button was chosen to close the dialog. The Show and Display methods return a value to indicate how the user closed them. Each dialog will return one of these values:

A –2 indicates that a Close button was used to close the dialog.

A –1 represents the OK button.

A 0 represents the Cancel button.

If the dialog has other buttons, they return numbers greater than 0 beginning with 1 and reading from left to right in the dialog.

Summary

In this hour, you have explored how to take advantage of auto executing code. You can use auto macros, as well as events that are triggered by user actions and application actions.

You learned that there are two levels of automation: You can work with auto macros and events that depend on a document or work with the Word application as a whole. You learned how to create an auto macro that is a procedure in a standard module with one of the defined auto macro names. You also learned how to design event procedures that are created in a class module.

You also learned one way to avoid using the InputBox to get information. If you are attempting to get information that can be selected from one of the existing Word dialogs, you can display the dialog, retrieve the information, and work with it.

Q&A

Q What if I need information that can't be entered in a built-in dialog box?

A In case there is no built-in dialog, you can use a User Form. For more information, refer to Hour 17, "Working with User Forms."

Q Is there any way to display the Properties window in its entirety?

A No, some of the components of the Properties window aren't part of Word. You will have to refer to the built-in constants to determine which component is in which dialog.

Workshop

Here are some questions and exercises to help you review the material covered in this hour. The answers to the quiz questions can be found in Appendix A, "Quiz Answers."

Quiz

1. What procedures automatically execute when a document is opened?
2. What is the benefit of using event procedures compared to auto macros?

Exercises

1. Modify the NewDocument event created in this hour (in the section "Using the Display Method") to acknowledge and respond to the Cancel button in the dialog and to exit the loop without completing the information. (Hint: Don't forget to re-initialize after making changes.)
2. Evaluate your automation checklist and see where you need to automatically execute code.

16

HOUR 17

Working with User Forms

In Hour 16, "Working with Auto Macros, Events, and Built-In Dialogs," you examined how to take advantage of built-in forms, but sometimes there isn't a built-in form that meets your needs. This hour will teach you how you to create a user form when you need a custom dialog.

The highlights of this hour include

- Understanding user forms
- Creating user forms
- Working with controls on a user form
- Working with additional controls
- Accessing the user form

Understanding User Forms

A user form is a custom dialog box that can be created in Microsoft Forms and displayed with your Visual Basic for Applications code to solicit information from the user.

As you have worked through the hours of this book, you have seen different approaches to getting information from the user. Beginning with Hour 5, "Exploring VBA," you used the InputBox to provide flexibility in your code. In Hour 14, "Working with Large Documents," the InputBox and MsgBox were used to gather information to fill-in the blanks for a software proposal.

Although the InputBox and MsgBox functions perform the task of information gathering, there is a great possibility that these methods might either allow incorrect information to be input or annoy your user because of the large number of prompts they use.

One of the common problems with data input is user inattention. The user may anticipate the next InputBox and type more than asked for. He or she might skip a prompt. One solution is to create a form template as illustrated in Hour 15, "Working with Forms."

A form template enables you to use fields to gather information from the user. When the user creates a new document based on a form template, the first form field is selected automatically. The user enters information in it and uses the Tab or Enter key to move to the next field.

Form fields work out well for replacing paper-based forms because the user responses on paper are usually short and don't require editing after entry. Form fields don't work as well when the user must be able to edit the text he inputs.

The proposal used as the sample template in Hour 14, for example, couldn't have been created as a form template. After the user filled in the information at the appropriate spots, he also had to create and edit the custom text for the proposal. The document also need to have spell check completed. This can't be done with a form when it is protected.

In Hour 16, you explored how to open the Word dialogs to gather information. A built-in dialog is great for customizing settings, but not for filling in unique information. When you need more than two or three answers from a user, and there isn't a built-in dialog to retrieve that information, you can create a user form.

To create a user form, you must complete three general steps:

1. Create a user form in your template.
2. Add controls for the information needed.
3. Write a procedure to display the form and process the information gathered.

To give you an idea of what you need to do to use user forms, create a user form that will prompt for information in a preschool parent-teacher conference report, as shown in Figure 17.1.

FIGURE 17.1
The template has the boilerplate text as well as the bookmarks in place.

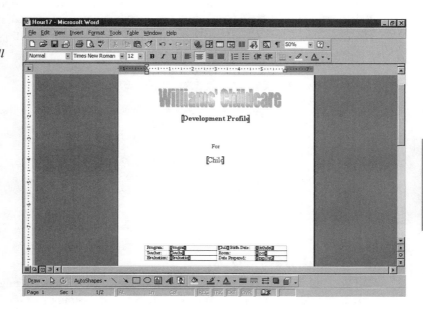

The template has been formatted with its text and bookmarks to assist with the completion of the document after the user answers the questions in the user form. Now you will create the form.

Creating User Forms

When you need a custom dialog to gather information from the user, you create a user form. This task isn't done with Word. You create the user form in the Visual Basic Editor. After the form is inserted into your project, you will set its size and properties; then you will add controls to create the user interface.

Adding a User Form

If you determine you need a user form, you insert a blank form into your Word project using the Visual Basic Editor. To add a new form to your project, complete these steps:

1. Open your template.
2. Select Tools, Macro, Visual Basic Editor.

3. Right-click on your template in the Project Explorer.

4. Select Insert, User Form.

The Visual Basic Editor will insert a blank user form for you to modify as shown in Figure 17.2. A user form begins as a blank window. You can control its appearance and behavior as you develop it. You can adjust property settings as well as add controls.

FIGURE 17.2

A blank user form is the foundation of your dialog.

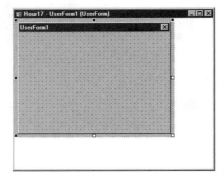

Sizing a User Form

Because the user form added to your project is a standard size, it might not have enough space to hold your interface. You aren't locked into keeping it at the standard size. You can adjust it using your mouse or by setting its properties.

To adjust the size of the dialog with the mouse, use the handles surrounding the form. When you place the mouse pointer on top of one of the handles, your pointer will change to a standard resizing arrow as shown in Figure 17.3.

FIGURE 17.3

Resizing a form is like resizing any of the drawing objects.

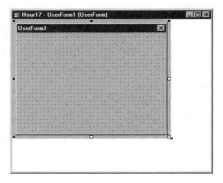

Resizing forms is similar to resizing any drawn objects with the mouse. After you have selected the resizing mouse pointer, you hold down the left mouse button and drag the border to the size required.

When you are working with a user form, you are developing in the User Form window. It is just a tool to assist with development. You may have noticed that some of the handles are open boxes and others are solid boxes. The solid handles indicate that you are as far to the left and top of the window as you can move the form.

As you begin developing your form, you'll learn that sizing isn't an exact science. You will probably find you are adjusting the size of the form frequently. Anytime you want to adjust it, you can do so.

If you would prefer to size a form to specific dimensions, the Properties window gives you greater precision. To set the dimensions of the form with the Properties window, follow these steps:

1. Make sure the handles are around the form.

2. Using the scrollbar in the Properties window locate the `Height` property and click to select it as shown in Figure 17.4.

FIGURE 17.4

The `Height` *property is selected.*

3. Enter the desired height in points such as `216` for a height of 3 inches.

4. Using the scrollbar move down and click on the `Width` property.

5. Enter `216` as the `Width`.

Finishing the Property Settings for the User Form

Properties, which were introduced in Hour 3, "Working with VBA and the Visual Basic Editor," are settings that control the appearance and behavior of objects. You already know that the Height and Width properties are just a few of the properties you can set for a user form.

As you scroll through the list of properties in the Properties window, you can see the possibilities available for the user form. As you develop more forms, you will become familiar with more of these properties, as well as those for other objects.

In most cases, you won't adjust most of the properties shown. There are only two that you set every time. You must set the Name and the Caption properties for your form.

The Name property provides a name to reference the form from your code. When the form is first created, it is assigned a name consisting of the name of the object with a number to make it unique in the project.

Just as you changed the names of bookmarks assigned to the form fields in Hour 15, you will also want to change the name of the user form to make your code easier to read. When you changed the bookmarks, you used a prefix of characters to designate the type of form field followed by a unique identifier. You can use the same approach with user forms. For example, you might change this form's name to frmProfile.

The Caption is another property you will want to change. It is the text that will appear in the title bar of the form to identify it to the user. In this case, you could enter Development Profile Information as the Caption. The Name is displayed in the User Form Window title bar, and the Caption appears in the title bar of the user form itself, as shown in Figure 17.5.

Working with Controls on a User Form

After you have set the properties for the form, you are ready to begin building your interface. This is accomplished by adding controls to the form. A control is an object that can be used to interact with the user. To build your form, you are going to complete the following general steps:

1. Place the controls on the user form.
2. Move and resize the controls as needed.
3. Set the controls' properties.

Examining the Controls

The controls that you can use to build your user interface are accessed from the Toolbox. It is the second window that opened when you inserted the form, as shown in Figure 17.6.

FIGURE 17.5

The Name *and* Caption *properties are set.*

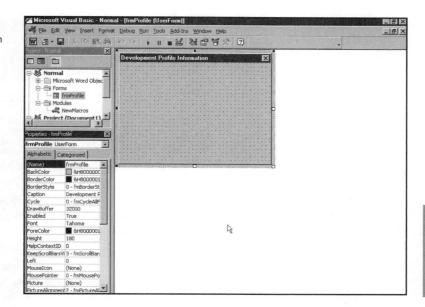

FIGURE 17.6

The Toolbox displays all the controls that can be added to your user form.

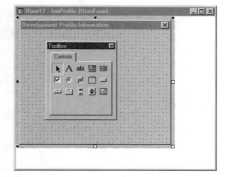

17

The Toolbox contains tools that can be used to add controls to your form. When you first create a user form, the Toolbox contains the standard set of controls. Some of the tools should be familiar to you after completing Hour 15.

You aren't restricted to using only the controls shown. You can work with any ActiveX control. An ActiveX control is any control that can be added through the Toolbox to provide choices for the user or used in automation through VBA or any programming language.

Microsoft has many controls that are shipped with Microsoft Office, but it only loads the standard controls initially to reduce the size of your project. The standard controls are listed in Table 17.1, in order from left to right and top to bottom.

TABLE 17.1   The Standard Controls

Control	Description
Pointer	This button enables you to unselect a tool if needed.
Label	This control enables you to display text that the user can't change. It is often used for headings or descriptions for other controls.
TextBox	This control is similar to the text form field. It gives the user an entry area for information needed for automation procedures.
ComboBox	This control is similar to the drop-down list form field. Instead of the user typing an answer, she can select the answer from a list. The ComboBox gives you more control over how the user works with the list than does the form field.
ListBox	This control is similar to the ComboBox except that it is a fixed size in the dialog and doesn't have the drop-down feature.
CheckBox, OptionButton, ToggleButton	These controls behave in a similar manner to the check box form field. They give the user a chance to indicate a Yes/No response by selecting the control. They can also be used in conjunction with the Frame to present the user with a multiple choice question.
Frame	This control is used to provide a visual as well as functional group for your form. You place it on the form and place other controls inside of it. When used with the CheckBox, OptionButton, or ToggleButton, it acts as a multiple choice control, with each CheckBox or button serving as one of the choices.
CommandButton	This control provides a mechanism to run a procedure. You can use it to add your own OK, Cancel, and other buttons.
TabStrip, MultiPage	These controls enable you to place more than one set of controls on one user form.

Control	Description
ScrollBar	This control enables you to gather information from the user without requiring the user to know a specific measurement type.
SpinButton	This control enables you to add a mechanism for incrementing and decrementing a value. Normally it is used in conjunction with the TextBox.
Image	This control is used to add graphics to your form.

Adding Controls

Now that you have been introduced to the standard controls you are ready to begin building your form. The first item needed to complete the development profile template is the name of the child. This is unique information and would be best represented on the user form as a TextBox control.

To help the user fill in the information, you can use a Label control to indicate what information is required in the TextBox. To add a Label and TextBox, complete the following steps:

1. Click on the Label tool in the Toolbox.
2. Move your mouse to the place where you want the control's upper-left corner to appear on the form. Notice that your mouse pointer has changed to help you keep track of what control you are working with, as shown in Figure 17.7. It appears as a crosshair pointer with an *A* to represent the selected tool.
3. Hold down the left mouse button, drag to the position where you want to place the lower-right corner of the control and release the mouse button to add the control.
4. Click on the TextBox tool in the Toolbox.
5. Repeat steps 2 and 3 to place a TextBox next to the Label on the form as shown in Figure 17.8.

Adjusting the Controls

After the controls are on the form, you can adjust their appearances with your mouse or with the Properties window. You can resize them using the same techniques shown for the user form. You can also move them if you don't get the placement correct. To move a control, point in the center of the control and drag it to a new location or set the Left and Top properties.

FIGURE 17.7

The mouse pointer changes to indicate that you are adding a control to the form.

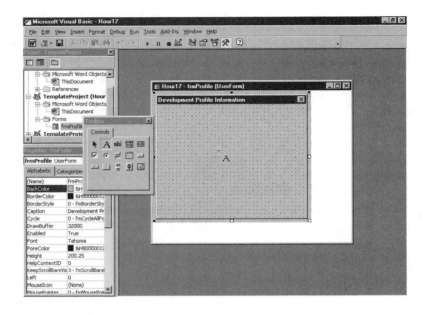

FIGURE 17.8

The Label *and* TextBox *are in place.*

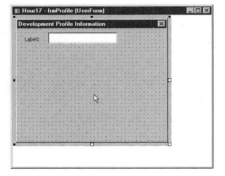

You will often adjust other properties as well. For example, you will set the Name and Caption properties of the Labels control. In this case, you can set the Label's Name to lblChild and its Caption to Child:. You do not use Labels in VBA very often, but doing helps you form good development habits.

The TextBox is a control that is more important for your automation because it will enable the user to enter information needed in the document. Usually, you will only set the Name property. In this case, you will set it to txtChild.

After this `Label` and `TextBox` are complete, you can add another `Label` and `TextBox` for the teacher. You can use the appropriate prefix with the word `Teacher` for the name and use `Teacher` for the `Label` `Caption`.

Working with Additional Controls

You can use some of the other controls to create your user form. The process is very similar to adding a `TextBox`. You could use a `CheckBox` to indicate whether the child is in kindergarten, a `ComboBox` to indicate which program the child attends, and the `OptionButtons` to indicate which evaluation is being completed. When you have completed adding controls, the form should resemble the one shown in Figure 17.9.

FIGURE 17.9
The completed design uses several types of controls.

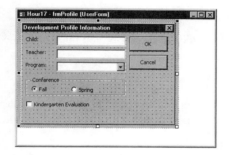

17

In addition to working with the standard controls, you can add any ActiveX control to your project. You will also have an opportunity to add one to the Toolbox.

Adding a `CheckBox`

A `CheckBox` control is used when the user needs to make a choice where the answer is Yes or No; or in programming terms `True` or `False`. With this example document, you want to change the title of the evaluation to Kindergarten Profile, if it is the final kindergarten evaluation.

Adding a `CheckBox` is easier with user forms than it is with form templates because there is a `Label` attached to the `CheckBox`. To set up the `CheckBox`, complete these steps.

1. Click on the `CheckBox` tool in the Toolbox.
2. Point to the form at the desired location and drag the `CheckBox` to the needed size.
3. Set `chkKindergarten` as its `Name` property.
4. Set Kindergarten Evaluation as its Caption property.

Notice that the `CheckBox` is not directly under the `Labels` and `TextBoxes` you created. You can create your controls in any order and reorganize them as needed.

Adding a `ComboBox`

The next control to set up is the `ComboBox` control for the program the child is participating in. Setting up a `ComboBox` is more complex than setting up a drop-down list field because you are can't populate its list with properties. To set up the `ComboBox` for the programs, complete these steps:

1. Place a `Label` and a `ComboBox` on the form as shown earlier in Figure 17.9.

2. Change the `Name` property to `lblProgram` and the `Caption` property to `Program:` for the `Label`.

3. Change the `Name` property for the `ComboBox` to `cboProgram`.

After the `ComboBox` control is added to the form, you must populate its list. To populate its list, you use the `AddItem` method. Its syntax is

```
expression.AddItem itemtext
```

The expression represents the control you are adding items to, followed by the `AddItem` keyword. This is followed by a string of text for the list.

The trick is determining where to place this code. When you were populating the drop-down form field in Hour 15, you used the `Exit` event for the previous control because the list changed depending on what was chosen in that control. In this case, the list is not affected by choices made on the user form. You want the list available from the moment the user views the form.

To populate the list as the form becomes visible, you are going to add your code, not to the control itself, but to the user form. When a form is called from your code, it is initialized. To add the items to the list, you are going to use the `Initialize` event. To create the `Initialize` event, follow these instructions:

1. Double-click on the background of the form to open its code window.

2. Notice that it automatically creates the `UserForm_Click` event.

3. Select `Initialize` from the Procedures list.

4. Add the following code:
```
1: Private Sub UserForm_Initialize()
2:     With cboProgram
```

```
3:          .AddItem "Infant"
4:          .AddItem "Toddler"
5:          .AddItem "Preschool"
6:          .AddItem "Kindergarten"
7:      End With
8: End Sub
```

5. Close the Code Window.

ANALYSIS When you are adding items to a list for either the ComboBox control or the
ListBox control, you will find that a loop or a With structure (as shown with the
Initialize event beginning on line 2) is most effective. The With statement is working
with the program ComboBox named cboProgram.

Each item is added with the AddItem method on a line within the structure on lines 3–6.
You can use strings as shown in this example as well as string variables.

Adding Frames and OptionButtons

The next choice that needs to be made by the user is the conference for which this profile
is being completed. Is it the fall or spring conference? When there are small number of
choices, you might consider creating an option group using the Frame and either the
OptionButtons, CheckBoxes, or ToggleButtons.

OptionButtons, CheckBoxes, and ToggleButtons act as True/False selectors unless they
are placed in a Frame. When they are placed in a Frame, they are mutually exclusive.
Only one of the group can be True at one time. To create the conference selection, complete these steps:

1. Select and place a Frame on the form, sizing it so it can hold the two conference
   choices.

2. Double-click on the OptionButton.

3. Click and drag an OptionButton within the Frame.

4. Notice the OptionButton tool is still selected. The OptionButton is still selected
   because you double-clicked instead of single-clicking the tool. It will stay until you
   click on another tool such as the Pointer tool.

5. Click and drag the second OptionButton within the Frame.

6. Click the Pointer tool to release the OptionButton tool.

17

7. Set the following properties:

Control	Property	Setting
Frame1	Name	fraConference
	Caption	Conference
Option1	Name	optFall
	Caption	Fall
	Value	True
Option2	Name	optSpring
	Caption	Spring

The Frame and its options are now set up to be used in the document. The Value property for optFall is set to True to indicate a default choice.

Adding CommandButtons

All the controls that have been placed in this user form are designed to collect information. The last two controls that need to be placed on the form are CommandButtons. The CommandButton provide one visual way for the user to take action. After the settings are entered, the data must be placed in the document.

To take advantage of a CommandButton, you have to add it to the user form and set its properties, as well as add code to indicate what action must be taken. To set up the two CommandButtons and add their functionality, complete these steps.

1. Double-click on the CommandButton tool in the Toolbox.

2. Drag two CommandButtons in the upper right of the form and select the Pointer to release the tool.

3. Set the following properties for each CommandButton:

Control	Property	Setting
Command1	Name	cmdOK
	Caption	OK
	Default	True
Command2	Name	cmdCancel
	Caption	Cancel
	Cancel	True

4. Double-click on cmdOK to open the Code window and create the cmdOK_Click event.

5. Add the following lines of code:

```
1: Private Sub cmdOK_Click()
2:     frmProfile.Hide
3:     If ActiveDocument.Bookmarks.Exists("Profile") Then
4:         If chkEvaluation = True Then
5:             ActiveDocument.Bookmarks("Profile").Range.Text = _
6:             "Kindergarten Evaluation"
7:         End If
8:     End If
9:     If ActiveDocument.Bookmarks.Exists("Child") Then
10:         ActiveDocument.Bookmarks("Child").Range.Text = _
11:         txtChild.Text
12:     End If
13:     If ActiveDocument.Bookmarks.Exists("Teacher") Then
14:         ActiveDocument.Bookmarks("Teacher").Range.Text = _
15:         txtTeacher.Text
16:     End If
17:     If ActiveDocument.Bookmarks.Exists("Program") Then
18:         ActiveDocument.Bookmarks("Program").Range.Text = _
19:         cboProgram.Text
20:     End If
21:     If ActiveDocument.Bookmarks.Exists("Evaluation") Then
22:         If optFall.Value = True Then
23:             ActiveDocument.Bookmarks("Evaluation").Range.Text = _
24:             "Fall"
25:         Else
26:         ActiveDocument.Bookmarks("Evaluation").Range.Text = _
27:         "Spring"
28:         End If
29:     End If
30:     Selection.GoTo What:=wdGoToBookmark, Name:="BeginEntry"
31:     Unload frmProfile
32: End Sub
```

6. Select cmdCancel from the object list and enter the following lines of code in its click event:

```
Private Sub cmdCancel_Click()
    Unload frmProfile
End Sub
```

ANALYSIS   With these steps, you have created a standard OK and Cancel button combination that is used in many dialogs. After placing the controls on the form, you set their properties. You set the Name and Caption properties for both buttons.

You also set the Default and Cancel properties. The Default property places a slightly darker border around the control and sets it to be automatically clicked when the user presses the Enter key. The Cancel property doesn't change the appearance of the control, but it sets up the button to be automatically clicked when the Esc key is selected.

17

After the properties are set, you begin developing the code to execute what happens when one of these buttons is clicked. The user selects the cmdOK button when she wants to take the dialog contents and place or use the information to set up the document.

On line 2, the Hide method is used to remove the form from display yet keep it in memory with its contents so they can be used to complete the document. Lines 3–29 populate the bookmarks in the document using the contents of the controls. With the TextBoxes and the ComboBox, you set the bookmark's Range object's Text property. With the OptionButtons and the CheckBox, you are testing the Value property to determine what text to place at the bookmarks.

Line 30 moves you to another bookmark to begin entering information for the profile. Line 31 uses the Unload statement to remove the form from memory when you have placed all the information. This same line is the only code in the cmdCancel event because when the user selects Cancel, he wants to close a dialog and take no action.

Adjusting the Tab Order

The form is now complete except for one small housekeeping step. If you like using your keyboard in dialog boxes, you are used to pressing the Tab key to move from control to control.

The path that is taken through the controls is referred to as the tab order. It is controlled by the TabIndex property. As you create controls, an index number is assigned to this property automatically. If you rearrange your controls, as you did with the Checkbox (placing it at the bottom of the form), you must adjust the tab order.

Rather than having to adjust the TabIndex property for each control, you can use the Tab Order dialog as shown in Figure 17.10 to correct the order.

FIGURE 17.10

The Tab Order dialog enables you to set the path when the user is tabbing through the controls.

Select View, Tab Order to display the dialog. You can then select the control to be moved. After the control is selected, you can click on the Move Up or Move Down buttons to move it within the order. In this case, you must move the chkKindergarten to before the cmdOKbutton. With this step, the user form is ready for use.

Adding a Control to the Toolbox

In some cases, the standard controls might not be enough. There are many other controls provided with the Visual Basic Editor that you can add to your project. You can also use any ActiveX provided by another company.

To add another control to the Toolbox, select Tools, Additional Controls. This will display the Additional Controls dialog as shown in Figure 17.11. Then you click in the Checkbox for the control (such as the Calendar 9.0 control) and click OK. The control will appear at the bottom of the Toolbox.

FIGURE 17.11

The Additional Controls dialog lists all the ActiveX controls loaded on your system.

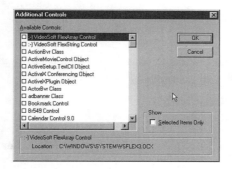

17

After the control is added to the Toolbox, it can be used as are any of the other tools. In this hour, you have been introduced to the standard controls. You will have to experiment to learn which controls best suit your needs.

Accessing the User Form

After the form is complete, you still aren't finished with the Visual Basic Editor. You must display the form for the user. This is accomplished with the Show method. If you create the following procedure in a standard module for this template, you can display the form as the document is created.

```
Sub autoNew()
    frmProfile.Show
End Sub
```

To see this form in action, save the template and close it. Select File, New. Then select this template. The completed user form will be displayed as shown in Figure 17.12. Answer all the questions and then click OK. After a moment, you will be looking at your document with the information from the dialog inserted at the bookmarks.

FIGURE 17.12
The user form has all
the controls added and
is ready for the user's
first setting.

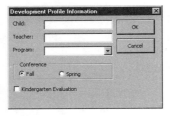

Summary

In this hour, you explored how to create a custom dialog, known as a user form, which is used to gather information from the user. You learned that user forms are created in the Visual Basic Editor.

You learned how to add a user form to your project, add controls, and set properties. You also learned how to work with your user form with VBA.

Q&A

Q What can I do to make aligning and sizing controls easier?

A The UserForms window is very much like working with the Drawing objects. You can drag your mouse across more than one control to select them and right-click or click on one and Shift+click on the others. The shortcut menu enables you to align and size controls using one of them as a model. The handles on the one to be used as a model are shown as empty handles instead of solid handles.

Q Why would I use the Calendar control?

A If the user must enter a date, there is a great chance of a typographical error. The Calendar control enables the user to select a date instead of typing it.

Workshop

Here are some questions and exercises to help you review the material covered in this hour. The answers to the quiz questions can be found in Appendix A, "Quiz Answers."

Quiz

1. What property identifies a control on a form?
2. What is the difference between a Label and a TextBox?
3. What method is used to populate a ComboBox or ListBox?
4. What is the Default property for a CommandButton?

Exercises

1. Revise the form to enable the user to select an Evaluation Date using the Calendar control.

2. Review your automation checklist to determine where you need user forms.

17

Hour 18

Working with Mailings

Creating letters or completing mail merges can be time consuming procedures, but they need not be. Many of the components of letters remain the same from letter to letter. With Visual Basic for Applications, you can streamline the process of creating a single letter or creating a mass mailing.

The highlights of this hour include

- Modifying a letter created with Letter Wizard
- Creating a letter without Letter Wizard
- Automating envelope creation
- Automating mail merge
- Creating a catalog or directory
- Working with email

 Part of this hour will take advantage of Outlook. If you aren't using Outlook, just pass over these sections.

Modifying a Letter Created with Letter Wizard

In Hour 1, "Introducing Automation Fundamentals," you had an opportunity to try out the Letter Wizard as a means for automating your letter creation. The benefit of using the Letter Wizard is that, after you answer a few questions, it generates the structure of the letter.

The downside of working with the wizard is the time required. You have to wait for the wizard to go through its routine before you can begin writing, regardless of what changes you made to the information. This can manifest itself two ways: The first situation arises when you create letters using the same settings. If you are creating letters for yourself or one sender, you will probably use the same letterhead and the same settings for what is included on a letter. You spend a great deal of time waiting to set the recipient.

Another problem also involves the wizard settings. If you are supporting letters for more than one sender, the settings must be changed each time the sender is changed. It would be nice to have those settings placed automatically.

With VBA, you can minimize the time it takes to answer the questions and still get the benefit of the wizard. Both problems involve the settings in the wizard.

To take advantage of the Letter Wizard with VBA, use the `RunLetterWizard` method. It can run the Letter Wizard with or without specific settings. The syntax is

```
expression.RunLetterWizard(LetterContent, WizardMode)
```

The expression represents the document you are in when the code is executed. It is followed by the `RunLetterWizard` method. This method has two arguments. The `LetterContent` argument specifies the settings for the wizard. The second argument, `WizardMode` indicates whether the wizard will perform as it does if you select it from the new dialog with the Next and Back buttons or whether it will perform as it does when it is selected from the Tools menu with an OK and Cancel button set.

The key to getting the most of the Letter Wizard is the `LetterContent` argument. It represents the `LetterContent` object which stores all the settings in the Letter Wizard. If, as the wizard is accessed, you send this method the settings that don't change, you can concentrate on the settings that need to be changed.

There are two methods that can be used to populate the `LetterContent` argument. There is the `GetLetterContent` which retrieves an existing `LetterContent` object from a document and the `CreateLetterContent` which enables you to create a new `LetterContents` object. The syntax is

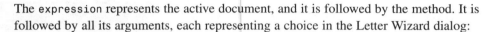

```
expression.CreateLetterContent(DateFormat, IncludeHeaderFooter, _
PageDesign, LetterStyle, Letterhead, LetterheadLocation, _
LetterheadSize, RecipientName, RecipientAddress, Salutation, _
SalutationType, RecipientReference, MailingInstructions, _
AttentionLine, Subject, CCList, ReturnAddress, SenderName, _
Closing, SenderCompany, SenderJobTitle, SenderInitials, _
EnclosureNumber, InfoBlock, RecipientCode, RecipientGender, _
ReturnAddressShortForm, SenderCity, SenderCode, SenderGender, _
SenderReference)
```

The `expression` represents the active document, and it is followed by the method. It is followed by all its arguments, each representing a choice in the Letter Wizard dialog:

- The `DateFormat` is a string to represent how the date should appear when inserted. The `IncludeHeaderFooter` can be set to `True` or `False` depending on whether you want a header and footer on the letter.

- The `PaperDesign` argument is a string that indicates the template you want to use. It includes the filename as well as the complete path.

- The `LetterStyle` argument can indicate what type of paragraph formatting you want for the letter. It is set with built-in constants representing the three styles such as `wdFullBlock` for the standard letter style with no paragraph indention.

- The `Letterhead`, `LetterHeadLocation`, and `LetterHeadSize` arguments control whether you are using pre-printed letterhead. `Letterhead` is a `True/False` argument indicating its use. `LetterheadLocation` indicates the location of the letterhead on the page, and `LetterHeadSize` indicates how much space needs to be reserved.

- The `RecipientName`, `RecipientAddress` are strings that provide information about who the letter is going to. `Salutation` and `SalutationType` indicate the string of the salutation and what style of salutation you are using.

- The third tab in the Letter Wizard has several optional text inclusions for your letter. These are represented by string arguments, `RecipientReference`, `MailingInstructions`, `AttentionLine`, `Subject`, and `CCListing`.

- The last tab of the Letter Wizard is the information about the sender. You have the `ReturnAddress` for the address string. The `SenderName`, `SenderCompany`, `SenderJobTitle`, and `SenderInitials` are used to insert information about the person sending the letter.

- The `Closing` argument is a string with the text that should appear at the end of the letter. There is also an `Enclosure` argument to indicate whether there are any enclosures.

18

The remaining arguments are used to support other languages. If you are creating your documents in English, these documents aren't necessary.

To illustrate the use of this method, you could create a procedure called LettersWithWizard shown in Listing 18.1. It shows how to deal with multiple senders and still get the benefits of the wizard without wasting any time.

LISTING 18.1 The LettersWithWizard Procedure

```
 1: Sub LetterwithWizard()
 2:     Dim strInitials As String
 3:     Dim strSender As String, strTitle As String
 4:     Dim strCompany As String
 5:     strInitials = InputBox("Enter sender initials.", _
 6:         "Sender Information")
 7:     Select Case strInitials
 8:         Case "jb"
 9:             strSender = "John Barnes"
10:             strTitle = "Account Representative"
11:             strCompany = "James Manufacturing"
12:         Case "ds"
13:             strSender = "Donna Smith"
14:             strTitle = "Customer Service Representative"
15:             strCompany = "James Manufacturing"
16:         Case Else
17:             strSender = ""
18:             strTitle = ""
19:             strCompany = "James Manufacturing"
20:     End Select
21:     ActiveDocument.RunLetterWizard ActiveDocument.CreateLetterContent( _
22:         DateFormat:="May 19, 1999", IncludeHeaderFooter:=True, _
23:         PageDesign:= _
24:         "C:\Program Files\Microsoft Office\Templates\1033\
            ⮡Contemporary Letter.dot" _
25:         , LetterStyle:=wdFullBlock, _
26:         Letterhead:=False, LetterheadLocation:=wdLetterTop, _
27:         LetterheadSize:=InchesToPoints(1), _
28:         Salutation:="", SalutationType:=wdSalutationFormal, _
29:         RecipientReference:="", MailingInstructions:="", _
30:         AttentionLine:="", Subject:="", CCList:="", _
31:         ReturnAddress:="James Manuafacturing" & Chr$(13) & Chr$(10) & _
32:         "12 Any Street" & Chr$(13) & Chr$(10) & "AnyTown, ST 55555", _
33:         SenderName:=strSender, Closing:="Sincerely,", _
34:         SenderCompany:=strCompany, SenderJobTitle:=strTitle, _
35:         SenderInitials:=strInitials, EnclosureNumber:=0, _
36:         RecipientName:="", RecipientAddress:=""), False
37: End Sub
```

ANALYSIS The LetterwithWizard procedure is designed to prompt the user for the sender initials. It then calls on the wizard and plugs in the information for that sender. Lines 2–4 set up variables to store the information that is set for each sender.

Lines 5–20 retrieve the initials of the sender using an InputBox and test against two sets of initials using a Select Case structure. There is a Case Else in case the initials are unknown.

After the sender information is obtained, the Letter Wizard is called on lines 21–36, using CreateLetterContent to populate the LetterContent argument. You could have set up an object variable for the LetterContent argument and then used that same variable for the RunLetterWizard method. The resulting behavior of the Letter Wizard is different, however.

> Line 24 provides the path for the template. You might need to modify that line to reflect the path of your Contemporary Letter template.

If you use an object variable, it sets up the wizard and displays the first tab of the wizard to the user. If you look at the arguments specified in the CreateLetterContent, you'll notice that they aren't in order. The recipient information is at the very bottom. By placing the CreateLetterContent method inside of the RunLetterWizard method as an argument, the wizard populates the dialog and leaves you at the Recipient tab, which is the information that needs to be changed.

When you run this macro, you will be prompted for the initials as shown in Figure 18.1. You can enter one of the choices such as jb.

18

FIGURE 18.1

The InputBox *asks for the initials.*

After the choice is entered, the Letter Wizard is displayed as shown in Figure 18.2. The user can then use the Address book or type in the recipient information.

FIGURE 18.2
The Letter Wizard is displayed with the second tab selected.

Creating a Letter Without Letter Wizard

In Hour 1, you explored how to set up a custom letter template. It is great when most of the elements of the letter, except for the recipient and the contents, don't change. With the custom letter template, however, you lose the capability to use the Address book to plug in the recipient information.

With an `AutoNew` macro or the `Document_New` event, you can still retrieve the recipient information from the Address Book. You use the `GetAddress` method to retrieve the information. The syntax is

```
expression.GetAddress(Name, AddressProperties, UseAutoText, _
    DisplaySelectDialog, SelectDialog, CheckNamesDialog, _
    RecentAddressesChoice, UpdateRecentAddresses)
```

The expression represents the application followed by the `GetAddress` keyword. This method can use up to eight arguments.

The `Name` argument indicates the name for which you want to retrieve an address. If this argument is left blank, the dialog will be displayed.

The `AddressProperties` argument enables you to control the formatting of the address by indicating the AutoText entry that controls the format. This argument is only used if the `UserAutoText` argument is set to `True`. Otherwise, it uses the default address layout.

The `DisplaySelectDialog` and `SelectDialog` arguments control the display of the dialog and what you can do with it. In most cases, you won't set these arguments because you want to select an address and control the placement in your document.

The CheckName argument determines if the Check Name dialog opens when the Name argument doesn't provide enough information. RecentAddressesChoice and UpdateRecentAddresses determine if only the recent addresses will be listed and whether the select address should be added to the recent list.

To try this out, you can create an AutoNew procedure just to display the dialog and insert the name and address selected. You must complete these steps:

1. Open the template you created in Hour 1.

2. Select Tools, Macro, Visual Basic Editor to open the Editor.

3. Right-click on the template from the list in the Project Explorer.

4. Select Insert, Module.

5. Add the following code:

```
1: Sub AutoNew()
2:     Dim letRecipient
3:     letRecipient = Application.GetAddress
4:     Application.Browser.Target = wdBrowseField
5:     Application.Browser.Next
6:     Selection.MoveRight Unit:=wdCharacter, Count:=1, Extend:=wdExtend
7:     Selection.TypeText letRecipient
8: End Sub
```

6. Save the template and close it.

7. Select File, New.

8. Double-click on the template to create the document and launch the AutoNew macro, which displays the Select Name dialog shown in Figure 18.3.

FIGURE 18.3

The recipient can be selected from the list.

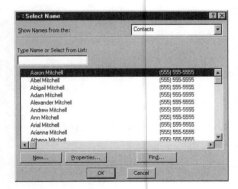

9. Select a name and click OK.

10. Notice the name and address are inserted in the document as shown in Figure 18.4.

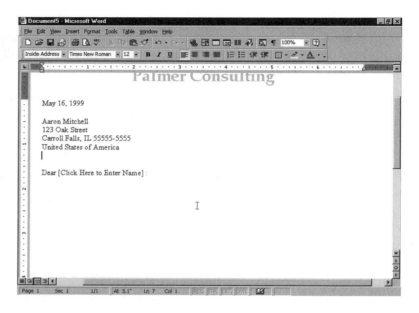

FIGURE **18.4**

The name and address are now a part of the document.

As you look at what is inserted as the address, you might not be happy with the formatting. A country name, which you probably don't need, is part of the address, and no company name is included. This format is the default layout. You can create an AutoText entry to specify another format and use AddressProperties to declare it.

To use AddressProperties, you will need to create the AutoText entry and then modify the code. To add the company and telephone number and remove the country information, complete these steps:

1. Type the following text into your document:

```
<PR_GIVEN_NAME> <PR_SURNAME>
<PR_COMPANY_NAME>
<PR_STREET_ADDRESS>
<PR_LOCALITY>, <PR_STATE_OR_PROVINCE> <PR_POSTAL_CODE>
<PR_OFFICE_TELEPHONE_NUMBER>
```

2. Select this text and choose Insert, AutoText, AutoText to open the AutoText dialog.

3. Enter CustomAddress as the name of the entry.

4. Select Add and Close.

5. Delete the text.

6. Switch to the Visual Basic Editor and change the code as shown in the following:

```
1: Sub AutoNew()
2:     Dim letRecipient
3:     letRecipient = Application.GetAddress( _
```

```
4:            AddressProperties:="CustomAddress", UseAutoText:=True)
5:       Application.Browser.Target = wdBrowseField
6:       Application.Browser.Next
7:       Selection.MoveRight Unit:=wdCharacter, Count:=1, Extend:=wdExtend
8:       Selection.TypeText letRecipient
9: End Sub
```

7. Switch back to Word and try out the new procedure.

The AutoText entry is the key to custom formatting. It uses set tag IDs for the fields in your address book to give you the information you need. You can create several AutoText entries to meet specific information needs in your documents with this approach. For more information concerning the tag IDs available, look up the AddAddress method in online help.

Automating Envelope Creation

After a letter is complete, an envelope has to be printed. You can use selected text to print the envelope.

To accomplish this task, you are going to use the PrintOut method for the Envelope Object of the active document. The syntax is

```
expression.PrintOut(ExtractAddress, Address, AutoText, _
    OmitReturnAddress, ReturnAddress, ReturnAutoText, PrintBarCode, _
    PrintFIMA, Size, Height, Width, FeedSource, AddressFromLeft, _
    AddressFromTop, ReturnAddressFromLeft, ReturnAddressFromTop, _
    DefaultFaceUp, DefaultOrientation)
```

The PrintOut method must be preceded by an expression that represents what to print. In this case, you can use the ActiveDocument.Envelope to represent the Envelope object.

When you are printing out the envelope, the PrintOut method has eighteen arguments that control the envelope's appearance:

- The first argument is ExactAddress. It can be set to True if you want to use a bookmark to indicate what to print as the address on the envelope. The bookmark must be named EnvelopeAddress. The Address argument would be a string to use as the address. It is ignored if ExactAddress is set to True. The AutoText argument can be used indicate an AutoText entry that can be used for the address.

- The next three arguments control the return address of the envelope. OmitReturnAddress indicates that you don't want a return address on the envelope. If it is set to False, the ReturnAddress can hold a string with the return address, or the ReturnAddressAutoText can indicate the AutoText entry that has that information.

18

- The `PrintBarCode` and `PrintFIMA` arguments control whether these items are included on the envelope. If you are mailing outside of the country, these can be omitted.

- The next four arguments control the dimensions of the envelope. You can specify a size using a built-in constant with the `Size` argument, or you can use the `Height` and `Width` arguments to provide measurements. The `FeedSource` indicates where the envelope is going to feed into the printer. This is also set with built-in constants.

- The `Addressfromleft`, `AddressfromTop`, `ReturnAddressfromLeft` and `ReturnAddressfromTop` all control the placement of these items on the envelope. This is especially helpful if you have to adjust these items because of a graphic border on an envelope.

- The `DefaultFaceUp` and `DefaultOrientation` arguments also indicate information about how the envelope feeds through the printer. These arguments are tied to a particular printer. You might need to walk through the process manually to get the right parameters for your printer.

In the following example, you take the text highlighted in the document and print an envelope adjusting the return address to accommodate a graphic border on the envelopes. You create the following procedure shown in Listing 18.2.

LISTING 18.2 The `PrintEnvelope` Procedure

```
 1: Sub PrintEnvelope()
 2:     If Selection.Range.Text = "" Then
 3:         MsgBox "No text is selected, please select the address.", _
 4:         vbInformation + vbOKOnly, "Address Missing"
 5:         Exit Sub
 6:     End If
 7:     ActiveDocument.Bookmarks.Add "EnvelopeAddress", Selection.Range
 8:     ActiveDocument.Envelope.PrintOut ExtractAddress:=True, _
 9:         OmitReturnAddress:=False, _
10:         ReturnAddress:=Application.UserAddress, _
11:         PrintBarCode:=True, _
12:         Height:=InchesToPoints(4.13), _
13:         Width:=InchesToPoints(9.5), _
14:         AddressFromLeft:=wdAutoPosition, _
15:         AddressFromTop:=wdAutoPosition, _
16:         ReturnAddressFromLeft:=InchesToPoints(1), _
17:         ReturnAddressFromTop:=InchesToPoints(0.5), _
18:         DefaultOrientation:=wdLeftClockwise, DefaultFaceUp:=False
19: End Sub
```

ANALYSIS This procedure begins by testing to make sure that there is a selected range with an address on lines 2–6. If there is no text selected, a message box displays and you exit the procedure.

Line 7 places a bookmark around the selected text so you can use the `ExactAddress` argument for the `Printout` method. The bookmark must be named `EnvelopeAddress` to be recognized by the method.

Lines 8–18 call the Printout method and set its arguments. Notice that `ExactAddress` is set to `True` to pick up the bookmark. Notice the `ReturnAddress` is set using the `UserAddress` property from the Options dialog.

The adjustments to the placement of the return address are made on lines 16–17. The `InchestoPoints` function is used to convert a standard measurement into points which is required by the argument.

Automating Mail Merge

In addition to doing a single letter, many people do mass mailing using the Microsoft Word mail merge feature. This feature leads the user by the hand to complete the project. If you are doing frequent mailings, you may want to cut down the time it takes to create a letter with VBA. With Mail Merge, you can let VBA select a source automatically, work with the records, or even build documents.

18

Selecting a Source

One way to save time with Mail Merge is to speed up the process of setting the source of the records. Selecting the source of the mail merge records varies depending on what type of data source you are working with.

If you are working with a Word document, Access database, or Excel worksheet, you can use the `OpenDataSource` method. Its syntax is

SYNTAX
```
expression.OpenDataSource(Name, Format, ConfirmConversions, ReadOnly, _
    LinkToSource, AddToRecentFiles, PasswordDocument, PasswordTemplate, _
    Revert, WritePasswordDocument, WritePasswordTemplate, Connection, _
    SQLStatement, SQLStatement1)
```

The `OpenDataSource` method is preceded by the expression that represents the `MailMerge` object for the document. It has fourteen arguments that you can set, and all but three apply to Word:

- The first argument is `Name`. It is a string that contains the name of the file as well as its path. You can indicate a file or you can use a MS Query file name. MS Query is an Microsoft application that enables you to manipulate data sources.

- The `Format` argument indicates what format the file is in. It is specified by built-in constants. The `wdOpenFormatAuto` is the default, and it indicates that it will auto-detect the format.

- `ConfirmConversions` and `ReadOnly` can be set to `True` or `False`. They indicate how the file is treated after it is opened.

- The `LinkToSource` is an important argument. If this is set to `True`, the data source will be refreshed when the main document is opened. This makes sure you are working with the latest data stored in the data file.

- The `AddtoRecentFiles` indicates whether the file will be added to the list on the bottom of the File menu. In most cases, the user isn't working with the document itself and you won't want it added.

- You also have control over the security of the document. If you use password protection on your documents, the `PasswordDocument` and `PasswordTemplate` enable you to pass the password with VBA to open the document. Revert can be set to `True` to indicate that you want to revert to the file on the drive if the file is already open when you try to open it.

- The `WritePassworddocument` and `WritePasswordTemplate` enable you to send the password needed to save the file if changes are made. It gives you the power to edit the data with VBA.

The last three arguments aren't applicable to a Word document as the source. The `Connection` argument is a string that provides additional information for accessing the data when you are working with an outside source such as Microsoft Access, Microsoft Excel, or an ODBC source.

With Access, you are providing the name of the table or query you want to access. With Excel, you provide the name of the worksheet. The last data source mentioned is Open Database Connectivity (ODBC) It is a widely accepted method for working with different types of data, especially data on a server.

Working with an ODBC source requires a better understanding of how outside data sources work. This topic is not within the scope of our material. Please refer to the on-line help for more information on what is required with an ODBC connection.

The last two arguments `SQLStatement` and `SQLStatement1` enable you to create a Structured Query Language (SQL) statement to indicate what information you want to work with from an outside source. SQL is a standardized language for retrieving and modifying data within most databases.

If you want to work with only those customers in a particular city, you could use SQL to retrieve only those records. Each of these SQL arguments can hold only 255 characters.

You build the SQL statement using the first argument, SQLStatement, and then add the remaining characters in the second one, SQLStatement1.

If you wanted to automate the selection of a data source other than an ODBC source, the syntax is very simple. You can create procedures like these shown in Listing 18.3 to set a Word or an Access source.

LISTING 18.3   The SelectWordSource and the SelectAccessList Procedures

```
 1: Sub SelectWordSource()
 2:     ActiveDocument.MailMerge.OpenDataSource Name:= _
 3:         "C:\My Documents\Toys Employees.doc", _
 4:         LinktoSource:=True, Revert:=False
 5: End Sub
 6:
 7: Sub SelectAccessList()
 8:     ActiveDocument.MailMerge.OpenDataSource Name:= _
 9:         "C:\My Documents\You Name It Toys.mdb", LinktoSource:=True, _
10:         Format:=wdOpenFormatAuto, Connection:="TABLE Employees", _
11:         SQLStatement:="SELECT * FROM [Employees]"
12: End Sub
```

18

ANALYSIS   The SelectWordSource in lines 1–5 is very simple because you don't have to worry about the format of the document being used. It uses the MailMerge object for the active document. It sets the Name property on line 3 to indicate the filename and path. It also sets the LinktoSource on line 4 to make sure that you get the current data and the Revert so you won't trash any changes made to the data if the file is already open.

The SelectAccessList is a little more complex. It also sets the Name and LinkToSource arguments to indicate what data is used. It has the Format argument on line 10 to control the what type of information is expected.

The difference is in the Connection and SQLStatement arguments. On line 10, the Connection indicates what object within Access you want to use. There are two types of data objects in Access you can use. The Table object is the object that stores the data. There is also a Query object which is a definition (description) of the subset of records. Here the Table object is used with the Employees table referenced.

The SQLStatement is used on line 11 in this case to indicate that all the fields and all the records will be used. SQL language, designed specifically for manipulating and managing databases, has its own syntax.

In this case, the SELECT keyword indicates that you are selecting a subset of records. The asterisk indicates you want to use all the fields. The FROM keyword indicates the source and `Employees` is the table name. SQL is also needed for sorting or filtering the data as shown in the next two sections.

You can also select an Address Book as your source. An Address Book doesn't use the same method to make the connections. You use the `UseAddressBook` method. It has one argument, `Type`. `Type` is a string that indicates the type of address book. For example, the `TYPE` for Outlook is `olk`. The procedure resembles the following:

```
Sub SelectOutlookList()
    ActiveDocument.MailMerge.UseAddressBook Type:="olk"
End Sub
```

This procedure initiates the connection, but the user will be prompted for some information. To handle address book data, Microsoft Word creates a virtual document to control the merging.

For this sample template, this data source isn't compatible with the field settings because the Outlook fields are fixed. You will get errors as you attempt to merge with the current merge fields in place. If you are going to be switching between Outlook and other sources with different type of the fields, you might want to consider adding the fields with VBA as part of the routine of switching. This is accomplished with the `Add` method for the `Fields` collection for the document.

At this point, you want to make sure that you are using the Word document to minimize the resources you are using.

Setting a Sort Order

After you have selected a data source, you can adjust the query options using the Mail Merge Wizard. One of these query options gives the capability to adjust the order of the records based on one or several fields. This procedure is referred to as Sorting.

After the data source has been accessed with the `OpenDataSource`, you modify its characteristics with the `DataSource` object. In this case, you need to modify the `QueryString` property. You could create a procedure like the `SortbyDepartment` shown in Listing 18.4 to handle the modifications.

LISTING 18.4   The `SortbyDepartment` Procedure

```
1: Sub SortbyDepartment()
2:     Select Case ActiveDocument.MailMerge.DataSource.Type
3:         Case wdMergeInfoFromWord
4:             ActiveDocument.MailMerge.DataSource.QueryString = _
```

```
 5:                "SELECT * FROM C:\My Documents\Toys Employees.doc
                ➥ORDER BY Department" & ""
 6:          Case wdMergeInfoFromAccessDDE
 7:              ActiveDocument.MailMerge.DataSource.QueryString = _
 8:                "SELECT * FROM [Employees] ORDER BY Department" & ""
 9:          Case Else
10:              'No Action
11:      End Select
12: End Sub
```

ANALYSIS This procedure sets up a Select Case statement to test the DataSource's type on line 2. In both cases, it sets up the QueryString with the appropriate SQL statement on lines 4–5 and 7–8. The first part is identical to that shown earlier which opened the data source.

The QueryString begins with the SELECT keyword followed by an asterisk to indicate that all fields should be included. That is followed by the FROM clause to indicate the data source.

To sort, you have added a new clause. It is called the ORDER BY clause. In this clause, the keywords are followed by the field or fields to sort by.

Setting a Filter

Setting a filter is identical to setting the sort order except the clause is not the ORDER BY clause. It is the WHERE clause. The WHERE clause contains an expression to indicate a criteria to create a subset of the records.

The rules for the expressions are the same for the WHERE clause here as they were for the one in Hour 5, "Exploring VBA." You can use the WHERE clause, for example, to filter out all the records except those of the Marketing Department, as shown in Listing 18.5.

LISTING 18.5 The MarketingDepartment Procedure

```
 1: Sub MarketingOnly()
 2:      Select Case ActiveDocument.MailMerge.DataSource.Type
 3:          Case wdMergeInfoFromWord
 4:              ActiveDocument.MailMerge.DataSource.QueryString = _
 5:                  "SELECT * FROM C:\My Documents\Toys Employees.doc WHERE
                   ➥((Department = 'Marketing'))  & """
 6:          Case wdMergeInfoFromAccessDDE
 7:              ActiveDocument.MailMerge.DataSource.QueryString = _
 8:              "SELECT * FROM [Employees] WHERE ((Department = 'Marketing')) & """
 9:      End Select
10: End Sub
```

ANALYSIS The structure of this procedure is identical to Listing 18.4 except for the change in the SQL statement. It has the WHERE clause. On lines 5 and 8, it begins with the WHERE keyword followed by the expression. Notice that Marketing is surrounded by apostrophes. This takes the place of the quotations when you are building the argument. When the code executes they will be treated as quotations.

After this procedure has executed, you will see that there are fewer records to work with, and the records are only of those people in Marketing, as shown in Figure 18.5. This is clear because Caroline Fisher is the first person instead of Mark Mitchell. He is assigned to Accounting and isn't a part of the filtered list.

FIGURE 18.5

The records selected are all employees from the Marketing department.

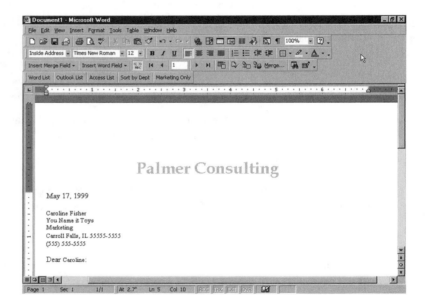

You can create separate procedures to filter specific groups of information or use the User Forms to create a choice to automate filters. You have a great deal of flexibility.

Automating Printing

In the preceding example, you had the toolbar available to print the letters. If you are automating the entire process with VBA you will also automate the printing of the letters. You will use the MailMerge object's Destination property and the Execute method. The code is simple for printing. You can create a procedure like the one below:

```
Sub PrintLetters()
   With ActiveDocument.MailMerge
       .Destination = wdSendToPrinter
```

```
        .Execute
    End With
End Sub
```

The `Destination` property is set with built-in constants. To go to the printer, you use the `wdSendToPrinter`. You can also send the letters to another document by using a different constant.

Creating a Catalog or Directory

You sometimes want to create a document that shows all records in a single list, not reserving a separate page for each record as you do when creating letters. This is referred to as creating a Catalog. This is an area where you will find many opportunities to use VBA for two reasons:

- The process completed by the Mail Merge Helper creates a static list and requires rebuilding if the data changes.
- The document generated by the helper can require extensive formatting to meet your needs.

The task of creating a catalog can be fully automated. You could create a procedure called `CreateEmployeePhoneList` as shown in Listing 18.6 to create a call list.

LISTING 18.6   The `CreateEmployeesPhoneList` Procedure

```
 1: Sub CreateEmployeeCallList()
 2:     Dim objDocument As Document
 3:     Set objDocument = Documents.Add(DocumentType:=wdNewBlankDocument)
 4:     objDocument.Activate
 5:     ActiveDocument.MailMerge.MainDocumentType = wdCatalog
 6:     ActiveDocument.MailMerge.OpenDataSource Name:= _
 7:         "C:\My Documents\Toys Employees.doc", _
 8:         ConfirmConversions:=False, ReadOnly:=False, _
 9:         LinkToSource:=True, AddToRecentFiles:=False, _
10:         Revert:=False, Format:=wdOpenFormatAuto
11:     ActiveDocument.MailMerge.EditMainDocument
12:     Selection.ParagraphFormat.TabStops.Add _
13:         Position:=InchesToPoints(6), _
14:         Alignment:=wdAlignTabRight, Leader:=wdTabLeaderDots
15:     ActiveDocument.MailMerge.Fields.Add _
16:         Range:=Selection.Range, Name:="FirstName"
17:     Selection.TypeText Text:=" "
18:     ActiveDocument.MailMerge.Fields.Add _
19:         Range:=Selection.Range, Name:="LastName"
20:     Selection.TypeText Text:=vbTab
```

18

continues

LISTING 18.6 continued

```
21:      ActiveDocument.MailMerge.Fields.Add _
22:      Range:=Selection.Range, Name:="Phone"
23:      Selection.TypeParagraph
24:    With ActiveDocument.MailMerge
25:         .Destination = wdSendToNewDocument
26:         .MailAsAttachment = False
27:         .MailAddressFieldName = ""
28:         .MailSubject = ""
29:         .SuppressBlankLines = True
30:         With .DataSource
31:             .FirstRecord = wdDefaultFirstRecord
32:             .LastRecord = wdDefaultLastRecord
33:         End With
34:         .Execute Pause:=True
35:    End With
36:    Selection.TypeParagraph
37:    Selection.MoveUp Unit:=wdLine, Count:=1
38:    Selection.ParagraphFormat.Alignment = wdAlignParagraphCenter
39:    With Selection.Font
40:         .Name = "Arial"
41:         .Size = 16
42:         .Bold = True
43:    End With
44:    Selection.TypeText Text:="Employee Call List"
45:    Selection.TypeParagraph
46: End Sub
```

ANALYSIS   The first thing that is accomplished with this code is the creation of a new document with the Add method and assigned to the objDocument variable on line 3. After the document is created, you activate it so you can work with it.

After the document is created, the OpenDataSource method is used on lines 6–10 to assign it to the Word document with the records in it. After the connection is completed, you have to set up the appearance of the document by editing the main document.

The Add method is used with several collections during this code. It was used to add a new document, and it is used now to add a new tab at the right margin for the phone number on lines 12–14.

After the formatting is set up, the fields are inserted into the document. On lines 15–23, the structure of the document is built using the Add method to add the mail merge fields, as well as the TypeText and TypeParagraph methods to place the fields on the page as needed. The TypeParagraph method is used on line 23 to end the line with the record on it.

Lines 24–36 have a `With` structure to merge the data with the structure in the new document. On line 25, the `Destination` property is set to create a new document with the `wdSendToNewDocument` constant. Lines 31–34 set up the scope of the data, you are working with. Line 35 uses the `Execute` method to merge it into another document. The `Pause` argument is set to `True` to indicate that if there are any problems with the merge, the procedure should stop and notify the user of the problem.

Lines 37–46 work with the new merged document. They add a simple title. You could add any formatting desired at this point. At this point, you have automated the procedure to create a catalog. When this procedure is executed, the catalog shown in Figure 18.6 will be automatically generated.

FIGURE 18.6

The catalog is completed by the procedure.

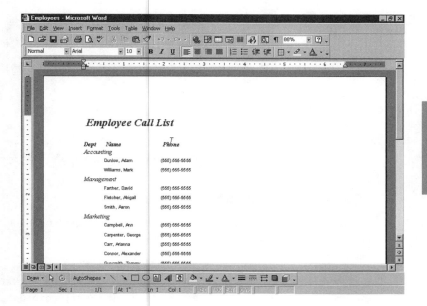

Working with Email

Another method for mailing documents is to use email instead of regular or interoffice mail. You can create a procedure to automate that process, with either single letters or as part of a merge operation.

Sending a Single Letter

If you want to prompt the user to send a document via email with VBA, there are two approaches. If you want the users to fill in the information for the transmission, use the `SendMail` method:

```
ActiveDocument.SendMail
```

With one line of code in a procedure, you can prompt for the email information. This line of code opens the email message window, as shown in Figure 18.7, so the user can manually enter information to accompany the document.

FIGURE 18.7

The Message window shows the document as an attachment.

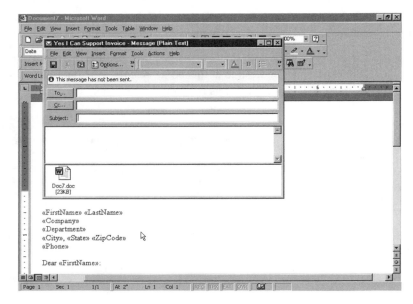

Merging to Email

The other approach to using Email is to use the `MailMerge` object and work with the `Destination` property. You indicate a field that stores the email addresses as well as a subject line.

You might also want to check to make sure mail exists on the machine before attempting this operation. You could create a procedure called `EmailRecipients` to automate email as shown in Listing 18.7.

LISTING 18.7   The `EmailRecipients` Procedure

```
1: Sub EmailRecipients()
2:     Dim lMailSystem As Long
3:     lMailSystem = Application.MailSystem
4:     If lMailSystem = wdNoMailSystem Then
5:         MsgBox "This machine doesn't have a mail system.", _
6:             vbInformation + vbOKOnly, "Missing Mail System"
7:         Exit Sub
8:     End If
```

```
 9:      With ActiveDocument.MailMerge
10:          .MailAddressFieldName = "Email"
11:          .MailSubject = "Office 200 Training"
12:          .Destination = wdSendToEmail
13:          .Execute
14:      End With
15: End Sub
```

ANALYSIS   This procedure checks to make sure email is set up on the machine, and then it creates email messages to the recipients and places them in your Outlook Outbox. The next time you send mail, those messages will be sent.

Lines 2–8 use the `MailSystem` property to check to see if there is a mail system set up on the machine the user is working on. It checks that property against a built-in `constantwdNoMailSystem`. If a match is made, a message is displayed, and the procedure terminates without attempting to send the messages.

Lines 9–14 construct and send the messages using a `With` structure and the `MailMerge` object for the document. Line 10 sets the `MailAddressFieldName` that gives the name of the field in the data source that has the email addresses.

Line 11 indicates the string to use as the title for these messages. Line 12 indicates that you want to merge to email. After the parameters are set up, the `Execute` method is used. This carries out the merge.

Summary

In this hour, you have explored how to use VBA to speed up your correspondence and merging. You learned how to get more from a letter created with the Letter Wizard by passing it some of the settings that never change. You can also display a specific tab to speed up the entry of the information that does change.

You explored how to add the Address Book loop up to your own custom template. You also learned how to speed up the creation of envelopes.

Another area where you can use VBA is merging. You looked at how to add a source automatically that can eliminate the need to search a hard drive or network for a file. You also learned how to manipulate the data after it is attached with sorting and filtering.

Last, but not least, you learned how to get the most from your merging output. You looked at automatically sending the merge to the printer, controlling the creation of a catalog, and sending email.

18

Q&A

Q Can I automate the use of the Memo Wizard?

A You can automatically launch the wizard by using the Add method to add a document to the Documents collection, but you can't affect the settings as you can with the Letter Wizard because it doesn't use the LetterContent object.

Q Can I automate the printing of labels as well as Envelopes?

A Yes, you can. Instead of working with the Envelope object, you use the MailingLabel object.

Workshop

Here are some questions and exercises to help you review the material covered in this hour. The answers to the quiz questions can be found in Appendix A, "Quiz Answers."

Quiz

1. What property can be used as the ReturnAddress for the sender?
2. If you want to get rid of a country or add a company name when you use the GetAddress method, what should you do?
3. If you want to build your merge main document with VBA, what method should you use?
4. If you want to merge to email, do you have to include the email field in the document?

Exercises

1. Create a procedure to print a mailing label for the selected address.
2. Review your automation checklist to see where merging is needed.

HOUR 19

Managing Large Documents

In Hour 14, "Working with Large Documents," you explored some techniques for making large documents easier to work with and update. In this hour, you are going to explore more techniques for large document management.

The highlights of this hour include

- Working with subdocuments
- Formatting a master document
- Using AutoCaption, cross references, and summaries
- Controlling field updating
- Working with revisions

To enable you to concentrate on the concepts of large-document management, the companion Web site has several large documents and a template with sample procedures. There is a finished example of the template, as well as one for you to work with.

Place the template, Landscaping Proposal, in your default templates directory, and the remaining documents in your default documents directory. There are four supporting documents, All Season Color.doc, Birds and Butterflies.doc, Landscape Design.doc, and Lawn Care.doc.

Working with Subdocuments

If you frequently work with large documents that need to be updated on a regular basis or maintained by more than one person, you might find having only a single document is a problem. You may also find, as the document grows larger and larger, it becomes more difficult to work with. This book, itself, is a good example. In addition to the author, there are editors who need to make changes to the text of the book. Also, it is quite cumbersome for anyone to work with the whole book—a document more than 400 pages in length—at one time.

For this book, the text is broken down into smaller units—hours; but the book must still be treated as one unit to ensure consistent formatting, such as page numbering. This makes editing difficult.

Microsoft Word has a solution: a master document with subdocuments. To make writing and managing easier, you first decide what topics need to be treated as a unit. When you are working on a book or manual, chapters provide set dividing points. Each unit can be placed in a separate document. In addition, although it isn't required, basing all documents on the same template makes working with the documents even easier.

To review the entire contents or create a final printout, each part of the documents is inserted as a subdocument into a master document. A master document is any Word document that has subdocuments included.

To create a master document, begin by creating a new document. Remember it is best to base the document and its subdocuments on the same template. Select the Outline view. When the Outline view is active, Word displays the Outlining toolbar. It is used to manage the subdocuments. You can use it to insert a subdocument, remove a subdocument, take selected text and create a subdocument, or merge subdocuments together for ease of management. You can also lock documents to prevent anyone from making additional changes.

Working with a master document enables you to collapse the document to just see heading levels or expand particular sections. These tools can make management of large text easier.

If you create many long documents that share common elements, such as a description of products, master documents can help you guarantee everyone is using the most up-to-date version. When the file is opened, the subdocuments are linked to provide the latest content. This saves a lot of proofreading.

In many cases, you can use Visual Basic for Applications to automate the construction and maintenance of all these types of documents. If you use VBA, you must be able to add, open, and delete subdocuments.

Adding Subdocuments

One of the major benefits of using VBA with master documents is the ease with which you can change information in the document. You only have to edit the master document, inserting the subdocuments that are required. The example used in this hour illustrates how VBA can let you choose what subdocuments to include in a master document. If you include various materials, such as marketing packets, training materials, or informational documents for different occasions, you want a way to select specific subdocuments each time you put together a master document. Rather than manually creating a master document with the appropriate subdocuments, you can use VBA to create an insert system so you can pick and choose which subdocuments to insert.

One method is to create a toolbar with buttons (see Figure 19.1). Each one represents a different subdocument. The user can select which ones to insert into the existing document.

When you click on one of the buttons, the document is inserted as a subdocument at your insertion point. This is accomplished with the AddFromFile method. The syntax is as follows:

```
expression.AddFromFile(Name, ConfirmConversions, ReadOnly, _
PasswordDocument, PasswordTemplate, Revert, _
WritePasswordDocument, WritePasswordTemplate)
```

The expression represents the subdocument collection for the range that you are working with, and it is followed by the AddFromFile keyword. It can use up to eight arguments. These include the following:

- The *Name* argument is required by this method. It holds the filename with its path.

- The *ConfirmConversions* argument can be set to True if you want Microsoft Word to prompt when a document must be converted before it is inserted.

- The *ReadOnly* argument can be set to *True* if you want to prevent the user from changing the contents of the document. This is useful if the user should never change the document.

- The *PasswordDocument*, *PasswordTemplate*, *WritePasswordDocument* and *WritePasswordTemplate* give you more flexibility. Instead of inserting a file as read-only so no changes can be made on it, you can also indicate a password to be used when the file is inserted.

- The *Revert* argument, between the two sets of password arguments, can be set to *True* or *False*. It indicates what will happen when a document is inserted that is already open at the time. If *Revert* is set to *True*, the copy of the file in the folder is used. If it is set to *False*, the document that is currently being edited will be included with its unsaved changes.

FIGURE 19.1

The toolbar has four buttons representing the documents.

Document toolbar

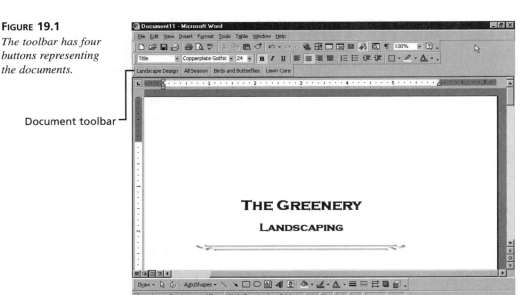

For use in this hour, the Web site has a template called Landscape Proposal.doc that already has a title page and a table of contents with one entry in it. There are also four documents that can be inserted. If you haven't done so already, download these files from the companion Web site. Place the Landscape Proposal.doc in your default templates directory and the remaining documents in your default documents directory.

To insert the Landscape Design document, complete these steps to create the
InsertLandscapeDesign procedure:

1. Open the Visual Basic Editor.

2. Right-click on the template project in the Project Explorer and select Insert,
   Module.

3. Enter the code for the procedure as shown in Listing 19.1.

LISTING 19.1   The InsertLandscapeDesign Procedure

```
 1: Sub InsertLandscapeDesign()
 2:     On Error GoTo InsertError
 3:     Selection.Range.Subdocuments.AddFromFile Name:= _
 4:         "c:\My Documents\Landscape Design.doc", _
 5:         ConfirmConversions:=False, ReadOnly:=False, _
 6:         Revert:=False
 7:     Exit Sub
 8: InsertError:
 9:     Select Case Err.Number
10:         Case 4605    'Not in Outline View
11:             ActiveWindow.View = wdMasterView
12:             Resume
13:         Case Else
14:             MsgBox Err.Number & " " & Err.Description, vbInformation
15:     End Select
16: End Sub
```

ANALYSIS   The first step in this procedure on line 2 is to initialize the error handler because
there are several problems that might arise with this procedure. You must be able
to deal with the errors if they occur.

Lines 3–6 set up the InsertFromFile method to insert the file. It uses the Name argument
to specify the file with its path, as well as the ConfirmConversions, ReadOnly, and
Revert arguments to handle how the document was inserted.

Line 7 marks the end of the code to be executed on a regular basis. Line 8 is the line
label for the error handler.

The error handling code takes up the remainder of the procedure on lines 9–13. The first
error code that is checked by the Select Case is 4605. To insert a subdocument, you must
be in the master view. If this error is triggered, the view is switched, and the Resume keyword is used to execute the InsertFromFile method again.

19

Any other error is handled by the `Case Else` clause. You can add a specific case for error 5273, which is an invalid path or filename. If you're working with a network, you might want special testing for that case as well.

There is one error that isn't tracked separately in this procedure that may create a special situation. Error 5174 is triggered when you attempt to insert a file that doesn't have the same template as the master document. If you aren't using error handling, the message `Subdocument <Name> has a different template than its master document. The master document template will be used` is displayed, and the user has to click OK.

When you develop your subdocuments, take special care to make sure that they are based on the same template as the master document they will be used with. Another option is to change the template of any document before insertion. Open the document, set its `AttachedTemplate` property to match the `AttachedTemplate` property of the master document (which is the `ActiveDocument`), and then, save and close it. The `Resume` keyword is used to attempt the insert again.

This process isn't one I would recommend on a regular basis because it adjusts the document without allowing the user to look at the consequences first. Try to catch the template problem as you are creating the procedure. You can then make the change and verify the results before insertion.

Collapsing Subdocuments

After the subdocument is inserted into the master document, the user can make changes to it. When you are editing a master document, you have additional ways of viewing the document using Outline view. Although you don't have to create special procedures to work with the Outline view (because of the toolbar and default shortcut keys), you can control the Outline view with VBA. For example, if you want to insert several subdocuments and automatically collapse them to show only their top-level headings (in order to give you an overview of the entire document), you can use the `ShowHeading` method. It takes one line of code:

```
ActiveWindow.View.ShowHeading 1
```

The `ActiveWindow.View` references the window you are working with and its view. It is followed by the `ShowHeading` method with a 1 to indicate the level of headings you want to see.

Expanding Subdocuments

After the master document is collapsed, you can automatically display a subdocument by working with the `Subdocuments` collection. For example, you could expand just the Landscape Design subdocument with the following code shown in Listing 19.2.

LISTING 19.2 ExpandLandscapeDesign Procedure

```
 1: Sub ExpandLandscapeDesign()
 2:     Dim objSub As Subdocument
 3:     For Each objSub In ActiveDocument.Subdocuments
 4:         If objSub.Name = "Landscape Design.doc" Then
 5:             objSub.Range.Select
 6:             For I = 1 To 9
 7:                 ActiveWindow.ActivePane.View.ExpandOutline
 8:             Next I
 9:         End If
10:     Next
11: End Sub
```

ANALYSIS Line 2 declares an object variable to represent a subdocument. This can be used in the rest of the code. Lines 3–10 use the For Each...Next structure to cycle through the subdocuments collection and test each one's Name property.

After the subdocument with a matching name is found using the If structure, it is selected on line 5. The ExpandOutline method is used to expand the subdocument. It is placed in a For...Next loop because you have to expand though each level in the subdocument.

Opening Subdocuments

There are times when expanding a subdocument isn't enough. You want to open the source document. To open a subdocument, you use the Open method. For example, to open the subdocument that currently has the insertion point in it takes one line of code.

```
Selection.Range.Subdocuments(1).Open
```

When this line is executed, the subdocument will be opened in a separate window. You could use a For Each...Next loop to open all the documents when the master document is opened, but you have to watch your resources.

Deleting Subdocuments

You can also automate the deletion of a subdocument. The subdocument can be deleted with the Delete method. By modifying the procedure shown above to expand the Landscape Design document, you can also delete it from a master document as shown below:

```
 1: Sub DeleteLandscapeDesign()
 2:     Dim objSub As Subdocument
 3:     For Each objSub In ActiveDocument.Subdocuments
 4:         If objSub.Name = "Landscape Design.doc" Then _
```

19

```
5:            objSub.Delete
6:      Next
7: End Sub
```

The `For Each...Next` loop tests for the Landscape Design document. When it is located, the `Delete` method on line 5 is executed. It is a quick way to eliminate old subdocuments from a master file.

One good use for the `For Each...Next` loop with the subdocument collection is to update a reference to a subdocument. If a subdocument needs to be replaced in each one of a group of documents, you can open each document and replace it with code. You might find this helpful with price lists, bonus rate sheets, discount rate sheets, and so forth.

Formatting a Master Document

After you begin using a master document to manage larger documents, you will find that there are some additional formatting issues to consider. You must manage sections, control headers and footers, and work with a table of contents and indexes.

Using Sections with Subdocuments

Sections are used with subdocuments to control how a subdocument is integrated into the whole. As a subdocument is inserted into the master document, you can see two section breaks are added to the document as well. (You can only see these section breaks if you are viewing your document marks. To view your document marks, click on the Show/Hide button on the standard toolbar.)

Inserting a subdocument places a section break above the insertion point to begin the section on a new page. A section break is also inserted after the subdocument as a continuous break. The section breaks affect the flow of the document after the subdocument's insertion. You can see how these two breaks follow each other with two subdocuments as shown in Figure 19.2.

These breaks can be a factor when inserting subdocuments automatically. The contents of the subdocument might require special attention. If the subdocument has headers and footers as part of the document, these must be placed in their own section. You might want to use VBA to make the process easier. You can create a procedure called `ModifyNextPageSections` as shown here:

```
1: Sub ModifyNextPageSections()
2:     Dim objSection As Section
3:     For Each objSection In ActiveDocument.Sections
4:         If objSection.PageSetup.SectionStart = wdSectionNewPage Then
```

```
5:            objSection.PageSetup.SectionStart = wdSectionContinuous
6:         End If
7:     Next
8: Sub
```

FIGURE 19.2

The breaks are inserted automatically.

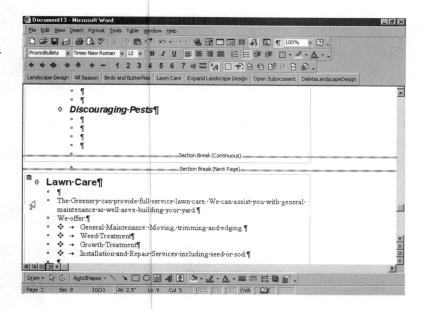

ANALYSIS In this case, the `For Each...Next` structure makes checking the sections easy. On line 2, an object variable, `objSection` is declared as a section.

Lines 3–7 check each section in the active document. The `SectionStart` property for the PageSetUp of each section is tested to see if it is set to begin on a new page. If it is, the property is set to `wdSectionContinuous`. After the procedure is executed, there are now two continuous section breaks in between the subdocuments as shown in Figure 19.3.

Controlling Headers and Footers

Eliminating the breaks between sections is only half of the problem. Now as you scroll through the document, you will notice the headers and footers aren't consistent as shown in Figure 19.4.

On the page in Figure 19.4, the header shows the title, Landscaping Services Summary, but the Landscape Design section does not begin until the middle of the page. You can control the headers and footers with VBA.

19

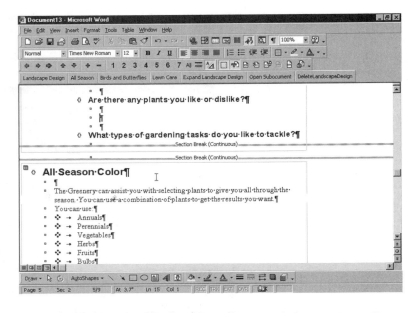

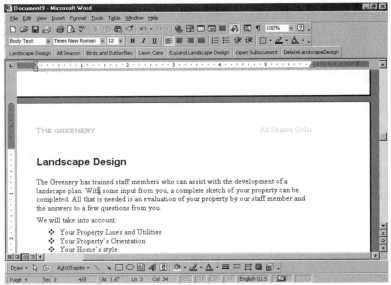

When you create a fresh document using the Landscaping Proposal template, you have a general header and footer set up. You might set up this header and footer for the whole master document. That means that you have to remove the headers and footers of the subdocuments before you adjust the section breaks.

The `SetGeneralHeader` procedure shown in Listing 19.3 uses VBA to remove the headers and footers in each subdocument and then changes the section breaks to give a general header and footer for the entire document.

LISTING 19.3   SetGeneralHeader Procedure

```
 1: Sub SetGeneralHeader()
 2: '    Change View
 3:     If ActiveWindow.ActivePane.View.Type = wdNormalView Or ActiveWindow. _
 4:         ActivePane.View.Type = wdOutlineView Then
 5:         ActiveWindow.ActivePane.View.Type = wdPrintView
 6:     End If
 7: '    Test for Header/Footer
 8:     Dim objSub As Subdocument, objTestStory, objSection As Section
 9:     For Each objSub In ActiveDocument.Subdocuments
10:         objSub.Open
11:         Documents(objSub.Name).Activate
12:         For Each objTestStory In ActiveDocument.StoryRanges
13:             If objTestStory.StoryType = wdPrimaryHeaderStory Or _
14:                 objTestStory.StoryType = wdPrimaryFooterStory Or _
15:                 objTestStory.StoryType = wdEvenPagesHeaderStory Or _
16:                 objTestStory.StoryType = wdEvenPagesFooterStory Or _
17:                 objTestStory.StoryType = wdFirstPageHeaderStory Or _
18:                 objTestStory.StoryType = wdFirstPageFooterStory Then
19:                 ActiveDocument.StoryRanges(objTestStory.StoryType) _
20:                 .Delete
21:             End If
22:         Next
23:         ActiveDocument.Close SaveChanges:=wdSaveChanges
24:     Next
25:     For Each objSection In ActiveDocument.Sections
26:     If objSection.PageSetup.SectionStart = wdSectionNewPage Then
27:         objSection.PageSetup.SectionStart = wdSectionContinuous
28:         End If
29:     Next
30: End Sub
```

ANALYSIS   This procedure shifts view, deletes any headers or footers in the subdocuments and closes them. Lines 2–6 change the view to the Print Layout because you can't work with headers and footers unless you are in the Print view. This code is the same code that was introduced in Hour 11, "Working with Page Appearance and Printing."

Lines 7–24 open each subdocument and activate it. After all are activated, the headers and footers are deleted and the documents are closed.

19

Line 8 declares the variables needed for testing. Line 9 sets up the `For Each...Next` loop to cycle through the subdocuments. Line 10 opens the document, and line 11 activates it so you can work with it.

Lines 12-21 test the stories in the `StoryRanges` collection for this document. This code is also the same as the code introduced in Hour 11 except for line 20. It uses the `Delete` method to get rid of the header and footers.

Line 23 closes the documents. The `wdSavechanges` setting makes sure the document is saved as it closes.

Lines 25–29 are duplicated from the earlier procedure to change the New Page section into continuous ones. When this procedure is executed, the subdocuments will end up with the same header as shown in Figure 19.5.

FIGURE 19.5

All subdocuments show the header of the master document.

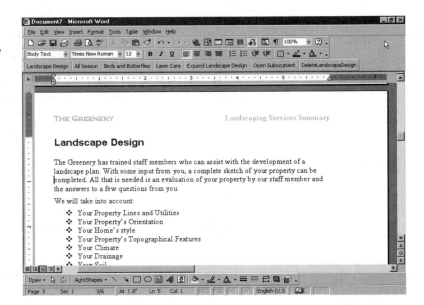

Using AutoCaption, Cross References, and Summaries

In addition to controlling headers and footers, you might also want to add automation for some of the other document elements that are useful with larger documents. You might want to turn on AutoCaption, add References, or add a Document Summary to your text. All these can be controlled with VBA.

Controlling AutoCaption

The AutoCaption feature can save you a lot of time when preparing a document or sub-documents. It enables you to reference different objects, such as graphics, in the same manner. The AutoCaption feature enables you, as you create the document, to predefine which objects you to which you will add a caption. When you insert an object (such as a graphic) into the document, AutoCaption automatically adds a number in the text for easy referencing. You might have noticed the formatting in this book; all the figures for a chapter are numbered sequentially. Letting AutoCaption take care of this for you prevents problems when you insert a graphic in your text. The numbers will renumber automatically.

You can set up AutoCaptioning with VBA so that it functions same way every time you need it, and it can be turned off when you don't need it. You can create a procedure like SetUpAutoCaption shown in Listing 19.4.

LISTING 19.4   The SetUpAutoCaption Procedure

```
 1: Sub SetUpAutoCaption()
 2:     On Error GoTo CaptionError
 3:     Dim objAutoCaption As AutoCaption, lAutoTrue As Long
 4:     For Each objAutoCaption In Application.AutoCaptions
 5:         If objAutoCaption.AutoInsert = True Then lAutoTrue = vAutoTrue + 1
 6:     Next
 7:     If lAutoTrue > 0 Then
 8:         AutoCaptions.CancelAutoInsert
 9:     Else
10:         AutoCaptions.CancelAutoInsert
11:         With AutoCaptions("Word.Picture.8")
12:             .AutoInsert = True
13:             .CaptionLabel = CaptionLabels("Figure")
14:         End With
15:         With AutoCaptions("PBrush")
16:             .AutoInsert = True
17:             .CaptionLabel = CaptionLabels("Figure")
18:         End With
19:         With CaptionLabels("Figure")
20:             .Position = wdCaptionPositionBelow
21:             .NumberStyle = wdCaptionNumberStyleArabic
22:             .IncludeChapterNumber = False
23:         End With
24:         With AutoCaptions("wfwTable")
25:             .AutoInsert = True
26:             .CaptionLabel = CaptionLabels("Table")
27:         End With
```

19

continues

LISTING 19.4 continued

```
28:        With CaptionLabels("Table")
29:            .Position = wdCaptionPositionAbove
30:            .NumberStyle = wdCaptionNumberStyleArabic
31:            .IncludeChapterNumber = False
32:        End With
33:    End If
34:    Exit Sub
35: CaptionError:
36:    Select Case Err.Number
37:        Case 5941, 438, 91
38:            Resume Next
39:        Case Else
40:            MsgBox Err.Number & " " & Err.Description, vbInformation
41:    End Select
42: End Sub
```

ANALYSIS This procedure checks to see if any item has been selected for automatic insertion. If items have been selected, the procedure clears the settings. If no item is selected, it sets up AutoCaptioning for Word pictures, Paintbrush pictures, and tables.

Line 2 turns on error handling in case one of the items doesn't exist. Lines 4–6 test if any items in the AutoCaptions collection have AutoInsert set to True. If so, it increments a variable. Lines 7–33 constitute an If...Then...Else structure to set the variable. If the lAutoTrue variable is greater than 0, AutoCaptioning is shut off on line 8 with the CancelAutoInsert method.

If no items are selected, lAutoTrue = 0. In that case, lines 10–32 set up AutoCaptioning and turn it on. Lines 11–14 turn on AutoCaption for Word Pictures by setting the AutoInsert property to True and by specifying a Captionlabel property as a string.

Lines 15–18 do the same thing for Paintbrush pictures. Lines 19–23 set up the caption label Figure. Its Position property is set to below the pictures with a built-in constant. The NumberStyle property is set the same way, and the IncludeChapterNumber is set to False indicating that you don't need a chapter number.

If you wanted to include a chapter number, this property would be set to True, and you would need to set the ChapterStyleLevel or HeadingLevelforChapter properties. Using these properties requires some input from the user. You might also want to use the document properties to assist with setting these values.

Lines 24–32 accomplish the same settings for tables. Line 34 has the Exit Sub statement for the end of the procedure, if everything proceeds as expected.

Lines 35–41 contain the error handling. They use a standard `Select Case` statement for error handling. Line 37 tests for three errors. 5941 will be triggered if the object you are trying to set an AutoCaption for doesn't exist . Errors 438 and 91 occur when VBA tries to execute the statements within the `With` structures for a missing object.

Line 38 just tells the code to resume at the line below the error. This enables the code to set up the objects it can. Another approach would be to display a message to the user and set up none of the objects.

Adding Cross References

References within larger documents can also be of great assistance to the user. You can use VBA to automatically insert the references for different subdocuments. For example, throughout this book, you have seen references to other hours when a topic was mentioned that gets more coverage elsewhere. The cross-reference cuts down the time it takes to find more information. To insert a cross-reference, use the `InsertCrossReference` method. The syntax is

SYNTAX

```
expression.InsertCrossReference(ReferenceType, ReferenceKind, _
    ReferenceItem, InsertAsHyperLink, IncludePosition)
```

The expression represents a selection or a range that you are working with, and it is followed by the `InsertCrossReference` keyword. There are up to five arguments that can be used to set up the reference.

- The *ReferenceType* argument is set with a built-in constant and represents the type of object you are referencing. For example, `wdRefTypeBookmark` indicates you are looking at a bookmark. For automation purposes, this is easiest to use.

- The *ReferenceKind* argument indicates what type of reference you want in your text. It is set with a built-in constant as well as `wdPageNumber` to make the page number appear in your text.

- The *ReferenceItem* argument indicates the index of the item you are referencing. When you set the reference manually, Microsoft Word figures this out for you. If you are using it in VBA, you have to know the index of the item. You can use the `GetCrossReferenceItems` and use a loop to determine which index number you need. If you are using a bookmark, this is the bookmark name.

- The *InsertAsHyperlink* argument lets you set up a reference to automatically jump to the reference when it is clicked. This is great for online documents. It is set to `True` or `False`.

19

- The *IncludePosition* argument can be set to True or False to indicate that you want to see the word above or below in order to establish a relative position from the point of reference.

With VBA, you can use this method to insert cross-reference text automatically. In AddColorReference, shown in Listing 19.5, the code searches for the All Seasons subdocument, and if it is in this master document, the code inserts a reference at a bookmark.

LISTING 19.5 The AddColorReference Procedure

```
 1: Sub AddColorReference()
 2:     Dim objSub As Subdocument, bExists As Boolean
 3:     For Each objSub In ActiveDocument.Subdocuments
 4:         If objSub.Name = "All Season Color.doc" Then bExists = True
 5:     Next
 6:     If bExists = False Then Exit Sub
 7:     ActiveDocument.GoTo What:=wdBookmark, Name:="ColorReference"
 8:     Selection.TypeText "If you like lots of color, please refer to "
 9:     Selection.TypeText "the All Season Color section on page "
10:     Selection.InsertCrossReference ReferenceType:=wdRefTypeBookmark, _
11:         ReferenceKind:=wdPageNumber, ReferenceItem:="AllSeason", _
12:         InsertAsHyperlink:=False, IncludePosition:=False
13:     Selection.TypeText "."
14: End Sub
```

ANALYSIS Lines 2–5 set up and test an object variable representing subdocument to determine if the All Season Color document is a part of this master document. It also sets a variable equal to True.

Line 6 tests this variable. If it is False, no reference is needed and the procedure is terminated. If the document exists, line 7 moves to the spot for the reference using a bookmark and the GoTo method. Lines 8–9 use the TypeText method to place the text for the reference, and lines 10–12 place the reference itself.

This is followed by line 13, which places a period after the page reference. Line 14 is the end of the procedure. When the procedure is run, the document has a reference in the Landscape Design document as shown in Figure 19.6.

Adding Summaries

Depending on the style of your larger documents, you may want to include a summary. A summary is a synopsis of the contents of a longer document. It is a formatting technique that is frequently used with proposals, legal documents, and technical articles. It provides a quick overview to help the reader get ready to read the document (or in some cases, determine whether reading it would be useful).

FIGURE 19.6

The reference is in place.

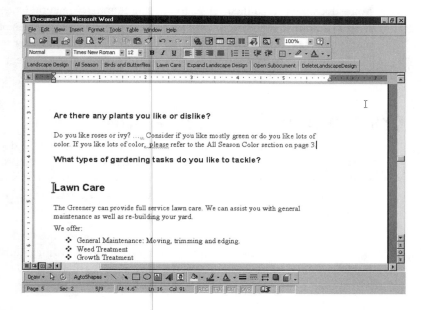

Microsoft Word has an AutoSummarize feature to help you get started. You can experiment with this feature to find the settings that work best for your type of document.

After you find the settings to use, you might want to consider a procedure to save you some time. To use the summary feature, you can use the AutoSummarize method. Its syntax is

expression.AutoSummarize(*Length*, *Mode*, *UpdateProperties*)

19

The expression represents the document, and it is followed by the AutoSummarize keyword. There are three arguments:

- The *Length* argument is a number representing a percentage, which the text is reduced to. For example, 25 would make the summary 25% of the size of the whole document.

- The *Mode* indicates how you want to summarize. It is set with a built-in constant. You can highlight the points in the document, create a summary at the beginning, create a separate document, or hide everything but the summarized points.

- The *UpdateProperties* is a `True`/`False` argument. It indicates whether the document properties are updated to reflect the summary.

Some documents lend themselves to the AutoSummary feature. Others do not. When you want to automate the process with a master document that includes other document elements (such as a title page and table of contents), you might prefer to create the summary in a separate document and then insert the summary document into the master document.

Controlling Field Updating

When you are adding and deleting subdocuments within a master document, be sure the master document is kept completely up-to-date. When you use fields, their values do not always automatically update to reflect changes in your document, such as the table of contents or the cross-reference fields. It is a good idea to update your fields after editing with VBA.

This is very easy to do. You use the `Fields` collection and the `TablesofContents` collection. The `ReconcileFields` procedure (shown in the following) illustrates what is needed.

```
1: Sub ReconcileFields()
2:     Selection.WholeStory
3:     Selection.Fields.Update
4:     ActiveDocument.TablesOfContents(1).Update
5: End Sub
```

The first step on line 2 selects the text of the entire document. This is done using the `WholeStory` property. Then you use the `Update` method on line 3 for the `Fields` collection to cycle through all the fields and update their status.

Line 4 also uses the `Update` method, only this time it is with the `TableofContents` collection for the document. The `1` in parentheses indicates you want to update the first table of contents. You could use the `For Each...Next` structure if you were supporting more than one table of contents. If you are using Indexes or any of the other tables, you can update them as well.

The reason tables of contents and similar elements are handled differently is because of the complexity of the information stored in them. The `Update` method completes a full update. It essentially regenerates the table. If you know the topics in the table are still correct, you can use another method that updates only the page numbers.

This is done with the `UpdatePageNumbers`. Its syntax is

SYNTAX

```
Expression.UpdatePageNumbers
```

The expression represents the table collection item you want to update. For example, you could use the same `TableofContents` collection shown above on line 4. If you wanted to update the page numbers of the existing table instead of regenerating the entire table, the line could be changed as shown below.

```
ActiveDocument.TablesofContents(1).UpdatePageNumbers
```

Working with Revisions

Even when the document is complete, the creation process isn't over. You usually have to edit the document. With larger documents and master documents, more than one person might be doing the editing. You can track changes made by each individual with Word.

You can automate the set up of your revision options. Automatically setting your revision options is similar to setting any of the other options. Using properties, you can control how revisions appear in your document.

There are eight properties that control the appearance of revisions in your document. You can set `DeletedTextColor`, `InsertedTextColor`, `RevisedLineColor`, and `RevisedPropertiesColor` to set the color of any change you make in your document. These properties are all set with built-in constants for the basic color set.

You also have `DeletedTextMark`, `InsertTextMark`, `RevisedLineMark`, and `RevisedPropertyMark`. These enable you to select a built-in constant to indicate a mark to use for these changes as well as the color. For example, the following procedure sets the color of your changes to a dark red:

```
Sub RevisionSettings()
    Application.Options.InsertedTextColor = wdDarkRed
    Application.Options.DeletedTextColor = wdDarkRed
    Application.Options.RevisedLinesColor = wdDarkRed
End Sub
```

You can also turn on revisions with VBA. This is also controlled with properties. You have the `TrackRevisions`, `PrintRevisions`, and `ShowRevisions` print for the document. The `SwitchRevisions` procedure illustrates how one macro can switch between two states. In this case, you are switching between two states—tracking and not tracking changes.

19

```
Sub SwitchRevisions()
    With ActiveDocument
        .TrackRevisions = Not .TrackRevisions
        .PrintRevisions = Not .PrintRevisions
        .ShowRevisions = Not .ShowRevisions
    End With
End Sub
```

You can also use VBA to work with Version control. You can create one procedure that prompts for a comment for the version, saves it, and then saves the document:

```
Sub SaveVersion()
    Dim strComment As String
    strComment = InputBox("What Comment should be used for the Version?")
    ActiveDocument.Versions.Save Comment:=strComment
    ActiveDocument.Save
End Sub
```

After getting the comment with an InputBox, the version is saved with the Save method for the Versions collection and the string becomes its comment. Then the Save method is used for the ActiveDocument.

Summary

In this hour, you have explored many ways to make working with larger documents easier. You learned that you can automate the management of a master document, as well as control AutoCaption, Referencing, summaries, and revision marking.

You investigated how you can automate the management of the subdocuments within master documents. You also learned how to add, collapse, expand, and delete subdocuments from your master document.

You were shown how VBA can assist with the formatting of a master document. You learned how to do more with headers and footers, as well as work with various tables.

Q&A

Q Do you have to delete the headers and footers from the subdocument?

A No, you can leave the headers and footers. The example in this hour illustrates the importance of section breaks that are automatically inserted with the document. You can also use the subdocument collections and modify each of the header and footer stories.

Q Can you apply one of the versions with VBA?

A Yes, you can apply a version with VBA. Instead of the Save method, you use the Open method.

Workshop

Here are some questions and exercises to help you review the material covered in this hour. The answers to the quiz questions can be found in Appendix A, "Quiz Answers."

Quiz

1. When expanding a master document's subdocuments, is it required to expand all levels with the setting of 1–9 in a For...Next loop?

2. What happens if you attempt to set an AutoCaption for an object that doesn't exist in the collection?

3. What argument for the InsertCrossReference method indicates what type of cross-reference is needed?

Exercises

1. Create a comprehensive procedure that asks what documents are needed and inserts them and then modifies the header and footer to meet your expectations.

2 Review your automation checklist to see where master documents and the techniques outlined in this hour are needed.

19

HOUR 20

Working with Other Office Applications

One of the benefits of working with Microsoft Word is that it is a part of Microsoft Office, and Visual Basic for Applications (VBA) is the standard language for automation with Office. This means you can use functions from other applications and exchange information between Word and other Office applications.

The highlights of this hour include

- Working with Excel
- Working with Graph
- Working with Access
- Working with PowerPoint

Working with Excel

In Hour 12, "Working with Tables," you experimented with different methods and properties to control table set up and formatting. The Word table capability is considerable and gives you a great deal of control over formatting information, but it isn't designed for in-depth numerical analysis or calculations (such as financial information or statistical calculations).

When you need in-depth numerical manipulation, consider using Microsoft Excel. It provides many features to facilitate your work with numbers.

Unfortunately, using Excel doesn't eliminate the need to use the information stored in your Word documents. When you need the power of Excel, but also access to the information and features in Word, you have two choices. You can integrate the data as a file or as an object. You can also control Excel with VBA remotely from Word. Each of these choices is discussed below.

Importing a Worksheet as a File

The first approach for integrating data from an Excel workbook is to insert a worksheet as a file. This approach uses the same method you worked with in Hour 9, "Working with Text," when you inserted a Word document into another Word document.

The `InsertFile` method enables you to get information from a file and place it in your document. Its syntax is

```
expression.InsertFile(FileName, Range, ConfirmConversions, _
Link, Attachment)
```

SYNTAX

The expression represents the range or selection, and it is followed by the `InsertFile` keyword. There are five arguments.

The `FileName` is the name of the file with its path. The second argument is the `Range`. This isn't used frequently with Word documents because normally you want to include the entire document. If you want a portion of a document, you can indicate the name of a bookmark that includes the text you want.

With Excel, the `Range` argument is more important. If you omit the `Range` argument when your file has more than one worksheet, you will get a dialog (see Figure 20.1) prompting for what worksheet or named range you want to include.

FIGURE 20.1

You are prompted for the worksheet or range.

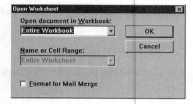

In most cases, you will complete the range argument for the `InsertFile` method with Excel files. You can indicate the worksheet's name with the range of cells, such as `Summary!A1:F9`.

The `ConfirmConversions` argument enables you to prompt the user for confirmation on the conversion of the file. `Link` enables you to insert the file while establishing a link to the file.

The `Attachment` argument is used when you want to attach a file to an email message. You won't need it to insert an Excel worksheet into your document.

You can create the `InsertExcelAsFile` procedure shown below. It inserts the total sales for 1999 into your document.

```
1: Sub InsertExcelasFile()
2:     Selection.InsertFile FileName:= _
3:         "C:\My Documents\You Name It Toys.xls", _
4:         Range:="Summary!A1:F9", ConfirmConversions:=False, _
5:         Link:=False, Attachment:=False
6: End Sub
```

When this procedure is executed, it inserts the summary worksheet without a prompt and without a link. The summary information is inserted and formatted as a table as shown in Figure 20.2.

There are some problems that occur when the Excel worksheet is converted. For example, the worksheet loses the center across formatting for the first row. You can correct this by merging the first row of cells.

The alignment in the first column is also lost when the file is inserted because of the column's identification with the first row. You need to correct by adjusting the `Alignment` property for the first column.

The key thing to remember about this insertion is that the worksheet now becomes a part of the document. You can make changes to it without harming the original Excel

20

workbook file. The reverse is also true. Any changes you make to the workbook won't register in the original file. To have complete editing capability, you can import the worksheet as an object.

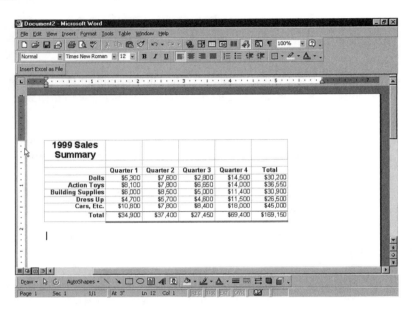

Importing a Worksheet as an Object

If you want to be able to maintain the worksheet from your Word document, you can bring the data in as an object instead of a file. To utilize this approach, use the `AddOLEObject` method for the `Shapes` or `InlineShapes` collection. If you want greater control over the object's placement, use the following syntax for the `Shapes` collection:

```
expression.AddOLEObject(ClassType, FileName, LinkToFile, DisplayAsIcon, _
    IconFileName, IconIndex, IconLabel, Left, Top, Width, Height, Anchor)
```

SYNTAX

The expression represents the `Shapes` collection for a document followed by the `AddOLEObject` keyword. If you are using the `Shapes` collection, you can set up to twelve arguments:

- The `ClassType` argument indicates what type of object is being inserted. In this case, Excel must be installed on the system.

- The `FileName` argument is described above. It stores the name and path of the document.

- `LinkToFile` can be set to `True` if you want to maintain a connection to the original file. If it is set to `False`, it will create a new copy of the file.

- The `DisplayAsIcon`, `IconFileName`, `IconIndex`, and `IconLabel` can all be used to display a file as an icon in the document. This is especially useful with a document that will be accessed online.

- The `Left`, `Top`, `Width`, `Height`, and `Anchor` are identical to those arguments discussed in Hour 13, "Working with Graphics." They control the placement and size of the object.

To insert the Excel workbook as an object, use following procedure. It inserts the file with a link.

```
1: Sub InsertExcelAsObject()
2:     ActiveDocument.Shapes.AddOLEObject ClassType:="Excel.Sheet.9", _
3:         FileName:="C:\My Documents\You Name It Toys.xls", _
4:         LinkToFile:=True, DisplayAsIcon:=False
5: End Sub
```

This code, which inserts the file as a link, is the simplest version of this procedure. In addition to this code and the code shown earlier that inserts the worksheet as a file, you will probably want to add the error-handling code in case there is a missing file. Error-handling code was introduced in Hour 9.

You might also want to add a `Case` clause for a missing class type of an object. This is only needed if you are creating a new object. If you are inserting a file, it automatically picks up the type from the file.

The benefit of using this approach is that it you can double-click on it at any time and make changes. The disadvantage is that the sheet you want to insert must be the one that is currently selected at the time of insertion. This can mean more work for you.

> Inserting a workbook as an object, with a chart sheet as the active sheet, is a quick way to get the chart into your document.

20

Storing Information in an Excel Database

Another method for working with Excel is to use VBA to access the data directly. In Hour 15, "Working with Forms," you learned how to take data from a form and enter it into your Word table. You don't have to use a Word table. You can also place it in an Excel worksheet.

Microsoft Excel can act as a database. You can set up columns to serve as your fields, and each record can be placed in a separate row as shown in Figure 20.3. You can then use VBA to populate the rows.

FIGURE 20.3

*The Excel database is
ready for input.*

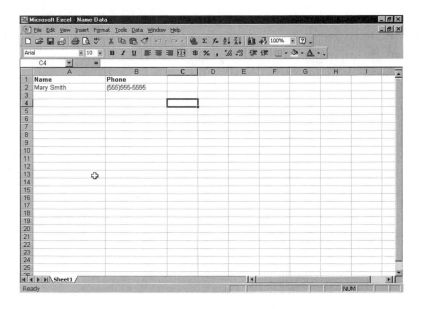

When you want to work with another application, there are some additional steps required before you write your code. You have to make sure you have access to the object library for that application.

To minimize the typing, you will work with a smaller form than the one used in Hour 15. Complete these steps to create your form, or you can open the Update to Excel Database.Doc file from the companion Web site.

1. Create a new file using the Hour20 template from the companion Web site.

2. Add a one-row, four-column table to your document.

3. Enter Name in the first cell and Phone in the third cell.

4. Add text fields in the second and fourth cells from the Forms toolbar.

5. Change their bookmark names to txtName and txtPhone.

6. Protect the form and enter a name and phone number in the fields.

7. Save the document as shown in Figure 20.4, and you are ready to begin programming.

8. Open the Visual Basic Editor and open the module.

Figure 20.4

The form is now ready for programming.

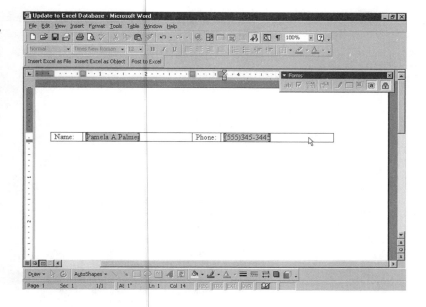

Before you begin writing the code, you must prepare the project to access Excel. You have to set a reference to Excel's object library. If Excel is installed properly, this is a simple task with the References Dialog.

1. Select Tools, References, the References Dialog (see Figure 20.5) will open. From it, you can select the references you need.

Figure 20.5

The References Dialog lists the applications you are accessing in your code.

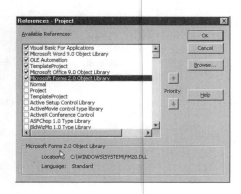

20

2. Scroll down the list of choices, select the Microsoft Excel 9.0 Object Library, and select OK.

Now you can begin adding code to use the functions in Excel. You can create a procedure like PostToExcel shown in Listing 20.1.

LISTING 20.1 The PostToExcel Procedure

```
 1: Sub PostToExcel()
 2:     Dim objExcel As Excel.Application
 3:     Dim strDoc As String
 4:     strDoc = ActiveDocument.Name
 5:     On Error GoTo PostErr
 6:     Set objExcel = CreateObject("Excel.Application")
 7:     With objExcel
 8:         .Workbooks.Open _
 9:             ("C:\My Documents\Name Data.xls")
10:         .ActiveSheet.Range("A1").Select
11:         .Selection.End(xlDown).Select
12:         .ActiveCell.Offset(1, 0).Select
13:         .ActiveCell.FormulaR1C1 = Documents(strDoc) _
14:             .FormFields("txtName").Result
15:         .ActiveCell.Offset(0, 1).Select
16:         .ActiveCell.FormulaR1C1 = Documents(strDoc) _
17:             .FormFields("txtPhone").Result
18:         .ActiveCell.Offset(0, 1).Select
19:         .ActiveWorkbook.Close SaveChanges:=True
20:         .Quit
21:     End With
22:     MsgBox "You have successfully posted this information", _
23:         vbInformation + vbOKOnly, "Posting Complete"
24:     Exit Sub
25: PostErr:
26:     Dim strErr As String, strTitle As String
27:     Select Case Err.Number
28:         Case 1004   'Excel's missing file
29:             strErr = "The posting can't continue because "
30:             strErr = strErr & "Name Data.XLS can't be found."
31:             strTitle = "Missing File"
32:         Case 5941   'Fields Missing
33:             strErr = "There are no fields in this document. "
34:             strErr = "So posting can't continue."
35:             strTitle = "Missing Fields"
36:         Case Else
37:             strErr = "Error " & Err.Number & "," & _
38:             Err.Description & "has occurred. Processing was halted."
39:             strTitle = "Unexpected Error"
40:     End Select
41:     MsgBox strErr, vbExclamation + vbOKOnly, strTitle
42: End Sub
```

ANALYSIS When you take advantage of another application, such as Excel, your general VBA training will be transferable, but you must also learn about the specifics of the application represented by its object library.

With Excel, there is an `Application` object for controlling the applications as a whole. It has a `Workbooks` collection for accessing workbooks, and each `Workbook` object has a `Sheets` collection for accessing a specific sheet.

In the `PostToExcel` procedure on line 2, the first step is to declare an object variable to represent Excel. This is accomplished by setting up the variable as `Excel.Application`.

Line 3 declares a string variable that will hold the name of the document. Line 4 assigns the `Name` property for the active document to a string variable for use later.

Line 5 sets up error handling. Error handling is important here because there are several places where you can run into trouble. A document without fields, based on this template, will generate an error. Another error can occur if a user is unable to locate the workbook he is attempting to open.

Line 6 points the variable to Excel by using the `CreateObject` function. This function creates a new instance of Excel for use in this procedure. It won't be visible on the desktop because you have to make it visible with the `Visible` property. In this case, it isn't necessary for you to see it.

Lines 7–21 use a `With` structure to work with the instance of Excel to place the field data in the worksheet, Name Data.XLS, which is already set up to store this data as shown in Figure 20.3.

Lines 8–9 use the `Open` method with the `Workbooks` collection of Excel to open the Names Data workbook. After the workbook is open, the code begins to navigate and place data in the worksheet.

Line 10 uses the `Select` method with the `Range` object specifying the cell address A1, which is the top of the worksheet. Line 11 also uses the `Select` method with the `Selection` object. It uses the `End` property with the `xlDown` index constant to reference the last cell in the first column and select the first column of the last record entered.

After the last record is selected, move to the empty row below. This is accomplished with the `Select` method with the active cell. It uses the `Offset` property to indicate that you want to select the cell that is one row down and in the same column. Line 13 places the contents of the `txtName` form field in that cell using the form field's `Result` property.

Lines 15–8 repeat the placement process for the contents of `txtPhone`. Line 19 uses the `Close` method to close the active workbook and save the changes. Line 20 uses the `Quit` method to exit this instance of Excel.

20

Lines 22–23 display a message for the user indicating that the posting process is complete. It is followed by the `Exit Sub` statement to end the execution of the procedure.

Lines 25–41 have a `Select Case` structure to tackle the error handling. Notice the errors 5273 or 5174, which indicate a missing Word file, are not the ones triggered. Because you are using an Excel method, Error 1004, an Excel error, is triggered if the workbook can't be located.

Error 5941 is the error generated by Word when an object referenced can't be located in the collection. There is also a `Case Else` for any other problem that might occur.

This example gives you a chance to see how to gain access to functions that are part of another application. The application must provide an object library and support the use of VBA. This procedure doesn't check to see if the information has already been posted in the workbook. When you are working with Excel, doing that would require more code. If you want to learn more about working with Excel and VBA, see *Sams Teach Yourself Excel 2000 Programming in 24 Hours*.

Working with Graph

Another tool you can access through Word is Microsoft Graph. It is one of the applets that ships with Office, but you can't use it separately. In Microsoft Excel, working with charts is very easy. Because charting of numerical data is often necessary in Excel, it has special objects for charting. In Microsoft Word, it isn't as simple to chart because the Word table isn't as full featured as the Excel worksheets.

If you frequently create charts from a tables, you might consider using VBA. You can use VBA to insert a chart and then modify it. For example, earlier in this hour, you inserted some data from Excel as a file to get a table. You can create a pie chart of the totals as shown in the Listing 20.2. After you select Tools, References, and the Microsoft Graph 9.0 Object Library, you are ready to add your code. The `InsertChartFromTable` procedure, shown in Listing 20.2, illustrates how to create a chart and input the data from the row heading column and the totals column.

LISTING 20.2   The `InsertChartFromTable` Procedure

```
1: Sub InsertChartFromTable()
2:     Dim objShape As InlineShape, strData(5, 5) As String
3:     Dim objTable As Table
4: '   Get Selected Table Data with omissions
5:     Set objTable = Selection.Tables(1)
6:     strData(0, 1) = objTable.Cell(4, 1).Range.Text
7:     strData(0, 2) = objTable.Cell(5, 1).Range.Text
```

```
 8:        strData(0, 3) = objTable.Cell(6, 1).Range.Text
 9:        strData(0, 4) = objTable.Cell(7, 1).Range.Text
10:        strData(0, 5) = objTable.Cell(8, 1).Range.Text
11:        strData(1, 0) = objTable.Cell(3, 6).Range.Text
12:        strData(1, 1) = objTable.Cell(4, 6).Range.Text
13:        strData(1, 2) = objTable.Cell(5, 6).Range.Text
14:        strData(1, 3) = objTable.Cell(6, 6).Range.Text
15:        strData(1, 4) = objTable.Cell(7, 6).Range.Text
16:        strData(1, 5) = objTable.Cell(8, 6).Range.Text
17:        Selection.EndKey Unit:=wdStory
18:
19: '    Add Chart
20:        Set objShape = Selection.InlineShapes.AddOLEObject _
21:            (ClassType:="MSGraph.Chart.8", FileName:="", _
22:            LinkToFile:=False, DisplayAsIcon:=False)
23:        objShape.OLEFormat.Activate
24: '    Format Chart
25:        With objShape.OLEFormat.Object.Application
26:            .DataSheet.Range("00:D5").ClearContents
27:            .DataSheet.Range("01").Value = _
28:                Left(strData(0, 1), Len(strData(0, 1)) - 2)
29:            .DataSheet.Range("02").Value = _
30:                Left(strData(0, 2), Len(strData(0, 2)) - 2)
31:            .DataSheet.Range("03").Value = _
32:                Left(strData(0, 3), Len(strData(0, 3)) - 2)
33:            .DataSheet.Range("04").Value = _
34:                Left(strData(0, 4), Len(strData(0, 4)) - 2)
35:            .DataSheet.Range("05").Value = _
36:                Left(strData(0, 5), Len(strData(0, 5)) - 2)
37:            .DataSheet.Range("A0").Value = _
38:                Left(strData(1, 0), Len(strData(1, 0)) - 2)
39:            .DataSheet.Range("A1").Value = _
40:                Left(strData(1, 1), Len(strData(1, 1)) - 2)
41:            .DataSheet.Range("A2").Value = _
42:                Left(strData(1, 2), Len(strData(1, 2)) - 2)
43:            .DataSheet.Range("A3").Value = _
44:                Left(strData(1, 3), Len(strData(1, 3)) - 2)
45:            .DataSheet.Range("A4").Value = _
46:                Left(strData(1, 4), Len(strData(1, 4)) - 2)
47:            .DataSheet.Range("A5").Value = _
48:                Left(strData(1, 5), Len(strData(1, 5)) - 2)
49:            .Chart.ChartType = xlPie
50:            .PlotBy = xlColumns
51:            .Chart.HasTitle = True
52:            .Chart.ChartTitle.Text = "Total Sales for 1999"
53:        End With
54: End Sub
```

ANALYSIS Lines 2–3 set up several variables that are needed to create the table. The
objShape will act as a pointer to the chart after it is created. The strData isn't just

a variable. It is an array to store more than one value with the same name using the index to keep them straight. It is a two-dimensional array so that you can create the data as it appears in the table. The objTable variable represents the table where the insertion point will appear when this macro is executed.

Lines 4–17 get the data from the table and place it in the array. Line 5 sets up the objTable variable to point to the active table to retrieve the data. Lines 6–17 use the Text property for the Range of a specific cell to fill in the exact spot in the array.

You are not using every possible slot in the array for data. This makes the transfer to the chart easier. Line 17 moves to the end of the document. After all of the values are placed in the array and the insertion point is moved, you are ready to add the chart.

To insert a chart, the AddOLEObject method is used as it was for an Excel object on lines 20–22. The difference is, because this is a new object, a filename isn't needed.

Line 23 uses the Activate method for the new OLE object represented by objShape to make sure that you can edit the chart. You can begin placing data and formatting the chart.

When you want to work with a Microsoft Chart inserted in your Word document, you are working with the Microsoft Graph object model. The Word object model provides the access. The real difference between Excel and Word is apparent here. Because Word doesn't include the Chart object, the code isn't as clean as it is when you use Excel.

Lines 25–53 use a With structure to modify the contents and the type of chart added to your document. On line 25, you have to set up the object you want to work with. When you are working with an OLE object, you are accessing an object model that isn't part of Word. The objShape object is your InlineShape object that holds the OLE object.

The OLEFormat property represents the OLEFormat object. This object provides a method for controlling the inserted object. Its Object property enables you to access the object model with its properties and methods. With Microsoft Graph, the Application object referenced at the end of line 25 serves the same purpose as the Application object in Word. It is the top of its object model.

Line 26 uses the Datasheet object's Range object, specifying the entire range of default data created as the default chart appears in the object. You will notice the first address of the range is 00 instead of A1. With Microsoft Graph, you specify your own Column and Row headings. The first cell for values is A1, so your headings appear in Row 0 or Column 0. The ClearContents method deletes all the information.

Lines 27–48 transfer the data from the strData array to the Datasheet of Microsoft Graph using the Range object and its Value property. You'll notice that you aren't just taking the data and transferring it to the cells. The `Left` function is used to strip two characters from the end of the data.

When you are working with a table in Word, a major difference is that the table cell has an end of cell marker that isn't a factor in Excel. Using both the `Left` function and the `Len` function to get the length of the string and strip out the marks enables you to clean the data as it is placed.

After all the data has been entered into the Datasheet, line 49 sets the `ChartType` property for the `Chart` object to change the default column chart to a pie chart with the built-in constant.

Line 50 adjusts the `PlotBy` property. When you set up a pie chart manually, you select whether your data will appear in rows or columns. This is taken care of with the `PlotBy` property. In this case, the property establishes the setting `xlCoumns`, making each row represent a pie slice.

Lines 51–52 set up a title for the chart. The `HasTitle` property must be set to `True` to indicate that there is a title before you begin setting it up. In this case, only the chart title's text is adjusted. You can change its appearance with VBA.

To see this procedure work, insert the Excel file and place your insertion point in the table. When you run this procedure, you will get the chart shown in Figure 20.6.

FIGURE 20.6

The chart is inserted and some formatting has been completed.

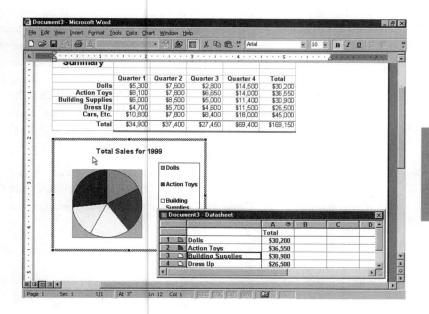

20

The chart is left active to allow for additional changes. You could add code to deactivate, resize, or move the chart. Just as you did when using Excel from Word, you must learn more about the object model of Microsoft Graph. The easiest way to get more information is to place your insertion point in the word, Chart, in the code and press F1. The Microsoft Graph VBA online help file will appear in the Help browser. You can select the Microsoft Graph Objects topic to learn more about the structure of its object model.

Working with Access

In the Excel section earlier in the hour, you explored how to use an Excel worksheet, instead of a Word table, as a database to store information. Another alternative is to use Access to store the information. You can still use VBA to retrieve and place information in the database.

Using Access Records

Accessing information in an Access database is different from working with data in Excel. With Excel, the data is stored in cells, and you may have to do some hunting to find what you need. With Access, the information is stored in records in tables, and this can be very helpful when you are accessing information from another source.

If you want to retrieve a list of all of the employees, you might use VBA from Word to get that list. When you want to work with an Access Database, you will find it is more complex than Excel or Graph because there is more than one object model to work with. When you to use the data directly from the database, you don't use the Access object model. You want to use a data model. To confuse this issue even further, there are two object models. The Data Access Object model (DAO) is the older one, which doesn't offer much flexibility. With Office 2000, the Microsoft ActiveX Data Object model became the recommended method for accessing data directly, regardless of the source. You can use this same approach whether the data is in Access, FoxPro, SQL Server, or a third-party source. All that changes is the identifier for the source.

Before you can begin developing your code, you still have to set up the reference to the object library. You select Tool, References, Microsoft ActiveX Data Object Library 2.1. Then, you can create a procedure like RetrieveEmployees shown in Listing 20.3.

LISTING 20.3   RetrieveEmployees Procedure

```
Sub Ret 1: rieveEmployees()
  2:     Dim cnnEmployees As ADODB.Connection, rsEmployees As Recordset
  3:     Set cnnEmployees = New ADODB.Connection
  4:     cnnEmployees.ConnectionString = _
```

```
 5:            "Provider=Microsoft.Jet.OLEDB.4.0;Data Source=C:\My Documents\
              ➥You Name It Toys.mdb"
 6:        cnnEmployees.Open
 7:        Set rsEmployees = New ADODB.Recordset
 8:        rsEmployees.Open "Employees", cnnEmployees, adOpenStatic, _
 9:            adLockReadOnly
10:        rsEmployees.MoveFirst
11:        Do Until rsEmployees.EOF
12:            Selection.TypeText "Employee:" & vbTab
13:            Selection.TypeText rsEmployees!FirstName _
14:                & " " & rsEmployees!LastName
15:            Selection.TypeParagraph
16:            rsEmployees.MoveNext
17:        Loop
18:        rsEmployees.Close
19:        cnnEmployees.Close
20: End Sub
```

You also set up columns, called fields, for each item of information. After data is stored, you can access it by creating a Recordset. The Recordset can return all the records in a table, or it can be created with only the records that meet certain criteria. This capability is similar to the filter created in Hour 18, "Working with Mailings." In Access terms, this is known as a Query; some other databases refer to it as a View.

Line 3 assigns the connection variable as a New `ADODB.Connection` to create a new connection for this operation. Lines 4–5 set the `ConnectionString` property for the new connection to establish the database to use. The `ConnectionString` property is what stores the type of database, the name of the database, and other arguments that are required.

In this case, it is straightforward. You specify the Provider, which is what type of database, and the Data Source, which is the path and filename of the database .If you are using security or want to do more than just read data, you must add parameters for that access.

Line 6 opens the connection with the `ConnectionString` using the `Open` method. After the connection is established, you can retrieve the data.

Line 7 assigns the `rsEmployees` Recordset as a new Recordset and line 8 opens the Recordset using the `Open` method. The `Open` method for Recordsets has five arguments. Its syntax is

recordset.Open *Source, ActiveConnection, CursorType, LockType, Options*

The source indicates the table or query that has the data required. The `ActiveConnection` is the connection that is established to the database. The `CursorType`

20

is the type of access that is needed. In this case, the built-in constant is `adOpenStatic`, which means that you are reading data only and that you want to grab the records at a precise point in time. It indicates that you don't need to see all the changes made by other users as the code is processing.

The `LockType` indicates what type of use you need in the procedure. In this case, you are only retrieving information , so you just need to read data.

You don't need the last argument in this procedure because you are only retrieving data. This argument is most frequently used when other sources are involved. It indicates how the command to open the Recordset is to be interpreted by the source.

Lines 10–17 retrieve the information using a `Do Until` loop. Line 10 uses the `MoveFirst` for the Recordset to move to the first record. Line 11 begins the `Do Until` Loop. It uses the EOF property.In a Recordset, there is a marker at the beginning and end of the records. The BOF property will be `True` if the pointer located before the records; and the EOF property is `True` if the pointer located after the records. This loop will continue until there are no more records to add to the document.

Line 12 begins by entering some text and a tab. Line 13–14 use the `TypeText` method to add the employee. The information is from the fields in the `Employees` table in the database. To reference a field, use the Recordset variable followed by an exclamation and the name of the field.

Line 15 uses the `TypeParagraph` to end the line with the employee, and line 16 moves to the next record in the Recordset with the `MoveNext` method. Lines 18–19 close the database objects to finish the procedure. The ActiveX Data Object model provides complete access to any information stored in a database. You can retrieve information, as shown in this example, as well as perform other data operations. You can add and modify records. You can create queries to get a subset of the data or modify records. You can also create new database objects, such as a new table. For more information, you can use the online Help file for ADO. The easiest way to access it is to place your insertion point in the word *Recordset* on line 2 and press F1.

Retrieving a Report as a Word Document

In addition to accessing data in a database directly, you can also use other objects from Access directly with VBA. One feature of Access that you might want to use is its capability to export a report to Word.

As with the other sections in this hour, before you can begin you have to establish a reference to the correct library. Select Tools, References, and the Microsoft Access 9.0 Object Library. After that is set, you can develop your code.

In the previous section (in the You Name It Toys.mdb database), you used the ADO library to access the records directly. You can also use the information from the database by exporting an Access report as shown in Figure 20.7. To work with one of the Access objects, you can't use the ADO library. You must instead use the Access Object library.

FIGURE 20.7

The Report as it would be viewed in Access.

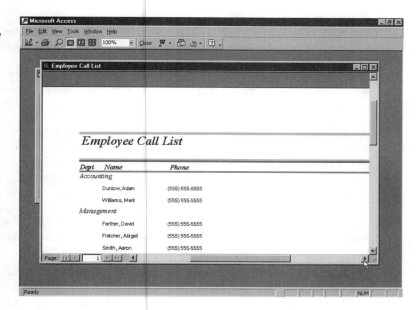

You can create the GenerateEmployeeList procedure listed in Listing 20.4 to send the report to a file and then insert the file into your current document. You can also add the new file as a subdocument in a master document.

LISTING 20.4 The GenerateEmployeeList Procedure

```
 1: Sub GenerateEmployeeList()
 2:     Dim objAccess As Access.Application
 3:     Set objAccess = New Access.Application
 4:     objAccess.OpenCurrentDatabase _
 5:         FilePath:="C:\My Documents\You Name It Toys.MDB", _
 6:         Exclusive:=False
 7:     objAccess.DoCmd.OutputTo _
 8:         ObjectType:=acOutputReport, _
 9:          ObjectName:="rptEmployeeCallList", _
10:         OutputFormat:=acFormatRTF, _
11:         OutputFile:="c:\my Documents\Employees.RTF", AutoStart:=False
12:     Selection.InsertFile FileName:="C:\My Documents\Employees.RTF"
13: End Sub
```

20

ANALYSIS Lines 2–3 declare a variable to reference the Access application. This is done by setting the variable as an `Access.Application` object and the setting it up as a new instance of Access.

Lines 4–6 use the `OpenCurrentDatabase` method to open the You Name It Toys database. The filename with the path is the first argument. The second argument indicates whether you want to be the only user with access to the database. In this case, the argument is set to `False`, because you aren't going to make any changes to the database.

Lines 7–11 use the `OutputTo` method for the `DoCmd` object to send a database object to a file in a format that can be opened in Word. The first argument indicates that you want to access a report object. The `objectName` is the name of the report in Access.

The `Outputformat` is set to `acFormatRTF` because it can be opened in Word. The `Outputfile` is the name of the file to be created. If it already exists, it will be overwritten by default. If it is left blank, you will be prompted for a filename. The `AutoStart` is set to `False` because you don't want to launch another copy of Word with this new document.

Line 12 uses the `Insertfile` method to bring the document into the current document. You can insert it as a subdocument, if you are using a master document. When this procedure executes, it brings in the report as shown in Figure 20.8. You need to be aware of some limitations of this process. If you compare Figures 20.7 and 20.8, you will notice that the graphic line elements are missing and the report header and footer have been converted to regular text. It might be simpler to create the original report using none of these elements and then use VBA to add the formatting when the report is in Word.

In this section, you explored how to use the data stored in an Access database, as well as one of its reports. It provides an introduction only. If you want to learn more about creating databases in Access or using VBA with the ADO or Access object models, see *Sams Teach Yourself Access 2000 in 21 Days*.

Working with PowerPoint

Another application that is part of Microsoft Office is PowerPoint. This is a powerful presentation graphics package, which enables you to create presentations that can be printed on transparencies, transferred to slides, or used as an online presentation. When you are using Word, you can send your Word document to PowerPoint to provide the text for your presentation. To send a document to PowerPoint, you need the `PresentIt` method. To send the active document requires one line of code:

```
Activedocument.PresentIt
```

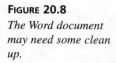

FIGURE 20.8

The Word document may need some clean up.

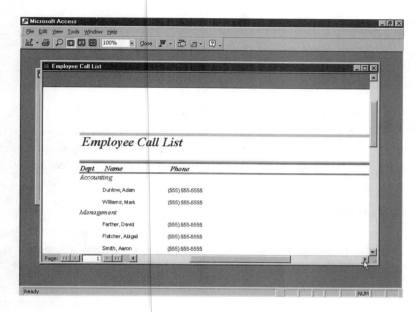

This works best if you create an outline in your document before you write your text. Word will send all the text to Powerpoint. If you create an outline, similar to a table of contents, for the document and then export it, the framework of the presentation might be more to your liking. You can also create a procedure that creates a new document from the original document containing only text with the Headings 1–9 styles to export.

Summary

In this hour, you have explored how to get the most of the other Office applications from within Word. You examined how to bring in data from Excel, as well as how to run the Excel application remotely with VBA.

You also took a look at how to integrate Microsoft Graph from Word. Word isn't as closely integrated with Graph as it is with Microsoft Excel; but if you use VBA, that difference isn't as noticeable.

You also looked at how to work with Access. You can use data from an Access database, or you can import an Access report directly. You also looked at how to get information into PowerPoint from your Word document.

20

Q&A

Q Can you bring in a chart from Excel?

A You can only integrate an Excel chart if it is the active sheet, and you bring it in as an object.

Q Can you control PowerPoint with VBA directly?

A Yes, you can control PowerPoint directly. You have to set a reference to its object library and define an object variable as `PowerPointApplication`. After that is defined and set up, you can begin accessing its object model.

Workshop

Here are some questions and exercises to help you review the material covered in this hour. The answers to the quiz questions can be found in Appendix A, "Quiz Answers."

Quiz

1. Which approach lets you edit an Excel workbook from your document?
2. Why do you need to use the Object property for the `OLEFormat` object to control an inserted graph?
3. Why are there two methods for working with Access databases?
4. What is a Connection?

Exercises

1. Create a procedure to bring in the information from the remaining worksheets in You Name It Toys.XLS.
2. Evaluate your automation lists to see where you can use this hour's techniques.

Hour **21**

Working with Microsoft Outlook, the Internet, and Windows

In Hour 18, "Working with Mailings," you looked at how to use the Address Book from Outlook to fill in the address of a letter or use names for a merge operation. You can also access other items from Outlook with Visual Basic for Applications (VBA).

Another area you will examine is how to work with the Internet. Because you can access the Internet from within Word or use Word to create Web pages, you will look at how to embed hyperlinks and automate the formatting of Web pages.

In addition, you will learn how to get more out of the Windows environment. You can use the information in the computer's registry and functions of Windows from Word.

The highlights of this hour include

- Working with Outlook's Calendar and Tasks
- Working with the Internet
- Understanding the Windows Registry
- Understanding the Windows API

Working with Outlook's Calendar and Tasks

In addition to creating email from Word and using the Contacts list for letters, memos, and merging, you can also manipulate other items in Outlook. You can work with the Calendar and Task List.

To work with any of the Outlook objects directly, you must have access to its object model just as with the other Office applications, such as Excel. When you work with Outlook, you must first set up the reference for your project. After you open the Visual Basic Editor and select the project, you can set the reference by selecting Tools, References. Scroll through the list, select Microsoft Outlook 9.0 Object Library, and click OK.

Be aware that, when selecting the library, there is a chance for confusion. Microsoft has Outlook and Outlook Express, which only has the email features of Outlook. Each of these has its own object library. If you are working with Outlook, be careful to select the Microsoft Outlook 9.0 Object Library. For Outlook Express, you must select the Microsoft Outlook Express 5.0 Object Library. This section will work with Outlook rather than with Outlook Express because Outlook has a more complete set of features.

Accessing the Task List

In Hour 7, "Understanding Repetitive Processing with Loops," you used the example of building of a task list to explore repetitive processing. If you are using Outlook to track tasks, rather than entering tasks from memory, you can retrieve this information.

Retrieving information from Outlook is similar to working with the other Office applications. After setting up a link to Outlook, you will use its objects, with their properties and methods, to get the information you need. If you want a list of the tasks for the current month, you can develop a procedure similar to the GetTaskEntries procedure shown in Listing 21.1.

LISTING 21.1   The GetTaskEntries Procedure

```
 1: Sub GetTaskEntries()
 2: '   Get Dates for processing
 3:     Dim lMonth As Variant, lYear As Variant, strDate As String
 4:     Dim dtFirst As Date, dtLast As Date
 5:     lMonth = Month(Now())
 6:     lYear = Year(Now())
 7:     strDate = lMonth & "/01/" & lYear
 8:     dtFirst = CDate(strDate)
 9:     dtLast = DateAdd("m", 1, dtFirst) - 1
10: '   Get Outlook tasks and build list
11:     Dim objOutlook As Outlook.Application, objNameSpace As NameSpace
12:     Dim objTaskFolder As MAPIFolder, objTask As TaskItem
13:     Set objOutlook = CreateObject("Outlook.Application")
14:     Set objNameSpace = objOutlook.GetNamespace("MAPI")
15:     Set objTaskFolder = objNameSpace.GetDefaultFolder(olFolderTasks)
16:     For Each objTask In objTaskFolder.Items
17:         If objTask.DueDate >= dtFirst AND _
18:             objTask.DueDate <= dtLast Then
19:             Selection.TypeText "Task: " & vbTab
20:             Selection.TypeText objTask.Subject
21:             Selection.TypeParagraph
22:             Selection.TypeText "Due: " & vbTab
23:             Selection.TypeText objTask.DueDate
24:             Selection.TypeParagraph
25:             Selection.TypeText "Status: " & vbTab
26:             Select Case objTask.Status
27:                 Case olTaskComplete
28:                     Selection.TypeText "Completed"
29:                 Case olTaskDeferred
30:                     Selection.TypeText "Deferred"
31:                 Case olTaskInProgress
32:                     Selection.TypeText "In Progress"
33:                 Case olTaskNotStarted
34:                     Selection.TypeText "Not Started"
35:                 Case olTaskWaiting
36:                     Selection.TypeText "Waiting"
37:             End Select
38:             Selection.TypeParagraph
39:             Selection.TypeText "Comments: " & vbTab
40:             Selection.TypeText objTask.Body
41:             Selection.TypeParagraph
42:             Selection.TypeParagraph
43:         End If
44:     Next
45: End Sub
```

21

ANALYSIS Before you begin retrieving the tasks, lines 2–9 set up the date range you want. In this case, you want all tasks for the current month. Lines 3–4 declare the variables for the date processing.

Line 5 uses the `Month` function to retrieve the current month digit for the system date retrieved with the `Now` function. Line 6 uses the `Year` function for the year.

Line 7 builds a string using the `Month` and `Year` variables and Line 8 converts it to a string using the `Cdate` function. After you have the first day of the month, you can calculate the last day with the `DateAdd` function on line 9.

You are adding one month to the first day of the month to get the next month and subtracting one to get the last day of the month. This is better than adding a specific number of days because you don't need to know how many days are in a specific month.

After you have the date variables, you can then begin looking at tasks in Outlook. Lines 11–12 declare the variables that will be needed for this process.

Line 13 assigns a value to the variable, `objOutlook`. This will be used to represent the Outlook application. It is assigned using the `CreateObject` method to indicate you want to work with an instance of Outlook with the Outlook Application string.

Line 14 sets up the `NameSpace` for Outlook. Excel and Access have a `Workspace` object. In Outlook, it is called a `NameSpace`. It is set up with the `GetNameSpace` method. With the MAPI string, you are indicating you want the default workspace.

Line 15 sets up the next variable, `objTaskFolder`. In Outlook, you store everything in folders. There are specific default folders, as well as personal ones. Line 15 uses the `GetDefaultFolder` method to point to the default task folder.

After the folder is located, you can begin processing tasks. Lines 16–44 use a `For Each Next` loop to examine each task in the `Task` collection. Lines 17–18 test the `DueDate` property for each task to determine if it should be included because it is in the current month.

If the task's `DueDate` property meets the criteria, its information is placed in the current document using the `TypeText` method and specific task properties. The `Subject` property provides the name of the task. `DueDate` indicates when it should be completed.

The `Status` property is a littler trickier. The `Status` for a task is stored as a long integer represented by built-in constants. A `Select Case` structure is used to determine which constant is returned. It also places corresponding text in the document. The last property included in the document is the `Body` property. It stores any of the free-form text from the task. You can enter notes or comments here.

When this procedure is run, it creates a format similar to the one created with loops in Hour 7. Your output might resemble that shown in Figure 21.1.

FIGURE 21.1

The procedure returns three tasks.

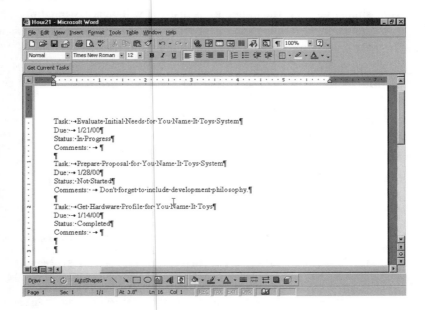

FIGURE 21.1

The procedure returns three tasks.

You can make this procedure more robust by adding custom formatting, or you can place this information in a table if desired. You can also include more information. Any information that can be set for a task in the Outlook Task form (see Figure 21.2) can be accessed with VBA.

FIGURE 21.2

The Outlook Task form has a lot more information that could have been included.

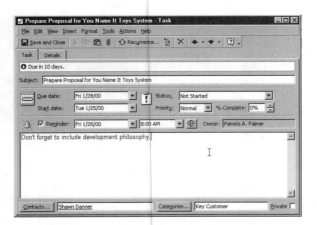

21

Accessing the Calendar

In addition to accessing tasks in the Tasks folder, you can also access appointments in a similar fashion. The difference is that you will be accessing different properties for the appointment. The GetAppointmentEntries procedure shown in Listing 21.2 illustrates the process for working with appointments instead.

LISTING 21.2 The GetAppointmentEntries Procedure

```
 1: Sub GetAppointmentEntries()
 2: '   Get Dates for processing
 3:     Dim lMonth As Variant, lYear As Variant, strDate As String
 4:     Dim dtFirst As Date, dtLast As Date
 5:     lMonth = Month(Now())
 6:     lYear = Year(Now())
 7:     strDate = lMonth & "/01/" & lYear
 8:     dtFirst = CDate(strDate)
 9:     dtLast = DateAdd("m", 1, dtFirst) - 1
10: '   Get Outlook appointments and build list
11:     Dim objOutlook As Outlook.Application, objNameSpace As NameSpace
12:     Dim objCalendarFolder As MAPIFolder, objAppointment As AppointmentItem
13:     Dim sngDuration As Single, strDuration As String
14:     Set objOutlook = CreateObject("Outlook.Application")
15:     Set objNameSpace = objOutlook.GetNamespace("MAPI")
16:     Set objCalendarFolder = objNameSpace.GetDefaultFolder(olFolderCalendar)
17:     For Each objAppointment In objCalendarFolder.Items
18:         If objAppointment.Start >= dtFirst And _
19:             objAppointment.Start <= dtLast Then
20:             Selection.TypeText objAppointment.Subject
21:             Selection.TypeParagraph
22:             Selection.TypeText "Begin: " & vbTab
23:             Selection.TypeText objAppointment.Start
24:             Selection.TypeText vbTab
25:             Selection.TypeText "End: " & vbTab
26:             Selection.TypeText objAppointment.End
27:             Selection.TypeParagraph
28:             sngDuration = Int(objAppointment.Duration / 60)
29:             If objAppointment.Duration - sngDuration * 60 > 0 Then
30:                 strDuration = sngDuration & " Hours, " & _
31:                 objAppointment.Duration - sngDuration * 60 & _
32:                 " Minutes"
33:             Else
34:                 strDuration = sngDuration & " Hours"
35:             End If
36:             Selection.TypeText "Expected Duration: " & vbTab
37:             Selection.TypeText strDuration
38:             Selection.TypeParagraph
39:             Selection.TypeText "Comments: " & vbTab
40:             Selection.TypeText objAppointment.Body
```

```
41:                Selection.TypeParagraph
42:                Selection.TypeParagraph
43:           End If
44:      Next
45: End Sub
```

ANALYSIS In the GetAppointmentEntries procedure, much of the code is the same as in the GetTaskEntries procedure. Lines 1–9 don't change because they perform the date calculations.

Lines 10–12 don't change that much. You still need variables to refer to the instance of Outlook, its NameSpace, the Calendar folder and each appointment. Appointments are a different type of object called an AppointmentItem. Line 13 sets up two new variables to deal with the Duration property.

Lines 14–16 are the same as the task procedure except for the Calendar default folder is represented with a different constant. Lines 18–44 use the For Each Next loop to evaluate each appointment in order to choose which appointments to include and to format them.

The If structure is different on lines 18–19 because appointments have a Start property instead of a DueDate. The rest of the code is structured in the same way as the Task example except for the Duration property.

With Tasks, the problem property was Status. Status was stored as a number so that you needed a Select Case structure to evaluate the value and create text. With Duration, the issue is different. Duration stores the allocated time in minutes. Lines 28–37 perform a conversion to translate the time to hours and minutes.

Line 28 takes the Duration and divides it by 60. It then strips the integer portion of the number to get the hours. Line 29 uses an If structure to test an expression. By subtracting the new variable from the Duration property, you can see if there are any minutes left over. If so, you can pick the appropriate format stored as a string. This string is then used to display the time in the document.

When the procedure is executed, its results resemble those shown in Figure 21.3. You could use the Format function to change the appearance of the dates and times, or you could place this information in a table.

The Appointment object is more robust than the Task object. Appointments have a different set of properties, and you can also access the objects related to meeting scheduling through the Appointment object. You might want to get a list of attendees from an Appointment object for inclusion in a document (such as a meeting agenda).

21

FIGURE 21.3

*There are two appoint-
ments in January.*

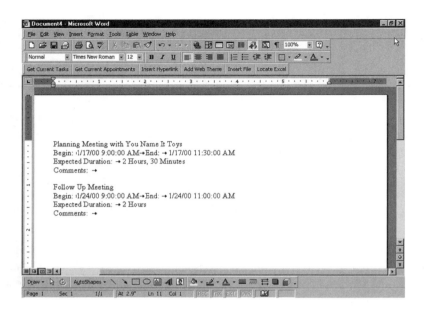

FIGURE 21.3

*There are two appoint-
ments in January.*

In addition to reading appointments or tasks, you can work with the Outlook Journal. The Journal enables you to track the time you spend on various activities. One of its options is to automatically track the time spent on Office documents. There are many fields available for journal entries as shown in Figure 21.4. When an entry is automatically created for a document, a shortcut for the document is also created in the entry. With VBA, you can read journal entries the same way you read the tasks and calendar items. You can create your own entries, appointments, meetings, and tasks because all of these collections support the Add method.

FIGURE 21.4

*The Journal Entry for
a Word document
includes a shortcut to
the file.*

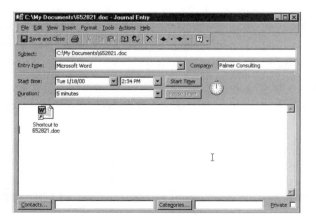

Working with the Internet

Another feature that was enhanced with Office 2000 was the support of the Internet. You can automate several tasks associated with working with the Internet. You can automate the embedding of hyperlinks, as well as the formatting of Web pages with VBA.

Embedding Hyperlinks

If there are hyperlinks that you want to include in your document on a regular basis, consider a procedure to insert them. To insert a hyperlink into your document, you use the Add method for the Hyperlinks collection. The syntax is

SYNTAX

```
expression.Add(Anchor, Address, SubAddress, ScreenTip, _
    TextToDisplay, Target)
```

The expression represents the Hyperlinks collection you want to add a link to. It is followed by the Add keyword. It can use up to six arguments:

- The Anchor indicates what paragraph the link is attached to. Like a graphic object, it has an anchor in the document.

- The Address and SubAddress provide the information to get to the Web address or file and a place in that page or document. These arguments must be surrounded by quotations.

- The ScreenTip argument is text that explains the link when the mouse pointer is over it. The TexttoDisplay is an alternative string shown in the document instead of the address.

- The Target is a location to load the hyperlink. If left blank it, it launches your browser.

For example, if you frequently reference the Macmillan Web site. you can create a procedure to add it and supporting text as shown in Listing 21.3.

LISTING 21.3   Adding a Hyperlink

```
1: Sub InsertMacmillanHyperLink()
2:     Selection.TypeText "For more information, please refer to "
3:     ActiveDocument.Hyperlinks.Add Anchor:=Selection.Range, _
4:         Address:="http://www.mcp.com/", SubAddress:="", _
5:         ScreenTip:="Open Macmillan's Web site", _
6:         TextToDisplay:="Macmillan Publishing"
7:     Selection.TypeText "."
8: End Sub
```

21

ANALYSIS Line 2 inserts some supporting text to lead into the hyperlink. It includes a trailing space to make space between the link and the text.

Lines 3–6 insert the hyperlink with the Add method. They anchor the hyperlink to the current location. They use the Web address for the Address argument, but don't include a subaddress.

The Add method uses the ScreenTip and TexttoDisplay arguments to change the appearance of the address and provide additional information when the user is about to click on the link. Line 7 just ends the sentence with a period. When this procedure is executed it appears in the document as shown in Figure 21.5.

FIGURE 21.5

The hyperlink is in place in its sentence.

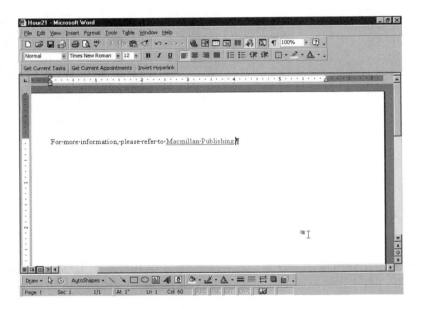

Setting Up the Web Page Layout

Another aspect of working with the Internet with Word is the capability you gain to create Web pages in Word. To support this capability, there are some special formatting choices that you can use for Web pages only. The application of these formatting choices can also be added with a procedure.

NEW TERM A *theme* changes the appearance of a document to format it as a Web page. You use the ApplyTheme method to add a Theme. Before you apply the theme to the document, be sure the document is viewed as a Web page. If it isn't, the theme will not be visible. To set the tone for a Web page as a corporate theme, you might create the `AddWebTheme` procedure shown in Listing 21.4.

LISTING 21.4   The AddWebTheme Procedure

```
1: Sub AddWebTheme()
2:     If ActiveWindow.View.Type <> wdWebView Then
3:         MsgBox "This is not in Web View, the Theme won't be applied", _
4:             vbInformation, "Not a Web Page"
5:         Exit Sub
6:     End If
7:     ActiveDocument.ApplyTheme Name:="corporat 011"
8: End Sub
```

ANALYSIS   Lines 2–6 check to see what view for the document is set. If it isn't set to Web View, the procedure will stop executing. Line 7 uses the `ApplyTheme` method to apply the chosen theme.

The `ApplyTheme` method has one argument which is the `Name` argument, but that isn't exactly accurate. The `Name` argument actually has four components. The first component is the name of the theme as represented in the folder. Getting the theme name isn't as easy as using some of the other formatting attributes. The themes display in the Theme dialog with complete names as shown in Figure 21.6. The chosen theme in this example is shown as Corporate. In the folder, it is shortened to *corporat*.

FIGURE 21.6

The Theme dialog enables you to choose a Web site theme.

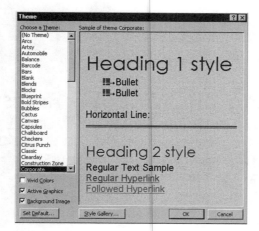

21

Following the folder's name for the theme, there are three numbers. These represent settings that are set with the three check boxes in the Themes dialog. The first number represents the Vivid Color settings, the second is the Active Graphics setting, and the third is the Background Image setting. You can set them to 1 or 0. A setting of 1 means that the feature is activated, and a 0 means that it is deactivated.

When this procedure is executed, it applies the settings you have chosen for the selected theme. With the Corporate theme and the heading entered, the page appears as shown in Figure 21.7.

FIGURE 21.7

The Web page has a corporate theme.

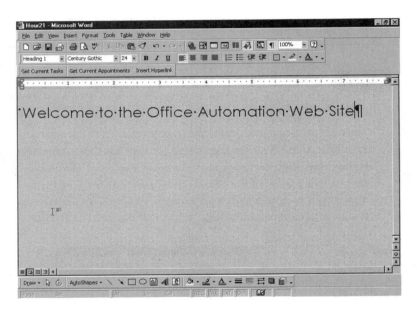

Understanding the Windows Registry

In addition to taking advantage of features that are inside of Word, you can also take advantage of features of Windows from within Word. One of these features is the Windows Registry. The Windows Registry is a special-use database that stores information about the user's computer. Its hardware, software, and settings are stored or registered.

As stated above, the Windows Registry stores the settings for your computer. If you adjust some of the settings incorrectly, it may cause problems with your hardware or software.

This section provides an introduction only. Please do not experiment without first researching the exact settings you want to change.

Examining the Registry

Before you begin examining how to take advantage of the Registry and its settings, you need to understand how the Registry is organized. The easiest way to view the Registry is to use a utility called REGEDIT. To run REGEDIT, complete these steps:

1. Select Start, Find, Files or Folders to display the Find dialog.

2. Type in `regedit*.exe` as the Named file to search for on your hard drive. It should locate REGEDIT.EXE or REGEDIT32.EXE depending on whether you are using Windows 95/98 or Windows NT.

3. Double-click on the file to launch the Registry Editor as shown in Figure 21.8.

FIGURE 21.8

REGEDIT enables you to view and change the Registry.

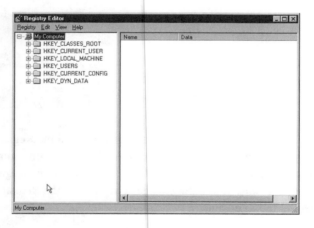

The Registry is displayed in a tree structure in the same way your folders are displayed in Windows Explorer. There are six folders shown in the Registry. Each of these controls a different aspect of your computer.

21

HKEY_CLASSES_ROOT stores information about the software installed on the system where the Registry is stored, and HKEY_CURRENT_USER stores information about the current user. HKEY_LOCAL_MACHINE stores information about the hardware and software on the machine that is accessing the Registry. HKEY_USERS has information about the users for this machine. HKEY_CURRENT_CONFIG stores information about your hardware. HKEY_DYN_DATA is on machines for Windows 95/98 to store information about Plug and Play.

Microsoft Word uses the Registry to store information about how you work with Word. For example, if you open the HKEY_CURRENT_USER\Software\Microsoft\Office\ 9.0Word\wizards\Memo Wizard in the Editor, you will see the choices are preserved from the last time you ran the Memo Wizard as shown in Figure 21.9.

FIGURE 21.9

The Memo Wizard stores its settings in the Registry.

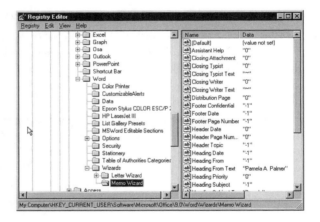

The benefit of storing information in the Registry is that the Registry is a part of the operating system. You don't have to depend on the user having something installed. The bad news is that unless you have a good understanding of the Registry, there is a great potential for problems. You might change something in the Registry that could cause your system to fail to operate.

Taking Advantage of the Registry

For the most part, you won't have a reason to edit the Registry directly. If you want to store and retrieve information for one of your projects, you have some tools within Word to assist with that task.

In Hour 9,"Working with Text," as you explored inserting files, you looked at placing files in a specific location on your hard drive. In that case, you created a special directory inside of your My Documents directory. This was a hard coded path. By working with the Registry, you can store any path and then call it from storage each time the procedure is run. You can use the `PrivateProfileString` property to store information in the Registry. Using it requires some information which identifies the setting you want to use or set in the Registry. The syntax is

expression.PrivateProfileString(*Filename, Section, Key*)

The expression references the system, and it is followed by the `PrivateProfileString` keyword. Within parentheses, you have the three components that identify the setting.

- `FileName` can contain a specific settings file. If you want to store your settings in the Registry, this component must be set to an empty string.

- `Section` gives the path in the Registry for the setting.

- `Key` indicates the specific key you want to retrieve or place.

With the `PrivateProfileString` property and the capability to open a dialog to use any choices made, you can make your code more flexible. You can rewrite the procedure to find the path for a filename in the Registry, as shown in Listing 21.5.

LISTING 21.5 The `InsertFilewithRegistry` Procedure

```
 1: Sub InsertFileWithRegistry()
 2:     On Error GoTo DevError
 3:     Dim strRegPath As String, strDir As String
 4:     Dim strFilePath As String
 5:     strRegPath = System.PrivateProfileString("", _
 6:         "HKEY_CURRENT_USER\Software\Microsoft\" & _
 7:         "Office\9.0\Word\Options", "InsertPath")
 8:     If Len(strRegPath) = 0 Then
 9:         MsgBox "The InsertFilePath isn't stored in the Registry." & _
10:             "Please use the Copy dialog to locate the " & _
11:             "Imagine.Doc file.", _
12:             vbInformation, "Missing Path"
13:         With Dialogs(wdDialogCopyFile)
14:             .Display
15:             strDir = .Directory
16:             If Len(strDir) = 0 Then
17:                 MsgBox "You didn't select a path, operation cancelled."
```

continues

21

LISTING 21.5 continued

```
18:                    Exit Sub
19:               End If
20:               strRegPath = Mid(strDir, 2, Len(strDir) - 2)
21:           End With
22:           System.PrivateProfileString("", _
23:               "HKEY_CURRENT_USER\Software\Microsoft\" & _
24:               "Office\9.0\Word\Options", "InsertPath") = strRegPath
25:       End If
26:       strFilePath = strRegPath & "Imagine.doc"
27:       Selection.InsertFile FileName:=strFilePath, Range:="", _
28:           ConfirmConversions:=False, Link:=False, Attachment:=False
29:       Exit Sub
30: DevError:
31:       Dim strMessage As String, strTitle As String
32:       Select Case Err.Number
33:           Case 5273        'Path or File not valid
34:               strMessage = _
35:               "Please verify the Insert Files folder exists and try again."
36:               strTitle = "Invalid Folder or File Name"
37:           Case 5174        'File Couldn't be found
38:               strMessage = _
39:               "Please verify the Development Cycle file is in the folder."
40:               strTitle = "Missing File"
41:           Case Else
42:               strMessage = "Error " & Err.Number & "," & _
43:               Err.Description & "has occurred. Processing was halted."
44:               strTitle = "Unexpected Error"
45:       End Select
46:       MsgBox strMessage, vbOKOnly + vbExclamation, strTitle
47: End Sub
```

ANALYSIS This procedure differs from the original because it looks to the Registry for path information. If it can't find the path, it prompts for the directory with a dialog. Line 2 initializes the error handler, and lines 3–4 define the variables to store the path from the Registry and for the file itself.

Lines 5–7 retrieve the InsertPath from the Registry. The PrivateProfileString property for the System object is used to get the path. The FileName is left blank to indicate the item is in the Registry and not a settings file. The section is set to point to a specific folder in the Registry, and the Key value is InsertPath.

Lines 8–21 test what value is retrieved from the Registry. Using the Len function, if the string is empty, the Dialogs collection is used to get the path. Lines 9–12 display a message box indicating there is a problem and informing the user he must use the Copy dialog to find the path.

Lines 13–21 set up a `With` Structure to work with the `Dialogs` collection. Line 14 displays the dialog. The display method is used because you don't want to actually copy data. You just want to use the settings. After the user selects a path, lines 16–19 test to make sure some folder was selected.

Line 20 sets the path using the `Directory` property for the Copy File dialog. You have to use the `Mid` function to strip extra quotations from the string.

Lines 22–24 use the new path to set the `InsertPath` setting in the Registry using the `PrivateProfileString` property. Line 26 uses the path to set the file path for the insert operation and the rest of the code is the same as the example in Hour 9.

With the `PrivateProfileString` property, you used the `System` object for the Application. Rather than using a resource internal to Word or using an object library of one of the Office applications, you rely on one of the Windows' resources, the Registry.

Understanding the Windows API

In Hour 20, "Working with Other Office Applications," you explored using functions from another application such as Excel. You set a reference to its object library and then began developing your code. That object library was stored in a dynamic link library (DLL). A DLL is any file that stores procedures in a separate file. That file can then be referenced, and its functions can be used in your code.

The Windows operating system includes many functions that can eliminate development time for specific actions. When Windows was initially introduced, one of its marketing points was that if you learned how to perform a task, you wouldn't have to relearn it for another application. Minimizing, Maximizing, Restoring, or Closing a window are all good examples. In every application, you can click the Close button to close a specific window. That function is part of the Windows operating system, not part of that application. You can access these standard functions with the Application Programming Interface (API).

With VBA, you don't have to use the API directly very often because VBA offers many functions and methods that call on Windows function for you. One of these is the Close method for a document. This built-in functionality doesn't prohibit you from using the Windows API for functions that are supported.

With the Windows API, there are six DLLs: COMDLG32.DLL, DLLLZ32.DLL, GDI32.DLL, KERNEL32.DLL, USER32.DLL, and VERSION.DLL. They each control different aspects of Windows. For example, COMDLG32.DLL provides functions to display and manipulate standard dialogs like the Print dialog. In your Word VBA

21

development, you probably won't have a need for these functions because you have the built-in dialog collection.

It isn't part of the scope of this book give you a complete tour of what is available with the Windows API. To give you a chance to see an API function in action in your code, you can use the FindWindow function.

In Hour 20, when you wanted to work with one of the other Microsoft Applications, you used the New keyword to create a new instance or the CreateObject function. You can also create a procedure to determine if the application is already open before you create a new instance. If you are able to determine this, you might be able to save some resources.

The first step is to declare the function for use in your project. The declaration must be placed in the general declarations section of the project:

```
Declare Function FindWindow Lib "User32" alias "FindWindowA" _
    (ByVal lpClassName as String, ByVal lpwindowsName as string) as Long
```

The Declare Function indicates you want to declare an outside function for use. The FindWindow keyword indicates how you are going to reference the function. The Lib keyword followed by the "User32" indicates that it is stored in the USER32.DLL file.

The Alias keyword followed by "FindWindowsA", gives the name of the function in the library itself. Inside of the parentheses, two arguments are needed—the class name and the window name for the application you are searching for. The as Long indicates that the procedure will return a Long value.

The ByVal keyword isn't one you have used in this book. It controls the way a value is passed to a function. By default, values passed to a function are passed by reference, which means that in the processing in the function, the value can change. The ByVal keyword passes a copy of the value to the function. The original value isn't altered by the function.

With string values, the ByVal keyword functions differently. Most API functions were created with C or C++, and for better or for worse, the functions do have a C-like or C++-like structure. C strings are different than the strings you are accustomed to working with in VBA. In C, you use null terminated strings. You will have to make sure to terminate your strings as you send them, and then remove the null terminator when you go to use what you get back.

After the function is declared, you can create your procedures using that function. To learn if Excel is already open on your system, you can create the LocateExcel procedure shown in Listing 21.6.

LISTING 21.6 The `LocateExcel` Procedure

```
1: Sub LocateExcel()
2:     Dim lExcel As Long
3:     lExcel = FindWindow(vbNullString, "Microsoft Excel - Book1")
4:     If lExcel <> 0 Then
5:         MsgBox "Excel Open"
6:     Else
7:         Msgbox "Excel Not Open"
8:     End If
9: End Sub
```

ANALYSIS   Line 2 declares a long variable for the return value of the function. Line 3 uses the `FindWindow` function. The class name argument isn't going to be used with this example, so the `vbNullString` constant is sent. The name of the application along with a workbook is sent as the application's name.

If the application isn't opened, the procedure returns a `0`. Otherwise, it returns the handle for the application. That enables you to work with the application. In the code for Hour 20, you located a worksheet that you wanted to use, and if it was open, you used the `GetObject` method instead of the `CreateObject` method.

With the Office Developer's edition, there are some additional resources to assist you with learning about the functions available and some tools to help you implement them in your code.

Summary

In this hour, you continued to explore how to take advantage of outside resources in your code. You looked at accessing other objects from Outlook, as well as preparing a document to work with the Internet.

You also looked at the Windows resources available. You learned to store and retrieve settings from the Windows Registry, as well as to use Windows functions with the application program interface (API).

You only received a brief introduction to the API. There are additional resources included with the Developer's Edition including a complete listing of `Declare` statements for the functions. The key thing to remember is most of the functions are accessed through methods and functions within VBA and the Word Object model. You don't want to go outside of Word for a function that is built-in.

21

Q&A

Q Can I access the Notes in Outlook?

A Yes, you can. You set up the `MAPIFolder` variable but you use the `olFolderNotes` constant.

Q Is the Registry the only place to store data to be used in a procedure?

A In addition to the Registry and the Document Properties, you can also set document variables for a document or a template. Where you place the data depends on the procedure.

An important aspect of this question is the user's habits. If the user utilizes the same machine every time a document is opened or created, any of these options work. If the user works on more than one machine, the question is more complex. In this case, you will probably use storage in the document or template.

Workshop

Here are some questions and exercises to help you review the material covered in this hour. The answers to the quiz questions can be found in Appendix A, "Quiz Answers."

Quiz

1. What is a `NameSpace`?
2. What property sets the text shown in the document for a hyperlink?
3. What settings are stored under the HKEY_CURRENT_USER folder of the Registry?
4. Why is the `ByVal` keyword important?

Exercises

1. Modify the procedure from Hour 20 that places data in an Excel worksheet using `FindWindow` to see if Excel is already open.
2. Review your automation checklist to see if you need to use any of the techniques covered in this hour.

Hour **22**

Adding Help

When you begin adding automation to your work in Word, you create procedures to speed up the creation of your own documents. After a time, you might find that you are creating procedures for other users, enabling them to complete documents for you in a timelier manner. Because these other users haven't developed the procedures they are using, it might be useful to provide them with information about what is occurring in your code.

The highlights from this hour include

- Using the status bar
- Programming the Office Assistant
- Evaluating other types of Help

Using the Status Bar

In many cases, you don't need to provide lengthy instructions, but you want to keep the user updated on the progress of a procedure. In these cases, one of the easiest approaches is to use the status bar.

If you are using a Word Form Field, setting the status bar text is easy. In the Field Options window, there is a button labeled Add Help Text. It opens a dialog with two tabs. The first tab, shown in Figure 22.1, enables you to add text that will be displayed on the status bar when the control has the focus. You can add text in this window or select an AutoText entry to display instead.

FIGURE 22.1

You can use an AutoText entry for the status bar or add text.

The text entered will be seen in the status bar when the form is protected and the field is active, as shown in Figure 22.2. You won't be able to see it when you are designing your form.

FIGURE 22.2

The status bar shows the text you entered in the Form Field Help Text dialog.

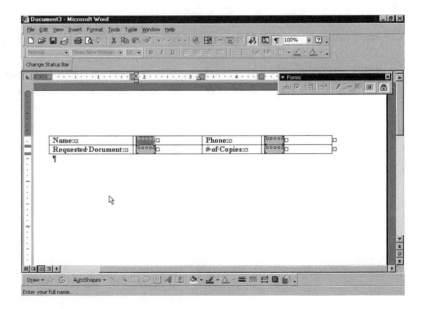

The Add Help Text dialog also gives you the capability to add F1 Help. If you select the second tab (see Figure 22.3), you can select an AutoText entry or enter text to be displayed when the F1 key is selected while the field is active.

FIGURE 22.3

*The F1 Help tab lets
you set the text to
respond if the F1 key
is selected when a field
is active.*

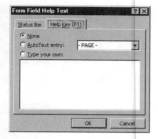

When the user presses F1, the text you entered is displayed in a special dialog, as shown
in Figure 22.4. Its appearance is set. You can only change the text.

FIGURE 22.4

*The Help text is
displayed.*

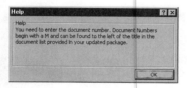

If you want to adjust the content of the status bar, there is no dialog to set the text for
objects in a standard document. When you want to change the status bar text during a
procedure, you set the StatusBar property as follows:

```
Sub ChangeStatusBar()
    StatusBar = "Inserting File..."
End Sub
```

The text will take over the text on the status bar, as shown in Figure 22.5. The status bar
text will remain until you change it with another setting, or until the procedure ends and
the user takes an action.

In some of the longer code examples you have seen, comments are used to explain what
certain lines of code are accomplishing. You might want to consider adding the
StatusBar setting at those points, as well, to help the user understand what is occurring.

Although they are not a part of adding Help, there are methods you can use, in conjunction with changing the status bar, to make the screen less confusing to the user as your
code executes. With longer procedures, you might have noticed that the executed actions
are visible on the screen. If you find their presence distracting, you can eliminate the
problem for your users by turning off screen updating with the ScreenUpdating property
for the application.

Set the ScreenUpdating property to False before the lines of code that will execute and
then change the setting back to True after these lines. This procedure freezes the screen
until all the processing is complete.

FIGURE 22.5

The status bar was changed with your code.

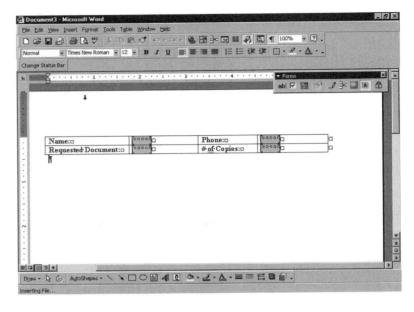

If you use the `ScreenUpdating` property, it is also a good idea to use the `ScreenRefresh` method before turning `ScreenUpdating` back on. If you do so, when you turn control back to the user, the document shows all the changes just made. Your code might resemble the structure shown in Listing 22.1.

LISTING 22.1 Using the `ScreenUpdating` Property and `ScreenRefresh` Method

```
 1: Sub LongProcedure()
 2:     StatusBar = "Begin Processing…"
 3:     Application.ScreenUpdating = False
 4: '   First Code block
 5:     Status Bar = "Text of Your Choice"
 6: '   Next Code Block
 7:     Status Bar = "Text of Your Choice."
 8: '   Next Code block
 9:     Application.ScreenRefresh
10:     Application.ScreenUpdating = True
11: End Sub
```

ANALYSIS Line 2 sets the initial status bar line, and line 3 turns off the screen updating so that your code can work on the document without displaying every step to the user. The code that does the actual work is shown on line 4. In reality, you will have multiple lines of code here.

Line 5 illustrates that you need to update the status bar periodically by setting the `StatusBar` property to new text. Because the user won't be seeing the result of each individual line of code in the document, updating the status bar will be his only visual clue that anything is taking place. Line 9 refreshes the screen manually, and line 10 turns on screen updating when you are finished.

Programming the Office Assistant

The status bar is a great way of showing the progress of a procedure as it executes, but there are times you need to provide more than a progress update. For these occasions, you can use the Office Assistant as a way to communicate with your users.

The Office Assistant probably greeted you when you first launched Word after upgrading. (To see it, choose Help, Microsoft Word Help.) The Office Assistant was designed to provide friendly assistance. You can use the Office Assistant for the same purpose in your projects.

Determining the Uses for the Office Assistant

Depending on the types of tasks you are automating, you might find several uses for the Assistant in your projects. If you are developing for other users, you can use it to provide some guidance about what functions have been automated.

The Assistant can provide instructions for the completion of a form. To do this, you can add code to use the Assistant in the `NewDocument` event procedure or the `AutoNew` procedure.

You can also use the Office Assistant with a User Form. It can provide step-by-step instructions for the completion of a form.

You can use Office Assistant to gather information from the user. You might have noticed that when the Assistant is displayed, many of the questions are shown as communications from the Assistant rather than being displayed with message boxes.

Accessing the Assistant Object

When you have a use for the Office Assistant, you can manipulate it with VBA. It is another Microsoft Office resource. Before you can add the Assistant to your code, you need to set a Reference:

1. Switch to the Visual Basic Editor.

2. Select Tools, References.

3. Select Microsoft Office 9.0 Object Library and click OK.

After the reference is set, you can begin using the Assistant. You can control its appearance and behavior. You can display it, change which Assistant is used or what actions are shown, display text, and take action based on what a user does with the Assistant.

Manipulating the Assistant

When a user begins using Office, he meets the Office Assistant almost immediately. Beginners find the Assistant helpful and often leave it displayed to answer questions and offer tips. Some more experienced users hide the Assistant until they have a question. Other users disable the Office Assistant because they prefer to work with the complete Help contents, rather than pose questions through the Assistant. If you are want to use the Assistant, keep in mind these three user approaches to its use. There are several steps to begin using the Assistant for communication with the user:

1. Determine whether the Assistant is running; if it is not, display it.

2. Determine whether you want to change the Assistant's personality.

3. Set up your message and display it.

4. Handle any user actions taken with the Assistant.

In this section, you will experiment with the Office Assistant by tackling a task to accommodate the more experienced users. You will give them an option to work without the Assistant.

Setting Up the Assistant

To get an answer about using the Office Assistant, you use the `AutoNew` procedure. Determine if the Assistant is displayed and display it if it isn't. You will then display a message asking if the user wants to have the Assistant's help.

With the other applications you have been working with, you set the reference and then you set up object variables for the application and its objects. When you are working with the Assistant, you must develop more than one procedure to manipulate the Assistant. You will create variables that can be accessed by more than one procedure:

1. Select General from the Object list and Declarations from the Procedures list.

2. Enter the following Declarations:

```
Private objAssistant As Assistant
Private objBalloon As Balloon
Private bEnabled As Boolean
Private bOriginalState As Boolean
Private bUseAssistant as Boolean
```

After the Declarations are set, you can begin writing the AutoNew procedure as shown in Listing 22.2. It will set up the object variables and preserve the user's current Assistant settings at the same time.

LISTING 22.2   The AutoNew Procedure

```
 1: Sub AutoNew()
 2:     Set objAssistant = Assistant
 3:     If objAssistant.Visible = True Then
 4:         bOriginalState = True
 5:     Else
 6:         bOriginalState = False
 7:         If objAssistant.On = True Then
 8:             bEnabled = True
 9:             objAssistant.Visible = True
10:         Else
11:             bEnabled = False
12:             objAssistant.On = True
13:             objAssistant.Visible = True
14:         End If
15:     End If
16:     Set objBalloon = objAssistant.NewBalloon
17:     objAssistant.Animation = msoAnimationBeginSpeaking
18:     With objBalloon
19:         .Heading = "Welcome to Hour 22"
20:         .Text = "Do you wish assistance with this template?"
21:         .Icon = msoIconTip
22:         .Button = msoButtonSetYesNo
23:     End With
24:     Dim lReturn As Long
25:     lReturn = objBalloon.Show
26:     objAssistant.Animation = msoAnimationIdle
27:     If lReturn = msoBalloonButtonNo Then
28:         objAssistant.Animation = msoAnimationDisappear
29:         objAssistant.Visible = False
30:     End If
31: End Sub
```

ANALYSIS   The first step is to assign the object variable for the Assistant. This is set with line 2. Notice that unlike some of the object variables you have set in the past, this one doesn't create a new instance with the New keyword. There is only one Assistant at any given time. You can't create more than one of them on the screen, so you don't use the New keyword.

Lines 3–14 test the state of the Assistant with an If...Then...Else structure before you begin altering its current settings. Line 3 tests the Visible property for the Assistant to see if it is currently in view. If the `Visible` property is `True`, the `bOriginalState` variable is set to `True` on line 4, and no more action is needed.

If the Assistant isn't visible, you are required to do some work. Line 6 sets the `bOriginalState` to `False` so that you know how to reset the state when the document is closed.

Lines 7–15 tests the `On` property of the Assistant. Testing the `Visible` property takes care of the user who displays the Assistant only when there is a question. The users who prefer to use the complete Help file may have disabled the Assistant altogether. In that case, you have to turn the Assistant on.

Line 7 tests the `On` property. If it is `True`, line 8 sets the `bEnabled` variable to preserve that state, and line 9 displays the Assistant.

If the `On` property is `False`, you have more work to do. Line 11 sets `bEnabled` to `False` to preserve the value, and line 12 sets the `On` property to `True`. Then the `Visible` property is changed on line 13.

The next step is to manipulate the Assistant to show your message. When you want to display a message with the Assistant, you use a `Balloon` object. Line 16 uses the `NewBalloon` method to create a new `Balloon` object for your message.

When you work with the Assistant, you can decide what actions are shown for the Assistant. Line 17 sets the `Animation` property for the Assistant using a built-in constant. There are thirty-five actions that can be shown for the Assistant, regardless of what personality is chosen.

Lines 18–23 uses a `With` structure to format the `Balloon` object to behave as a message box. Line 19 sets the `Heading` property. It is the first line in the balloon and is shown in bold. Line 20 sets the text for the message itself.

Lines 21 and 22 set the urgency. Line 21 indicates it is a low-level message by formatting it as a Tip with the Icon property. Line 22 indicates that you want Yes and No buttons in the balloon. These features are all set with built-in constants.

After the balloon is set up, you are ready to display it. This part of the process is very similar to the use of the `MsgBox` function. Line 24 sets up a variable to store what button is selected in the balloon, and line 25 uses the `show` method to display the balloon.

Line 26 adjusts the Assistant's animation to indicate that the Assistant is finished talking. It uses the `msoAnimationIdle` constant. You can use any of the Animation constants.

There are several constants, such as msoAnimationLookRight, that enable you to change the direction the Assistant is facing. Keep in mind the Right used in this constant refers to the Assistant's right, not yours.

Lines 27–34 test the user's response to the balloon. If the user selected No with the balloon (which means he doesn't want to work with the Assistant), the Animation is set to show the disappearing action, and the Visible property is set to False.

The AutoNew procedure is executed when a new document is created based on this template. If you want to use the Assistant whenever a document is opened, regardless of whether it is new, you must use this code in the AutoOpen event.

Giving Instructions with the Assistant

Now that the Assistant has been set up, you can use it to communicate with this form when protection is enabled. You can create procedures and use the Field Options dialog to assign the procedure to execute when a field is entered.

For example, if you want to instruct the user to enter his name as it appears in the company roster, you can create a procedure, as shown in Listing 22.3, to use the Assistant to tell him what to do.

LISTING 22.3 The txtName_Enter Procedure

```
 1: Sub txtName_Enter()
 2:     If objAssistant.Visible = False Then Exit Sub
 3:     With objBalloon
 4:         .Heading = "What's your Name?"
 5:         .Text = "Enter your name as it appears on the company roster"
 6:         .Icon = msoIconTip
 7:         .Button = msoButtonSetOK
 8:     End With
 9:     objAssistant.Animation = msoAnimationCheckingSomething
10:     objBalloon.Show
11:     objAssistant.Animation = msoAnimationIdle
12: End Sub
```

ANALYSIS Line 2 checks to see if the Assistant is Visible. If it isn't, this procedure has no need to execute, and the Exit Sub stops it.

Lines 3–8 set up the balloon's contents using the same structure. Line 9 animates the Assistant, and line 10 displays the balloon. Line 11 changes the Animation.

After the procedure is created for the template, it needs to be assigned with the Text Form Field Options dialog, as shown in Figure 22.6.

FIGURE 22.6

The procedure is assigned to run as the field is entered.

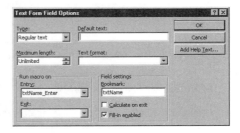

Now when the user Enters the field, the new balloon will be displayed as shown in Figure 22.7. The user will press Enter and begin inputting information. You can create procedures for each field or only the ones that need further explanation.

FIGURE 22.7

The new balloon is displayed, showing your message to the user.

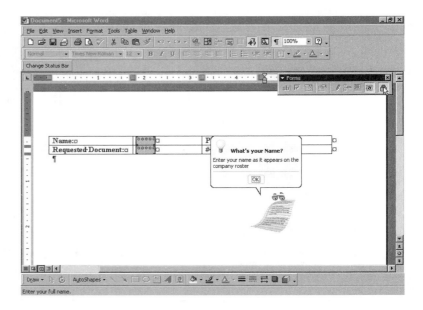

Resetting the Assistant's Settings

When you are using the Office Assistant as shown, with the AutoNew procedure and the Enter setting for fields, you need to use an AutoClose procedure, as shown in Listing 22.4, to reset the Assistant's settings to what they were before you started.

22

LISTING 22.4 The AutoClose Procedure

```
1: Sub AutoClose()
2:     If bOriginalState = True Then
3:         Exit Sub
4:     Else
5:         objAssistant.Visible = False
6:         If bEnabled = False Then objAssistant.On = False
7:     End If
8: End Sub
```

 ANALYSIS Line 2 tests the bOriginalState variable. If it is True, no action is needed. If it is False, you set the Visible property to False on line 5. Line 6 tests the bEnabled variable and adjusts the On property.

The Assistant can be a very friendly way to communicate with your users. In addition to the uses you have seen earlier in this chapter, you can also use the Assistant as an alternative user form for simple selections. You can include check boxes or options in the balloons. You can also change the personality of the Assistant, if needed.

> If you are using the Assistant to gather information with a longer procedure, remember it can also act as a message box. Consider using an If...Then...Else structure to see if the Assistant is visible. If it isn't, you can use the MsgBox function. If it is, you can use the Assistant. This technique is illustrated in Hour 23, "Creating A Global Template or Add-In."

Evaluating Other Types of Help

You have learned to use the Status Bar, MsgBox function, and the Assistant to exchange information with the user, but those aren't your only choices to communicate. You can add text to the template. You can display another document or create a complete Help system with the Office Developer's Edition.

Adding Text to the Template to Provide Help

Some templates include description about the template used as text. If you use the Contemporary Memo template to create a new document, for example, the new document isn't created empty, as shown in Figure 22.8.

There are fields to be filled in, as well as text instructing users to add additional text in specific locations. The user simply clicks to enter the information needed and deletes what isn't needed.

FIGURE 22.8

*The contemporary
memo template has
instructions as text.*

This is the easiest way to communicate the purpose of the template and the steps needed
to use this template. There is, however, the disadvantage that, as the user deletes text, he
permanently loses it as a reference.

Creating Another Document with Help Information

Another approach is to use VBA to create another document to serve as a reference. The
Contemporary memo also shows this approach. In the paragraph where the user is
instructed to enter text, he is advised to double-click on an icon to get additional details.

If you point to the icon and right-click, you can select Toggle Field Code. Doing so displays the code, which indicates that it is a MACROBUTTON field, as shown in Figure
22.9. When double-clicked, this field is set to run the ShowExample macro procedure.

When this icon is double-clicked, it runs the ShowExample procedure listed in Listing
22.5. It creates a new document and loads an AutoText entry with a sample.

FIGURE 22.9
The field code will launch a procedure.

22

LISTING 22.5 Microsoft's ShowExample Procedure

```
 1: Public Sub ShowExample()
 2:
 3:     Dim oDoc As Document
 4:
 5:     Application.ScreenUpdating = False
 6:     Set oDoc = Documents.Add(Template:=
➥ActiveDocument.AttachedTemplate.FullName)
 7:     oDoc.Content.Delete
 8:     oDoc.AttachedTemplate.AutoTextEntries("Gallery Example").
➥Insert Where:=Selection.Range, RichText:=True
 9:     ' oDoc.Content.ParagraphFormat.Reset
10:     Selection.HomeKey Unit:=wdStory
11:     Application.ScreenUpdating = True
12: End Sub
```

ANALYSIS Line 3 sets up the document object variable. Line 5 turns off screen updating. Line 6 creates a new document based on the same template, and line 7 deletes the contents.

Line 8 uses an AutoText entry to create a sample memo. Line 10 takes you to the top of the document, and line 11 turns on the screen updating.

> The one change that you might want to consider is using the MsgBox function after line 11 to tell the user they can use Alt+Tab to switch between the documents.

The benefit of using VBA to create a separate document is that it leaves the instructions intact. The user can see a sample of the template, but he does not have to do a lot of work to create the text of the document. This approach is great if you have many custom styles with specific uses.

Evaluating a Help File

The last alternative for providing assistance to the user is one that requires quite a bit more effort on your part. If you have a template with many macros that automate much of the document creation process, or if you are creating a Wizard, you might want to create a Help file.

Most applications use a Help file to assist with learning about various actions. (To see Word's Help, chose Help, Contents, and Index.) A Help file isn't a part of your template. It is a separate file, and to display it, you use the Windows Help API functions. It appears in a window by itself with a Table of Contents in one pane and the topics in a second pane.

Creating a Help file is not a quick process. There are five steps. It also requires some tools that are only available with the Microsoft Office Developer's Edition. Those steps are

1. Create the Help topics.
2. Create the Table of Contents and Index.
3. Create the Help Project.
4. Compile the Help File.
5. Create procedures to access the new Help file.

This type of Help isn't something you add for simple templates. Creating a separate document with information or having text in the template for instructions are much easier methods to provide Help in uncomplicated situations. The effort it takes to create a Help file and the fact that you must have the Developer's Edition to create it probably make this your last choice for providing Help. You only want to use a Help file if you support your own wizards or if you have some very complex templates.

22

Summary

In this hour, you have explored how to provide assistance for your templates and procedures. You learned about several alternatives.

The chapter begins with the easiest method to implement. You looked at how to change the status bar to indicate what is happening within your procedures. Then you explored how to use the Microsoft Office Assistant to communicate with your users. This is a very friendly approach to helping inexperienced users.

You also examined three additional approaches that provide instructions or help with more complex templates. These included directions as text, creating a new document with instructions, or creating a complete Help file.

Q&A

Q Can I change the appearance of the mouse when I change the status bar?

A No, You can use the `MousePointer` property to change the appearance of the mouse when you are working with User Forms only.

Q How do I change the Office Assistant?

A If you want to change the personality of the Office Assistant, use the `FileName` property. Each personality is stored in a separate file with an ACS extension. You can simply add a line of code changing that property.

You must careful when changing the `FileName` property. Not all the ACS files are loaded as part of a standard installation. You will probably want to use VBA to check if the file exists before you change the property.

Q What do I use to create a standard Help file?

A The Microsoft Office Developer's Edition has a tool called the HTML Help Workshop. It assists you with creation of Help files. It has a Help file of its own to walk you through the process.

Workshop

Here are some questions and exercises to help you review the material covered in this hour. The answers to the quiz questions can be found in Appendix A, "Quiz Answers."

Quiz

1. Can you change the Help dialog for form fields?
2. Why would you want to adjust screen updating?
3. What object controls the text of the Assistant?
4. When is creating a new sample document better than having instructions in the template?

Exercises

1. Create procedures to be executed when they are entered for the remaining fields for this template.
2. Examine your automation list to determine what kind of Help you want to provide for each template.

Hour **23**

Creating a Global Template or Add-In

As you begin creating procedures to automate tasks, you will find there are procedures or actions that you use frequently. Rather than include the code for these procedures in each template, you can place it in a global template. You will now learn about global templates and how to use them.

The highlights of this hour include

- Understanding the Normal template
- Examining global templates
- Developing global templates
- Connecting a global template

Understanding the Normal Template

When you first started working with Word, you weren't even aware that a type of document called a *template* existed. You launched Word, and a document opened with it. You could begin typing your document immediately. As you learned more about Word, you might have found yourself changing specific settings, such as your page margins, every time you created a new document. When you located the Default buttons in the Page Setup and/or Font dialogs, you had already begun working with templates.

The Normal template is the base template for all of your work in Microsoft Word. The Normal template is different from any other template in one important way. If it is missing on your hard drive, Microsoft Word automatically creates another one, with all of the default settings, as you open a new document.

When you first began experimenting with Visual Basic for Applications (VBA), your macros were probably saved in the Normal template (the default location for macros) when you used the Macro Recorder. It is easy to do this, even after you know about templates, because Word encourages you to save the macros in the Record Macro dialog (see Figure 23.1).

FIGURE 23.1

The Store Macro In prompt defaults to the Normal template.

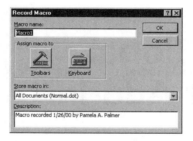

The Store Macro In defaults to All Documents (Normal.dot) as the choice. The "All Documents" phrase assists with your decision to use the Normal template because you think, of course, that you want to be able use the macro with all documents.

Using VBA, the procedures on the Normal template are available to all documents regardless of the template a document is based on; however, there are several problems with storing all of your procedures in the Normal template.

The first is the size of the file. As you add code to the Normal template, its file size grows. As the file gets larger, it will take longer to load. Because it is always loaded, you may experience some delay in creating a new document or launching Word with it.

The second problem has to do with sharing your code with others. If you develop a procedure to complete a task that you want to give to another user, you don't want to give him your Normal template along with the procedure. If your Normal template is copied over the recipient's Normal template, he will have your code, but he will also lose all his own custom settings, including any code of his own.

One alternative is to create a template with the code and have the recipient use the Organizer to copy your procedures into his Normal template. The drawback to this approach is that if you change your procedure, the user who copied it won't have your changes. A better solution is to use a global template.

Examining Global Templates

A *global template* is a template that is attached to your current document to provide access to its project with its code and objects. For example, the template created for Task Update reporting could be attached manually with the following steps:

1. Select Tools, Templates and Add-ins to display the Templates and Add-ins dialog, shown in Figure 23.2.

FIGURE 23.2

The Templates and Add-ins dialog enables you to manage the attached files.

2. Select Add to display the File dialog.
3. Use the file browser to locate the Task Update.Dot template you want to include and select it.
4. Click OK to load the template.

After the template is loaded, there isn't any visual change on your screen. In Word, this standard template is used as a global template. The file format is the same. In other Microsoft Office applications like Excel, this is known as an add-in. Add-ins have a special file format in the other applications.

When you attach a template, you only have access to its project. You can't see any of the boilerplate text, or use any of the page settings or styles. You only have access to those objects displayed in the Visual Basic Editor—the procedures and the user forms.

When you select Tools, Macro, Macros to display the Macros dialog (see Figure 23.3), you can see the additional macros in the list. There are several versions of the macro that set up tasks like `TaskSetUpFor`.

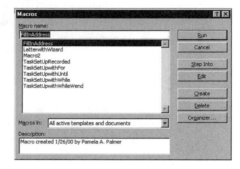

When you select a macro procedure, you can run it. If you run the `TaskSetUpWithFor`, the `InputBox` displays as it did when you created a new document, and it places the task lines in the document as shown in Figure 23.4.

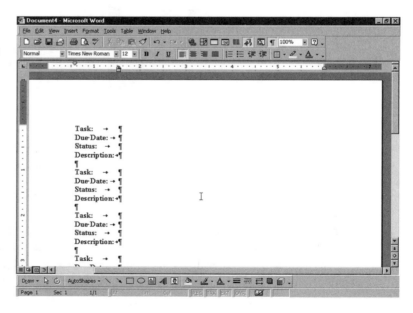

Global templates offer several benefits when you share your code with others. The first benefit is protection. When you open the Macro dialog, you can click the Run button for one of the macros, but the Edit button is disabled. You can't edit a global template when it is attached.

If you are in the Visual Basic Editor, the user will be able to see the macro listed in the Project Explorer, but if he attempts to open it, a message box appears informing him that it isn't viewable. This gives you a certain degree of protection against unauthorized editing. There are also some additional ways of protecting your template shown later in this hour.

The second benefit is that you can limit the size of the Normal template. Rather than having all of your procedures in the Normal template, you can store related procedures in different templates and load them only when they are needed.

The third benefit is the ease of update. If you change the code in a procedure in your Normal template, you must send the revised Normal template to everyone and have each recipient use the Organizer to move the macro from one template to the other. With a global template, you can make any changes as needed and then send the file to the other user. He just copies it over his existing template file without harming his Normal templates.

Developing Global Templates

Using a global template makes maintenance of your code much easier, but you must take some special care when you are constructing the procedures. When you create code for a template, the code references objects within the same file. When you begin creating global templates, you use code from one file to work with another file.

The first precaution is to make sure that you put the correct information in your code. In many of the procedures you have created, you took advantage of properties, such as the `ActiveDocument` property, to make your code simpler. This property will serve you with global templates as well as it did when you were working with a single template, but you must make sure that it is what you want.

Even though the user can't use the content of an attached global template, your code can. To get to objects in the template, you can't use the `ActiveDocument` property. You will use the `Templates` collection.

For example, you want to use an AutoText entry from the host template. You can't use the `ActiveDocument` property because it isn't the active document. If the template

Marketing Support is stored in your default template directory, you can use the following lines of code to reference an AutoText entry called `ProductList`.

```
Dim strTemplate as string
strTemplate = Options.DefaultFilePath(wdUserTemplatePath) & "\" _
    & "Marketing Support.Dot"
ActiveDocument.Templates(strTemplate).AutoTextEntries("ProductList") _
    .Insert Where:=Selection.Range, RichText:=True
```

The second precaution is to make sure that any data that is needed is available for the procedure. When you are working with an attached template, you can't guarantee that a piece of data is set in the active document. You must use more error handling to test information before taking action.

You will probably develop more functions in global templates. You can specify the data required as arguments and then send the information when you call the user-defined function from another template.

The third precaution is to minimize the risks of duplicate names with procedures. If you have any suspicion about the existence of another procedure with the same name, include the template name as you reference the procedure you want.

Creating a Procedure

When you create procedures for a global template, the process is essentially the same as for creating any other template. Keep in mind that the user won't have access to any boiler plate text or styles, so minimize these items.

One example of a procedure that might be better placed in a global template than in a standard template is one that gives you a standard messaging interface. In Hour 22, "Adding Help," you were introduced to the Office Assistant and how to manipulate it with VBA. If you have used the Office Assistant for any length of time, you may have noticed that, if it is visible, messages are shown in a balloon with the Assistant. If the Assistant isn't visible, these messages are shown in a message box.

In VBA, that display must be managed manually. You can create a function as shown in Listing 23.1 to display the message in the appropriate format.

LISTING 23.1   The GenMessage Function

```
1: Public Function GenMessage(strMessage As String, strTitle As String, _
2:     lIcon As Long, lButtons As Long, lMode As Long) As Long
3: '   This function displays a message in a Msgbox or with the Assistant
4: '   depending on whether the Assistant is visible.
5:     If Assistant.Visible = True Then
```

```
 6:        Dim objBalloon As Balloon
 7:        Set objBalloon = Assistant.NewBalloon
 8:        With objBalloon
 9:            .Heading = strTitle
10:            .Text = strMessage
11:            .Icon = lIcon
12:            .Button = lButtons
13:            .Mode = lMode
14:        End With
15:        GenMessage = objBalloon.Show
16:    Else
17:        Select Case lIcon
18:            Case msoIconAlert, msoIconAlertCritical
19:                lIcon = vbExclamation
20:            Case msoIconAlertInfo, msoIconAlertTip
21:                lIcon = vbInformation
22:            Case msoIconAlertQuery
23:                lIcon = vbQuestion
24:            Case msoIconAlertWarning
25:                lIcon = vbCritical
26:            Case msoIconNone
27:                'no action needed, they match.
28:        End Select
29:        Select Case lButtons
30:            Case msoButtonSetAbortRetryIgnore
31:                lButtons = vbAbortRetryIgnore
32:            Case msoButtonSetOK
33:                lButtons = vbOKOnly
34:            Case msoButtonSetOkCancel
35:                lButtons = vbOKCancel
36:            Case msoButtonSetRetryCancel
37:                lButtons = vbRetryCancel
38:            Case msoButtonSetYesNo
39:                lButtons = vbYesNo
40:            Case msoButtonSetYesNoCancel
41:                lButtons = vbYesNoCancel
42:            Case Else
43:                GenMessage = 16
44:                Exit Function
45:        End Select
46:        lMode = vbApplicationModal
47:        Dim lTempMessage As Long
48:        lTempMessage = MsgBox(strMessage, _
49:            lButtons + lIcon + lMode, strTitle)
50:        Select Case lTempMessage
51:            Case vbAbort
52:                GenMessage = msoBalloonButtonAbort
53:            Case vbCancel
54:                GenMessage = msoBalloonButtonCancel
```

continues

23

LISTING 23.1   continued

```
55:              Case vbIgnore
56:                  GenMessage = msoBalloonButtonIgnore
57:              Case vbNo
58:                  GenMessage = msoBalloonButtonNo
59:              Case vbOK
60:                  GenMessage = msoBalloonButtonOK
61:              Case vbRetry
62:                  GenMessage = msoBalloonButtonRetry
63:              Case vbYes
64:                  GenMessage = msoBalloonButtonYes
65:          End Select
66:      End If
67: End Function
```

ANALYSIS   The creation of a general message handler is trickier than it seems because there isn't an exact match between components for the Assistant's `Balloon` object and the arguments for the `MsgBox` function.

Lines 1–2 declare the function in your code. This function is expecting five arguments. The `strMessage` and `strTitle` are string for the message and the title of the message box or balloon. The `lIcon`, `lButtons`, and `lMode` control the appearance and behavior of the message box or balloon.

Line 5 sets up the If structure to determine which way the message will be displayed. It tests the Assistant's `Visible` property. If it is `True`, a balloon for the Assistant will display the message.

Lines 7–8 declare a `balloon` object and set it to equal to the `NewBalloon`. Lines 8–14 use a `With` structure to set up the balloon. Line 15 displays the message setting the result up as the name of the function. Line 16 is the `Else` statement to indicate what lines should be executed if the Assistant isn't visible.

When you create a general message handler, there are some problems to overcome because the Assistant's `Balloon` object supports so many more settings and returns different values than the `MsgBox` function. The first difference is in the icons that can be displayed. The `Balloon` object has seven types of icons that can be displayed, whereas the `MsgBox` function only has four. Lines 17–28 use a `Select Case` structure to reset the `lIcon` argument with one of the icon constants for the `MsgBox` function.

Lines 29–45 complete the same translation for the button constants. You will notice that lines 42–44 constitute the `Case Else` clause. There are fourteen button combinations with the `Balloon` object compared to the six button combinations for the `MsgBox` function. The balloon also has other combinations to enable the balloons to function as a wizard.

Line 43 sets the function equal to 16 which isn't one of the valid return values for either the balloon object or the MsgBox function. This means that you will have to deal with the instance of this message when you call this function.

Line 46 sets the MsgBox mode to be application modal because there are no matches except Modal for the operation of both. Lines 48–49 set the name of the function equal to the MsgBox function using these arguments.

Lines 50–65 convert the return code from the MsgBox to one of the codes for the Balloon object so that you only have to test for one set of values when you call this function. The template is ready to be attached unless you want to add protection against modification.

Naming and Protecting the Template Project

When you are creating a template to be used as global template, make sure that it can be identified in your code. By default, all templates begin with a name of TemplateProject. This can cause problems when you begin working with global templates. You want to make sure that each template has a unique identifier and that you have changed each template's name.

Although it isn't required, you may find it convenient to name the Template Project the same as the filename, except don't include any spaces. If you don't change the name, you will receive an error message when you attempt to reference the template in your code.

Also make sure that the template is safe from changes. Earlier in this hour, you saw that an attached template's code couldn't be edited. That will stop most users from attempting to change your code, but not all. Some will open the template directly to make changes.

To guard against the more creative users, you can protect any module. With any module, whether it is in an attached template or a standard template, the code can be protected against changes without harming the function of the template. With a few simple settings, you can name and protect a project:

1. Remove the attached template using the Templates and Add-ins dialog.
2. Open the Visual Basic Editor.
3. Right-click on the template you want to protect, such as Hour23.Dot.
4. Select TemplateProject Properties to display the TemplateProject—Project Properties dialog as shown in Figure 23.5.

23

FIGURE 23.5

FIGURE 23.5

The template project properties can be edited with this dialog.

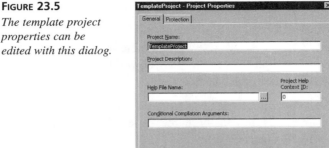

5. Change the name to Hour23 and select the Protection tab as shown in Figure 23.6.

FIGURE 23.6

The Protection tab lets you set a password to enable the user to edit the code.

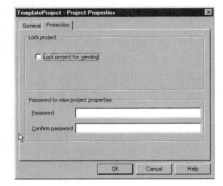

6. Select the Lock Project from Viewing check box.

7. Type a Password for Viewing and type the same password to verify.

8. Save and close the template.

The project is now protected from viewing without the password specified. Now if you open the template and it isn't attached as a global template, you must enter the password as shown in Figure 23.7 when you attempt to edit the project.

After you have created the template and, if necessary, protected the project, the template is ready to be used as a global template. You must determine when it is needed and load the template at that time.

FIGURE 23.7

*When you have pro-
tected the project,
users must enter the
password before they
can even view its
objects.*

Connecting a Global Template

After the template is created, you need to create a connection to it. To minimize the overhead with Word, a global template is attached on a session-by-session basis. Word has no
memory of what was in use in the last session. If there is a global template you use every
time you work with Word, the best solution is to place it in the startup folder for Office.
With a standard installation, this folder is C:\Program Files\Microsoft Office\Office\Startup.

If a global template is placed in this folder, it will automatically be loaded every time
you launch Word. If there are global templates that aren't needed every time, or you just
want to make sure that the template is loaded before you attempt to use any of its functions, you must learn how to work with global templates in VBA.

Verifying and Loading a Global Template

One good safety precaution with global templates is to make sure the template is loaded
before you begin calling its objects. This can be accomplished by working with the
AddIns collection and each add-in's Installed property.

Earlier in this hour, you created a template to store the GenMessage function, and you
may have named it Hour23.Dot. If you want to make sure that global template is
attached when you are working with another template like Hour23Use.Dot, complete
these steps:

1. Create a new template and save it as Hour23Use.Dot.

2. Open the Visual Basic Editor.

3. Right-click on the Hour23Use.Dot template and select Insert, Module.

4. Add the procedure shown in Listing 23.2 to the module.

5. Save and close the template.

6. Create a new document on this template.

LISTING 23.2 The AutoExec Procedure

```
 1: Sub AutoExec()
 2:     On Error GoTo GlobalError
 3:     AddIns
      ➥("c:\Windows\Application Data\Microsoft\Templates
      ➥\Hour23.dot").Installed = True
 4:     Exit Sub
 5: GlobalError:
 6:     Select Case Err.Number
 7:         Case 5941   'Template Not in Collection
 8:         AddIns.Add _
 9:             "c:\Windows\Application Data\Microsoft\Templates\Hour23.dot", _
10:             True
11:         If Err.Number = 5180 Then   'File doesn't exist.
12:             MsgBox "Unable to locate the Hour23 template." & _
13:                 "Please verify it is in your default template " & _
14:                 "directory and try opening this document again.", _
15:                 vbInformation, "Missing Global Template"
16:             Exit Sub
17:         End If
18:     End Select
19: End Sub
```

ANALYSIS This procedure executes when a new document is created based on the template or as a document created with this template is opened. It checks the global template to make sure it is attached.

Line 2 sets up error handling because there are two situations in which you can encounter problems. The first situation occurs if the template isn't listed and the second if the file doesn't exist in the specified folder.

Line 3 attempts to install the template. You are using the AddIns collection that lists all registered global templates. A template becomes registered the first time it is attached. You indicate which template by using its path and filename. Line 3 also sets the template's Installed property to True. If the template has been registered already, all requirements have been met, so line 4 exits the procedure.

If the template hasn't been added to the AddIns collection, an error will be generated. Line 5 is the line label for the error handler, and line 6 begins the Select Case structure to check the error number.

Line 7 tests for the first error number, 5941. This error number means that the item referenced isn't a part of the collection. In that case, the template hasn't been registered.

Lines 8–10 use the Add method to register the template in the collection. It requires two arguments. The first is the path and filename. The second is True indicating that you want to install it as you add it.

Lines 11–17 tackle another problem that might occur. It is possible that template can't be added because it doesn't exist on the drive. In that case, another error number, 5180 occurs. This uses inline error handling to inform the user that the template doesn't exist. You can, if you want, close the document to minimize the potential for additional problems if a user attempts to use any of the template's project.

> You need to make sure that you have the template attached before you proceed with the rest of this hour.

Using the Template

After the template is attached, you can begin using the procedures. In this case, you have created a function for message processing. To call procedures and functions from one of the global templates, you must establish a reference to it and then add your code.

Without a reference, your code won't compile. It will generate an error telling you that the function or procedure isn't recognized. To establish a reference, select Tools, References, and select Hour23 from the list.

After the reference is set, you can use its procedures from your code in this template. To test the GenMessage function, you can add the procedure listed in Listing 23.3.

LISTING 23.3   The MessageTest Procedure

```
1: Sub MessageTest()
2:     Dim lReturn As Long
3:     lReturn = GenMessage("Do you wish to insert the Title?", _
4:         "Add Title", msoIconAlertQuery, msoButtonSetYesNo, msoModeModal)
5:     If lReturn = msoBalloonButtonYes Then _
6:         Selection.TypeText "My Title"
7: End Sub
```

ANALYSIS   Line 2 sets up the return variable for the value that is received from the function. Line 3–4 use the GenMessage function from the global template to show the message to the user. Notice that the last three arguments are sent with the Assistant's balloon constants to make it easier to read.

On lines 5–6, the value returned is tested and if it is yes, then text is entered into the document. You need to execute this procedure with and without the Assistant to see the balloon and the message box.

Summary

In this hour, you have explored the value of global templates. You have learned that if you only need to share procedures or user forms with other users, you can create a global template.

You learned that the Normal template is the base template for all of the work you do, but it might not be the best place to store procedures that need to be shared. You might want to consider a global template instead. It makes maintaining your code much easier.

If you decide that a global template is the approach you want to take, you have to complete two steps: prepare the template and attach it when you want to use it.

Q&A

Q Are Word templates the only thing you can attach to Word?

A No, templates aren't the only files you can attach to Word. You can also attach other add-ins. You can work with add-ins created with Excel or PowerPoint or any dynamic link library (DLL) that can be manipulated with VBA.

Q Can I create my own DLLs?

A Yes, you can create your own DLLs. You can create your own Project as shown in this hour, and then you can use the `MakeCompiledFile` method for Visual Basic to compile it.

Workshop

Here are some questions and exercises to help you review the material covered in this hour. The answers to the quiz questions can be found in Appendix A, "Quiz Answers."

Quiz

1. What are the three benefits of using a global template?
2. Why is it important to rename the `TemplateProject` when you are developing a global template?

3. What is the problem if I enter the name of a procedure in a global template in my code and a message states that my procedure won't compile because it isn't defined?

Exercises

1. Create a global template with two functions to get the first and last days of a month. Modify the template created for Hour 21, "Working with Microsoft Outlook, the Internet, and Windows," to retrieve appointments to use these procedures.

2. Evaluate your automation checklist to see where you are going to need global templates.

23

HOUR 24

Creating a Wizard

In several of the hours in this book, you have used Microsoft Word wizards, such as the Memo Wizard, to generate a starting point for a document. In this hour, you will examine what makes up a wizard and how to create one of your own.

The highlights of this hour include

- Running wizards
- Examining a wizard
- Planning a custom wizard
- Developing your own wizard

Running Wizards

If you hadn't discovered it before picking up this book, Microsoft provided many templates to assist with document creation. When you select File, New to display the New dialog, you get a list of possible document types to choose from. There are even more possibilities out there on the Internet. On some of the tabs in the New dialog, such as the Memos tab (see Figure 24.1), there are two choices shown—a template icon and a wizard icon.

FIGURE **24.1**

The Memos tab offers both templates and wizards.

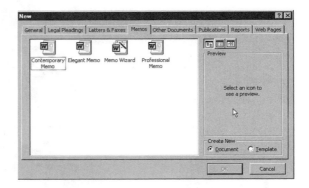

FIGURE **24.1**

The Memos tab offers both templates and wizards.

In Hour 1, "Introducing Automation Fundamentals," you explored the differences between these two types of methods for creating new documents: The templates give you a framework for the document, and the wizards ask a series of questions to fill in part of the new document for you.

If you select the Contemporary Memo template, a new document is created as shown in Figure 24.2. This document has many fields where information must be filled in.

FIGURE **24.2**

The contemporary memo has many fields that require information to be filled in.

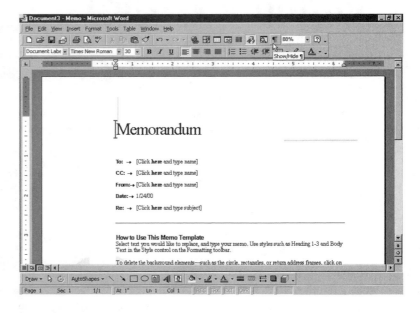

If the user selects the Memo Wizard, the process of creating a memo is much more directed. The Memo Wizard creates a new document and displays a user form, which prompts the user for information, as shown in Figure 24.3.

FIGURE 24.3

The Memo Wizard asks the user for information that will complete the memo.

The Memo Wizard has a flashy format for a user interface. It asks for the style, title, heading, recipients, closing, and header and footer information, and then it creates the memo with far fewer fields that must be filled in manually than does the template. It even pulls up the Assistant to help with completing the memo.

There are many wizards available to meet your document-creation needs. Another wizard that you examined in this book is the Letter Wizard (see Figure 24.4). When you select it, this wizard uses the same process as did the Memo Wizard—this time helping you complete a letter. There are several steps prompting you for information to generate the document.

FIGURE 24.4

The Letter Wizard also prompts for information.

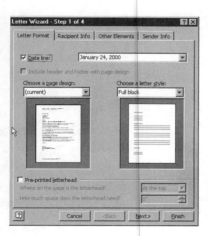

In both cases, the user is asked for information with a tab or page. After all the questions are answered, the document is created using the information provided. The user doesn't have to make any decisions about what information must be completed. The questions take care of placement.

24

Examining a Wizard

When you work with a wizard, you are not working with a special part of Word. A wizard is really only another template with its extension changed to display the special icon. It is, however, a more complex template than most. To get a better idea of what makes up a wizard, look at the Memo Wizard:

1. Select the Open icon from the toolbar.

2. Select Document Templates from the File Type list. You automatically move to the templates folder specified in your File Locations options, but the Microsoft templates won't be placed there.

3. Move to the main template folder. For a default installation, it is C:\Program Files\Microsoft Office\Office\1033.

4. Change the File Type to All Files to view the wizards as well as the templates.

5. Double-click on the Memo Wizard to open it.

When it opens, the document itself shows nothing but a blank page. It is a document like any other. What makes this a wizard can only be seen in the Visual Basic Editor. If you open the Visual Basic Editor and look in the Project Explorer (see Figure 24.5), you will see the objects that make this a wizard.

FIGURE 24.5

The Memo Wizard project uses many objects to get information from the user.

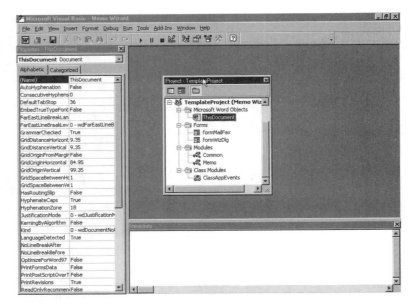

The wizard uses the Word objects, two forms, two standard modules and one class module to create the user interface shown when a new document is created. Don't let the number of objects shown in this wizard frighten you. In earlier hours, you learned all the skills you need to create a wizard of your own.

The first element that makes this a wizard instead of a plain template is the Word object, `ThisDocument`. If you double-click on it to open the Code window, you see two event procedures. The `Document_New` event is the first element. When a new document is created, the user isn't left to his own devices. The `StartWizard` procedure is launched.

If you open the Common module and use the Procedures list to select the `StartWizard` procedure, you see that `StartWizard` calls several procedures to set up the wizard for use. Towards the bottom of the procedure, you see the second element that makes this a wizard. It displays a user form, `formWizdlg` (see Figure 24.6), enabling the user to make choices.

24

FIGURE 24.6

The `formWizdlg` user form is more complex than those you have created to date.

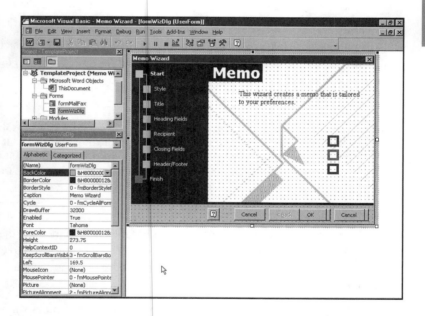

This form may look complicated, but it is constructed in the same way as the one you created earlier. If you click on the black background, you see that the background is an `Image` control when you look at the Properties window. If you click on one of the choices on the left, you will see that each choice is a label.

You might be confused by the fact that several controls appear to be stacked on each other. This is especially evident when you look at the command buttons. When you develop your wizard, you can use separate controls with different procedures and use the `Visible` property to control which buttons can be accessed at one point of the process. You can also use one set of buttons and change the `Caption` property to indicate function and use a `Select Case` structure to test the `Caption` to indicate what statements to execute.

This dialog also uses a control you haven't worked with yet. If you click on the white area where the page graphic is shown, you will see that this control isn't an image. It is the `Page` control.

When you want to have multiple sets of questions for the user, you can use two approaches. You can use the Page control. If you click on the object list in the Properties window, you are looking at Page0. There are actually eight pages numbered 0 to 7 in the Page control. As you select each one of them from the list, you see each step for creating a memo has its own page.

Another alternative is a Tab control. Instead of separate pages, this control has a tab for each step of the process, as shown in the Letter Wizard. Both the Page and Tab controls give you separate work areas for input.

If you like the appearance of the Memo Wizard, Microsoft has a white paper titled, "Creating Wizards in Microsoft Office 97." It comes with a blank version of this form and the steps on how to use it to create your own wizard. You can download it from the Microsoft Office Developer's Web site at http://www.microsoft.com/officedev/.

This wizard uses a special type of module, called a class module, that you have not yet worked with. A class module is a code module that enables you to create your own custom objects with events, properties, and methods. This class module creates three events for this wizard.

Creating class modules isn't a requirement for wizards, but class modules can come in handy as your code becomes more complex. Creating class modules is not within the scope of this book.

Planning a Custom Wizard

To get an idea of what is involved in creating wizards, you will now create a wizard to solve some problems that occurred in an earlier example. In Hour 14, "Working with Large Documents," you created the Proposal Sample template to look at how you could work with larger documents, The `DocumentCompletion` procedure gathered information using the `InputBox` and `Msgbox` functions. Creating a wizard is a better option than these because there are so many prompts required.

Determining What Information Is Needed

The `DocumentCompletion` procedure only needs five answers to automatically complete aspects of the document. It is easy to move too fast with the `InputBox`, however, and miss one of the questions. Consider a more complex example. You want to automate the creation of response letters for phone calls to an Organizational Specialist firm.

You need the customer's name, address, what he called about, and what information to include in his marketing package. What seems to be four questions actually breaks down to many more. If you are completing a standard letter, you want to have a greeting such as, "Dear Mr. Smith." Doing this requires that the caller's name to be broken down into its components. You might also want to break down the address if you want to add it to a mail merge source such as a table, Excel workbook, or Access Database. You can also indicate in the letter if the person called about a home or office problem.

Determining the Steps

After you have isolated all the information, determine how that information can be broken down in your wizard. For example, you can put all the mailing information in one step and the call-specific information in a second step.

You can separate the call information from the document components if desired. Each wizard you create will have a different number of steps. In this case, you will work with three steps, to give you a chance to see the code involved in managing the form with a multiple-step wizard.

Developing Your Wizard

After you have determined what steps you need and the information necessary for each step, you can begin automating your wizard. As in the previous examples of user forms, you will design the form, and then you will add the code to automate the form.

24

Designing Your Form

When you have compiled your list of steps and the information required to automate a document, turn it into a user form. You can use any of the controls shown in Hour 17, "Working with User Forms," to represent the information required, but you will use a special control to create your steps.

When you add a user form to your project, the Visual Basic Editor displays the Toolbox. One of the standard controls is the MultiPage control. It is a single control that can act as a container for other controls. These controls can be placed on separate pages as needed.

If you prefer, you can open Hour24, which is available from the companion Web site.

Before you can begin adding controls to the MultiPage control, place it on the form and set its properties. To set up the MultiPage control for your wizard, complete these steps:

1. Create a new Template in Microsoft Word.
2. Save the template as Marketing Letter.
3. Open the Visual Basic Editor.
4. Right-click on the project in the Project Explorer and select Insert, User Form.
5. Set the form's Name property as frmResponse and its Caption to Marketing Letter Wizard.
6. Select the MultiPage control (the icon that resembles tabbed index cards) from the Toolbox.
7. Point to the upper-left corner of the form, hold down the left mouse button, and drag the control on the form as shown in Figure 24.7.

When the MultiPage control is placed on the form, it has two pages as the default. If you click on the Page2 tab, you will see the second page come to the front. If you click on Page1, that page will move to the front of the stack.

Before you can begin adding other controls, set up the MultiPage control itself by determining its properties. This is trickier than it might seem. As you just clicked on Page1, notice the selected object in the Object list of the Properties window is Page 1. You will have to click on the border of the control to select the entire control, or select the entire control from the Object list in the Properties window.

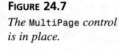

FIGURE 24.7

The MultiPage *control is in place.*

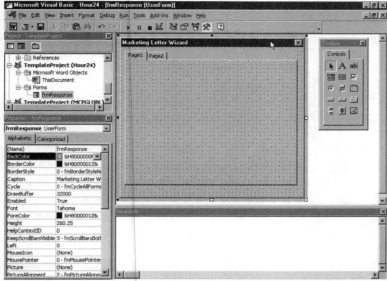

You should set the Name property, such as mpWizard, to reference the control in your code. You can also alter its appearance with properties. The MultiRow property indicates whether the tabs will move to a second row if there isn't room to display them in the first row. The Style property controls what types of tabs are shown, if any. In the Memo Wizard, no tabs were used. There is also a TabOrientation property. This controls where each tab is placed. A tab can be on top, at one of the sides, or on the bottom of the control.

After the MultiPage control properties are set, you can begin to set up the pages. Each page is treated separately in the wizard, but they are also part of a group or collection.

Notice that the Name property indicates the tab's placement in the sequence, and the Caption mirrors that. You might want to leave the Name alone and only change the Caption. For Page1, you can change the Caption to Recipient Information. Notice that this page is referenced by an Index number of 0.

There are also some properties to control the page's appearance and behavior. If desired, you can add a picture as a background. You can also add an effect when the user moves to another page with the TransitionEffect property.

After you have set the properties for Page1, set them for Page2. In this case, change the Caption to Call Information.

24

Now you have a problem. You have established that this wizard has three steps, but you just ran out of pages. To add a page, you point to the Caller Information tab, right-click, and select New Page from the menu. You can change its Caption to Include.

If you prefer to work with a completed form that is ready for code, you can import the frmResponse.frm file from the companion Web site.

After the pages are in place and their properties are set, you add the controls for each page. For this example, you are going to use labels, text boxes and check boxes for the interface. You can use any of the other controls to complete the interface. For the text boxes, change the Name property for each. Set the Caption property for the labels; for the check box, set both Name and Caption properties. See Figures 24.8, 24.9, and 24.10 for the layout of these pages. Table 24.1 shows the property settings.

FIGURE 24.8

The Recipient Information is the first page in the wizard.

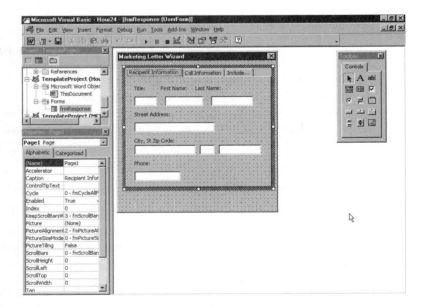

FIGURE 24.9

The Call Information fills in some of the content of the letter.

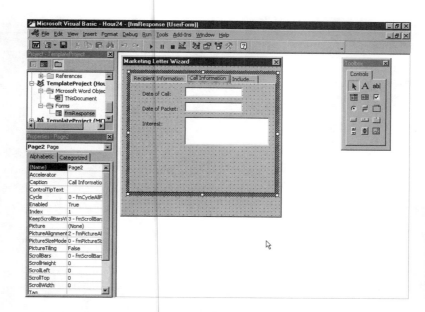

FIGURE 24.10

The Include tab shows what text will be included in the document.

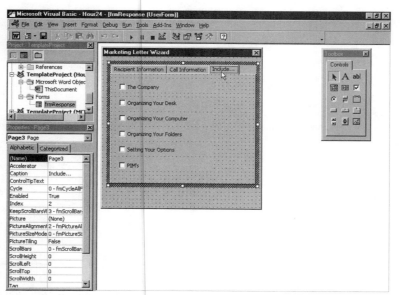

24

TABLE 24.1 The Properties for the Wizard Controls

Type of Control	Name	Caption
Page1 Controls		
8 Labels		Title
		First Name
		Last Name
		Address
		City
		State
		Zip Code
		Phone
8 Text boxes	txtTitle	
	txtFirst	
	txtLast	
	TxtAddress	
	TxtCity	
	TxtState	
	TxtZipCode	
	txtPhone	
Page2 Controls		
3 Labels		Date of Call
		Date of Packet
		Interest
3 Text Boxes	txtCallDate	
	txtDate	
	txtInterest	
Page3 Controls		
6 Check boxes	chkCompany	The Company
	chkDesk	Organizing Your Desk
	chkComputer	Organizing Your Computer
	chkFolders	Organizing Your Folders
	chkOptions	Setting Your Options
	chkPIMs	PIMs

In addition to the controls created to solicit information, you also need four command buttons to assist with navigation. They are placed below the MultiPage control. You need Cancel, Back, Next, and Finish buttons. Use the captions with cmd in front as their names. You also need to set the Cancel property to True for the Cancel button and the Default button to True for Finish. When all the controls are in place, the form appears as shown in Figure 24.11.

FIGURE 24.11

The form shows the command buttons below the page.

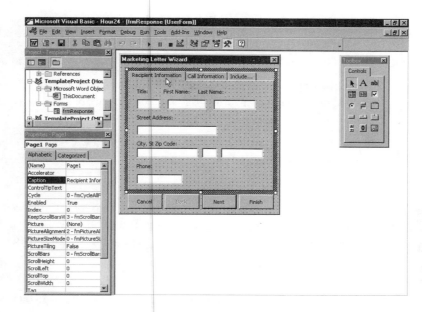

If you set the `Accelerator` property for a control, you can underline a character in the caption to be activated by the Alt key plus a chosen accelerator.

Developing the VBA to Generate the Document

After the interface is designed, you can begin adding code. Add code to start the wizard, automate the completion of pages, and use the data to complete the document.

Start the Wizard

The first step is to add code that will start the wizard as the new document is created. Do this with an event procedure. To create the New event, complete these steps:

1. Double-click on the `ThisDocument` object in the Project Explorer.
2. Select Document from the object list to automatically create the New event.
3. Add the following code:

   ```
   frmResponse.Show
   ```

That one line of code will display the user form when a new document is created. The user can then begin entering the data to complete the form.

Navigating Between Pages

When the user is completing the form, he will need to move between the pages. Using the tabs is one method, but many wizards have command buttons to make the task easier.

To provide functionality to the command buttons, add code. The Cancel button is first. It must be close to the user form without taking any action. This is accomplished with the Unload method.

If you right-click on the Cancel button and select View Code, the Visual Basic Editor will create the Click event and you can add:

```
Unload frmResponse
```

In many circumstances, especially when there is a lot of information, you might want to use the MsgBox to verify closing the dialog. You set up a Boolean variable and set it to True as a user enters data. You can test it and use the MsgBox only if it returns True.

The second two buttons are very much alike. One moves the user to the next page, and the other moves the user to the previous page. When you are at the first page, you can't move to the previous page, and when you are on the last page you can't move to the next page. You can declare a module level variable to keep track of the current page and create Click events for each button to tackle that navigation.

1. Press Ctrl+Home to get to the top of the module and enter this declaration:
   ```
   Private bytSelectedPage as Byte
   ```

2. Select the User Form from the object list and select Initialize Event from the procedures list. Add this line of code to initialize the new variable.
   ```
   BytSelectedPage = 0
   ```

3. Select cmdBack from the object list and complete the Click event as shown below:
   ```
   Private Sub cmdBack_Click()
       mpWizard.Value = bytSelectedPage - 1
       bytSelectedPage = bytSelectedPage - 1
       If bytSelectedPage = 0 Then cmdBack.Enabled = False
       If bytSelectedPage < 2 Then cmdNext.Enabled = True
   End Sub
   ```

4. Select cmdNext and complete the Click event as shown below:
   ```
   Private Sub cmdNext_Click()
       mpWizard.Value = bytSelectedPage + 1
       bytSelectedPage = bytSelectedPage + 1
       If bytSelectedPage > 0 Then cmdBack.Enabled = True
       If bytSelectedPage = 2 Then cmdNext.Enabled = False
   End Sub
   ```

The variable, bytSelectedPage is initialized as 0. This is because you are on the first page of the control, and its index number is 0. Then the cmdBack_Click event sets the value of the MultiPage control to one number lower and adjusts the variable. After the variable is adjusted, it is tested with an If statement to determine if the Enabled property must be adjusted for the current page.

The Next button is identical, except that you add to the variable, and the test is reversed. You need to enable the Back button when the page is greater than 0.

Creating the Document

The last button that requires code is the Finish button. It is the one that does the work of creating the document. It determines if any prompts necessary to have the user complete the form are missing. When all the information is present, it fills in the document. The cmdFinish_Click event is shown in Listing 24.1.

LISTING 24.1   The cmFinish_Click Event

```
 1: Private Sub cmdFinish_Click()
 2: '    Test the Data
 3:      StatusBar = "Verifying Data"
 4:      Dim bDataError As Boolean
 5:      If Len(txtTitle) = 0 Then bDataError = True
 6:      If Len(txtFirst) = 0 Then bDataError = True
 7:      If Len(txtLast) = 0 Then bDataError = True
 8:      If Len(txtAddress) = 0 Then bDataError = True
 9:      If Len(txtCity) = 0 Then bDataError = True
10:      If Len(txtState) = 0 Then bDataError = True
11:      If Len(txtzipcode) = 0 Then bDataError = True
12:      If Len(txtPhone) = 0 Then bDataError = True
13:      If bDataError = True Then
14:          mpWizard.Value = 0
15:          bytSelectedPage = 0
16:          cmdBack.Enabled = False
17:          cmdNext.Enabled = True
18:          MsgBox "You haven't completed your recipient information.", _
19:          vbInformation, "Missing Data"
20:          Exit Sub
21:      End If
22:      If Len(txtCallDate) = 0 Then bDataError = True
23:      If Len(txtDate) = 0 Then bDataError = True
24:      If Len(txtInterest) = 0 Then bDataError = True
25:      If bDataError = True Then
26:          mpWizard.Value = 1
27:          bytSelectedPage = 1
28:          cmdBack.Enabled = True
```

continues

LISTING 24.1   continued

```
29:          cmdNext.Enabled = True
30:          MsgBox "You haven't completed your Call information.", _
31:          vbInformation, "Missing Data"
32:          Exit Sub
33:      End If
34:      If chkCompany.Value = True Or chkDesk.Value = True Or _
35:          chkComputer.Value = True Or chkFolders.Value = True Or _
36:          chkOptions.Value = True Or chkPIMS.Value = True Then
37:          bDataError = False
38:      Else
39:          bDataError = True
40:      End If
41:      If bDataError = True Then
42:          mpWizard.Value = 2
43:          bytSelectedPage = 2
44:          cmdBack.Enabled = True
45:          cmdNext.Enabled = False
46:          MsgBox "You haven't completed your Include Information.", _
47:          vbInformation, "Missing Data"
48:          Exit Sub
49:      End If
50:
51: '    Begin Letter Format
52:      On Error GoTo WizardError
53:      frmResponse.Hide
54:      StatusBar = "Beginning Letter Format..."
55:      Application.ScreenUpdating = False
56:      Selection.EndKey Unit:=wdStory
57:      Selection.TypeText Text:=txtDate
58:      Selection.TypeParagraph
59:      Selection.TypeParagraph
60:      Selection.TypeParagraph
61:      Selection.TypeText Text:=txtTitle & " " & txtFirst & " " & txtLast
62:      Selection.TypeParagraph
63:      Selection.TypeText Text:=txtAddress
64:      Selection.TypeParagraph
65:      Selection.TypeText Text:=txtCity & ", " & txtState & " " & txtzipcode
66:      Selection.TypeParagraph
67:      Selection.TypeText Text:=txtPhone
68:      Selection.TypeParagraph
69:      Selection.TypeParagraph
70:      Selection.TypeText Text:="Dear " & txtTitle & " " & txtLast & ":"
71:      Selection.TypeParagraph
72:      Selection.TypeParagraph
73:      ActiveDocument.AttachedTemplate.AutoTextEntries("Intro") _
74:          .Insert Where:=Selection.Range
75:      Selection.TypeParagraph
76:      With ListGalleries(wdBulletGallery).ListTemplates(7).ListLevels(1)
77:          .NumberFormat = ChrW(61492)
```

```
78:            .TrailingCharacter = wdTrailingTab
79:            .NumberStyle = wdListNumberStyleBullet
80:            .NumberPosition = InchesToPoints(0.25)
81:            .Alignment = wdListLevelAlignLeft
82:            .TextPosition = InchesToPoints(0.5)
83:            .TabPosition = InchesToPoints(0.5)
84:            .ResetOnHigher = 0
85:            .StartAt = 1
86:            With .Font
87:                .Color = wdColorTeal
88:                .Size = 13
89:                .Name = "Wingdings"
90:            End With
91:        End With
92:        ListGalleries(wdBulletGallery).ListTemplates(7).Name = ""
93:        Selection.Range.ListFormat.ApplyListTemplate  ListTemplate:= _
94:            ListGalleries(wdBulletGallery).ListTemplates(7), _
95:            ContinuePreviousList:=True, ApplyTo:= _
96:            wdListApplyToWholeList, DefaultListBehavior:=wdWord9ListBehavior
97:        If chkCompany = True Then
98:            Selection.TypeText Text:=chkCompany.Caption
99:            Selection.TypeParagraph
100:        End If
101:        If chkDesk = True Then
102:            Selection.TypeText Text:=chkDesk.Caption
103:            Selection.TypeParagraph
104:        End If
105:        If chkComputer = True Then
106:            Selection.TypeText Text:=chkComputer.Caption
107:            Selection.TypeParagraph
108:        End If
109:        If chkFolders = True Then
110:            Selection.TypeText Text:=chkFolders.Caption
111:            Selection.TypeParagraph
112:        End If
113:        If chkOptions = True Then
114:            Selection.TypeText Text:=chkOptions.Caption
115:            Selection.TypeParagraph
116:        End If
117:        If chkPIMS = True Then
118:            Selection.TypeText Text:=chkPIMS.Caption
119:            Selection.TypeParagraph
120:        End If
121:        Selection.Range.ListFormat.RemoveNumbers _
122:            NumberType:=wdNumberParagraph
123:        Selection.TypeParagraph
124:        Selection.Style = ActiveDocument.Styles("Body Text")
125:        ActiveDocument.AttachedTemplate.AutoTextEntries("Close") _
126:            .Insert Where:=Selection.Range
```

continues

LISTING 24.1 continued

```
127:        Selection.TypeParagraph
128:        Selection.InsertBreak Type:=wdPageBreak
129:        ActiveDocument.Bookmarks("Focus").Range.Text = txtInterest
130:        ActiveDocument.Bookmarks("Focus2").Range.Text = txtInterest
131:        ActiveDocument.Bookmarks("CallDate").Range.Text = txtCallDate
132:        Selection.EndKey Unit:=wdStory
133:
134: '    Insert Additional Information
135:        StatusBar = "Inserting Additional Information"
136:        Dim strDir As String, strFile As String
137:        strDir = Options.DefaultFilePath(wdDocumentsPath) & "\"
138:        If chkCompany = True Then
139:            strFile = strDir & "Our Company.doc"
140:            Selection.InsertFile FileName:=strFile
141:            Selection.TypeParagraph
142:        End If
143:        If chkDesk = True Then
144:            strFile = strDir & "Organizing Your Desk.doc"
145:            Selection.InsertFile FileName:=strFile
146:            Selection.TypeParagraph
147:        End If
148:        If chkComputer = True Then
149:            strFile = strDir & "Organizing Your Computer.doc"
150:            Selection.InsertFile FileName:=strFile
151:            Selection.TypeParagraph
152:        End If
153:        If chkFolders = True Then
154:            strFile = strDir & "Organizing Your Folders"
155:            Selection.InsertFile FileName:=strFile
156:            Selection.TypeParagraph
157:        End If
158:        If chkOptions = True Then
159:            strFile = strDir & "Setting Your Options.doc"
160:            Selection.InsertFile FileName:=strFile
161:            Selection.TypeParagraph
162:        End If
163:        If chkPIMS = True Then
164:            strFile = strDir & "PIMS.Doc"
165:            Selection.InsertFile FileName:=strFile
166:        End If
167: '    Resetting the Screen
168:        Application.ScreenRefresh
169:        Application.ScreenUpdating = True
170:        MsgBox "Marketing Letter Wizard Complete.", vbInformation, _
171:            "Automation Complete"
172:        Selection.HomeKey Unit:=wdStory
173:        Unload frmResponse
174:        Exit Sub
175: WizardError:
```

```
176:    Dim strMessage As String, strTitle As String
177:    Select Case Err.Number
178:        Case 5273       'Path or File not valid
179:            strMessage = _
180:            "Please verify the Insert Files folder exists and try again."
181:            strTitle = "Invalid Folder or File Name"
182:        Case 5174       'File Couldn't be found
183:            strMessage = _
184:            "Please verify the marketing files are in the " & _
185:                "Insert Files folder."
186:            strTitle = "Missing File"
187:        Case Else
188:            strMessage = "Error " & Err.Number & "," & _
189:            Err.Description & "has occurred. Processing was halted."
190:            strTitle = "Unexpected Error"
191:    End Select
192:    Application.ScreenRefresh
193:    Application.ScreenUpdating = True
194:    MsgBox strMessage, vbOKOnly + vbExclamation, strTitle
195: End Sub
```

24

ANALYSIS After the user has entered the information for the letter, the Finish button will be clicked. The cmdFinish_Click event procedure takes all the information and creates the letter with its additional information. Creating the letter wizard is the longest procedure you have worked with in this book. The first step is on line 3. The procedure sets the StatusBar property to indicate that the procedure is testing the data.

Lines 4–21 test the information entered on the first page for the recipient information. Line 4 declares a variable to keep track of any problems with the data. Lines 5–12 use the Len function to test each text box to make sure data of some type was entered. If nothing was entered bDataError is set to True.

After all the text boxes are evaluated, the variable is tested. If any of the text boxes are empty, this variable is now True. Lines 13–21 will be executed if there is missing data. Line 14 sets the Value for the MultiPage control to 0, which sets it to the first page and resets the variable that tracks the pages. Lines 16–17 tackle which buttons should be enabled when you are on the first page. Line 18 displays a message box, and line 20 terminates the execution.

In this simple version, you are only testing to make sure something was entered. In a more sophisticated example, you might restrict the user to specific state abbreviations with a combo box, verify the zip code and phone number as valid entities, and so on.

Lines 22–33 complete the same process for the second page. Lines 34–49 complete the same task for the third page, but the logic is different. In this case, only one of the items need be included. The Or operator is used to find out if any of the check boxes have been selected. If the variable is set to False, it means one of the items was selected.

If there is an error, the process is the same. The page is selected, and a message is displayed. Then the users can make selections. When that the information is collected, the procedure is ready to complete the document beginning on line 51.

Line 52 sets up an error handler to deal with the insertion of the files. Line 53 hides the form to keep it out of the way, but in memory, as needed. The remainder of the code uses techniques you have seen in other hours to complete the marketing letter.

Line 54–55 set up the screen to keep it from flashing, and line 56 moves to the end of the document. Line 57 inserts the contents of txtDate and line 58–60 add blank lines below it.

Lines 61–72 builds the mailing address and greeting from the contents of the text boxes on the form. Line 73 inserts an AutoText entry for the introduction of the letter.

Lines 75–96 set up a bullet style and apply it to the empty paragraph. Line 75 creates a blank paragraph after the introduction, and lines 76–92 set up a new bullet style with a stack of papers. Lines 93–96 apply the bullet style.

Lines 96–120 add items to the bulleted list. This is accomplished by evaluating the Value of each check box. If the Value is True, The TypeText method is used to add the Caption of the check box to the document as a bullet.

Line 121 removes the bullet from the last paragraph that was added, and Line 123 adds a new paragraph. Line 124 changes the style back to Body Text for the next paragraph.

Line 125 inserts another AutoText entry for the letter's closing, and line 127 adds a blank line. Line 128 inserts a page break so the included information begins on a new page.

Lines 129–131 set the Text property for several bookmarks, using the contents of three of the text boxes on the form. You can fill in as many entries as needed. Line 132 moves to the end of the document.

Lines 135–166 insert the information indicated with the check boxes. Line 135 updates the status bar, and line 136 defines two variables that are required for this task. Line 137 sets the strDir variable using the DefaultFilePath property.

Lines 138–142 illustrate what happens with each check box. The check box is tested to see if it is True on line 138. If it is True, line 139 sets the strFile variable using the strDir variable and a set string with the name of the document. Line 140 uses the Insertfile method to insert the text from the specified file, and a blank line is added with line 141. Each check box is evaluated and taken care of in the same manner.

Lines 167–174 return the Word settings to normal after the run of the procedure. Line 168 uses the ScreenRefresh method to repaint the screen after all the changes. Line 169 turns the screen updating back on. Line 170 displays a message with the MsgBox statement to indicate that the procedure is complete.

Line 172 takes the user to the top of the document. Lines 173–174 unload the form and exit the procedure when the procedure executes normally. Lines 175–194 provide error handling in case there is a problem with inserting the selected files. It is identical to the error handling introduced in Hour 9, "Working with Text."

Lines 192–193 differ from the code in Hour 9. They are added to take care of the screen. Because this procedure turns off screen updating, you need to turn it back on when responding to an error. Otherwise, you will leave the user with a screen that won't move. Line 194 displays the message.

When this procedure runs, the user enters all the information in the user form, and then the procedure builds the document. When you look at the completed letter, it has many of the components added for you, as shown in Figure 24.12. You might now want to edit the letter to make it more personal, but the basic foundation is complete.

24

FIGURE 24.12

The document is already partially complete.

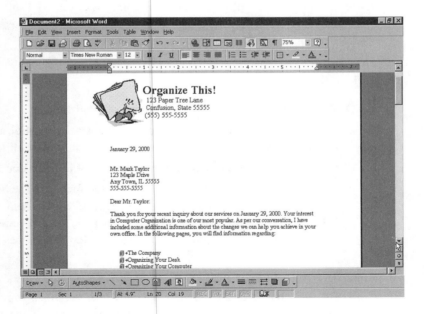

The last step is to change its extension to wiz. That will change the icon shown in the New dialog. This can be done with the File Save As command or through the Windows Explorer.

Summary

In this hour, you focused on how to create a custom wizard to build documents. You examined some of the wizards that ship with Microsoft Word—only to find that they are only templates in disguise.

To create a wizard of your own, determine what information is required to complete a document and plan the steps for your wizard. After you have a plan, you are going to use several tools you learned about in other hours.

You are going to create a user form to prompt the user for information. This can use standard controls to prompt for different types of information or steps. You also learned that there is a special control called the MultiPage control. This gives you different pages for each step.

After the form is created, you create a Document_New event to display the form as a new document is created and write the code. This code will take the user's answers to build the document using techniques you have seen throughout this book.

Q&A

Q Can you create wizards only in Microsoft Word?

A No, you can create wizards in the other Microsoft applications. The process is slightly different because templates work differently in the different applications.

Q Should you avoid the InputBox function to get information from the user?

A No, you don't have to stop using the InputBox function. The benefit of the user form approach to getting information is that it is less likely to confuse the user. When there are more than two or three questions, the user might accidentally skip one of the questions by pressing the Enter key too many times or clicking too early.

Q Why is planning a big part of creating a wizard?

A Because you are creating a more complex form here than you did in Hour 17, planning is a very important factor. You can minimize the amount of work on the form if you anticipate everything that is needed before you begin.

Q **Is using the `MultiPage` control the only way to create steps?**

A No, you can use the `TabStrip` control or separate forms.

Workshop

Here are some questions and exercises to help you review the material covered in this hour. The answers to the quiz questions can be found in Appendix A, "Quiz Answers."

Quiz

1. What property controls the appearance of the `MultiPage` control?
2. How do you add, remove, or move a page in a `MultiPage` control?
3. How do you switch between pages?

Exercises

1. Change the State text box to a combo box.
2. Add a prompt for Home or Office and plug it into the HO bookmark.
3. Evaluate your automation checklist and identify areas that could utilize a custom wizard.

24

APPENDIX A

Quiz Answers

Hour 1

1. If I want access to an automated task from more than one type of document, where is the automation saved?

   The automation needs to be placed in the Normal template or a global template.

2. If I use a custom style in a global template, but the formatting is not displayed, what is wrong?

   If you create a custom style with the same name as a style in the Normal template, the settings for the style in the Normal template will be used. Word will look for the style in the document, its attached template, and the Normal template before searching any global templates.

3. Can I include graphics in an AutoText entry?

   Yes, you can select the graphic to be included and proceed as you would with text. If you only select a graphic, you will not see a ToolTip as you type the AutoText entry's name.

4. Could the close of a letter be boilerplate text instead of an AutoText entry?

Yes, you could have the close of the letter as boilerplate text. This is a preference issue. If you want to be able to press Ctrl+End and begin typing the body of the letter, an AutoText entry is better because the close text isn't in your way.

If you add a MacroButton field for the body of the letter, the close as boilerplate text is not an issue. You would be using Ctrl+Page Down to move to the body of the letter.

Hour 2

1. Why is it a good idea to walk through the steps before recording the macro?

Walking through the steps gives you a chance to see what is involved in automating the task as well as to isolate areas where you can't use the mouse.

2. Why can't I just put all the macros in the Normal template?

Technically, you could place all the macros in your Normal template. You may experience problems with this approach. You may suffer a delay when executing these macros, if there are a lot of macros in the file. You may experience errors if the macro is expecting a specific document to be accessible.

3. What happens if I type in a name for the macro that is invalid?

The Macro Recorder will create an error. It will open the Visual Basic Editor and display a message box that displays the message Invalid procedure name. You will have to switch back to Word and begin recording again.

Hour 3

1. What is an object?

An object is a component of Microsoft Word or another application that can be manipulated in VBA.

2. What are properties, methods, and events?

A property is a characteristic of an object that can be read and in some cases changed. A method is a built-in procedure that can be called for an object. An event is an action that will affect an object.

3. Why are constants a better choice than entering the numeric settings for arguments and properties?

Instead of having to memorize the numeric setting for all the arguments and properties in VBA, you can look at the constant name. It increases the readability of your code.

4. What window displays the list of documents currently active?

The Project Explorer displays a list of documents and templates currently open or accessed.

Hour 4

1. What is a collection?

A collection is a group of objects that are alike.

2. Why are all objects a component of the `Application` object?

The `Application` object acts as the container for all the objects to control the access and provide access to the Word features from other applications.

3. Why is the `Selection` object so important in your automation?

The `Selection` object is the one that enables you to manipulate text.

Hour 5

1. Which keyword is used to declare a variable that needs to be shared between modules?

You will use the `Public` keyword.

2. If you need to use a variable in several procedures, where does it need to be declared?

To share a variable between procedures, it needs to be placed in the General Declarations for a module.

3. What does the `WeekDay` function do?

The `WeekDay` function allows you to test a date to see what day of the week it falls on. It is very useful when you want to make sure that a date isn't on a weekend.

4. Why is the `MsgBox` so valuable?

Most users are used to seeing communications from the application in a `MsgBox`. This enables you to use a predictable means of communication.

Hour 6

1. What statement needs to be in the code to disregard a character's case when evaluating it, and where does it need to be placed?

The statement is `Option Compare Text`, and it needs to be placed in the General Declarations of the module.

A

2. Which logical operator would be used if you wanted to make sure that several conditions were met before executing your code?

The And operator can be used to make sure all conditions are met before executing your code.

3. What property holds the document properties?

The BuiltInDocumentProperties stores these properties as an array. You access each individual one by indicating the index for that specific property.

4. How would the Case clause for a Select Case structure be worded to see if a value was less than or equal to 10?

Case Is <= 10

Hour 7

1. How can I increment the counter in the For...Next loop by more than one?

Include the Step keyword followed by the increment, such as For I = 0 to 100 Step 5 to count by fives.

2. How do I decide whether to place the While or Until at the top or bottom of the loop?

You have to decide if you need to execute the actions at least once. If the answer is Yes, then you will place the While or Until expression at the bottom of the loop.

3. Is there a time when the While...Wend is used?

It is unlikely. It is not as flexible as the Do...While loop because you can't test the condition after executing the actions once. You can only test the condition on entering the loop.

Hour 8

1. How can I halt the execution of my procedure for debugging?

You can add the Stop statement before the line you want to halt before executing, or you can add a breakpoint.

2. If you have the Locals window to view the values for the variables, why would you want to use the Immediate window?

The Immediate window allows you to change data as well as look at it.

3. What is the first step for error handling?

You have to initialize the error trap with the On Error statement.

Hour 9

1. What argument is needed to make sure that the formatting is inserted in the document with the text of an AutoText entry?

   PreserveFormatting needs to be set to True to insert the text and its formatting.

2. Why is error handling needed when inserting a file?

   The directory might not exist or the file might be deleted. You do not want to end up in the Visual Basic Editor if one of these issues occur.

3. How would you access the Company property (another one of the Document properties) and place it in the document?

   The following line of code:

   ```
   Selection.Fields.Add Range:=Selection.Range, Type:=wdFieldCompany
   ```

4. How would you access the Checked by property (another one of the custom properties) and place it in the document?

   The following line of code:

   ```
   Selection.Fields.Add Range:=Selection.Range, Type:=wdFieldEmpty, Text:= _
   "DOCPROPERTY ""CheckedBy"" "
   ```

Hour 10

1. To change the indention of the first line of a paragraph, what properties do you need to set?

   You need to set both the LeftIndent and FirstLineIndent properties.

2. What method is used to clear the tab stops for a selection?

   The ClearAll method for the TabStops collection is used.

3. What collection stores the different numbering and bullet styles?

   The ListGalleries collections stores the different styles.

Hour 11

1. How can you add a page border to the first page only?

   Create a section for the first page and then only apply the page border to that section.

A

2. How would you add a comment to the document?

You would use the `Add` method to create add a comment to the document and the `TypeText` method to add the comment text. You would also need to close the comments view when you were finished, such as

```
Selection.Comments.Add Range:=Selection.Range
Selection.TypeText Text:= _
    "This illustrates how to add a comment."
ActiveWindow.ActivePane.Close
```

Hour 12

1. What is the advantage of setting the `NumRows` argument as 1 for the `Add` method when inserting a table?

The advantage is that choosing 1 eliminates the guesswork about the number of rows needed. As you add text in the cells and tab to the next cell, rows will be added as needed.

If you are going to have set column headings, you might consider using 2 as the setting. This would enable you to format the headings without disturbing the formatting of the rest of the cell entries.

2. Where are columns inserted?

Unlike rows, which are inserted by several methods, there is only one method for inserting columns: `InsertColumnsRight`. The new column will be created to the right of the insertion point.

3. Can you save time in formatting when converting text to a table?

Yes. You can specify an `AutoFormat` style when you are using the `ConvertToTable` method with the `Format` argument. This can be set with the built-in constants for the desired style.

Hour 13

1. What is the method for inserting pictures into your document?

The `AddPicture` method.

2. What is the difference between placing the picture in the `Shapes` collection or `InlineShapes` collection with the `AddPicture` method?

The difference has to do with which layer the picture is placed in. The `InlineShapes` collection contains those objects that are placed in the text layer. They are treated as characters and will wrap as any text element.

The Shapes collections is more flexible. It stores the object placed in the drawing layer of the document. This enables you to move the picture in relation to the page instead of acting as part of the text. It also provides more formatting options.

3. Why are object variables so important when you are working with shapes?

They help you identify the shape after it is created so that you can adjust its formatting properties. They also assist with managing shapes in the collection.

Hour 14

1. What property stores the text in a bookmark?

The Bookmark has a Range that has the selected text within the bookmark. Its text property stores the contents.

2. How do you create columns with different widths?

You set up the first column using the TextColumn object for the PageSetUp object for the document. Then you use the Add method to add additional columns.

3. Why is the Bookmarks collections Exists method important?

It allows for error handling. Before you try to use the contents of a bookmark, the Exists property can be checked to make sure that the bookmark referenced is a part of the document.

4. Why would you use the MarkEntry method for inserting an index item instead of a standard field?

It gives you a greater control over formatting the item.

Hour 15

1. Why is it important to change Bookmark text for a field?

If you change the bookmark using the same structure you are using elsewhere with automation, it will make it easier to write code to use the field.

2. How do you access the contents of a field with VBA?

You are going to use the Result property for the field in the FormFields collection for the document. If you are working with the active document, the syntax is

```
Activedocument.FormFields("fieldbookmark").Result
```

This approach will work except with the check box. You will use the CheckBox object's Value property.

A

3. What collection do you manipulate when you want to change a drop-down list's choices?

A drop-down list has a DropDown property that references its DropDown object. You will use its ListEntries collection.

4. Why wasn't a fixed path added for the Open method in lines 6–14 of Listing 15.2?

If you are creating a form to be used by more than one user across the network, you may not have a set path that can be used. Here you see how to use one of the file locations from the user's options.

Hour 16

1. What procedures automatically execute when a document is opened?

If code exists for the following procedures, they will be executed in the following order: the Deactivate event for the current document, the Activate for the new window, the Change event to indicate you have switched to a different document, the Open event, and finally the AutoOpen macro.

2. What is the benefit of using event procedures compared to auto macros?

The event procedures are more flexible for managing events with the same name within the operating environment. It will execute the one closest to the document and then move on to the next file. It checks the document, its template, the Normal template, and finally, any global templates.

Hour 17

1. What property identifies a control on a form?

The Caption property provides a description of a control.

2. What is the difference between a Label and a TextBox?

The TextBox can accept entry. The Label is used only for informational purposes.

3. What method is used to populate a ComboBox or ListBox?

The AddItem method.

4. What is the Default property for a CommandButton?

If the Default property is set to True, the CommandButton can be activated with the Enter key.

Hour 18

1. What property can be used as the ReturnAddress for the sender?

   You can use the application's UserAddress property.

2. If you want to get rid of a country or add a company name when you use the GetAddress method, what should you do?

   If you want to modify the template for information for the insertion of the address, you need to create an AutoText entry called AddressProperties. For more information concerning the contents of the AutoText entry, look up the GetAddress method in online help.

3. If you want to build your merge main document with VBA, what method should you use?

   To add fields to the document, you are going to use the Add method for the Fields collection for the active document.

4. If you want to merge to email, do you have to include the email field in the document?

   No, the email field must be a part of the source, but it doesn't need to be included on the letter.

Hour 19

1. When expanding a master document's subdocuments, is it required to expand all levels with the setting of 1–9 in a For...Next loop?

   You can use any number of levels between 1 and 9 to control the expansion.

2. What happens if you attempt to set an AutoCaption for an object that doesn't exist in the collection?

   VBA generates an error. You can create an error handler as shown in this hour to deal with that error.

3. What argument for the InsertCrossReference method indicates what type of cross reference is needed?

   The ReferenceType combined with the ReferenceItem enable you to indicate what is referenced.

A

Hour 20

1. Which approach lets you edit an Excel workbook from your document?

   To get editing capability, you need to insert it as an object.

2. Why do you need to use the Object property for the OLEFormat object to control an inserted graph?

   When you insert a chart, it is placed in a Shape control. You can't control the chart directly because it doesn't exist in a separate file. It only exists in this shape. You use its OLEFormat property to gain access to its OLE format. When you need to manipulate an object, you use the Object property to control the contents of the shape.

3. Why are there two methods for working with Access databases?

   There are two object models because not everyone stores their data in Access. There are many other databases. With the ActiveX Data Objects, you can access data stored in any database as long as it has a ODBC driver.

   It also reduces the overhead when you are accessing the data. You don't have to support all of the Access interface components if you only want to work with records.

4. What is a Connection?

   In the ActiveX Data Object model, the Connection establishes the link to the database application. After that connection is completed, you can then access the contents of a specific database.

Hour 21

1. What is a NameSpace?

   The NameSpace is an object in Outlook. It is similar to a workspace in Excel. It is the general application's work area.

2. What property sets the text shown in the document for a hyperlink?

   If you don't want to display the Web address, you can set the TextTodisplay argument for the Add method for the Hyperlinks collection.

3. What settings are stored under the HKEY_CURRENT_USER folder of the Registry?

   The settings for the user that is logged in to the system are stored here.

4. Why is the `ByVal` keyword important?

The `ByVal` keyword controls how variables are passed to functions. If the `ByVal` keyword is passed to an API function, the data stored is passed to the function, but the actual variable remains intact. It ensures that the variable values won't be disturbed.

With Strings, this is even more important because most API functions are written in C or C++. They are expecting a C formatted string. This is not the way strings are stored in VBA. Using the `ByVal` and also making sure you send null terminated strings will ensure the strings are processed correctly.

Hour 22

1. Can you change the Help dialog for form fields?

No, you can only enter text to be displayed using the Form Field Options.

2. Why would you want to adjust screen updating?

In longer procedures, setting the `ScreenUpdating` property to `False` eliminates the flickering of each action carried out on the screen. It makes the code run much faster.

3. What object controls the text of the Assistant?

You set up a `Balloon` object to display text for the Assistant. You have a `Heading` and `Text` property to control the contents. You also have labels, if you want to add options or check boxes to the balloon.

4. When is creating a new sample document better than having instructions in the template?

When you have many custom styles for which you want to display samples or when there are multiple procedures you want to explain, the separate sample document enables the user work on a document based on the template, as well as refer to a document with the template's instructions and additional information such as style samples.

Hour 23

1. What are the three benefits of using a global template?

Global templates reduce the size of the Normal template, make it easier to share code between templates and users, and make code easier to update.

A

2. Why is it important to rename the `TemplateProject` when you are developing a global template?

   All templates are initially referenced as `TemplateProject`. If you don't change the name, you are likely to get reference problems when you attempt to use certain procedures in your code.

3. What is the problem if I enter the name of a procedure in a global template in my code and a message states that my procedure won't compile because it isn't defined?

   You didn't set the reference to the global template. If you are going to use a procedure from Word manually, this isn't an issue. Without a reference, you can't access the procedure with VBA. Select Tools, References and select your template.

Hour 24

1. What property controls the appearance of the `MultiPage` control?

   The `Style` property.

2. How do you add, remove, or move a page in a `MultiPage` control?

   Point to one of the pages and right-click. A menu will drop down, and you can select one of those choices.

3. How do you switch between pages?

   You keep track of the current page with a variable and set the `Value` property for the `MultiPage` control with an offset. You can either add or subtract one from the variable.

APPENDIX B

Using the Templates from the Companion Web Site

If you decide that you want to view and run the sample macros provided on the companion Web site, you will download a self-extracting executable. This executable must be run to place the files in your Template directory. If you aren't sure where to place the files, select Tools, Options, and the File Locations tab to view the folder for your templates.

After the templates are placed in the folder, you are ready to use them. As you work through Hour 1,"Introducing Automation Fundamentals," you will learn that macros can be placed in several locations. One of these locations is your Normal template. It is the global template for all your work.

Because you customize that template as you work in Microsoft Word, you probably do not want to lose your settings. To avoid any possibility that you might overwrite this template, any hour in which a task creates a macro in your Normal template will also contain a special template named Hour and the hour number such as Hour02.dot.

After the templates are placed in the Templates folder, you can create a new document from the template and try out the macros from the hour. If your installation isn't standard, you might have to make changes to the macro. Any macro that you want to use in your own work can be moved to the Normal template.

Using One of the Sample Templates

Using a sample template is like using any other template. For example, to try out the Meeting Memo macro, you will

1. Copy the Custom Memo template and the Hour02 templates to the Templates folder.

2. Select File, New.

3. Double-click Hour2 (see Figure B.1).

FIGURE B.1

The Hour2.Dot template has the MeetingMemo *macro.*

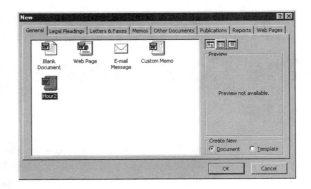

4. Select Meeting Memo button from the toolbar.

If you do not have a standard installation, the macro may not work until you change the path of the template in the macro.

5. View the completed memo created with the macro.

Making Changes to a Macro

If your installation of Microsoft Office isn't standard with its folders on your C drive in the \Programs Files\ folder, some of the macros created for the sample templates won't work. You must edit them to point them to the correct files.

To edit a macro, do the following:

1. Select Tools, Macro, Macros.

2. Select the macro and select Edit.

3. Highlight the code to change and type the change as you would a new folder name (see Figure B.2).

FIGURE B.2

The folder name is highlighted and ready for the change.

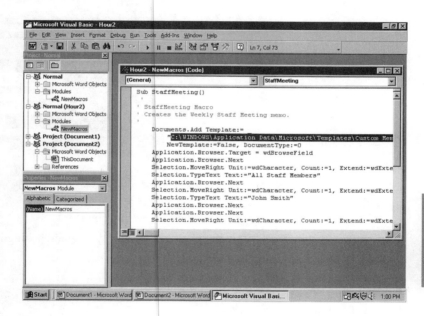

4. Save your work.

Moving a Macro to Your Normal Template

Macros in one of the Hour templates were originally intended to be located in your Normal template. If you want to use one of these macros in your regular work, it will be easier if it is located in the Normal template. To move a macro, perform the following steps:

1. Select the macro lines. Make sure you highlight the Sub and End Sub lines (see Figure B.3).

FIGURE B.3

The Sub and End Sub lines indicate the beginning and end of the macro.

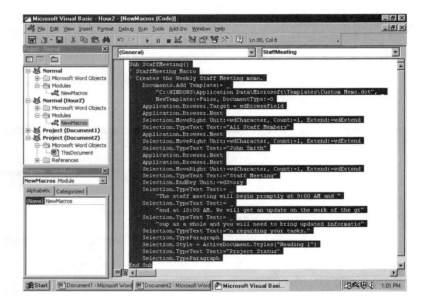

2. Select Edit, Copy to place the lines on the clipboard.
3. Open the module for the Normal template by double-clicking it in the Project Explorer (see Figure B.4).

FIGURE B.4

The Normal template is always listed in the Project Explorer.

4. Press Ctrl+End to move to the bottom of the code module.
5. Select Edit, Paste to retrieve the procedure from the clipboard.
6. Save the Normal template.

You can also use the Organizer to move macros.

After the macro is copied into the Normal template, it can be run from the Macros dialog. If you want to be able to access it from the toolbar, you will have to re-create the toolbar button by dragging the macro from the Customize dialog's Commands tab to the toolbar.

B

INDEX

Symbols

< (Less Than operator), 105
<> (Not Equals operator), 104
<= (Less Than or Equal operator), 105
>= (Greater Than or Equal operator), 105
= (Equals operator), 104

A

accelerators, 461
Access (Microsoft). *See* Microsoft Access
activation event procedures, 301
ActiveDocument property, 196, 272, 437
ActivePrinter property, 213
ActiveX controls
  add to Toolbox, 329
  Data Object model, 390
  user forms, 319

Add method
  Fields collection, 172
  hyperlinks, 405
  indexes, 273
  tables, 218
  tables of contents, 272
Add Watch command (Debug menu), 150
add-ins, 444-446
AddColorReference procedure, 370
AddFromFile method, 357-360
AddHorizontalLine method, 238, 240
AddItem method, user forms, 325
AddOLEObject method, 380-381, 388
AddPicture method, 237-245
Address Book, mail merge, 346
AddShape method, 247-248
Alignment, 187, 191
AllCaps property, 183

Anchors, hyperlink, 405
And operator, 107
Animation property, 184
apostrophes, 41
Apple Macintosh, 66
application event procedures, 301-302
Application object, 73, 173
Application Programming Interface. *See* Windows API
ApplyTheme method, 406-408
arguments, 50, 61, 70
  Auto Quick Info, 96
  specify by position, 71
arrays, 86
Art properties, 208
As keyword, 85
Auto List Members, 96-97, 138
auto macros, 296-300
Auto Quick Info, 96, 137
Auto Syntax Check, 96-98, 138
auto-executing macros, 35, 51
AutoCaption, 367-369

Get **FREE** books and more...when you register this book online for our Personal Bookshelf Program

http://register.samspublishing.com/

SAMS

 Register online and you can sign up for our *FREE Personal Bookshelf Program*...unlimited access to the electronic version of more than 200 complete computer books—immediately! That means you'll have 100,000 pages of valuable information onscreen, at your fingertips!

 Plus, you can access product support, including complimentary downloads, technical support files, book-focused links, companion Web sites, author sites, and more!

 And you'll be automatically registered to receive a *FREE subscription to a weekly email newsletter* to help you stay current with news, announcements, sample book chapters, and special events, including sweepstakes, contests, and various product giveaways!

 We value your comments! Best of all, the entire registration process takes only a few minutes to complete, so go online and get the greatest value going—absolutely FREE!

Don't Miss Out On This Great Opportunity!

Sams is a brand of Macmillan Computer Publishing USA.

For more information, please visit *www.mcp.com*